THE WORLD'S
ELITE
FORCES

**The men, weapons and operations
in the war against terrorism**

THE WORLD'S
ELITE FORCES

**The men, weapons and operations
in the war against terrorism**

MILITARY PRESS
New York

A SALAMANDER BOOK

This Edition published by
Military Press, distributed by
Crown Publishers, Inc.,
225 Park Avenue South,
New York, New York 10003,
United States of America.

© Salamander Books Ltd., 1987.

ISBN 0-517-64643-9

All correspondence concerning the content of this
volume should be addressed to Salamander Books Ltd.,
52 Bedford Row, London WC1R 4LR, United Kingdom.

h g f e d c b a

Printed in Italy by G. Canale & C. S.p.A. Turin

CREDITS

Editor: Ray Bonds
Designer: Barry Savage
Filmset by SX Composing Ltd.
Color reproduction by Rodney Howe Ltd.,
Magnum Graphics, and Melbourne Graphics Ltd.
Color artwork: Terry Hadler, and TIGA.
Printed in Italy.

THE AUTHORS

Walter N. Lang is Consultant Editor of the American Defense Preparedness Association's *National Defense* magazine, and Chief of the Editorial Services Branch, American Forces Information Service, based near Washington, DC. An MA in Political Sciences, and MS in English, he has also been Chief, Internal Information Division, Office of Public Affairs, Aeronautical Systems, at USAF's Wright-Paterson AFB, Ohio. He has written extensively for important international publications, including *Air Force Magazine, Seapower*, and *International Combat Arms*. He was a Contributing Editor to Salamander's *The Modern US War Machine*, and is co-author of their *Computers in Warfare*.

Peter Eliot, who contributed the section on ammunition and helped otherwise with the weapons and equipment section of this book, is Managing Director of Delta Firearms Ltd., specializing in training bodyguards, embassy personnel and civilian firearms owners in house defense and close quarter battle techniques with handguns. A former British Army small arms instructor and sniper, and police firearms user and instructor, with combat experience in Northern Ireland, he has been involved with the training of special forces groups internationally, including the SBS.

Keith Maguire, who contributed the section on Northern Ireland, was born in Belfast in 1959 and lived there until 1986. He received his BA and MSSc from Queen's University Belfast, and intensively researched terrorist groups in Northern Ireland, meeting most of the senior figures in these organizations. He also worked as a courier for a security company collecting and delivering money and dangerous drugs round the province. He has written a number of academic papers on terrorism in Ireland, and also written on South African defense matters.

Acknowledgements

Books are easily the total of the contributions of many people and organizations, and this one is no exception. For example, much valuable material and help was provided by Current News Analysis & Research Service of the Office of the Secretary of the Air Force in the Pentagon. Its former head, Harry Zubkoff, was also most generous with his time and reviewed the manuscript. Others who shared their time with equal generosity were, of course, General Bob Kingston, who provided the foreword and read the script as well; R. Lynn Rylander, Deputy Director, Special Planning, under the Assistant Secretary of Defense for International Security Affairs; Ross Kelly, Special Operations Division, IEAL, and a major, United States Army Reserve, one of the true experts in the international arena of special operations forces; Cpl. Bob Mountel (USA, Ret.) and Bob Haskell of the John F. Kennedy Special Warfare Center, Fort Bragg, North Carolina; and Alex Kemos, a consultant who was particularly helpful with the aspects of the book dealing with terrorism and counterterrorism.
On a more personal note, there was the contribution of my daughter, Kristin Brendel, who did a lot of typing and just as much proofreading. Finally, of course, there is the "glue" that pulls it all together and somehow makes sense of it, the patient wife who puts up with odd hours and a somewhat distracted husband so a book of this kind can be put together. To Paula, a special thanks for these virtues; this is dedicated to her.

Walt Lang

The publishers would also like to thank all the official organizations, press agencies, commercial companies and private individuals who have provided information and illustrations for this book. Picture research was undertaken by John and Diane Moore, of Military Archive and Research Services (MARS), and a full list of picture credits is given on page 224.

CONTENTS

FOREWORD   8

INTRODUCTION
THE VIOLENT PEACE   10

SECTION ONE
ELITE FORCES   18

SECTION TWO
THE ENEMY: TERRORISM   86

SECTION THREE
OPERATIONS:
THE VISIBLE PAYOFF   114

SECTION FOUR
WEAPONS AND EQUIPMENT   148

INDEX   220
PICTURE CREDITS   224

FOREWORD

THIS IS not the first book that has been written about the elite forces that exist in various countries throughout the world. However, this highly researched and authoritative volume is certainly one of the most definitive of its kind written to date, and most likely will remain so for the foreseeable future.

The author has compiled an extensive presentation of organizations that have often been exaggerated, misunderstood or misrepresented. He guides the reader through the complex multi-missions of some of the forces he writes about, including conventional military, special operations, terrorist and counter-terrorist organizations.

Organizations are included that I, a retired professional soldier with experience in special operations and with long associations with many of the foreign and all of the United States organizations listed, would not define nor include as elite forces. However, if one is to discuss them in the context presented by the author – that is, as ". . . selected elite forces established for conventional warfare operations, including paratroop formations, dedicated counterterrorist units and historic formations" – all are, and rightly should be, classified as elite forces.

The establishment of elite forces has greatly increased since the end of World War II – a fact recognized and documented by this book. There are many reasons for this growth, among them:

●Improvements in the sophistication and lethality of weapons and the quantum jump in the complete spectrum of conducting conventional warfare, concomitant with the increased costs required to man and equip sizable modern forces.

●The recognition by many nations that a highly trained, truly professional force, committed in a timely and judicious manner, could possibly deter an aggressor. This has the added benefit of preventing the commitment of much larger conventional forces at a later time.

●Recognition that a requirement exists to have a highly trained organization that can rapidly respond to terrorist threats or acts.

Many nations recognize the requirement to form, organize, equip, train and support elite or special operations forces in peacetime so they can operate, when directed to do so, in all phases of pre-conflict and conflict.

They must be prepared to conduct operations during this period of "violent peace", and they must also be ready to conduct their wartime missions without having to take the time for extensive training after conflict starts, as was the case during World War II.

Many of the requirements are discussed in this book which differentiate elite forces from conventional forces. This is as it should be since selection and training are so critically important to the successful performance of any elite unit. Personnel in these units are volunteers who undergo some form of selection process which greatly tests individual physical ability, stamina and the capability to plan and operate under great mental and physical strain.

In most organizations, this selection process serves as an assessment system which helps determine whether individuals measure up to the standards of the organization. In fact, it is during this initial selection process that those who aren't likely to meet those standards are separated from the unit.

Some organizations, when not selecting certain individuals within their ranks (for whatever reason) return them to their parent unit or to another organization, usually a support type, with high praise and as much good will as possible. This is done to ensure that non-acceptable volunteers do not poison the recruiting well throughout the regular formations.

Those who do go forward are language-trained, area-oriented forces capable of providing sustained assistance to individual countries. This is vital to any nation whose national policy it is to assist in obtaining or preserving freedom.

Many nations control their elite forces at the highest national levels, and, when committing them externally, they are called upon to perform strategic missions. Some forces are controlled and supported by operational commanders, while others may be committed independent of the conventional force chain of command.

Whatever the mode of commitment, there exists in all phases of special operations the need for extensive planning so that psychological and deception operations are an integral part of the overall operation whenever possible. I believe that some of the most important factors in planning and conducting these kinds of operations are the need for timely, accurate intelligence and good security.

The author has done exceptional research on the various elite forces. While some information is readily available from open sources in the Western countries, the Communist nations have not been as open with information in this area. Despite this limitation, Mr. Lang has produced a work that should be indispensable for the practitioner and student of elite forces and special operations organizations.

I predict that anyone associated with special operations, terrorism or counterterrorism will welcome this book and use it as a reference many times.

Robert C. Kingston,
General, US Army (Ret.)

GENERAL ROBERT C. KINGSTON,
US Army

General Kingston enlisted in the US Army in 1948 and has commanded a platoon, a company, a battalion, two brigades and special operations forces in two conflicts. He wears 16 battle stars and also earned the Combat Infantry Badge (two awards); the Master Parachutist Badge (US); Ranger Tab; Gliderman Badge; Korean Parachutist Badge; Parachute Wing (UK); Cambodian Parachutist Badge; Vietnamese Jumpmaster Badge; Vietnamese Ranger Badge; and 12 overseas bars.

His special operations experience includes a tour in Korea as commanding officer, Far East Command Special Mission Group. He was executive officer of the Ranger Mountain Camp, Dahlonega, Georgia (1954-55). In 1960-1961, he served as the exchange airborne officer with the 16th Independent Parachute Group, UK.

General Kingston was also senior advisor to the Vietnamese Ranger Command (1966) and commander of the 3rd Special Forces Group (Airborne), 1st Special Forces, Fort Bragg, North Carolina.

In January 1973, General Kingston assumed command of the Joint Casualty Resolution Center, Nakhon Phanom, Thailand. In October 1975, he became commander of the US Army John F. Kennedy Center for Military Assistance and the US Army Institute for Military Assistance at Fort Bragg.

The general pinned on his fourth star and assumed command of the United States Central Command, MacDill Air Force Base, Florida, on 1 January, 1983. He retired from active duty on November 30, 1985.

THE
VIOLENT PEACE

A CERTAIN fascination exists on this planet – it always has – with the exploits of uniformed warriors who dash deep into enemy territory, create utter havoc and, having successfully completed the mission, return to camp to prepare for yet another foray. It is the stuff from which literature and legend spring.

Even at that, these warriors – usually members of special or unconventional military formations – are viewed with skeptical ambivalence. When they are successful, a certain aura of glamor attaches to that success; when they are not – particularly when the failure is publicized – opprobrium comes all too swiftly.

Make no mistake about it: there is an inherent distrust of secret operations and those associated with them, particularly in open and democratic societies. It is a distrust that runs deep and which causes the fortunes of elite forces to wax and wane.

"Elite", of course, is simply one of several ways to describe special or unconventional military and paramilitary formations. Other labels that have been applied are commando, paratrooper, cowboy, irregular, guerrilla, or simply – and perhaps more embracing – special operations forces. Whatever the choice of designation, however, these forces have always had an important role to play in their nations' defense forces, and their historical legacy is particularly rich.

The Roman legions, for example, were denied success by irregular African forces using camels and arrows. They were also thwarted in Great Britain by the guerrilla tactics of a female warrior named Boedicia. In America, the sharpshooting Minutemen played an undeniably significant role in the outcome of the American Revolutionary War. General George Washington's famous crossing of the Delaware on Christmas Eve just prior to the Battle of Trenton was a special operation. And in Britain, what we now know as the Special Air Service had its genesis in North Africa in 1941, where it performed daring raids behind German lines during World War II.

The post-World War II era saw a decline in elite forces; in fact, many were disbanded. Without a war, the argument went, there was no mission. Marry to that the historical distrust of elite forces, as well as the uneasy tolerance accorded them by the regular forces, and it's easy to see why elite forces seemed to be approaching their nadir.

But the mission for special forces can never truly go away for one very basic reason. They are and must be an integral part of any nation's defense forces and, as such, will always have a role in defending the sovereign. These forces are now stronger than they ever were, and the reasons for this are both practical and historical.

In the 1960s, a netherworld existed in which a state of neither "true peace" nor "true war" developed. It featured so-called "wars of national liberation" characterized by conflict in which the postwar process of decolonization played itself out. By the 1970s, these postwar spasms were over in Africa, East Asia, and the Middle East and hands previously at the tiller of revolutionary movements were now firmly on the reins of power.

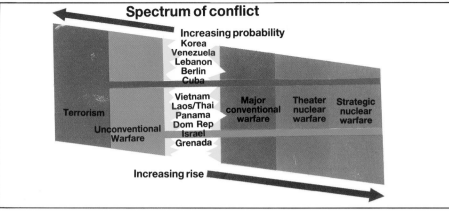

Spectrum of conflict

Increasing probability

Korea
Venezuela
Lebanon
Berlin
Cuba

| Terrorism | | Vietnam Laos/Thai Panama Dom Rep Israel Grenada | Major conventional warfare | Theater nuclear warfare | Strategic nuclear warfare |

Unconventional Warfare

Increasing rise

Left: *This diagram is based on a US Department of Defense view of the "spectrum of conflict", showing how terrorism is a form of warfare at the opposite end of the scale from strategic nuclear warfare, but cutting across the entire spectrum. The use of elite forces could occur throughout the spectrum, also, and examples of actual or potential hot-spots are given.*

Below: *One of the hot-spots that has actually caught fire: a typical scene from the Lebanon, where political extremists, rioters and outright terrorists have taken their politics to the streets. This could be the battleground for special, or elite, forces.*

But that did not mean that the use of upheaval and instability had been abandoned. Far from it. In fact, the distorted and grotesque outrages of terrorism, state-sponsored and otherwise, plagued the globe. As an instrument of national will, it represented a more deliberate type of conflict with severe consequences for the security of nations.

Since 1962, conflict of one form or another has led to violent changes in the governments of 17 countries. In the late 1980s, there were active insurgencies in more than 20 nations; and, counting wars of various stripe under way, nearly one out of four countries was engaged in some sort of conflict.

In the space of just one recent month:

● Iraq used its air force to launch bombing attacks against troop trains in the Khuzestan province in Iran and to hit targets near the city of Esfahan. Iran reported that the attacks killed more than 80 people.

● UNITA rebels and government forces clashed in 11 of Angola's 15 provinces, with UNITA claiming to have killed more than 100 Angolan and Cuban troops.

● On the other side of the globe, clashes between government forces and communist Shining Path guerrillas in Peru left more than 80 rebels dead in the Ayacucho region.

● In Sri Lanka, 65 rebels and 14 soldiers were killed as the army continued to root out Tamil guerrillas in the Mannar area.

These incidents only begin to reveal what went on during the month! In the words of one observer, "World War III has already begun and ... is comprised of brush-fire conflicts, assassinations, terrorist bombings, coups, revolutions, and civil strife". The prophetic views of George Orwell come pretty close to the mark. War may not be peace, he claimed, but the peace of our time has assumed some unmistakably warlike characteristics.

That is unlikely to change in the near future. The next few decades seem certain to bear witness to an increasing number of situations requiring responses short of full mobilization to address. There is no clean and easy way to categorize these crises and the types of conflict they represent. However, it is clear that terrorism, special operations and what has been dubbed "low intensity conflict" need to be considered together. Nobody has devised a universally acceptable definition of that last term, although an understanding of what it represents is critical to understanding elite forces and their roles.

One definition claims that low intensity conflict is a political-military confrontation between contending states or groups below the level of conventional war and above the routine, peaceful competition among states. It involves protracted struggles of competing principles and ideologies and ranges from subversion to the use of armed force. It is waged by a combination of means employing political, economic, informational and military instruments. Such conflicts are often local in nature, but contain regional and global security implications. Accepting this definition, imperfect though it may be, at least provides a working framework in which to put low intensity conflict. It gives it a place in the spectrum of conflict shown in the diagram (location).

In this scheme, both mid- and high intensity conflict can be readily recognized since they involve the application of conventional military power. Elite forces, in this model, can be employed anywhere across the spectrum. Significantly, terrorism also cuts across the spectrum since it is properly identified as a form of warfare.

But even the most elite of special forces can deal with only a small portion of the threats posed by subversion, international criminality and terrorism. This is why more of these forces have come into being; it is why nations are cooperating in framing strategies to deal with the problems of conflict; it is why there is increasing recognition that terrorism is a form of conflict that must be met by forces specially trained for the counterterrorist mission.

Above: *A typical use of elite forces is here epitomized by France's GIGN special "police" unit: that of hostage rescue in an urban environment. Special training (both physical and psychological) and equipment are necessary for a satisfactory outcome.*

Above right: *Another task for special forces is the training of friendly nations' elite units; here Ecuadoran Commandos are practising lessons taught them by US Army Special Operations Forces. Britain's SAS and Germany's GSG 9 are among other organizations which train foreign "friendlies".*

Below: *US Army Ranger on advanced training, in a situation common to elite forces throughout the world. Tough and resolute beyond the norm, these troops have to be ready and able to fight anywhere at any time, in any conditions.*

MAJOR SPECIAL OPERATIONS FORCES OF THE WORLD

The term "special operations forces" usually refers to small, carefully selected military, paramilitary, and civilian units manned by personnel with unique and unusual skills. They are extremely well trained for specific rather than general purposes and undertake unusual tasks that ordinary units might accomplish only with greater difficulty and far less effectiveness.

It should be made clear, however, that these forces are *not* needed for all special operations, which are essentially defined as (1) those involving insurgency, counterinsurgency, resistance, transnational terrorism, counterterrorism (specific counterterrorist units are listed separately); and (2) are unorthodox, comparatively low-cost, potentially high pay-off, often covert or clandestine methods that national, subnational, and theater leaders use independently in peacetime or to support warfare across the entire spectrum of conflict.

EUROPE

BELGIUM
The Paracommando Regiment (Belgian Army)
1st Special Reconnaissance Co. (Belgian Army)

DENMARK
Special Reconnaissance Company (Jaegerkorps)

FRANCE
1st Parachute Brigade
2nd Parachute Brigade
13th Dragoons Parachute Regiment

ITALY
Paratroop Saboteur Battalion (9th Airborne Assault Battalion – Folgore Airborne Brigade)

NETHERLANDS
104th Long Range Patrol Company (Royal Netherlands Army)

NORWAY
Special Forces Group

SPAIN
Spanish Foreign Legion/Special Operations Unit

TURKEY
Special Warfare Department

UNITED KINGDOM
Special Air Service
Special Boat Squadron

USSR
Spetsnaz
Soviet Naval Infantry

NORTH AMERICA

CANADA
Special Service Force

UNITED STATES
Army Special Operations Forces
SEALS
US Rangers

AFRICA

SOUTH AFRICA
Reconnaissance Commandos

SOUTH ASIA

INDIA
Parachute Commandos
Special Frontier Force
India-Tibetan Border Police

INDONESIA
Special Warfare Command

PAKISTAN
Special Services Group

THAILAND
Royal Thai Army Special Forces (Airborne)

TAIWAN
Amphibious Commandos

AUSTRALIA
1st Special Air Service Regiment

PEOPLE'S REPUBLIC OF CHINA
6th Special Warfare Group
8th Special Warfare Group
12th Special Warfarepecial Forces Detachment
Parachute Training Center

CHILE
1st Paratroop Battalion
Special Forces Companies (six)

DOMINICAN REPUBLIC
6th Regular Battalion
Special Forces Group

PERU
Special Commando Companies (six)

LATIN AMERICA

BOLIVIA
Special Forces Training Center

BRAZIL
Special Forces Detachment
Parachute Training Center

CHILE
1st Paratroop Battalion
Special Forces Companies (six)

DOMINICAN REPUBLIC
6th Regular Battalion
Special Forces Group

PERU
Special Commando Companies (six)

MIDDLE EAST

EGYPT
Special Forces

IRAN
23rd Special Forces Brigade

IRAQ
Special Forces

JORDAN
Special Forces

COUNTERTERRORIST UNITS WORLDWIDE

EUROPE

AUSTRIA
Gendarmerieeinsatzkommando (Gendarmerie Special Unit – or Cobra Unit)

BELGIUM
Escadron Special d'Intervention (ESI of the Gendarmerie Royale)

DENMARK
Fromandskorset unit of the Royal Danish Navy Combat Swimmers
Politiets Efterretningstejeneste (PE) of the State Police Intelligence Service.

FEDERAL REPUBLIC OF GERMANY
Grenzchutzgruppe 9 (GSG 9)
Speziale-insatz Kommando (SEK) – Units in major German cities

FINLAND
Osasto Karhu (Bear Unit) of the Helsinki Police Department

FRANCE
Groupement D'Intervention De La Gendarmerie Nationale (GIGN)
Regiment Etranger DE Parchutistes (2nd REP) – used only for large scale hostage rescue operations

GREECE
Dimoria Eidikon Apostolon (DEA Special Mission Platoon) of the Athens City Police

ITALY
Groupe Interventional Speciali of the Carabinieri
Nucleo Operativo Central di Sicureza (NOCS – or Leatherheads)

NETHERLANDS
Marine Close Combat Unit ("Whiskey Company", Royal Dutch Marines)
Brigade Speciale Beveilinginsopdrachtn (BSB)

NORWAY
Beredskapstrop (readiness troop) of the National Police

PORTUGAL
Grupo de Operacoes Especiais (The Special Operations Group) of the Policia de Seguranca Publica

SPAIN
Grupo Especial de Operaciones (GEO) of the Policia Nacional Unidad Especial de Intervention (UEI) and Grupose Antiterroristas Rurales (GAR) of the Guardia Civil

SWEDEN
National Rescue Unit, a part of the Stockholm Police

SWITZERLAND
Stern Unit (Bern)
Enzian Unit (Zurich)

TURKEY
Ozel Inithar Kommando Bolugu (The Jandara Suicide Commando companies)

UNITED KINGDOM
Comacchio Group of the Special Boat Service
London Metropolitan Police D11 Unit
Special Air Service
Special Branch of the National Police (Garda Siochana), Irish Republic

LATIN AMERICA

ARGENTINA
Halcon 8 (Falcon) of the Argentinian Army

BRAZIL
Projecto Talon of the Army Special Forces

CHILE
Grupo de Operaciones Especiales (GOPE) of the national police force
Unidad Anti-terrorista (UAT) of the national police force/Army
FACH of the Chilean Air Force

COLOMBIA
Special Operations Group (GOES) of the Policia Nacional
GAES (Anti Extortion and Kidnapping Groups) of the Colombian Army
GAJDA Teams of the Colombian Air Force

ECUADOR
Army Puma Unit

HONDURAS
Comando de Operaciones Especiales (COE) of the Honduran Army Special Forces Command

VENEZUELA
Special Intervention Brigade

FAR EAST

AUSTRALIA
Special Air Service

HONG KONG
Police Special Duties Unit (SDU) of the Hong Kong Police

INDONESIA
SATGAS GEGANA (Counterterrorist Task Force) of the Indonesia National Police
SATGAS ATBARA of the Indonesian Air Force
Detachment 81, Army Special Forces
KESATUAN GURITA of the Indonesian Navy

JAPAN
Police Special Action Units

KOREA
707th Special Mission Battaliom, ROK Army
Counterterrorist Special Attack Unit of the National Police

MALAYSIA
Unit Timpaan Khas (Special Strike Unit) and/or Unit Indak Khas (Special Action Unit) of the Royal Malaysian Police

PHILIPPINES
Aviation Security Commando (AVESCOM)
Light Reaction Force of the Philippine Constabulary
Special Operations Group of the Army Special Warfare Brigade
Integrated National Police Field Force (INPFF)

SINGAPORE
Police Tactical Team

THAILAND
Special Unit of the Royal Thai Air Force
Other Units of the Royal Thai Navy SEALs, 1st Army Division, Army Special Forces, and Royal Thai Police.

NORTH AMERICA

CANADA
Emergency Response Teams, Royal Canadian Mounted Police

UNITED STATES
Delta
Hostage Response Team (HRT) of the Federal Bureau of Investigation
Other Units with US Marshal's Service, National Park Police and Department of Energy (Nuclear Emergency Search Team – or NEST)

AFRICA

EGYPT
Force 777

KENYA
General Services Unit (GSU) Recce Company of the Kenya Police

MOROCCO
GIGN

SOUTH AFRICA
South African Police Special Task Force
Special Task Force of the South African Rail and Harbor Police

SUDAN
144th Counterterrorist Unit (CTU)

TUNISIA
Groupement de Commando of the Garde Nationale

SOUTH ASIA

INDIA
Special Counterterrorist Unit (SCTU) of the Special Frontier Force

PAKISTAN
Special Services Group (SSG) of the Army

SRI LANKA
Army Commando Squadron

MIDDLE EAST

BAHRAIN
U-Group

ISRAEL
Sayaret Matka (also known as the General Staff Recon Unit or Unit 269)

JORDAN
101st Special Forces Battalion

LEBANON
Maokafaha of the Lebanese Army

OMAN
The Sultan's Special Force

SAUDI ARABIA
Special Security Force
Unit of the National Guard

NB: This table was prepared by the Editor from international sources, many of them obscure and unattributable.

Above: *Wherever there are terrorist movements there will be the need for counterterrorist units. Here, Peruvian special forces, whose main enemy is "The Shining Path" movement, train with US special forces.*

Below right: *Soviet airborne troops parade beside their famed BMD vehicles. These are likely to be "first in" in any form of conflict short of nuclear.*

Below: *Portuguese counterterrorist police guard the Turkish Ambassador's residence in Lisbon following a bomb attack and siege involving hostages. Seven people were killed, including five terrorists.*

It is also why this book on elite forces worldwide is structured as it is. It recognizes the link between terrorism, insurgency, and other forms of conflict. It further recognizes that virtually any low intensity conflict can escalate to something higher and hotter, which only underscores the need for elite forces with which to deter and handle brush-fire wars and terrorist incidents and why that need has been recognized by governments throughout the world.

There are literally hundreds of elite formations in existence – some with a handful of members, some with a cast of thousands. Many, despite the sensitive nature of their missions, are relatively easy to identify, explain and describe in some detail. Most of these units operate in open societies – the French Foreign Legion, the Italian Alpini, the Special Air Service units in Britain, Australia and New Zealand are examples.

Formations in closed, but visible, societies like the Soviet Union also have enough information available about them and can therefore be detailed with relative thoroughness.

Information about the smaller units in closed societies – such as the Polish Blue Berets (naval infantry special forces) and the Czechoslovakian special purpose forces – is difficult, but not impossible, to come by. Given their close alignment with their Soviet sponsors, however, it can be fairly assumed that these units, most of which are found in the Warsaw Pact countries, operate in much the same fashion as their parents. But the place of Warsaw Pact forces in the pantheon of elite units – both worldwide and within the Soviet sphere of influence itself – is not the same category as, say, that of the SAS in relation to the Western world. For these reasons, Warsaw Pact special purpose forces (as they are labeled) have been summarized instead of profiled.

In some cases, the mission of an elite force is strictly military in nature – the US Rangers are a good example and most recently distinguished themselves in Grenada in 1983. In other cases, the mission is strictly counterterrorist. This category includes the West German GSG 9, the French GIGN, the Italian Leatherheads and others.

And in yet other cases, there is a mixture: the Australian Special Air Service, for example, has troopers dedicated to both the military and counterterrorist ends of the business – yet they can all be found under the same organizational umbrella.

And if that's not complex enough, units such as Italy's COMSUBIN are charged with military responsibilities first and counterterrorist activities second – unless that mission is reversed in the national interest. It does happen. As a British SAS trooper put it quite tellingly, "When Maggie (Margaret Thatcher, British Prime Minister) plays, we play".

It would be blatantly presumptuous to claim that one has come up with a comprehensive guide to elite forces; it's comparable to claiming that one has been able to nail jello to the wall. To begin with, there is no accepted definition of what an elite force truly is beyond the fact that it has a quite different mission from a conventional force. Moreover, these units are constantly being formed, disbanded and realigned to meet individual circumstances.

Bulking large in the overall equation is the security factor – perhaps best captured in the phrase used to respond to questions about America's premier counterterrorist force, Delta. That standard reply goes, "Delta is an airline".

This book attempts to give as much detail as possible about the better known, more prominent and representative elite forces worldwide. If omissions are perceived, one hopes it doesn't detract from its overall usefulness as a guide to these forces.

A chart is provided that attempts to catalogue special operations forces worldwide. This, of course, represents a value judgment in and of itself, but the chart at best can only provide a snapshot of the elite forces panorama worldwide.

Take the question of Islamic special forces, for example. Pakistan's Special Service Group, after taking heavy casualties in the war against India, has now regained its strength – it now consists of three battalions, each with four companies. Another Islamic country, Turkey, has both airborne and commando units, as well as a counterterrorist organization, the Ozel Intithar Kommando Bolugu.

Morocco has a parachute brigade; Tunisia has a well trained 100-man special operations unit, the Groupement de Commando; Algeria maintains close to a dozen desert commando units; Sudan has its 144th Parachute Battalion.

Jump across the ocean and the picture is just as complex. While many Latin American countries have no military special operations units as such, others do. Costa Rica, El Salvador and Panama, for example, maintain small counterinsurgency units that fit the traditional description of special operations units. Further south in the continent,

Above left: *One of the most-feared terrorist threats of all is an attack on a packed airliner, especially if it were in the air. (This is a simulated situation.) Such attacks can have no military value for terrorists and, while they might feel they bring attention to their cause, actions like the shopping car park bombing by Spanish Basque terrorist in June 1987 have proven counterproductive.*

Above: *"Skyjacking" has been seen by terrorists as a high-value propaganda weapon, or as a lever to force a government to accede to their political demands. Here, an Iranian official negotiates with one of three terrorists claiming to be members of the Islamic Organization for the Liberation of Jerusalem who have taken control of an Air France 737 bound from Frankfurt to Paris, in August 1984.*

Above right: *Terrorists often fight their political battles on the streets of other countries. This is the scene of a bomb outrage by the French Direct Action group in a Belgian city.*

Right: *Another example of air transport and passengers being the targets of terrorism: an Algerian terrorist of uncommon sartorial sophistication, wields a Communist-bloc rocket launcher at Orly Airport, France, on 28 June, 1973. Terrorists seemingly have little trouble obtaining lethal weapons, and smuggling them through security checks has occurred with alarming frequency, despite the increasing use of advanced-technology means of detection.*

there is Brazil's Special Forces Battalion of the Paratroopers Brigade, with headquarters in Rio de Janeiro.

The point in citing these units is not to overwhelm the reader, nor to single out the units involved; it is designed to help underscore the breadth of what it would take to get more than that snapshot of the world's elite forces.

With that caveat clearly in mind, this book describes selected elite forces established for conventional warfare operations, including paratroop formations, dedicated anti-terrorist units and historic detachments. It also covers how these units are organized, trained, and equipped as well as how they operate.

Terrorist organizations, the most common threat in the world today, are also listed and described. Nearly 800 terrorist groups in 88 countries are listed. Some major groups (various Irish units, the PLO, Red Brigades) are described in detail – because in many ways they typify the forces at work in this era of "violent peace".

The profiles show how these terrorist organizations arm themselves for hijackings, kidnapping and sabotage operations. Also shown in detail are nine operations that exemplify how specially trained and equipped special operations forces have combatted terrorists or been involved in general war operations, such as Entebbe, Mogadishu, the Falklands, the siege at the Iranian Embassy in London and so on.

And, finally, there is a section devoted to weapons – more than 70, some of them quite exotic – which are used on the field of strife by elite forces.

In a work like this, the question is never how much one should include, but when one should stop. One recent publication chose to profile the elite forces of the superpowers and nine units in eight countries. This book goes considerably beyond that, but doesn't nail jello to the wall.

The best approach was considered to be to quit when the flavor of the message had been delivered. One hopes that this will have been accomplished for the reader by the time the final page is turned.

Walter N. Lang

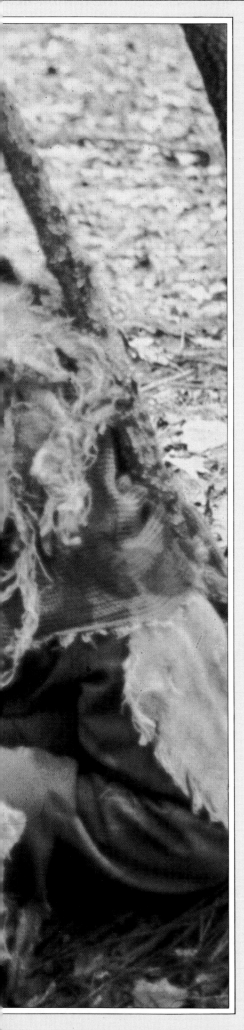

SECTION ONE
THE ELITE FORCES

UNITED STATES & NATO   20
CANADA: SPECIAL SERVICE FORCE   26
FRANCE: THE FOREIGN LEGION   28
FRANCE: PARATROOPS   31
FEDERAL REPUBLIC OF GERMANY: GSG 9   32
ITALY: ALPINE TROOPS   34
ITALY: COMSUBIN   35
ITALY: FOLGORE BRIGADE   37
SPAIN: FOREIGN LEGION   38
UNITED KINGDOM: GURKHAS   39
UNITED KINGDOM: THE PARACHUTE REGIMENT   41
UNITED KINGDOM: SPECIAL BOAT SQUADRON   43
UNITED KINGDOM: SPECIAL AIR SERVICE   44
UNITED STATES: 23rd AIR FORCE   48
UNITED STATES: US ARMY SPECIAL OPERATIONS FORCES   49
UNITED STATES: US ARMY RANGERS   54
UNITED STATES: 82nd AIRBORNE DIVISION   55
UNITED STATES: DELTA   56
UNITED STATES: US MARINE CORPS   56
UNITED STATES: US NAVY SEALS   60
USSR & WARSAW PACT   63
SOVIET UNION: AIRBORNE FORCE   65
SOVIET UNION: NAVAL INFANTRY   67
SOVIET UNION: SPETSNAZ   69
UNALIGNED FORCES   72
AUSTRALIA: SPECIAL AIR SERVICE   74
ISRAEL: PARATROOPS/ELITE UNITS   76
JORDAN: SPECIAL FORCES   76
NEW ZEALAND: SPECIAL AIR SERVICE   78
NORTH KOREA: SPECIAL PURPOSE FORCES   79
SOUTH KOREA: SPECIAL FORCES   80
SOUTH AFRICA: RECONNAISSANCE COMMANDOS   82
TAIWAN: LONG-RANGE AMPHIBIOUS RECONNAISSANCE
    COMMANDOS   84
THAILAND: SPECIAL ARMY FORCES   84

UNITED STATES & NATO

Above: *Grim and tough-looking these US Army SOF soldiers may look, at least their fatigues are clean and newly pressed!*

THE WORLD in general, and the United States in particular, because of its superpower status and global interests, has found itself dealing in shades of gray since World War II. That war was painted in two distinct colors: black and white. All Allied parties in the conflict knew the Nazi war machine was evil and were morally and materially dedicated to crushing it with every resource at their disposal. But a new type of conflict has dominated the world scene since then.

Categorized as low-intensity conflict, it is much more likely to occur now and into the forseeable future than its black and white counterpart. Included among these low-intensity scenarios are countering terrorism, assisting friendly nations in countering insurgencies, and assisting friendly resistance movements.

A resurgence of growth in special operations forces has accompanied the spread of low-intensity conflict. Nations facing threats by terrorists and insurgents have felt the need to develop or expand existing capabilities so that they can be directed against those threats, either through the formation of new forces or the expansion of existing capabilities.

The United States

The United States, despite its inherent distaste for a "warrior elite", has been adding muscle to its special operations forces. It has not been, and will not be, an easy task. The fortunes of US special operations forces have waxed and waned according to the military climate in the Pentagon and political pressures from Congress. Not only are many units involved, given the sheer size of the United States armed forces, but there are also rivalries to contend with between the individual services.

Notwithstanding, major strides have been made in beefing up and increasing the efficiency and responsiveness of American special operations forces. A US Special Operations Command (USSOC) was established on 16 April, 1987, and is headquartered at MacDill Air Force Base, Florida. It is headed by a four-star general.

All United States-based Army and Air Force special operations forces are assigned to this command, including the eight active and reserve special forces groups, the Rangers, and the special operations forces presently assigned to the 23rd Air Force. The only such forces *not* under this umbrella are the Naval Special Warfare Groups on the two coasts, which are expected to remain assigned to the US Pacific Command and the US Atlantic Command.

The US Readiness Command, a unified command that previously had elements of special operations forces assigned, was disestablished. Its SOF functions are to be transferred to the new command by 30 September, 1987, and its other functions assigned to other commands and agencies.

The principal function of USSOC – which will have headquarters manning of 250 people (446 by 1989) will be to prepare special operations forces to carry out their assigned missions. Moreover, its commander will also be responsible for directing selected special operations missions if directed to do so by the National Command Authority.

Theater upgrades are also part of the plan. There are five US special operations commands outside the United States, two of which (Special Operations Command, Europe, SOCEUR, and Special Operations Command, Pacific, SOCPAC) will now be headed by officers of general or flag rank. Other theater organizations are Special Operations, Atlantic, Central and South.

Like all unified commands, the chain of command runs from the President to the Secretary of Defense through the Joint Chiefs of Staff to the Commander-in-Chief, Special Operations Command.

From the policy and resource oversight standpoints, the office of Assistant Secretary for Defense for Special Operations and Low Intensity Conflict was also established on 16 April, 1987. Additional responsibilities include supervising preparation of SOF programs and budgets based on requirements identified by USSOC, and representing SOF interests within the decision-making councils of the Department of Defense. Significantly, there are three Deputy Assistant Secretary slots within the new organization, which is manned by 54

Right: *US Navy SEAL trainees struggle in a mud pit at the Naval Amphibious Base, Coranado, California. It's "hell week", conclusion of Phase I of their training, when trainees' physical, emotional and mental abilities are tested under the most severe conditions. Some even enjoy it!*

Below: *Members of US Army 5th Special Forces Group (Abn) practise rapelling from a tower with an injured comrade. SOF troops need to combine the skills of paratrooper, ranger and teacher.*

Bottom: *An instructor from US Navy Special Warfare Team 2-SEAL-Caribbean, 11th Military Intelligence Bn, instructs a member of 11th Special Forces Group (Abn) in foreign-manufactured and opposing forces weapons.*

Below right: *US Army Rangers paddle ashore. Experts in infiltration and deep recce into enemy territory, they also have anti-terrorist expertise.*

personnel. These include deputies for special operations, low-intensity conflict and resources.

As a further indication of the growth and momentum in US special operations capabilities, one need only look at the appropriate sections of the budget. In fiscal year 1981, funding was $440 million for all programs. By fiscal 1986, the figure was $1.2 billion, by fiscal 1988 $2.5 billion, and programs over the period fiscal year 1988-1992 are expected to account for $10.5 billion. To provide some perspective: the money dedicated to US special operations forces in an average year would fund the entire annual military requirements of Sweden.

The current composition of SOF and the presently identified improvements are shown in the accompanying table. It does not include Delta, nor does it include the US Marine Corps. They are not considered a part of SOF capability, even though the latter maintains an infrastructure of Force Reconnaissance Marines and is currently developing limited special operations skills in the Marine Amphibious Unit (Special Operations Capable).

SOF are viewed as having a particularly valuable role because of the skills and knowledge they have for dealing with low-intensity warfare. To this end, they are trained to understand this type of warfare and to be able to train the armed forces of the victims of such aggression. For example, the Army has sent hundreds of teams to 60 nations in the past six years, more than twice as many as it sent overseas during a comparable period in the 1970s.

In no way does this deny or negate the potential role of SOF in general war, where all forces would be involved in operations in their fields of specialty. "This has been their classical mission," says Adm. William J. Crowe, Jr., Chairman of the Joint Chiefs of Staff. "In general war, we're going to use Special Forces for long-range reconnaissance, to attack certain key targets, to obtain intelligence, organize partisans and so forth. These are functions that they do very well."

SOF are capable of direct action in overseas crises for

which the use of other, higher profile forces would be inappropriate. This includes dealing with hostile acts against US citizens by terrorists, dissidents or even by governments themselves in what are commonly referred to as state-sponsored actions. SOF have been used in these roles: Teheran, for example. There have been similar operations: the raid on Koh Tang island to seek the release of the crew of the *Mayaguez*, the preemptive strike in Grenada, and the *Achille Lauro* incident.

UNITED STATES SOF FORCE STRUCTURE EXPANSION

MAJOR SOF UNITS	FY1981	FY1987	FY1992
Special Forces Groups[A]	7	8	9
Ranger Battalions	2	3	3
Psychological Operations Battalions	3	4	4
Civil Affairs Battalion	1	1	1
SEAL Teams	2	5[B]	6[B]
SEAL Delivery Vehicle (SDV) Teams	0	2[B]	2[B]
Special Operations Wings	1	1	3
Special Operations Aviation Battalions	1	2	3
Total	**17**	**26**	**31**

PRIMARY AIRCRAFT			
Air Force			
MC-130E/H Combat Talons	14	14	38
AC-130A/HU gunships[C]	20	20	22
MH-53H/J Pave Low helicopters	9	19	41
CV-22 Ospreys[D]	0	0	6
EC-130E Volant Solos	4	4	4
HC-130 Tankers (SOF-dedicated)	0	8	31
C-141s Special Ops Low Level II (SOLL II)	0	0	13
C-130s SOLL II	0	0	11
Total	**47**	**65**	**166**

Army			
MH-60X helicopters	0	0	23
MH-47E helicopters (Pave Low equivalent)	0	0	17
MH-60 FLIR (SOF-dedicated) helicopters	0	16	21
M/UH-60 (SOF-dedicated) helicopters	0	29	17
CH-47D (SOF-dedicated) (10 with FLIR) helicopters	0	16	0
UH-1 (SOF-dedicated) helicopters	0	23	23
A/MH-6 (SOF-dedicated) helicopters	29	54	29
Total	**29**	**138**	**130**
Navy			
HH-60H helicopters	0	0	18

PRIMARY NAVAL EQUIPMENT			
Seafox (special warfare craft, light)	12	36	36
Sea Viking (special warfare craft, medium)	0	0	19
High speed boat	0	0	7
Dry deck shelters (DDS)	0	2	6
Submarines modified to accommodate DDS	0	5	7
SEAL delivery vehicles (SDVs)	18	19	19
Advanced SDVs	0	0	1
Total	**30**	**62**	**95**

[A] Includes four Reserve Component Groups.
[B] Includes two Underwater Demolition Teams redesignated in 1983.
[C] Includes 10 AC-130A Air Force Reserve gunships in FYs 1981/87. FY 1992 number reflects decommissioning of AC-130As and addition of 12 AC-130U aircraft.
[D] Includes programmed procurement through FY 1992. Actual deliveries will not begin until FY 1994. Total to be procured for SOF will be 55.

NATO Forces

Because of the NATO Alliance's overall force structure, as well as its essentially defensive role, the special operations capabilities in the NATO environment have been characterized as a "Mulligan's stew". This doesn't mean, however, that individual strengths haven't been assimilated into the overall planning effort. They have. Detailed descriptions of the special/elite forces of seven of NATO's 16 members are contained elsewhere. Iceland, of course, has no armed forces, and Luxembourg, because of its size, has only 720 men in its entire armed forces and another 470 in its police establishment, the *Gendarmerie*. The remaining NATO countries have capabilities of varying range. In thumbnail form, these are as follows.

Belgium. Its special operations establishment is the Paracommando Regiment. An extremely flexible force, it is composed of three battalions and supporting artillery, light armored reconnaissance, antitank and administrative units. It has performed two postwar missions, both in Zaire, competently and professionally. The Regiment operates a Commando Training Center and a Parachute Training Center.

In addition to this regiment, the Belgian Army has a "Special Reconnaissance Company" assigned to its I Corps and a national-level counterterrorist force known as the Special Intervention Squadron (ESI, for *Escadron Special D'Intervention*).

Denmark. This country has a relatively small special operations force of 50 men in the *Fromandskorpset.* Its scout swimmer school is believed by many to be the best of its kind in Europe, and the unit has the usual missions such as mine clearance, underwater demolitions and rescue and recovery; it also has counterterrorist duties as well.

The Danish Army also has a Special Reconnaissance Company (Jaegerkorps) with a headquarters and four 10-man patrol units. They have both an Army support and a counterterror mission.

Above left: *Member of the US Marine Corps Force Recon Company. Though not officially listed as part of the US Special Operations Force, Force Recon is certainly "special" and elite, with small four-man teams operating clandestinely in much the same way as do British SBS units, including para operations.*

Above: *Royal Netherlands Marine Corps troops training in Scotland. Dutch Marines include special amphibious combat groups equipped for mountain and arctic warfare as well as amphibious operations. Under NATO organization, the Dutch 1st Amphibious Combat Group and the Whisky Infantry Company are fully integrated into Britain's Royal Marine Commandos for amphibious operations on the vulnerable northern and southern flanks of NATO's European area. Within the Dutch Marines there is also a counter-terrorist unit.*

Right: *Belgian Paracommandos man a special para-droppable, rough-terrain vehicle used for reconnaissance patrols.*

Greece. Greek elite units include the Army Special Forces and the Alpine Raiding Company as well as the Greek Paratroop Regiment. A special mission platoon with the Athens City Police functions in a counterterrorist role. In addition to this 50-man unit, there are two special anti-hijacking units stationed at the airports at Athens and Thessaloniki.

The Netherlands. The Dutch have the 104th Long Range Patrol Company assigned to its Army. It combines the remnants of several former commando companies. Highly regarded, it is organized into a headquarters, a signal platoon, and four operational platoons; it specializes in deep, detailed reconnaissance missions.

Within the Royal Netherlands Marine Corps is the major and best known Dutch special operations force, the Special Assistance Unit (BBE, according to its Dutch initials). It is part of the Marine Corps' 1st Amphibious Combat Group, has three operational 30-man platoons organized into five-man teams, and displayed its capabilities when handling several situations wrought by South Moluccan terrorists (including the Moluccan "train incident"). This unit is trained for close-combat assault operations in wartime.

Norway. The Norwegians maintain a counterpart to the Danish *Fromandskorpset* in a Marine *Jaeger* platoon. Not surprisingly, they are trained for kayak operations in fjords, underwater demolitions, the use of collapsible boats, and in amphibious reconnaissance techniques.

The platoon comprises half the Norwegian military's new joint counterterrorism unit; the other half comes from elements of the Parachute Jaeger group. Actual strength of both Jaeger units is authorized at 100 personnel.

In addition, the Norwegians have a "Readiness Troop" that is part of its National Police structure. The military unit of this troop is reported to have a headquarters section and six five-man commando squads.

Portugal. A Special Forces Brigade, the buildup of which began in mid-1984, is maintained by Portugal. It basically consists of light infantry units and has had extensive experience in Angola, Mozambique and Guinea. Permanent elements are the headquarters, two Commando battalions, and signal, engineer and service support detachments.

The Brigade has dual capability: that is, the performance of the normal tactical light infantry missions, and the accomplishment of special operations missions for which they are particularly suited.

Turkey. The Turkish Army's Special Warfare Department is unique. Its special operations capabilities are dedicated to organizing, training and supporting an in-place guerrilla warfare capability. The Department is set up in several elements, all of which are designed to provide support for predesignated unconventional warfare operational areas.

National counterterrorist efforts are contained in a commando brigade and the *Jandara.* The latter unit's troopers are known colloquially as the "Suicide Commandos", and they are found in a number of regional companies.

Above: *Commando of Portugal's Corpo de Fuzilieros, a marine unit whose responsibilities include ensuring security of specified zones and installations, and cooperating with naval, police and other armed forces units, national and international. Training is tough, efficiency is high and, as could be expected, exercises include a high degree of beach assaults/amphibious raids. Portugal's elite units, in addition to this special corps, include army and air force commandos, and a Special Forces Brigade which is of recent origin but which has operated extensively overseas.*

Left: *Norway is a vital area to NATO, both for training in winter warfare and for the protection of the northern flank should Soviet/Warsaw Pact forces in war try to push through and establish useful bases in support of operations in the North Atlantic. While counter-terrorism might not be a major problem, security against infiltration, such as this ski patrol reconnaissance platoon is carrying out, is extensively exercised.*

Right: *Commando training for Turkish Army Special Warfare soldiers. Tough and dogged, the Turks are well-versed in conducting and dealing with guerrilla warfare situations. Turkey is an important NATO nation, not least since she shares borders with the Soviet Union, Iran, Iraq, and Syria.*

CANADA
SPECIAL SERVICE FORCE

C ANADA'S Special Service Force is declared to NATO and with Canada concentrates on operations in the far north while producing special rescue teams to deal with civilian emergencies.

The core of the Special Service Force is the Canadian Airborne Regiment, which is the elite unit of the Canadian armed forces. The airborne regiment can trace its origins back to the 1st Canadian Parachute Battalion, which was raised at Camp Shilo in 1942, and the 2nd Parachute Battalion which later became part of the combined US/Canadian 1st Special Service Force. The modern organization takes its name from this force, known as the "Devil's Brigade" in World War II, even though there is no US involvement in it.

The Canadian parachute force was maintained at a low level following World War II up to 1968 when the Canadian Airborne Regiment was formed to be a light, independent combined arms unit for deployment in low-intensity operations.

It is Canada's standby force for rapid deployment anywhere in the world in support of United Nations operations and, as such, is required to train in desert and jungle operations.

Organization

The Special Service Force, a part of Canada's Mobile Command (St Hubert, Quebec), is organized as a light brigade, although with only two infantry units its tactical viability is open to some question. Teeth arm units are an armored regiment (8th Canadian Hussars), an infantry battalion (1st Battalion, the Royal Canadian Regiment) and the Canadian Airborne Regiment. Combat support comes from an airborne artillery regiment (2nd Royal Canadian Horse Artillery Regiment), an engineer regiment and a signal squadron. Combat service support comes from the Airborne Service Commando (ie, logistic regiment).

The Canadian Airborne Regiment itself consists of three airborne commandos, which

are equivalent to a company in size and organization. 1st Airborne Commando is French-speaking; the 2nd Airborne Commando is English-speaking; and 3rd is bilingual.

Weapons and equipment

Small arms used by the Canadian Airborne Regiment include a Canadian adaptation of the US M16A1 in a rifle and carbine configuration. The squad automatic rifle is the 5.56mm minimum and the general purpose machinegun is the 7.62mm Belgian FN MAG58. Being phased out of service are the C1A1 7.62mm rifle modified from the Belgian FN, and a sub-machine gun based on the British Sterling.

Uniform

The winter uniform is the rifle green service dress with gold rank badges; the summer version is tan, also with gold rank; and the combat uniform is of unique Canadian design in a solid olive drab color. Officer ranks are designated by gold stripes and NCO ranks are based roughly on the British system. One unusual feature with the airborne troops is that the parachute qualification badge is a pair of wings surmounted by a maple leaf; for those serving with the Canadian Airborne Regiment the maple leaf is white, but for all others it is red. All eligible troops wear the paratroopers' maroon beret.

All members of the Special Service Force wear a patch with a winged sword and the motto "Osons" ("We Dare") clearly derived from that worn by the British SAS.

Left: *This shot clearly shows the warm practical winter clothing used by the Canadians. This protection is absolutely essential since one of the Special Service Force's main roles is directed towards Arctic operations, protecting and recapturing isolated installations.*

Below: *Canadian Special Service Force member prepares for a night jump. About one-third of the Special Service Forces are parachute qualified. Air mobility is critical in a country as vast as Canada, which has thousands of miles of coastline on three oceans.*

Above: *The new rifle being used by the Canadian Special Service Forces is the C-7. A version of the Colt M16A2 modified to suit Canadians, it is being produced in Canada.*

Below: *Member of the Canadian Airborne Regiment, for whom a pack of 80 lb is standard. Jumping with Special Service Force engineers, they can produce a rough airstrip in days.*

FRANCE
THE FOREIGN LEGION

NO ELITE unit is surrounded by a more romantic image than the French Foreign Legion, and none is the subject of more misinformation and myth. Formed to help conquer and control Algeria (and also to clear riff-raff from the streets of Paris), the Legion's early days were troubled not only by repeated wars against Arabs, but also by ill-discipline and internal strife.

In 1835 the Legion was ceded in its entirety to Spain to "honour" a promise of aid, in a shabby and cynical political manoeuvre; of 5,000 despatched only 500 survived. Meanwhile a new Legion was formed in December 1835; it fought in North Africa, the Crimea (1854-46), Italy (1859), Mexico (1863-67), the Franco-Prussian war (1870) and in numerous colonial campaigns.

The Legion played a major role in both world wars, losing many men, but adding to its reputation. The Legion even had units fighting each other in World War II, especially in Syria. After the war, in which Legion losses were 40,000 men, the next battleground became Indo-China where the Legion operated with great distinction in an increasingly disastrous campaign against the Viet Minh. During this period the first Legion parachute units were formed: *Bataillon Etranger de Parachutistes (BEP)*. The war culminated in the epic battle of Dien Bien Phu, one of the West's great military tragedies, where the 14,000 men of the French

garrison (including no fewer than seven Legion battalions) were eventually overwhelmed (they never surrendered) on May 8, 1954.

No sooner was it out of Indo-China than the Legion found itself in another war, this time in Algeria. Six infantry regiments, two cavalry and two parachute regiments fought in Algeria, with four *Saharienne* companies, as always, operating in their deep penetration role. Some Legion units took a few months off for the Anglo-French Suez campaign, but basically the Legion was involved in Algeria right up to the bitter end. Sadly, *1er Regiment Etranger de Parachutistes (1REP)* became involved in the generals' coup in 1961 and was disbanded in disgrace as a result.

The departure from Algeria has not, however, proved to be the end for the Legion, as had once been forecast, and since 1963 it has been heavily involved in many African countries, including Chad, Somaliland, Zaire, Djibouti and Malagasy. Units of the Legion also serve in the Pacific and in Central America.

Organization

The French Foreign Legion exists today as an all-arms force, well equipped (with standard French Army weapons) and well organized to serve France. Its current strength is 8,000 men and organization is based on regiments of 10 companies, with the specialist com-

panies (reconnaissance, mortar, light armor, etc) increasing at the expense of the infantry companies – a trend by no means confined to the Legion, nor indeed to the French Army. Current major units are given below.

1er Regiment Etranger. Located at Caserne Vienot in Aubagne, this regiment is responsible for the administration of the whole Legion. It also runs the band, recruiting detachments, a company administering a large training camp, and in wartime produces three companies to defend the IRBM missile sites on the Plateau d'Albion.

2er Regiment Etranger d'Infanterie. A 1,000-strong infantry regiment based at Bonifacio, Corsica, its companies rotate through commando and other specialist schools and frequently serve on overseas detachments. It belongs to the 6th Light Armored Division, based at Nimes in the South of France.

3e Regiment Etranger d'Infanterie. This regiment left Malagasy in 1973 and moved to its present base in Kourou, French Guiana. It is the most decorated regiment in the French Army.

4e Regiment Etranger. This regiment trains recruits and junior NCOs; it is located at Castelnaudary in France.

1er Regiment Etranger de Cavalerie. Stationed at Orange, this regiment is the armored component of the 6th Light Armored Division. It consists of three armored car

Left: *French Foreign Legionnaires in a setting familiar to all who have heard about them. Easily one of the most famous elite units, it has fought in France's wars for more than 150 years, particularly on the African continent.*

Right: *Perhaps the most chilling weapon used by commandos of the parachute regiments is the crossbow. It is fitted with a telescopic sight and can be used silently by the commando to kill from long range.*

Below right: *The paras of 2 REP undertake advanced courses in counterterrorist measures. For assaults on terrorist-held buildings, techniques developed by the Regiment's 2d Company are used.*

Below: *Foreign Legionnaires are equipped with the 5.56 FA MAS rifle. Unlike other bullpup design weapons, it can be fired from either shoulder because of two extractor positions on the bolt face.*

squadrons and a lorried infantry company. It is also earmarked as one of the spearhead units of the French intervention force.

2e Regiment Etranger de Parachutistes. Stationed at Calvi, Corsica, this regiment comprises an HQ and four combat companies. It prides itself in its ability to mount an operation against any given point in the world within 24 hours. One company is usually detached to *13DBLE*, Djibouti, for support.

5e Regiment Etranger. Centered on Mururoa, this unit has detachments at Tahiti and Arue. Its task is to provide security, communications and a power station for the French nuclear and experimental test sites in the Pacific.

6e Regiment Etranger du Genie This engineer unit battalion was formed with Legionnaires to prepare training areas. The battalion comprises one Legion infantry company and one company of French Army engineers.

Detachment Legion Etrangere de Mayotte. This detachment of two companies, commanded by a lieutenant-colonel, is on the island of Mayotte in the Indian ocean. The island is a staging post on the route to Reunion and the 250-strong Legion unit guarantees its security.

Selection and training

It is a fact of life that the Legion is both as "French" and "foreign" as you can get it. The

largest proportion of Legionnaires (52 per-cent) *are* French – though they cannot join as such, and do so claiming to be Belgians, Swiss or French Canadians. On the other hand, one unit of the Legion has men of some 45 different nationalities serving in it.

When a legionnaire enlists, he is immediately given an alias, the use of which is mandatory for three years. If he gets through the first three weeks – and he may drop out any time, or be booted out – the gates close on him for the remainder of his mandatory five-year contract. Training is for one year and takes place at Bonifacio on Corsica's southern tip. Besides emphasis on obedience, importance is placed on physical conditioning. No one, it is claimed, goes through Legion training without more than once soaking his socks with his own blood. Forced marches are common, and marksmanship is emphasized.

Specialist and advanced training

Live firing practice is conducted two days a week for 13 weeks. Once the training is ended, most legionnaires are then sent to one of the specialty schools (communications, for example) operating in or near Castelnaudary. Advanced training is given only to those deemed fit by the company commander. This entails attending the Corporal's Course, an eight-week effort that is con-

sidered to be one of the most physically demanding run by the Legion and, by inference, by any of the world's armed forces.

Beyond that is the possibility of the 14-week NCO course, after which the Chief Corporal's rating is received prior to receiving NCO (Sgt.) stripes. It is considered exceptional to receive NCO stripes in the course of a five-year enlistment.

Uniform

The Legion wears standard French Army uniforms, but with some special items to denote its status. The most famous item is the white-topped *kepi (kepi blanc)*, which is actually a white cloth cover on a standard blue *kepi* (with red top and gold badge and chinstrap). The *kepi blanc* cover is not worn by *sous* officers and above. Parade dress is khaki battledress with a number of ceremonial additions, including green shoulderboards with red tassels, white belt and gaiters, blue waist sash, and white gauntlets. A green tie is worn and officers also wear a green waistcoat. Members of the pioneer platoon wear a white apron and carry a ceremonial axe; they are also permitted to grow a beard.

Regiments on operations use a *foulard*, a strip of colored cloth, to indicate companies. All Foreign Legionnaires wear the green beret.

Above: *Training unit of 2 REP paras shows variety of equipment, including the 5.56 FA MAS rifle (commando, second left), and AN PRC6 radio (next to him).*

Below: *A French parachutist just after being dropped from his Transall C-160 aircraft as it circled over wild mountains in Córsica.*

FRANCE
PARATROOPS

THE FRENCH paratroops have probably carried out more operational jumps than any other parachute corps in the world in their campaigns in Indochina, Suez (1956) and Algeria, with others since (eg, Kolwezi). They have also at times become heavily politicized, to their detriment.

They were among the landing units in the French campaign in Indochina and carried out some 156 operational drops. They harried the Viet Minh ruthlessly, but not without suffering heavy casualties themselves. This culminated in their jump into a small valley in the north-west corner of the country on November 21, 1954, near Dien Bien Phu. Most parachute units were withdrawn and replaced by heavy infantry once the position had been secured, but when General Giap and the Viet Minh tightened the noose, *les paras* returned. Five battalions jumped into the cauldron between March 13 and May 6, some on the day before the garrison fell. The paratroops and the Foreign Legion bore the brunt of the battle and fought with extreme courage – it was just that they were fighting the wrong war in the wrong place.

Following the Indochina ceasefire and the French withdrawal in 1955, the paratroop units went to Algeria, arriving just as the war there started. The paratroops had been staggered by their reverses in Indochina and by their experience in the Viet Minh prisoner-of-war camps, and they set out to develop an entirely new code for what they saw as a crusade against the Communist-inspired guerrilla threat. They studied Mao Tse-tung's writings avidly and trained their staff officers and soldiers in new ways.

10th Parachute Division took time off for a brief foray in the frustrating and short-lived Suez campaign and then returned to Algeria. In January 1957 this division took over the city of Algiers which was virtually in the hands of the FLN, and inside two months restored control. Their methods were seriously questioned, however, and there were many allegations of torture. The general frustrations of the French civilians and military in Algeria boiled over in May 1958 in an uprising which eventually led to the return of Charles de Gaulle to the presidency. The paratroops, and in particular their general – Massu – were in the forefront of this affair. They were all also involved in the attempted *putsch* in January 1960, which was very short-lived and ended in ignominious failure. To this day, an element of distrust of *les paras* remains; for example, the number of years an officer may serve with paratroop units is now limited.

After the Algerian war the paratroops returned to France, but the French have maintained a strong parachute capability, and have regularly used these excellent troops overseas in pursuit of French diplomatic policies. Units of what is now 11th Parachute Division have served in Zaire, Mauretania, Chad and Lebanon, among other locations.

One facet of the French parachute units is the enormous influence they have had on the French Army as a whole in the post-War

Above: *A French para colonel in Vietnam in the 1960s. Note the red beret, para cap-badge and the para wings on the colonel's right breast. French paras have served in many hot spots, including Beirut where their ill-conceived peacekeeping mission was to end in tragedy, with many lives lost in a huge terrorist bomb explosion.*

years. This has been due in large measure to some very powerful characters such as General Jacques Massu and General Marcel Bigeard. The latter entered the Army as a private soldier, was captured as a sergeant in the Maginot Line in 1940 and then escaped to join the Free French in England where he joined the paratroops. He was, without a doubt, one of the finest battalion commanders of his generation in any army, and his reputation was such that his return to Dien Bien Phu had an electrifying effect on the entire garrison. He went on to become a General, and arrived to inspect units by parachute, his arm at the salute as he landed in front of the honor guard.

Organization

The approximately 14,000-man 11th Parachute Division is based at Tarbes. At least one-third of the Division is abroad, either on training missions of one kind or another, or maintaining a visible presence in Africa or the Indian Ocean. It is part of the French rapid-intervention force, together with 9th Marine Light Infantry Division, 27th Alpine Division, 6th Light Armored Division and 4th Airmobile Division. 11th Parachute Division comprises two brigades, with seven battalion-sized parachute units, one of which (1ᵉRPIMa) is under divisional control and has a para-commando/special forces role.

The other six units are: 3, 6 and 8 RPIMa equivalent to the former "colonial" paratroop units); 1 and 9 RCP (*chasseurs* or light

infantry) and 2 REP (the Foreign Legion parachute unit). There are also two independent units: 2nd RPIMa and 13 RDP.

Selection and training

All French paratroops are volunteers and undergo the same sort of selection and training as other parachute forces. The standard of training is high and certain volunteers can go on to join one of the para-commando units (eg, 1ᵉRPIMa).

Weapons and equipment

For many years the French Army was using the MAS 49/56 7.5mm rifle, but they have now re-equipped with the revolutionary short, light but effective 5.56mm FA MAS "bullpup" assault rifle, with the parachute units being among the first to receive it.

Uniforms

French paratroops wear standard French Army uniforms. Their parachute status is indicated by their red beret (except for Foreign Legion paras who wear a green beret). Para wings are large and in silver, and are worn on the right breast.

FEDERAL REPUBLIC OF GERMANY
GSG 9

AN APPROPRIATE characterization of the special operations forces in West Germany would be "defensive", both with respect to its military elements (the long-range reconnaissance company – or *Fernspähkompanie*) and its paramilitary national police arm – the *Grenzschutzgruppe 9 (GSG 9)*.

The Fernspähkompanie, said to be about 140-150 personnel, is assigned to each German army corps. It is oriented toward stay-behind operations against forces that have passed beyond them . . . or insertions behind enemy lines. Apart from performing long-range reconnaissance, they can also carry out sabotage missions if required. In fact, their operational concepts closely parallel those of the missions of the US Special Operations Forces. Basic training is conducted at the parachute and ranger course in Schongau. Further training is conducted at the Long Range Reconnaissance Training Center at Neuhausen ob Eck.

Responsibility for countering terrorism and other threats to internal order are vested in the Ministry of the Interior Department P (Police Affairs), and the principal organizational force responsible for such efforts is the GSG 9.

When terrorist groups began operating extensively in Europe in the late 1960s the West Germans were very reluctant to be seen to form a dedicated antiterrorist squad because of the quite understandable fear of reviving memories of the Nazi regime. Such considerations were taken even further at the 1972 Munich Olympics where security was kept deliberately low-key in an attempt to promote a "pacific" image of the new Germany. Sadly, the West Germans were taught a dreadful lesson by the Black September terrorists who killed two members of the Israeli Olympic team and took nine others

Above: *GSG 9 man with a silenced MP-5 submachine gun. Standard equipment of every GSG 9 officer weighs 265lb (120kg) and includes everything from machineguns to running shoes.*

hostage. The West Germans staggered from crisis to crisis in their attempts to solve the problem, but it ended in tragedy when the nine hostages and the terrorists died together in a spectacular "shoot-out" at the Furstenfeldbruck military airfield.

Determined to avoid further national humiliation, the West Germans created a totally new counter-terrorist group, but as part of the *Bundesgrenzschutz* (the Federal Border Police), and designated it *Grenzschutzgruppe 9* (GSG 9). This unit proved itself in October 1977 at Mogadishu in Somalia when a team of 27 men took part in a six-minute assault on a hijacked Lufthansa airliner and

released the 87 hostages. Since then there have been no overt GSG 9 operations, although there have been rumors of clandestine successes.

Organization

Unlike virtually all other elite counter-terrorist units, GSG 9 is firmly a police unit, coming under the direction of the Federal Ministry of the Interior. The unit was 180 strong at the time of Mogadishu and as a result of that operation it was decided to increase it to 300, but recruiting difficulties keep strength at about 160 to 200.

GSG 9 is in the process of increasing the unit strengths of its four combat units to 42 each. Overall, GSG 9 consists of a headquarters unit; a communications and documentation unit; an engineer unit; a training unit that can be used as another combat unit; a helicopter flight of three helicopters and 11 pilots and mechanics; and a supply unit. Within the combat units are a headquarters unit and a number of "special action" teams.

Selection and training

All members of GSG 9 must be volunteers from the ranks of the police force. Thus, any soldier who wishes to join must first leave the Army and join the Border Police. The training course is 22 weeks long and is directed at mind *and* body. The first 13 weeks are devoted to police duties, legal matters, weapons skills and karate.

Training takes place in a variety of locations as befits a unit which does not necessarily know in advance where it will be committed. The second part of the course comprises a detailed examination of terrorist movements combined with a final development of individual skills, including new developments in the optics and communications industries. The students become

Above: *GSG 9 has an array of weapons and vehicles that make it the envy of other strike forces, including specially modified Mercedes automobiles, some with barrel "ports" in the windshields.*

Right: *Ikar descender used by GSG 9 forces during training. The GSG 9 physical training is combined with intense academic training, and stresses terrorist theory.*

Below left: *A training session for the GSG 9. A special problem for an elite unit like this is to maintain enthusiasm over long periods of training and rare action.*

Below: *Other elite units hold GSG 9 training in such high esteem that there are often members of such units – FBI, British SAS, GIGN – on exchange training with them.*

acquainted with sharpshooter tools such as night vision devices, observation glasses and the like. Evasive driving techniques are also taught.

Failure rate on the course is about 80 percent. There is a stronger emphasis on academic work than in most such counter-terrorist units.

Weapons and equipment

The basic weapon is the standard police sub-machine gun – the Heckler and Koch MP 9mm – but when used by GSG 9 it is fitted with a silencer. The Hek G3SG1 is used for sniper missions and can be equipped with a gre-nade launcher. The men also use Mauser 66 sniper rifles and carry pistols; they are allowed to select their own model, a rare degree of choice in such units. Most unusual of the weapons is the Hek P9P 9mm P7 pistol which features a unique cocking device operated by gripping the gunframe – release it and the gun is totally safe!

Uniforms

GSG 9 members wear standard *Bundes-grenzschutz* uniform – a green battledress with a dark green beret. On operations the standard West German paratrooper helmet is worn, together with a flak jacket where necessary. No special unit identification is worn, although the wearing of a parachute qualification badge by a policeman may be an indication of his role.

ITALY
ALPINE TROOPS

THE MAJOR land threat to Italy comes from the north and northeast, and virtually the whole of this strategically critical region is mountainous. For this reason the Italian Army has long maintained its units of crack mountain troops – the famous Alpini. There are five mountain brigades *(brigata alpina)*: Taurinese, Orobica, Tridentina, Cadore and *Julia*. They serve in three army corps: III Corps (HQ at Milan) includes one mountain brigade; IV Corps (Bolzano) is responsible for the defense of the crucial Brenner Pass and has three mountain brigades; and V Corps (Vittorio Veneto) is responsible for the northeastern border with Austria and Jugoslavia, and has one mountain brigade; finally, one Alpini battalion is permanently assigned to the Allied Command Europe Mobile Force (Land).

The Alpine Brigades consist of a signals company, an engineer company, an aviation flight, a parachute platoon, a mountain artillery regiment (three battalions of 105mm howitzers and one battalion of 155mm howitzers), and a mountain infantry (Alpini) regiment of three to four battalions, together with an APC company. All the troops of the brigades are mountain trained and the supply columns have mules.

Selection and training

The 2nd Alpine Regiment is responsible for basic training and there is also an Alpine warfare school. All soldiers in the mountain brigades must be trained in mountain warfare, which requires a very high standard of fitness and determination. The Italian Army as a whole has a major training problem, however, because it is made up of conscripts who serve only for 12 months, of which the first three (which includes one course modeled after US Ranger training) are devoted to basic training. Add in four months of platoon training, followed by company and specialist training, and there is not much time left for service with a combat unit.

Weapons and equipment

Standard weapon of the Alpini soldier is currently the Beretta BM59 Mark Ital TA 7.62mm rifle (TA = Truppe Alpini). This weapon is an Italian development of the US Garand M1 0.30in rifle. The basic rifle – the BM59 Mark Ital – weighs 10lb (4.6kg) and has an effective range of 656 yards (600m). The Mark Ital TA has a tubular metal folding butt, a pistol grip and a special winter trigger to enable it to be fired when wearing gloves. Standard SMG is the 9mm Model 38/49 Beretta, a sturdy and reliable weapon, although the design is a development of a weapon first produced in 1938.

One item designed for the Alpini artillery, which has become world famous is the Oto Melara 105mm Model 56 pack-howitzer. This gun can be broken down into eleven sections

ITALY
COMSUBIN

for transportation by pack-mules. It has a range of 11,565 yards (10,575m), and over 2,400 have been sold to some 25 armies.

Uniform

The most instantly recognizable feature of Alpini dress is the famous grey-green felt mountaineer's hat, with a black eagle feather and red pompom on the left-hand side. The cap badge is of black metal and depicts an eagle above a light-infantry bugle containing the regimental number. The eagle feather and pompom are also worn on the steel helmet. The Alpini collar-patch is green. In parade dress the officers wear the traditional blue sash.

There are various types of combat dress, varying from standard combat uniform to full mountain gear of white hooded overall and trousers with a white-covered steel helmet – which provides both warmth and camouflage in snow.

Above: *H&K P11 underwater pistol used by COMSUBIN. The pistols are used on very special underwater missions. Electrically operated with 224V batteries, they have a 5 round magazine. Out of water, the weapon has the same effect as a 7.26 5mm pistol.*

Above: *Given its nimble-footedness and adaptability to severe weather conditions, the pack mule is the basic means of meeting the logistics requirement of the Alpini. US special forces will need to work with mules and get training from this source.*

Top left: *Alpini soldier in a good firing position with his MILAN anti-tank missile. Note the snow shoes to the left of the tree; despite legends, snow shoes are of use only for short distances.*

Left: *Members of the Alpini Brigade fight their way up the side of a mountain. Snow tractors, motor sledges and helicopters lend mobility to these elite mountain units, for the basic ski trooper is still the essential element.*

Left: *COMSUBIN support team members being "rescued" by a Sea King helicopter from rubber raft after an assault exercise. They originally had been air-dropped (200m) with all their explosives and weapons in amphibious containers.*

THE USE OF swimmers in combat is anything but new – it has been a part of warfare since ancient times. But the Italian Naval Assault Divisions of World War I and World War II can rightfully be considered among the pioneers of modern warfare of this type. Their record at Trieste, Pola, Suda Bay, Gibraltar and Malta only serves to underscore the point. Heirs to this legacy are the Italian Navy's current special operations force, known formally as *Commando Raggruppamento Subacqui ed Incursori* (COMSUBIN), or the Navy Frogmen and Raider's Group.

As a special operations force, its missions include clearing mines, explosives and underwater obstacles from Italian waters; landings on friendly or foreign territory for reconnaissance purposes; clearing beaches of obstacles prior to amphibious landings; and commando raids to destroy ships, dry-docks and fuel storage areas.

Rumors of a counterterrorist role for COMSUBIN first came to the surface in 1978 and were substantiated the following year, when the unit was called out when a hijacked airliner from Beirut was brought to Rome. Involvement continues in this role: COMSUBIN elements, for example, were deployed on Italian vessels near Lebanon during the *Achille Lauro* incident.

Organization

The 200-man strong COMSUBIN reports to the Navy Chief of Staff and is headquartered just outside La Spezia. From an organizational standpoint, the Raider Operations Group has responsibility for offensive operations, while the Frogman Group provides Italian coastline support.

Personnel for both units are drawn primarily from the crack San Marco naval infantry battalion – the 1,000-man Italian "marine corps". San Marco battalion personnel receive general commando training from the COMSUBIN – but they must leave the battalion when they volunteer for service with it.

The Raider Operations Group *(Gruppo Operativo Subacquei)* support is provided by a schools group, research and study group, and a special naval group.

Above: *Special forces descend cliff using rapelling technique which requires fitness, teamwork, stamina and courage, especially under fire. Scaling techniques get special emphasis in the 10-month training program.*

Below: *Member of the Folgore parachute brigade. Note the green beret with the parachutist's red badge. The weapon is a 9mm model 12 Beretta submachine gun, which has an automatic rate of fire of 120 rounds per minute.*

Below: *Italian Navy special forces support team with Franchi SPAS 15 shotgun and Beretta 92S pistols. The Franchi is used as a multi-purpose weapon for assault operations and the Beretta is the standard pistol for these forces.*

Selection and training

Currently, the all-volunteer (mostly from the San Marco battalion) *Incursori* are required to complete a 10 month training course. Rigorous physical tests are a part of it and, in fact, are required every three months for everyone in the unit for as long as they remain in the unit. The program includes ranger, parachute, hand-to-hand, demolitions and, of course, weapons training. These are in addition to Scuba and other swimming skills.

Those who go on to be part of the Raiders Group get an additional 42 weeks of specialized training with emphasis on parachuting, mountain climbing and vigorous physical endurance tests. This is capped off with a six-week command course. The COMSUBIN unit, not surprisingly, is rated quite highly by those who have observed it.

The *Incursori* use the same weapons as other Italian units in the main, with the Beretta 9mm model 12 submachne gun a particular favorite because of its compactness.

ITALY
FOLGORE BRIGADE

THE LINEAGE of Italian airborne forces can be traced back to 1938 when the first Italian parachute battalion was formed. Italy's current principal unconventional warfare unit is the 9th Airborne Assault (Saboteur) Battalion of the Folgore Airborne Brigade. Although detachments existed prior to 1962 as part of an airborne brigade, the date of formation is not published.

The Brigade's mission is to gather information and to perform sabotage and guerilla operations in enemy territory. Because its missions are related to Italy's support role in NATO, mountain operations also receive emphasis. The ranks of the Folgore Parachute Brigade contain parachute troops trained as airborne Alpine troops, airborne commandos, airborne artillerymen as well as other specialists.

Organization

The Italian Army's V Corps (HQ Vittorio Veneto) controls the Folgore Brigade, which is based at Pisa under the commander, Territory VII. The *paracadutisti* brigade Folgore consists of an engineer company, an aviation flight, engineer flight, one artillery battalion and a parachute infantry regiment of two battalions, plus a Carabinieri battalion.

A militarized national police force which also handles the military police function for the Italian armed forces, the Carabinieri is one of four battalions in the brigade, but it also retains a limited amount of autonomy and an Italian counterterrorist unit reportedly draws its recruits from the Carabinieri. Although Folgore has been designated as a counterterrorist unit, it does not have the principal domestic counterterror responsibility in Italy.

Saboteur Battalion – which has an approximate strength of 225 men – is another of the four battalions (the remaining two serve more conventional roles although all units are parachutable or air-transportable). The battalion is comprised of an HQ, training company, and an operations company – with a third company authorized in wartime. The Saboteur Battalion normally operates in patrols of two to 20 men.

Selection and training

Military service is imposed on all fit Italian males by the Constitution of 1947. The Brigade's unit training is oriented toward individual and team skills, much like those of US special forces. Emphasis is placed on underwater operations, airborne-launched and overland sabotage operations, deep reconnaissance and support for partisan forces.

Battalion members are all volunteers and its enlisted personnel reach noncommissioned officer rank. More than 16 months are spent in training, which includes physical training (4½ months); communications (2½); underwater demolition training (3½); parachute training (1½); skiing (1); artillery (3); and alpine training (1).

The Italian special operations trooper is recognized by his counterparts from other nations as high in proficiency in individual skills. Proficiency in unit skills is rated lower, perhaps because those skills are exercised less frequently.

Weapons and uniform

Members of the Parachute Brigade wear a maroon beret with the parachutist's beret badge. The camouflage uniform is one of the most practical around, with built-in knee and elbow pads which are gathered at the wrists, ankles and waist. The patch of the Folgore Brigade is worn on a "hanger" at the left shoulder, together with appropriate chevrons. Parachutist's badges, when worn, are on the right breast.

Collar insignia consist of silver "Savoy" star and winged parachute with dagger. The color of the background the star rests on indicates unit function – eg, black with red edging for engineers, or medium blue for all Brigade members except specialists.

Weapons include the Beretta 9mm Corto (.380 ACP) automatic pistol and the folding stock BM59 "Paracadutisti" assault rifle, which has a detachable grenade launcher and comes equipped with a folding bipod.

Left: *Parachutists of the Folgore Brigade prepare for jump in full regalia. The camouflage pattern is one that is standard throughout the Italian armed forces. Their weapons are BM59 7.62mm rifles.*

Below: *The Folgore Brigade contains parachutists trained as airborne alpine troops, commandos, artillery men, as well as other specialties. A MILAN anti-tank missile system is used here.*

SPAIN
SPANISH FOREIGN LEGION

IN CONTRAST to the better-known French Foreign Legion, the Regiment of Foreigners (*Tercio de Extranjeros* – Spanish Foreign Legion) consists almost entirely (90 percent) of natives. Formed by the King of Spain in 1920, it was inspired by its French counterpart, but also drew from the example of foreign and Spanish volunteers who fought in the Carlist civil wars of the early 19th century.

In fact, Lt. Col. Jose Millan Astray, prime force in creating the unit, spent time in Algeria studying the French Foreign Legion's recruiting methods, organization and field operations. He also demanded that all legionnaires substitute its "Credo of the Legion" for their past allegiances. Drawn up in collaboration with legionnaire and future "Generalissimo" Francisco Franco, the credo blended a number of concepts. Basically, however, it amounted to a tough and die-hard approach to soldiering. The Legion offered atonement and redemption for all past sins through self-denial, suffering and death. As one of its songs proclaims, "We are the bridegrooms of death."

True to that belief, during the Moroccan War (1920-27), the Legion suffered 45 percent casualties among officers and 38 percent among enlisted men in the 845 engagements in which it fought. Following that war, it reverted to its role as a colonial army, guarding Spain's remaining African possessions. These included two small enclaves – Melilla and Ceuta – in northern Morocco, where Spanish Foreign Legion units are still based today.

Ultimately, the decolonization process played itself out, armed conflict erupted with the Algerian-backed Polisario Front, and by 1981 the last of the Legion's monuments commemorating African battles was dismantled.

Organization

Today's Foreign Legion is made up of four regiments with subunits called *banderas* (flags), which are units of less than battalion size. The battalion color of each bandera evokes an episode, person or symbol famous in Spanish history. One bandera emblem, for example, is the double eagle of the House of Hapsburg.

There are three rifle companies and a support element to each bandera. The smallest unit with the Legion company is a four-man section under the command of a corporal.

The 1st of the Legion (1st, 2nd, 3rd Banderas) is based at Melilla; 2nd of the Legion (4th, 5th and 6th Banderas) is headquartered at the enclave of Ceuta; and 3rd of the Legion (7th and 8th Banderas and the 1st Light Group) is deployed at Fuerteventura in the Canary Islands.

The recently activated 4th of the Legion is based at Ronda, Spain. Found there as well is the Legion's elite Special Operations Unit. It has officially replaced the unofficial Special Operations Platoons, which were an integral part of each bandera in the early 1970s. This unit trains in activities such as Scuba, military parachuting, unarmed combat and guerrilla

tactics, and counterinsurgency operations.

The Legion Special Operations Unit (OLEU) attracts some of the best personnel in the Legion and is essentially a commando unit.

In 1979, the Legion was a formidable military force of about 10,000 soldiers and some estimates place its strength today at around 7,200. However, in line with recent army modernization efforts by the Spanish government, the unit has been reduced to 2,000 men, who will be re-equipped and trained as a rapid deployment force.

Weapons and equipment

The Spanish Foreign Legion uses basic infantry weapons, which include the 7.62 CETME Model 68 rifle, the 9mm Star Z-70B sub-machine gun (which is rapidly replacing the Z-62), and the 60.7mm ECIA mortar.

The Legion also has M41 and AMX-13 light tanks, AML-90 light armored cars and M-3 armored personnel carriers, as well as a number of American eight-ton trucks and British Land Rovers.

Selection and Training

Enlisting in the Spanish Foreign Legion is an easy and relatively straightforward process. A passport will work, or the applicant need only certify to the information he gives. To enroll, he need only go to a military or government building, police station or civil guard station at any port, airport or city within Spanish national territory or its islands.

After a thorough briefing, the candidate is given the option to quit; however, after passing a medical examination and upon being accepted, he incurs a minimum obligation of three years – a term he can expand to four or five years if desired.

Training is short, intensive and strict. The Legion's objective is to instill basic military skills in as short a time as possible – the usual training period is three months. It takes place at Ronda and includes drill, physical courses and familiarization with the traditions and disciplines of the Legion.

Above: *Spanish Foreign Legionnaires with 7.62mm CETME Model 68 rifles. Willingness to die under the standard of the Legion, said its founder, is the only qualification for service. He said, "It will be the most glorious because it will be stained with the blood of the legionnaires."*

Discipline is harsh and based on fear. Offenders are liable to find themselves in prison (not a desirable thing since prisoners sleep on concrete slabs and can be beaten at whim by the guards), or the recipient of a rain of blows to the head for poor shooting at a standard target. All things being relative, however, this punishment is mild compared to earlier times when, under some circumstances and for certain offenses, the legionnaire could be shot.

Much time is devoted in the field to the route march. Long distances are covered over rough terrain – either in light order or with heavy pack, depending upon the individual commander.

The typical legionnaire, however, is heavily dependent upon his officers for such basic things such as navigation, tactics and first aid in the field. His training in advanced weaponry and modern forms of warfare is negligible, something that may change with the anticipated modernization of the army.

To become an officer, it is first necessary to become a Spanish citizen. The highest rank to which one can be promoted as a legionnaire is that of major.

Uniform

Green is the traditional color of the Legion's uniform. The caps are specially designed and have a small red tassel. Short sleeve blouses are worn, which are open at the collar. Breeches are like jodhpurs, and legionnaires wear gauntleted gloves and white-lined capes with a fur collar and hood for cold nights. Webbing straps and belts are used instead of the leather versions found in the rest of the Spanish Army.

UNITED KINGDOM
GURKHAS

THE BONDS which link the legendary Gurkhas from the hills of Nepal with the British Army are slightly difficult to understand, but their strength is self-evident. The British in India fought two short wars against the Gurkhas in 1813 and 1816, which resulted in a very hard-won British victory and considerable mutual respect for each other's martial qualities. As a result three battalions of Gurkhas were immediately raised (1815) and Gurkhas have served the British Crown ever since.

By World War II, they numbered almost 250,000 soldiers. For well over a century the Gurkhas were part of the British Indian Army, but when the British left the Indian subcontinent in 1947 the Gurkha units were split between the new Indian Army and the British Army. The British Gurkhas moved to Malaya where these redoubtable mountain warriors became highly respected jungle fighters, playing a significant role in the defeat of the Malayan Communists. These skills stood them in good stead when they took part in the "confrontation" campaign in Borneo against the Indonesians. The Gurkhas today number about 8,300 and are based in Hong Kong, the sultanate of Brunei and in Church Crookham, near the main British Infantry Training Center at Aldershot.

The Ghurkas' most recent campaign was in 1982 when 1st Battalion, 7th Duke of Edinburgh's Own Gurkha Rifles (1/7GR) went to the Falkland Islands as part of 5 Infantry Brigade. They landed in San Carlos Bay and spent their first week mounting patrols to round up Argentine stragglers. On June 8 they went to Bluff Cove and then on to join in the final attacks on the Argentine positions around Port Stanley. The Argentine soldiers were quite literally terrified of the Gurkhas, who they accused of being "high" on drugs

Above: *A radio operator of the 6th Gurkha Rifles (6GR) in the dense jungles of Malaya.*

and of mercilessly killing all prisoners. Nothing could be further from the truth; in fact, the sole death of a Gurkha was the result of an accident after the fighting had ended. But it would be idle to deny that the Gurkhas had a very poor opinion of the Argentine soldiers who fled at the first sign that they were facing the famed Gurkha Rifles.

Organization

The original three battalions expanded and changed titles over the years, but basically there have been 10 regiments (of varying numbers of battalions) for most of the Gurkhas' history. In 1947 when the British left India, the 1st, 4th, 5th, 8th and 9th Gurkha

Rifles went to the Indian Army, and the balance – 2nd, 6th, 7th and 10th Gurkha Rifles – to the British Army. Still serving in the British Army are the 2nd King Edward VII's Own Goorkhas (The Sirmoor Rifles), two battalions; 6th Queen Elizabeth's Own Gurkha Rifles; 7th Duke of Edinburgh's Own Gurkha Rifles, two battalions; and 10th Princess-Mary's Own Gurkha Rifles.

Individual battalions are on the standard British Army organization, with some very minor amendments to comply with regimental custom. Following their move to the British Army, the Gurkhas expanded their activities to include engineers, signals and transportation. At times there have also been Gurkha artillery, parachute troops and military police, but these have all been disbanded.

The infantry battalions have very few British officers, the great majority being Queen's Gurkha Officers who have worked their way up through the ranks to Warrant Officer before being commissioned. The most senior is the Gurkha Major, a figure of immense prestige, who is the Commanding Officer's adviser on all Gurkha matters.

The principal current formation is the Gurkha Field Force (equivalent to a brigade) which is located at Sek Kong Camp in the New Territories in Hong Kong. This comprises four Gurkha battalions, of which one is detached to Brunei where it serves (and is paid for by) the Sultan. There is one battalion in England, stationed near Aldershot, and another in a training role in Hong Kong.

Selection and training

Gurkhas are recruited from the hill tribesmen in the Himalayan kingdom of Nepal. They are signed up at the age of 17 by itinerant *gallah-wallahs* (ex-Gurkhas who get a bounty for

Below: *Jungle warfare training is always a top priority for the Gurkhas.*

Below: *Creating the universal Gurkha soldier. His rifle is the US M16A1.*

each successful sign-up) and serve a minimum commitment of 15 years.

Instead of being called by name, Gurkhas are referred to by serial numbers – the last two digits of this number becoming "nicknames". Gurkha tribal names are left behind for the new life. A concept called *kaida*, which translates into a system of order, ritual and loyalty to officers and each other that is unquestioned, is the secret of their training and fortitude. As might be expected, boot camp is rigorous and transforms the Gurkha recruit in nine months from an often illiterate and barefoot mountain tribesman into a solid member of one of the world's most unusual – and ferocious – fighting forces. Recruits arrive in Hong Kong in January of every year to begin training.

Uniform and weapons

Gurkhas wear their own variations of British Army uniform. Combat kit is standard camouflage pattern smock and trousers, with green canvas webbing, except, of course, for the addition of the famous kukri weapon. Parade uniform is rifle-green in temperate climates and white in the tropics, with black, patent-leather waist belts for soldiers and cross-belts for officers. Buttons and badges are black. Soldiers wear a black pill-box hat on parade or the Gurkha slouch-hat, and a green beret in other forms of dress.

The kukri is the subject of many myths. The knives come in various sizes, but the dog-legged shape is constant. The rear edge is thick and blunt, making the knife quite heavy, but the cutting-edge is razor sharp. The kukri is no way a throwing knife, but it is quite excellent for hand-to-hand fighting and is the Gurkhas' preferred close-combat weapon. It is therefore always carried in war and there are many stories of its use against Germans, Japanese and Malayan Communists, to mention but a few of the Gurkhas' more recent enemies.

The future

With the prospect of the British departure from Hong Kong in 1997 the future of the British Gurkhas is once more in doubt. One or two battalions might be sustained in the United Kingdom, but this would be very expensive. Nevertheless it would be a very sad day were the ties between these legendary soldiers and the British Crown they have served so well to be severed.

Nowhere is the depth of this unique relationship more clearly described than in (of all places) the introduction to a Nepali language dictionary compiled by Sir Ralph Turner some sixty years ago: "As I write these last words, my thoughts return to you who were my comrades, the stubborn and indomitable peasants of Nepal. Once more I hear the laughter with which you greeted every hardship. Once more I see you in your bivouacs or about your fires, on forced march or in the trenches, now shivering with wet and cold, now scorched by a pitiless and burning sun. Uncomplaining, you endure hunger and thirst and wounds, and at last your unwavering lines disappear into the smoke and wrath of battle. Bravest of the brave, most generous of the generous, never had a country more faithful friends than you".

Or, in the words of a Gurkha commander, "They are just bloody good soldiers".

Above: *John Stanley, UK Defence Minister, pays a visit to a Gurkha training site. At the end of this 32-week training period, the boys from the mountains of Nepal will become the men of the Gurkhas.*

Left: *Although Gurkhas are recruited from the hills – a real contrast to the environment of the jungle – they have become among the best and most feared jungle fighters in the world.*

Below: *All ranks of Gurkhas must be capable of absorbing vast quantities of military instruction, including an understanding of advanced weapon systems and equipment such as this MILAN anti-tank missile system.*

UNITED KINGDOM
THE PARACHUTE REGIMENT

Above: *Captured Argentine soldiers are searched by British paratroopers during the 1982 war in the South Atlantic.*

Below: *Paras on the Falkland Islands manning a 7.62mm general purpose machine gun mounted on a tripod in the sustained fire role.*

Above: *British paratrooper in a new landing zone. His rucksack is not carried on him during the jump, but is suspended on the 'chute.*

THE VERY name of The Parachute Regiment (the "Paras") has come to signify both a type of soldiering and a certain "style" – dramatic, forceful and with panache. Para-troops would, it seems, always need to be fighting against heavy odds and either suc-ceed brilliantly or suffer glorious defeats: the one performance that is never allowed is an indifferent one.

It was Winston Churchill who demanded that a slightly reluctant War Office establish a corps of parachutists on the German model, and after a somewhat hesitant start the first unit was formed in late 1940.

When World War II ended, the Paras found themselves involved in many small wars on virtually every continent. These con-flicts have taken the Paras to Malaya, Borneo, Palestine, Suez, Aden, Cyprus, Kuwait, North Borneo, Northern Ireland and the Falkland Islands.

There was a major reduction in parachute troops in the immediate post-war years, and again in the 1960s and 1970s. 16th Parachute Brigade existed in Aldershot from 1949 to 1977 when it was redesignated 6 Field Force in one of the British Army's endless series of reorganizations and only one battalion of The Parachute Regiment was left in the parachute role. On 1 January 1982 6th Field Force became 5 Infantry Brigade and included among its units 2nd and 3rd Battalions The Parachute Regiment.

The Paras have always been among the more successful units in Northern Ireland and thus naturally a target for hostile propaganda. This reached a nadir on January 30, 1972, in the so-called "Bloody Sunday" episode when a crowd of civilians attacked the Paras and in the ensuing action some 13 civilians were killed. There was an enormous outcry, but the battalions of The Parachute Regiment have continued to return to Northern Ireland.

With the South Atlantic War in 1982, these

two battalions were hived off to 3 Commando Brigade and sent south with the Marines. In the Falklands these two units performed very well, and at Goose Green 550 men of 2 Para took on 1,400 Argentines and defeated them utterly, even though their commanding officer, Lt. Col. "H" Jones, died in the battle. In the finest Para tradition he died at the head of his men, personally leading an attack against a machine-gun position that was holding up the entire attack. He was posthumously awarded the Victoria Cross.

In December 1982 the British Secretary of State for Defence, Michael Heseltine, went to Aldershot to announce in person that 5 Infantry Brigade was to be redesignated 5 Airborne Brigade forthwith, so it would appear that the existence of the British Parachute Regiment is secure for a few more years.

Organization

There are currently three battalions of The Parachute Regiment in the British Regular Army (1, 2 and 3 Para), and a further three battalions in the Territorial Army (4, 10 and 15 Para). Two of the three regular battalions are part of 5 Airborne Brigade.

A parachute battalion is organized simi-larly to a standard infantry battalion, with three rifle companies and a support com-pany. However, it has a far lighter scale of transport. Because the battalion depends on the physical fitness and fighting efficiency of the men, more emphasis is placed upon selection and effective training.

Selection and training

All officers and men must volunteer for the Parachute Regiment. Prospective recruits undergo thorough mental, educational and psychometric tests – and then only the most educationally and mentally alert are selected as candidates for the Regiment.

The extremely arduous training course of 23 weeks is similar in many ways to that for Royal Marine Commandos. The first eight weeks follow the lines of what is laid down for recruits for the Army: drill, weapons training, everything on the double, plenty of exercise and map reading. The 12th week is the dreaded "P Company" week, in which members are selected for further training. About 80 percent of the recruits who have gone this far will pass.

Following completion of training, the men, who pride themselves on being the 'Spearhead of the Army" and on their ability to fight in any terrain and climate, will join their battalions. Only 35 percent of those who started the course will have gained their "wings".

Weapons and equipment

When there was an independent parachute force (16 Parachute Brigade) there was sufficient demand for it to be economical to produce special equipment for paratroop units. When the commitment was reduced in the past few years to just two battalions in the parachute role, with virtually no back-up from parachute-trained and -equipped supporting arms and services, such special equipment virtually disappeared. Thus, UK parachute units currently use standard British Army weapons and equipment, such as the 7.62mm L1A1 rifle, 9mm L2A3 Sterling sub-machine gun and L7A2 7.62mm general-purpose machine-gun.

However, the British Army is shortly to be issued with the 5.56mm L70A1 Individual Weapon, also known as the Small Arm for the 80s (SA80), an excellent weapon using the "bull-pup" design. This rifle is neat, compact and well-balanced and has proved very popular in troop trials. It can be expected that the battalions of The Parachute Regiment will be among the earliest to receive this weapon and its light machine-gun version, the L73A1.

Obviously, the Parachute Regiment is also to take full advantage of advanced weaponry and equipment as it enters service with the British Army.

Uniforms

The British paratroops' red beret has been adopted around the world and has given rise to their nicknames of "The Red Devils" and "The Red Berets". (History has it that Major-General Browning and another general were arguing over the color of a beret for the paratroops and, unable to agree, they turned to the nearest soldier to ask his views. "Red, sir," came the instant answer.) The red beret can be worn only by members of The Parachute Regiment (throughout their service) and by members of other Corps who are parachute-qualified, but only when on service with a parachute unit. The sleeve badge is a winged Pegasus.

Above: *Men of the SBS, the Royal Marines' elite unit, emerge from the hatch of a submarine during training. The ability to deliver men from a submarine onto a hostile shore is a valuable capability and was used on a number of occasions during the South Atlantic war of 1982.*

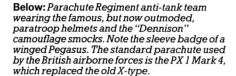

Below: *Parachute Regiment anti-tank team wearing the famous, but now outmoded, paratroop helmets and the "Dennison" camouflage smocks. Note the sleeve badge of a winged Pegasus. The standard parachute used by the British airborne forces is the PX 1 Mark 4, which replaced the old X-type.*

Below: *Swimmer-canoeists paddle towards the shore in a Klepper canoe. This lightweight canoe has replaced the Cockle type and is considerably more stable. It has tough rubber and polyester skin fitted over a wooden frame, which is tightened when bouyancy bags under the gunwale are inflated.*

UNITED KINGDOM
ROYAL MARINES SPECIAL BOAT SQUADRON

TO A LARGE extent, the whole of the 7,000 Royal Marines is an elite force in itself; every Marine would certainly claim it so. However, within the Royal Marines there are a number of smaller and more select groups of which the best known and most highly trained is the Special Boat Squadron (SBS). An elite within an elite, it is the Royal Marines equivalent to the British Special Air Service (SAS). It has its roots in the special units raised in World War II for raiding and reconnaissance on the shores of the European mainland. The techniques evolved so painfully in war were, fortunately, preserved in peace, despite many cutbacks and amalgamations. The Amphibious School of the Royal Marines at Eastney (now at Poole in Dorset) included a "Small Raids Wing", which was later redesignated the "Special Boat Company" and then, in 1977, the "Special Boat Squadron".

The SBS is the headquarters for the Special Boat Sections which are deployed under the operational command of Commando units, but can also act autonomously on special tasks. Its activities and organization are always secret. The mission of the SBS can roughly be equated with that of the Spetsnaz in the USSR and the SEALS in the US Navy. They are responsible for coastal sabotage operations and ground, surface, or underwater reconnaissance of potential landing beaches and enemy coastal facilities. Moreover, they are believed to have particular responsibility for security of Britain's off-shore oil and gas rigs.

The SBS has seen action in Oman, Borneo and during the Falkland Islands War. In the latter, the SBS were early ashore on South Georgia, having flown from the UK in a C-130 and then parachuted to a submarine in the South Atlantic. The submarine took them close inshore and they then completed their long journey in inflatable Gemini boats. The SBS is also rumored to have put patrols ashore on the Argentine mainland, landing from the conventional submarine, HMS *Onyx*, although this has never been confirmed. The SBS and SAS operated on the Falkland Islands twelve days before the amphibious landings, and the SBS reconnoitred the actual landing sites at San Carlos Bay. They welcomed the first landing-craft to reach the shore, and also silenced the Argentinian outpost on Fanning Head, overlooking the landings.

The way in which the SBS fits in with the much larger SAS organization is a matter for speculation, particularly as the SAS is known to have a Boat Troop, with similar equipment and capabilities to the SBS. Nevertheless, there is no known friction between the two units, and it must therefore be assumed that the responsibilities are not a problem in practice.

Selection and training

Recruitment to the SBS is from volunteers serving in the Royal Marine Commandos. All such officer and Marine volunteers undergo the usual physical and psychological tests, followed by a three-week selection test. Successful candidates then go on a 15-week training course in reconnaissance, demolitions, diving, and use of the Klepper canoe or Gemini craft. They then complete a four-week parachute course, following which they join an operational Special Boat Section.

SBS officers and Marines are not compelled to leave the SBS after a set period, as, for example, in the SAS, but like some other special forces they are usually forced to leave if they wish to obtain promotion past a certain point.

Uniforms

The SBS wear standard Royal Marine uniform and the commando green beret. The only indication in parade and barrack dress that a man belongs to the SBS is the wearing of Royal Marine parachuting wings on the right shoulder and of the "Swimmer Canoeist" badge on the right forearm. The latter has a crown above the letters "SC", flanked by laurel leaves. In parade dress both badges are embroidered in gold on a black backing. Officers of the SBS wear the wings, but not the "SC" badge (even though they are qualified to wear it by having passed the course).

Above: *These Avon Rubber dry diving suits and dry sacs are used by the Royal Navy. The sacs shield weapons, ammunition and provisions so that the swimmers can "come out fighting".*

Weapons and equipment

The SBS four-man half section patrols are usually armed with the US M16 Armalite rifle and M203 grenade launchers, although a special silenced version of the British Sterling sub-machine-gun (L34A1) is also used. Included in the patrol's equipment are plastic explosives, laser designators and burst-transmission radios.

SBS reconnaissance patrols travel light and have three-layered kits (escape and evasion, belt and pack). Very little is known about the escape and evasion kit, which presumably has survival devices and equipment hidden in clothing and other equipment. A handgun, knife, fishing line, water bottles, snares and a food pouch are in the belt kit. The pack kit contains some extra food, dry clothing and a waterproof poncho.

Boats used by the SBS include paddleboards (akin to surfboards), specially-produced Klepper Mark 13 collapsible boats, and the somewhat larger Gemini boats powered by 40bhp outboard motors. The SBS can also be transported by "Rigid Raider" boats, a militarized version of the glassfiber "Dory" fishing-boat, powered by outboards of up to 140bhp, operated by the specialists of the Royal Marines' Rigid Raider Squadron, with the capacity to carry 10 personnel.

There is also the "Kestrel", a three-man collapsible, which is small enough to be attached to the leg of a parachutist. Powered by a 9.5hp motor, which is dropped separately, the Kestrel is inflated by carbon dioxide.

UNITED KINGDOM
SPECIAL AIR SERVICE

IN DECEMBER 1975 a four-man "Active-Service Unit" of the Provisional IRA was cornered by London's Metropolitan Police in a flat in Balcombe Street, in the capital's Marylebone area. The four Irishmen held the owners – an understandably terrified couple – hostage, and the police were faced with the problem of resolving matters without physical harm coming to the elderly pair. The "Provos" were confident that they could strike a bargain with the police sooner or later. It was known that there was a radio receiver in the flat and, during a routine news broadcast, the BBC announced that an armed section of the Special Air Service (SAS) had arrived at the scene. Shortly afterwards, the Provos surrendered. They could cope with the police, but the SAS was something else again!

Foundation

The SAS was formed early in World War II with the appropriate motto "Who Dares Wins" at a time when many "special" units were being raised. Known originally as "L Detachment", the unit grew to 390 men in 1942 and was redesignated 1st Special Air Service Regiment (1 SAS). After various reorganizations and a period of further growth, an SAS

Brigade was formed in Scotland in January 1944, consisting of two British regiments (1 and 2 SAS), two French regiments (3 and 4 SAS), a Belgian squadron (later 5 SAS) and a signal squadron.

The SAS fought throughout the desert campaign, in Italy and in Northwest Europe, establishing a reputation for independent action by small groups of very highly trained men, operating deep behind enemy lines. At the end of the war in Europe the British Army divested itself of "private armies" (SAS among them), and it appeared the British Army had washed its hands of the "SAS idea" forever.

It takes more than that to keep a good idea down, however, and within months it was decided that there would be a future role for SAS-type activities. This led to the conversion of a Territorial Army (TA) unit, "The Artists' Rifles", into 21st Special Air Service Regiment (21 SAS) (Artists) – (Volunteers), the number 21 being obtained by combining and reversing the numbers of the two British wartime SAS regiments (1 and 2 SAS).

One of the early British post-war anti-colonial campaigns was the Malayan "Emergency" (1948-60). Brigadier Michael Calvert, a renowned ex-Chindit and commander of

the SAS Brigade 1944-45, arrived in Malaya in 1951 and formed the "Malayan Scouts (Special Air Service)" which quickly built up to regimental size. In 1952, the Malayan Scouts were redesignated 22nd Special Air Service Regiment (22 SAS), thus marking the official return of the SAS to the regular army's order of battle. The reputation of the SAS in Malaya was second to none. They spent very long periods in the deep jungle where they established particularly close links with the aboriginal peoples, and they also pioneered the techniques for parachuting into the trees and then abseiling down long ropes to the jungle floor.

When the conflict in Malaya began to wind down, the SAS were sent to the Oman in the Arabian peninsula in November/December 1958, where they carried out a daring attack on rebels in the 8,000ft (2,500m) high Jebel Akhdar, defeating the Arab dissidents on their own home ground. Following this success, 22 SAS moved to the UK where, after a short period in Malvern, they settled down in their now-famous home base at Bradbury Lines, Hereford. But by now they had been reduced to an HQ and two "sabre" squadrons.

The Far East soon beckoned again, how-

Left: *Clothed entirely and purposely in forbidding black – the uniform gives him a psychological edge – an SAS member practises abseiling down to a room housing "hostages". Special shoes help with the traction on the wall, his weapon is an MP-5A3, and the harness is specially developed for the SAS.*

Above right: *Special Air Service trooper practises tumble entry into a room where "hostages" are being held. In a lightning-fast, fluid movement he is firing as soon as he enters the room and picks out his target. The element of surprise itself is an effective "weapon".*

ever, with the "Confrontation Campaign" in Borneo, and a squadron of SAS arrived there in January 1963. Their success led to more demands for SAS and the third squadron was re-formed in mid-1963. This was just as well, because war broke out in Aden and from 1964-66 the three squadrons of 22 SAS were rotating between the UK, Borneo and Aden in a period known on the regiment as the "happy time". By 1967, these two wars were over and the SAS had a short period of consolidation and retraining.

In 1969 the situation in Northern Ireland exploded and the SAS began a long acquaintanceship with the Province. Simultaneously, renewed problems in Malaya and the Oman led to a return there. In July 1972, at the Battle of Mirbat in Oman, ten SAS soldiers, aided by a few local soldiers, defeated 250 dissidents in a memorable engagement. The SAS remained in the Oman for many years and there may be a few members there still. In August 1983 it was disclosed that the SAS was training a similar unit for the Sultan of Oman's "Special Force", composed of parachutists trained to exist for days on little food in desert conditions.

The anti-guerrilla campaigns of the 1950s,

1960s and early 1970s were succeeded by a new role in which the SAS quickly built up an unrivalled expertise – counter-terrorist actions. Spurred on by operations in Northern Ireland against the Irish Republican Army (IRA) and Irish National Liberation Army (INLA) the SAS has developed techniques which are copied throughout the Western world. This has led to the SAS not only being consulted by overseas governments and special forces, but also in being directly involved in some "foreign" operations. Thus, in October 1977, two SAS men were with the West German GSG-9 unit at the attack to recapture a hijacked German airliner at Mogadishu, and SAS members were also involved in the earlier Dutch operation against the Moluccan terrorists who had taken over a trainload of hostages.

Most famous of all such episodes, however, was the London Iranian Embassy siege of May 1980 when the SAS had perforce to conduct the operation in front of the world's TV cameras. In strict compliance with English law, the Metropolitan Police conducted the operation until the terrorists murdered one of the hostages and threw his body out on the street. The police then requested the SAS to take over, and the troops stormed in, using special weapons and tactics. The hostages were rescued, four of five terrorists killed, and not a single SAS man was lost.

This spectacular success, while a godsend for the hero-hungry world media, gave the SAS far more publicity than the Service would have preferred.

By 1982 the SAS seemed to be settled in a counter-terrorist role when the Falklands War broke out with Argentina. No. 22 SAS were immediately involved and were given the opportunity to remind the world that they are first and foremost professional soldiers, trained for war. They spearheaded the return to South Georgia island, although the first

reconnaissance landing in helicopters had to be aborted in truly appalling weather. The second landing was by inflatable boats and most men got ashore. One boat, however, broke down and the soldiers refused to compromise the operation by calling for help on the radio and were blown rapidly eastwards and were later rescued by helicopter. Meanwhile, at Grytviken, squadron headquarters and one troop of D Squadron took advantage of the crippling of the Argentine submarine "Santa Fe" to rush in and overwhelm the garrison, and South Georgia was quickly back under British control.

The first SAS soldiers were ashore on East Falklands by May 1 and remained there, close to the enemy and in foul weather, for some thirty days. They provided vital intelligence on troop movements and deployments, and also targeted enemy aircraft and naval gunfire support. On May 14 the SAS raided Pebble Island and blew up 11 Argentine aircraft; they also reportedly operated on the mainland of Argentina itself, although this has never been confirmed officially.

Their final role was to carry out a noisy and valuable diversionary attack on the eastern end of Wireless Ridge on the day before the Argentine surrender. That surrender was negotiated by Lieutenant Colonel Michael Rose, who had just handed over command of 22 SAS. He flew to Stanley to arrange the surrender terms with General Menendez and with his deep knowledge of the necessary techniques he was able to establish a total moral and psychological ascendency over the unfortunate Argentines.

As these examples make clear, the principal SAS mission is one of special operations – sabotage, raids, intelligence gathering, etc. – in denied areas. Contrary to popular belief, the counterterrorist mission in the UK is not the sole province of the SAS; it provides assault and rescue forces when facilities have been seized in the UK proper and operates covertly against the Irish Republican Army (IRA).

A secondary SAS mission is to organize and train friendly resistance forces, as well as to provide specialized security assistance training to friendly nations.

Organization

The present organization includes three regiments of approximately 600 to 700 men each. One regiment (22 SAS) is all-regular, while the other two (21 SAS (Artists Rifles) and 23 SAS) belong to the Territorial Army. There is a regular signal squadron with 22 SAS and another (63 (SAS) Signal Squadron) with the TA. These units are controlled by Director SAS Group, a brigadier whose headquarters are in London.

Each SAS regiment is composed of four squadrons, each having around four 16-man troops that work, operationally, in patrols of four. Some variations in size exist, of course, to accommodate special requirements for elements such as the Mountain Troop and Boat Troop.

Although they no longer operate together the SAS maintains close links with the New Zealand Special Air Service Squadron and the Australian Special Air Service. Fraternal links are also maintained with the 1st Para-

Above: *An SAS candidate in the hills of Wales. The going is tough. On a downhill slope, he runs; uphill, it's a quick walk. Ex-SAS soldiers have taken their considerable fighting and organizational skills to help form foreign security forces.*

chute Battalion of the Belgian Army which is descended from the wartime 5 SAS, and the Greek "Sacred Squadron (Helios Lokos)" which served with the SAS in North Africa and the Eastern Mediterranean in the last war.

There is a very close relationship between the present-day regular (22 SAS) and territorial (21 and 23 SAS) regiments. Both territorial regiments have a strong cadre of regulars, who ensure that professional standards are maintained, and who pass on the benefits of recent operational experience.

Selection and training

No officer or soldier enlists directly into the regular regiment (22 SAS). Instead, volunteers come from the other regiments and corps of the British Army, which sometimes leads to the accusation that the regiment is "poaching" some of the best and most enterprising young officers and soldiers. All volunteers for the SAS must first pass the selection course, which is based on the regimental depot at Hereford. The tests take place in the Brecon area of Wales and consist of a series of tasks designed to find out whether the individual has the qualities of mental resilience, physical stamina, self-discipline, initiative, independence and

spiritual toughness which the regiment has found necessary for its missions.

The process starts with 10 days of fitness and map-reading training in groups of 20 to bring everyone up to the same basic standards. Typical of such training: SAS members are not allowed to write down map references or to fold maps in a way that will reveal the area they are concerned with. This is followed by 10 days of solitary cross-country marching, culminating in a 40 mile (64km) march in 20 hours carrying a 55lb (25kg) Bergen rucksack. They must also demonstrate an aptitude for languages, since they will be expected to know at least two. Those who have not either voluntarily or compulsorily retired now undertake 14 weeks continuation training which includes a parachute course and combat survival training. At the end of this phase the survivors are presented with their beret and badge, and are at long last members of the SAS, although the training continues when specialist courses in signalling, languages, field medicine, demolition, shooting, free-fall parachuting and other military skills. Even after a soldier becomes a fully-fledged member of the regiment, there can be periods of high-intensity training for roles such as counter-revolutionary warfare commandos.

Unlike the earlier years of the SAS the emphasis today is on pulling and encouraging men to get through the tests and course, but without relaxing the high standards. Nevertheless, the pass-rate is only about 20 percent, although it must be appreciated that only rarely is there any reason for any of the other 80 percent to feel ashamed; the fact is that the SAS are, of necessity, looking for a very special combination of talents which is possessed by or can be developed in only a few people.

Once fully in the regiment, the normal tour of duty of several years is followed by return to the parent regiment or corps. This ensures that the regiment does not become too introspective and also serves to spread around the rest of the Army that curious blend of ideas and training which constitute the SAS.

Weapons and equipment

The SAS use standard British Army small arms such as the L1A1 7.62mm Self-Loading Rifle, Browning 9mm pistol and the 7.62mm General-Purpose Machine-Gun (GPMG). The Sterling 9mm machine-carbine is not used, the SAS preferring the Heckler and Koch 9mm SMG. In addition, the SAS specialize in training and using virtually any type of foreign weapon, either to take advantage of some particular attribute, or to blend in with some bit of local "scenery". Special "stun"

Left: *Trooper gets checked out on the M2 Carl Gustav 84mm antitank recoilless rifle. The SAS specialize in training with and using foreign weapons, which can help them take advantage of their attributes.*

Right: *The image of the SAS that has become burned in the minds of the world, the result of the successful and highly publicized siege of the Iranian Embassy in London. The weapon: an H&K MP5 silenced submachine gun.*

grenades have been developed for SAS use in which the blast effect has been maximized at the expense of damage potential.

It was announced in March 1984 that the SAS would use two Italian-built Agusta 109 helicopters captured from the Argentinians during the Falklands War. The aircraft are now part of the Army Air Corps inventory; they can carry up to seven troops and could be equipped for many roles, including anti-tank and electronic warfare.

The SAS have incorporated "high-tech" into their arsenal of tricks. Thermal imagers were used in the Falklands, for example, to verify the presence of personnel in buildings, or to identify their fighting positions. They have also used a satellite communications system, infrared night equipment and a host of surveillance, target acquisition and sensory devices.

Uniforms

The SAS deliberately shuns glamorous or flashy uniforms or embellishments, and wears standard British Army uniforms, as far as possible, with only the customary "regimental" items permitted under British practice. The three basic distinguishing marks of the SAS are the sand-colored beret, the cap-badge (a winged dagger with the motto "Who

Dares Wins") and SAS-wings worn on the right shoulder. In parade dress (No. 2 Dress) buttons, officers' Sam Browne belt, gloves and shoes are all black. Combat dress is standard British Army pattern with either the sand-colored beret or the peaked camouflage hat with no badge. With this latter hat on there is nothing about a soldier's uniform to show that he is a member of the SAS at all. One small idiosyncracy of SAS uniform is that in "pullover order" (the popular dress worn in barracks) the rank chevrons of NCO are worn on the shoulder straps, not on the right sleeve.

A unique combat uniform is available for use on anti-terrorist operations. This is an all-black outfit, with a black flak-vest, belt and boots. The standard issue respirator (which is made of black rubber) and grey anti-flash hood complete the outfit. Every item of this dress is worn for strictly practical reasons, but the overall effect is awe-inspiring.

The SAS wear uniforms on operations, though they do not wear insignia of rank. As one observer noted, "In no way are the members of the SAS 'a scruffy bunch of ruffians'. They are soldiers from whom a high standard of dress and cleanliness are required under normal conditions. All ranks fully understand and support the adage that a smart unit is a good unit."

UNITED STATES OF AMERICA
23rd AIR FORCE

Left: *Air Force special operations team members from the 1st Special Operations Wing are airlifted by Army UH-1H helicopter. This unit first won fame for providing fighter cover, air strikes, and air-lift for Wingate's Raiders, who operated behind enemy lines in Burma (they were known then as Air Commandos).*

Right: *Members of USAF's Special Operations Combat Control Team, Hurlburt Field, Fla., look at map in preparation for a training mission. The team is often called upon to instruct friendly foreign governments in their procedures as they apply to special air warfare.*

THE 23rd Air Force is not, in the strictest sense, an "elite" unit; however, its role in controlling special operations forces and resources is so essential that it must be included in any book on the subject. It is currently located at Scott Air Force Base, Ill.

On March 1, 1983, all combat and rescue and special operations forces were centralized under the Military Airlift Command, parent command of the 23rd and also headquartered at Scott.

Principal US Air Force special operations units include the 1st Special Operations Wing, Hurlburt Field, Fla.; the 1st Special Operations Squadron, Clark Air Base, Philippines; the 7th Special Operations Squadron, Rhein-Main Air Base, Germany; Detachment 1, Howard Air Force Base, Panama; and the Air Force Special Operations School, Hurlburt Field, Fla.

Air National Guard and Reserve units involved in special operations missions include 919th Special Operations Group, Duke Field, Fla.; 193rd Special Operations Group, Harrisburg International Airport, Pa.; and the 71st Special Operations Squadron, Davis-Monthan Air Force Base, Ariz.

Four EC-130E Volant Solos in the Pennsylvania Air National Guard are the only dedicated psychological operations aircraft suitable for broadcasts and leaflet drops.

1st Special Operations Wing

The 1st Special Operations Wing (SOW) had been under the Tactical Air Command prior to the 1983 reorganization. It organizes, trains, equips and operates assigned and attached forces for Air Force special operations. It also acts as the coordinating point for linking Air Force special operations with the other US military services.

1st SOW's lineage dates back to the 1st Air Commando Group, created on 29 March, 1944 at Reilakanda, India. It first won fame providing fighter cover, air strikes and airlift for Wingate's Raiders, who operated behind Japanese lines in Burma.

The present day 1st Special Operations Wing consists of three Special Operations Squadrons (SOS). Two are equipped with special versions of C-130 transport aircraft and the third with modified H-53 helicopters.

Units of this wing took part in Operation Eagle Claw (the attempted rescue of hostages in Teheran) as well as the Grenada rescue mission in 1983.

The three squadrons include the 8th SOS (MC-130E aircraft), which supports unconventional warfare and other Air Force special operations; 16th SOS (AC-130), which provides night close-air support, armed reconnaissance and interdiction, armed escort and limited command and control support; and 20th SOS (MH-53), which conducts day or night infiltration into potentially hostile territory for the purpose of resupply, reinforcement or exfiltration of ground units.

Aircraft

The equipment listed below was assigned to Air Force special operations at the close of 1986.

AC-130A/H/U gunships. There are 10 of each type, with the exception of the U model – the first of which will not join the fleet until fiscal year 1990. The AC-130A Spectre was developed for use in Southeast Asia and is armed with a variety of weapons ranging from Gatling guns to 40mm cannon. The AC-130H has greater range and payload, improved armament with a 105mm howitzer (known as the "Big Gun"), and fire control devices.

During the Grenada operation, AC-130Hs fired very close to US troops and with great accuracy. The question was not "Which building is the target?" It was, "Which window?"

MC-130E and MC-130H. There are 14 of the -E type, with 24 of the new -H models on order, with final delivery expected by fiscal year 1991. The MC-130E Combat Talon is a special operations version of the C-130E and has special avionics, ECM, and other devices that suit it for low-level operations. It is used for clandestine infiltration/exfiltration and airdrops.

The MC-130H Combat Talon II will be an improved H model with C-130 increased payload, improved command, control and communications fits, enhanced navigation and better avionics.

MH-53Hs Pave Low. Pave Low III helicopters perform missions similar to that of the

Combat Talon aircraft and provide the primary exfiltration capability for special operations forces. Including the eight now in the inventory, a total of 41 are programmed to be in operation by fiscal year 1990.

The Air Force's 1723rd Combat Control Squadron, also known as the Special Operations Combat Control Team (SOCCT), is an integral element of the 23rd Air Force and is located at Hurlburt Field. Its primary mission is to operate tactical communications equipment that controls drop and recovery zones, to perform forward air guide service, and to position navigational aids and target designation equipment.

Team members are rated parachutists with expertise in military free fall high altitude low opening and high altitude high opening techniques. They are also trained in demolition techniques; and selected personnel are quite capable of being used in amphibious and aquatic roles.

Other AF special operations units

Other organizations in support of Air Force special operations include:

Air Force Special Operations School (Hurlburt Field) – which was established in October 1964 and conducts academic training related to Air Force special operations.

1st Special Operations Squadron (Clark Air Base, Philippines) – which has flown a multitude of missions and aircraft since its inception in 1963 as the 1st Air Commando Squadron. Its missions include reconnaissance, unconventional warfare and training of indigenous forces.

7th Special Operations Squadron (Rhein-Main Air Base, West Germany) – the former 7th Air Commando Squadron is the only US Air Force Special Operations unit in Europe. It has its own medical team, intelligence, communications, avionics, aircraft, safety, Combat Control Team and other operational support functions.

Uniforms

Members of these special operations forces wear standard US Air Force uniforms, with appropriate shoulder and pocket badges. Combat Control Team members wear maroon berets and jump wings.

UNITED STATES OF AMERICA
US ARMY SPECIAL OPERATIONS FORCES

THE UNITED States has a long and rich history of military special operations which predate the Revolutionary War. However, the first truly integrated modern special operations organization in the United States Army did not begin until April 10, 1952, when the Psychological Warfare Center was established at Fort Bragg, N.C. Notably, psychological warfare in the Army at the time also consisted of unconventional warfare – a legacy of the special operations of the Office of Strategic Services (OSS) headed by Gen. "Wild Bill" Donovan during World War II.

The Special Forces were resuscitated in the early 1950s, with 10th Special Forces Group being activated at Fort Bragg, North Carolina on June 20, 1952, followed by 77th Special Forces Group on September 25, 1953. (The numbering appears to have been entirely at random.) These were followed by 1st Special Forces Group, which was raised on June 24, 1957 in Okinawa. This group sent a small team to train 58 men of the South Vietnamese Army at Nha Trang during this year, beginning a long association between the Special Forces and the Republic of Vietnam. Next, 5th Special Forces Group was raised on September 21, 1961, initially at Fort Bragg, but later it moved to Vietnam and became responsible for all Special Forces activities in that country.

President John F. Kennedy was fascinated with the Special Forces and visited Fort Bragg, where he authorized the wearing of the distinctive and symbolic headress – the green beret in the autumn of 1961. (Green berets are a form of headgear, and not – as some have assumed – a US Army military unit.) Also a result of the Kennedy visit: the first troops of the Special Forces deployed to South Vietnam in November 1961.

The original idea when the Special Forces were raised in the 1950s was that they would wage guerrilla operations against regular enemy troops in a conventional war. It soon

became clear, however, that in Vietnam the enemy himself was a guerrilla and so the Special Forces had to revise their methods. One of the principal programmes was the raising and training of Civilian Irregular Defense Groups (CIDG), with more than 80 CIDG camps being set up in the years 1961-65.

The Special Forces eventually operated throughout South Vietnam in a variety of roles, only some of which have so far been revealed. They had more extensive dealings with the ARVN (South Vietnamese Army) – and particularly with the Montagnard, or mountain people – than any other element of the US forces. They received awards for heroism and for dedication to duty far out of proportion to their numbers. Despite this, their relationship with some elements of the US chain-of-command was not always easy, with mistrust and suspicion sometimes interfering with their operations, an all too frequent problem for any elite force. The last soldier of the Special Forces left South Vietnam on March 1, 1971.

The Special Forces have always operated throughout the US areas of responsibility. An early deployment was to Bad Toëlz in

Above: *To qualify for Army Special Forces, a soldier must make it through Qualification Course. The trainers work ridiculous hours to ensure students make the grade.*

Below: *Underwater infiltration is one way that men of US Army Special Forces can enter enemy territory. They could also be paradropped or delivered by submarine.*

Above: *Army Special Operations Forces trainees carry ashore their inflatable raft. Infiltration/ exfiltration by water are essential skills to be learned*

Left: *Ranger training ensures that Special Operations Forces troopers, like these carrying M16 rifles, can operate in all terrains, including this dense swamp area.*

ORGANIZATION OF US ARMY SPECIAL FORCES "A TEAM"

Commanding Officer		Captain	Intelligence NCO		Sergeant (E7)
Executive Officer		Warrant Officer	Medical NCO	(2)	Sergeant (E5-E7)
Operations NCO		Sergeant (E8)	Communications NCO	(2)	Sergeant (E5-E7)
Weapons NCO	(2)	Sergeant (E5-E7)	Engineer NCO	(2)	Sergeant (E5-E7)

NOTE: In the US Army, ranks are graded from E1, which is the lowest, to E9, the highest enlisted rank. Grades E5 and above carry with it the designation of sergeant.

Below: *Unarmed combat training at the US Army John F Kennedy Special Warfare Center, Fort Bragg, California. Physical demands here are high, but it is not all "brute force and ignorance", for Special Forces personnel are expected to be proficient at signals, medical, engineering, intelligence, weapons handling, escape and evasion, and several other skills.*

Above: *Field training includes arctic and mountain warfare and survival. Such exercises may take the Special Forces soldier to foreign regions, where he might train with "friendly" specialists, like Italy's Alpini. He becomes familiar here with the use of skis and snow shoes and other special equipment.*

Bavaria, Federal Republic of Germany. Other groups operate in the Panama Canal Zone. Special Forces have long been involved in "advising" friendly armies in Asia, Africa, Central and South America, as well as in other parts of the world. They have thus tended to be always just on the edge of the limelight. They are now very firmly a part of the US Army's order of battle and likely to remain so for a very long time.

Organization

There are currently eight known Special Forces Groups (Airborne) – four of them active and four of them reserve units. Active units are: 1st Special Forces Group (Airborne) SFGA, Ft. Lewis, Wash., with 1Bn/1 forward-deployed to Torii Station, Okinawa; 5th SFGA, Fort Bragg, N.C., with 1Bn/5th at Fort Campbell, Kentucky; the 7th SFGA, Fort Benning, Ga., with 3Bn/7th in Panama; and the 10th SFGA, Fort Devens, Mass., with 1Bn/10th at Bad Toëlz, Germany.

Reserve units are: 11th SFGA (US Army Reserve), Fort Meade, Md; 12th SFGA (USAR), Arlington Heights, Ill.; 19th SFGA (National Guard), Salt Lake City, Utah; and 20th SFGA Birmingham, Ala. (National Guard).

The 1st Special Operations Command (Airborne) has the task of consolidating the management of all Army special operations forces assets. Not only does it manage and command these active Army Special Forces Groups, but it has the readiness training and preparedness responsibilities for the US

Army Reserve and National Guard units.

The traditional organization pattern of the Special Forces has been based on the Operations Detachment A, more popularly known as the "A Team".

While the individual elements that make up the profile of a typical special group may change from time to time, the group profile itself does not. Ideally, five A Teams are commanded by a B team, commanded by a major, with a further five officers and 18 soldiers.

Selection and training

All officers and soldiers in the Special Forces must be airborne qualified, and many are also trained in free-fall parachuting and/or for swimming roles. All enlisted personnel must also have at least two specializations, eg, engineering, intelligence, weapons, communications, demolitions, in addition to the primary or military occupational specialty. Many must also be trained in foreign languages.

The training for the Special Forces is both thorough and tough. To some extent, the normally rigorous training standards declined following the Vietnam War – for a

variety of reasons, including political. With the increasing emphasis of recent years that has been placed on special forces, this decline is in the process of being reversed and training attrition rates (now in the 60 percent plus range) are about what would be anticipated for a special force.

Further, like many Western special troops they will frequently attend courses with other armies; other armies also train with them.

Weapons and equipment

The US Special Forces are tasked to be the repository of knowledge on the world's small arms, and they are therefore trained on virtually every weapon likely to be found on operations anywhere in the world. Their own personal weapon, however, is the famed M161A1 rifle (the "Armalite") which has survived its period of controversy to become a very reliable and effective weapon.

Production of the M16A1 ended in 1975, but the US Army's stock is, in general, much older; the Army has twice put-off procuring new rifles, but is now almost certain to opt for the improved M16A2 and the Special Forces will be one of the earliest recipients. The M16A2 does away with the full automatic feature which enabled riflemen to blaze away using up vast amounts of ammunition, in favor of a 3-round burst capability.

A new barrel will make better use of the

Left: *Special Operations Forces have available to them the whole range of communications eqipment. There are specialist operators trained to encode and decode messages on equipment designed to conceal their unit's positions from "eavesdropping" by enemy communications experts.*

Below Left: *Many Army Special Operations personnel undergo training with US Navy SEALs in diving, with open and closed breathing apparatus, and in underwater demolitions.*

Below: *Submachine gun-armed Special Forces soldier in dense jungle training. Vietnam was a good training ground for present-day instructors, especially in combat survival escape-and-evasion techniques.*

new standardized NATO 5.56mm round (which is slightly longer and heavier than the previous US 5.56mm round) and new sights will utilize this new capability better, giving an effective range out to 875 yards (800m). Other, more esoteric small arms are on the drawing boards, but will not see service until after the year 2000.

Uniform

The basic hallmark of the Special Forces is the green beret, which was approved by President Kennedy, and has given rise to the "Green Berets" monicker. The Special Forces crest, which is worn on the flash in a beret, combines these crossed arrows with a dagger. The motto in the scroll surrounding the dagger is "De Oppresso Liber" ("Freedom from Oppression") which reflects their mission. This crest is normally set on a patch whose colours vary with the groups. Officers show their rank in the flash itself.

As with other special forces the basic uniforms are those of the US Army, although particular items may be added to fit in with a role. In fact, crossed arrows have started appearing on the jackets of US Army Special Forces in place of the branch insignia. The Special Forces are, however, fairly high-visibility troops and tend not to act or dress covertly, leaving that to other and more recently formed units.

Above: *Leader of a Special Forces patrol group, armed with Colt Commando. Trainees are also familiarized with foreign weapons, those of both allied and "enemy" forces, in case of loss or damage to their own.*

Left: *Special Forces personnel preparing for rapelling exercise. Apart from the "green berets', uniforms are standard US Army fatigues.*

Below: *Special Forces trooper with the Colt Commando, shorter derivation of the M16 carbine favored for its shorter barrel and lighter weight, which are useful for close quarters battle conditions. Red tip on the barrel reveals this as a training exercise.*

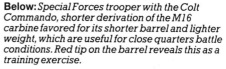

UNITED STATES OF AMERICA
US ARMY RANGERS

Above: *Rangers are kept wet half the time during their training phase in Florida, which puts them close to that prized "Ranger" tab.*

Left: *Post-Grenada ceremonies for men of 2/75th Rangers. The Grenada operation was carried out swiftly and effectively, particularly by the Rangers contingent.*

GENERAL Creighton Abrams, former US Army Chief of Staff, described the Rangers as follows: "The Ranger battalion is to be an elite, light and the most proficient infantry battalion in the world, a battalion that can do things with its hands and weapons better than anyone. Wherever the Ranger battalion goes, it is apparent that it is the best".

The US Army Rangers are the spiritual descendants of the old Indian fighters led by Major Robert Rogers in the pre-revolutionary colonial army, a tradition which was revived in World War II by Merrill's Marauders in Burma and by Darby's Rangers in Europe. The latter comprised six battalions raised and trained in the United States, and which fought with distinction in Sicily and Italy. Ranger units remained in the US Army's order of battle until the end of the Korean War, when they were quietly disbanded and most of their tasks picked up by the special forces.

In the post-Vietnam trauma, the special forces were reduced drastically, and devoted most of their energies to a simple fight for survival. The Ranger School had been operating for many years to maintain a high standard of leadership in the Army and in 1975 it was decided that two Ranger battalions should be re-formed, to perform a number of unique missions.

The Rangers were prepared to take part in the Iranian hostages rescue mission and were about to fly into Iran when the mission was cancelled due to the disaster of Desert One. Their first operational opportunity did not, therefore, arise until Grenada in 1982, when they spearheaded the landing on Port Salines airfield.

Ranger tasks are quick strike and shock action deep in enemy territory. These include ambushes, raids, interdiction and temporary seizure of priority targets. A less common mission for the Rangers is recovery of captured personnel and equipment.

Organization

The US Army lists one Ranger regiment – which has been described as an "elite light infantry organization" – with three subordinate 575-man battalions. Total Ranger strength is approximately 2,300 men. The Ranger regiment reports to the 1st Special Operations Command, Fort Bragg, N.C.

75th Regimental Headquarters and 3/75 are located at Fort Benning, Ga; the 130-man regimental headquarters has three teams skilled at the use of Scuba equipment and in HALO techniques. 1/75 and 2/75 are based, respectively, at Hunter Army Airfield, Ga., and Fort Lewis, Wash.

All men in the battalions are volunteers and come from other units of the Army. They do a standard two year tour, which can be extended by six months, subject to a recommendation by the commanding officer.

Weapons and equipment

The Ranger regiment is simply not equipped to take on sustained combat missions in a high threat environment. Its "artillery" comes from the two 60mm mortar squadrons in each company. Dragon anti-tank missiles and 90mm recoilless rifles are also part of armament. Some individuals such as radio operators, senior NCOs and officers carry the CAR-15 short-barreled weapon. All ranks are trained on foreign weapons, especially those of the Warsaw Pact and NATO.

Selection and training

Volunteers for the Ranger battalions must be airborne-qualified, and many go straight from the Ranger School course. Attendance at that course is not a prerequisite, however, and young soldiers can go direct to the three-week Ranger Indoctrination Program (ominously abbreviated to "RIP"). This starts with physical (including swimming) tests, and some eight parachute jumps from a CH-47.

The course concentrates on basic military skills and brings weapon-handling and infantry tactics up to a very high standard. The students are deliberately put under considerable stress. Courses are usually about 30 strong (minimum is 10) and an average of some 70 percent pass and go on to one of the battalions. Those who have not already done so will normally go on the Ranger School course after some 6 to 9 months in the unit; their pass rate is very high.

The two battalions have a very arduous training schedule, and divide their year into two 5½-month periods, separated by two-week block leaves. Training exercises are conducted all over the USA, and abroad wherever possible, with the particular aim of finding different climates and environments.

The 58-day US Army Ranger School is an unusual institution. It has existed for many years, even when there were no Ranger units as such, with the aim of training officers and NCOs. The whole gamut of "Ranger skills" is taught, including land navigation, patroling, weapon handling, hand-to-hand combat, survival, and mountaineering. The underlying purpose of the course, however, is to improve the standards of self-confidence and leadership throughout the Army as a whole (a few students also attend from the USAF and USMC). The course is intense – 18-hour days – and consists of three-week modules, and those who pass can wear the Ranger flash.

Uniform

Dress is standard US Army uniform, complete with badges and embellishments. Those who wear the "Ranger" flash on their right sleeve do so because they have passed Ranger School and not because they are in a Ranger unit. Trainees wear jungle fatigues and the patrol hat during training, while qualified members of the battalions wear camouflage suits. The only obvious item of Ranger dress is the black beret with the Ranger badge.

UNITED STATES OF AMERICA
US ARMY 82nd AIRBORNE DIVISION

THE US ARMY'S only division-size parachute formation is the 15,000 strong 82nd Airborne Division, based at Fort Bragg in North Carolina. It is part of XVIII Airborne Corps.

The mission of 82nd Airborne Division includes as its primary task (as should every parachute formation) that of seizing from the air important ground objectives and holding them until conventional ground troops can join up and relieve them. As currently tasked, 82nd Airborne Division is at the forefront of the US Rapid Deployment Force, its unique contribution being its jump capability.

One battalion is always at 18 hours readiness to deploy, with one of its companies at 2 hours notice. This is backed up by the remainder of the Division's Ready Brigade, nearly 4,000 strong, which would follow up within 24 hours.

The US forces can actually achieve this ambitious goal, and the 82nd is backed up by an enormous force of USAF parachute-capable aircraft, including many hundred Lockheed C-141 StarLifters and C-130 Hercules. The C-141s regularly display their ability to fly from the United States across the Atlantic and insert paratroops direct onto drop zones (DZ) in West Germany. Once committed to such an operation, 82nd Airborne Division has sufficient material supplies (ammunition, rations, water and fuel) for three days at combat rates, but aerial resupply would then become essential.

A Container Delivery System (CDS) has been developed which enables a fully stocked resupply container to be delivered with great accuracy within a 109×437 yard (100×400m) area. Fixed resupply DZs are thus no longer necessary, thus absolving the ground troops from a major defensive problem which has caused great difficulties in previous parachute operations. Each CDS container can carry 20,000lb (9,072kg) of stores; C-130s can carry up to 16 and C-141s 28.

The airlift capability is improving. Stretched C-141s are now in service and the rewinging of the giant Lockheed C-5 Galaxy aircraft is well in hand. Also a future possibility is the C-17 transport, which is intended for both strategic and tactical airlift, and would include an in-flight refueling capability, currently lacking on USAF C-130s.

Organization

82nd Airborne Division is made up of three brigades, each with three parachute battalions, together with an integral Divisional Support Command. There are three field artillery battalions, each with eighteen 105mm towed howitzers. The divisional tank battalion has 54 M551 Sheridan armored reconnaissance vehicles, which have the great advantage of being air-droppable. They have not been an outstanding success in US Army service, however, nor could they provide the airborne division with a genuine anti-armor capability.

Aviation support integral to 82nd Airborne Division is considerable. This includes 48 AH-

Above: *Trooper is rigged out with the new MC1-1B steerable parachute. The primary fighting* *element of the heavily armed and equipped 82nd Airborne is still the paratrooper.*

1S Cobras armed with TOW missiles, 90 UH-1H Huey transport helicopters (to be replaced by Black Hawk UH-60s, some of which have already been delivered) and 59 OH-58 Kiowa reconnaissance helicopters.

Selection and training

Soldiers can enter the US airborne forces direct, but must pass a rigorous selection, training and parachute course before being a full member of the division. Training of the units within the division is particularly intense and the three brigades rotate through a three-cycles-per-quarter system. There is also a host of exercises ranging from divisional down to company level, all aimed at keeping the fighting edge of the units razor sharp. Every soldier and officer, including women, in the division must be (and remain) parachute-qualified, the standard equipment currently being the MC1-1B steerable 'chute.

Weapons and equipment

Crucial to the equipment policy of the division is the tactical concept, which is based upon the Airborne Anti-Armor Defense (AAAD). Terrain, coupled with natural and man-made obstacles, is used to create "islands" of mutually-supporting anti-armor weapon teams, supported, of course, by artillery and close air support. Enemy armor would be canalized into killing zones where they would be destroyed piecemeal from the flanks and rear.

This concept requires an anti-tank system capable of air delivery and with effective ranges out to 3,280 yards (3,000m). There is also a requirement for integral air support and for an armored counter-attack force. Any sophisticated enemy can also be expected to throw considerable air assets at any major airborne landing, making air defense a major

requirement for the 82nd.

To meet these needs 82nd Airborne Division is equipped with light, effective weapons systems, although most of it is standard Army issue, and there is nothing like the range of specially developed equipment available to the Soviet airborne forces. Main anti-armor weapon is the highly effective TOW crew-served missile system, backed up by the M47 Dragon, and Light Anti-tank Weapon (LAW), both of which are shoulder-launched.

The M551 Sheridan soldiers on with the 82nd, but is overdue for replacement by a more satisfactory system. This is a major deficiency area, as any large airborne force is at its most vulnerable in the early few days of deployment, especially from armored attack. Anti-tank systems such as TOW can go part of the way to meeting the requirement, but a mobile reserve striking force is essential, and this is currently lacking.

As described above there is a large helicopter component in the division and the AH-1S could be expected to make a significant addition to the anti-tank capability. For air defense the division is armed with 48 six-barrel Gatlings (the Vulcan system) on wheeled mounts, backed up by Stinger, a man-portable shoulder-launched missile.

Uniforms

The uniforms and insignia of the 82nd Airborne Division are remarkably conventional. Normal US Army camouflage combat uniforms are worn, with the standard helmet. "Subdued" rank and qualification badges are worn, together with the "AA" (All-American) divisional patch on the left sleeve. A maroon beret is now being worn again, having been discontinued in the years 1978-80, greatly to the indignation of the airborne officers and soldiers.

UNITED STATES OF AMERICA
DELTA*

US ARMY Colonel Charlie A. Beckwith served with the British SAS in 1962-63 and on his return to the US Army sought to form a unit with the same organization, ideals and functions as the SAS. After numerous attempts spread over many years he succeeded, and the new force – named 1st Special Forces Operational Detachment-Delta (Delta, for short)–was authorized on November 19, 1977. Its credo was "surprise, speed, success".

This unit should not be confused with the Delta Project (Detachment B-52) set up by the Special Forces in Vietnam in the mid-1960s (and at one time commanded by Beckwith),

which was a totally different organization and concept. Delta is intended for use overseas, but only by invitation of the host government. The organization requires a high degree of specialization; its warfare focus is on counter-terrorism, and its priority tasks are barricade operations, hostage rescue and specialized reconnaissance.

Following its setting up, Delta proceeded to select and train its men, and various unit tasks were successfully undertaken. Then, on November 4, 1979, Iranian "students" broke into the US Embassy in Teheran, taking all the staff hostage, and from then on Delta was

increasingly deeply involved in planning a rescue operation, culminating in the actual attempts on April 24/25, 1980.

Organization

Delta is one of four units and elements reporting to the Joint Special Operations Command, Fort Bragg, N.C. JSOC was activated in 1981 to consolidate control over, help develop doctrine for, train, deploy and employ hostage rescue and other counterterror elements within the US Department of Defense.

Multi-service in resources, JSOC's principal components – in addition to Delta – are

UNITED STATES OF AMERICA
US MARINE CORPS

THE US Department of Defense does not formally list the Marine Corps as a part of its Special Operations Forces. In some respects, however, it is one and it would therefore be unfair not to include them in viewing such capabilities. More specifically, Reconnaissance Marines (and Force Reconnaissance in particular) have similar training and missions as special operations forces – with training in parachute and other airborne operations, as well as in scuba and other underwater operations. Their mission, however, is different in that it consists of tactical reconnaissance activities. There are roughly 1,400 Force Reconnaissance Marines, with more than 400 assigned to each of the three Marine Corps divisions.

The Marine Corps is the world's largest elite force. With a strength of some 198,000 men and women in three divisions and three air wings, it is even bigger than the total armed forces of most countries. Since it was raised by order of Congress on November 10, 1775, the USMC has taken part in every major war fought by the USA, as well as in numerous "police" actions and armed interventions all over the world.

These fine traditions have merged to produce an amphibious assault force whose maintenance is the *raison d'être* for today's Corps. Further, the evolution of Marine aviation units has provided the Corps with its own air force. This overall capability enables the USMC to claim to be a unique, combined-arms, ground-air force with a special competence in amphibious warfare.

The missions assigned to the USMC fall into three broad categories. The principal mission is to maintain an amphibious capability for use in conjunction with fleet operations, including the seizure and defense of advanced naval bases and the conduct of land operations essential to the successful execution of a maritime campaign. In addition, the Corps is required to provide security detachments for naval bases and the Navy's

Above: *Marine in Lebanon, where a terrorist attack on the Marine Battalion Landing Team Headquarters on 28 October, 1983, killed 241 military personnel. The equivalent of 12,000lb (5,440kg) of TNT were used.*

principal warships. Finally, the Corps carries out any additional duties placed upon it by the President.

A major feature of the USMC's position in the US defense establishment is unique in that it is the only service to have its basic corps structure defined by statutory law. The amended National Security Act of 1947 tasks the Marine Corps with maintaining a regular Fleet Marine Force of no less than three divisions and three aircraft wings, with the additional support units necessary.

Organization

The Marine Corps strength – 198,000 active duty personnel, including 9,300 women, and

40,000 reserves – is organized into four divisions and four aircraft wings (three regular and one reserve of each), but both organizations are larger than their counterparts in the other services. This is particularly apparent, in the division which, with a strength of 17,000 is some 20 percent larger than a US Army division.

The basic structure of the Marine division is essentially the traditional "triangular" model, with three infantry regiments, each of three battalions. The new infantry battalion, however, is smaller than before, with a headquarters company, weapons company, and three rifle companies, each of the latter being 20 percent smaller than its predecessors. Manpower and financial constraints prevented a fourth rifle company from being formed. Each Marine division has an artillery regiment, a tank battalion, an armored amphibian battalion, a light armored assault battalion (equipped with the new LAV), and other supporting units.

The standard Marine aircraft wing (MAW) has 18 to 21 squadrons with a total of 286 to 315 aircraft, ranging from fighter/attack (F-4, F-18), through medium attack (A-4, A-6, AV-8) and a tanker/transport squadron (KC-130), to helicopter squadrons (AH-1, CH-35, CH-46, UH-1) plus supporting squadrons of electronic warfare, observation and reconnaissance aircraft.

Weapons and equipment

The single dominant characteristic of Marine tactical doctrine is the emphasis on the principle of offensive action, which applies to all aspects of the Corps' activities. This ethos has a major effect on the way the USMC is equipped. Improved M16 rifles are being issued as the basic infantry weapon, while each squad, 13 strong, has the new 5.56mm Squad Automatic Weapon (SAW) (M249) in each fire team. The battalion weapons company will also acquire a new heavy machine-gun platoon with eight firing teams, each of the 160th Aviation Group, Fort Campbell, Ky.; SEAL Team 6, Dam Neck, Va., which "comes aboard" if their special skills are needed for a mission; and elements of the 23rd Air Force.

Following the SAS pattern, the basic building block of Delta (reportedly manned by more than 100 "operators", as they call themselves) is the four-man squad. Four squads make up a troop, and two or more troops form a squadron.

Selection and training

Under Colonel Beckwith's command, Delta's selection and training processes were essentially similar to those used by the SAS. These processes have been refined but are probably fundamentally unaltered.

The selection process includes an assessment by a psychologist, in addition to an interview of several hours' duration with officers and noncommissioned officers. Col. Beckwith was not looking for the "gung ho" adventurist for Delta, but for loners who could operate independently, follow strict constraints and endure monotony ... men who could be "extremely patient" and then "extremely aggressive".

Members of the first group were required to be fit enough to perform an inverted crawl across 40 yards (36.6m) in 25 seconds, swim 110 yards (100m) fully dressed (with boots), and do 37 situps and 33 pushups, each within one minute. Very high shooting standards are set; for example, snipers must achieve 100 per cent shots on target at 600 yards (545m) and 90 per cent at 1,000 yards (915m).

Training occurs in such unusual skills as the ability to drive a locomotive; to hot-wire cars and trucks; to handle hysterical hostages; to refuel a jetliner; as well as others.

*Note: This entry was prepared by the Editor.

Weapons and equipment

Very little is known of Delta's equipment and weapons, although clearly they will be able to get most of what the most technologically advanced country in the world can provide. It is certainly known that their snipers use the Remington 40XB rifle with 12x Redfield telescopic sights, and for the Teheran operation two out of three machine-gunners were armed with M60s while the third had a Heckler and Koch HK21.

All personnel, according to some accounts, have "accurized" Colt .45 semi-automatic pistols and a few carry M3A1 "grease guns" or M16s. CAR 15 rifles as well as various shotguns and grenade launchers (M203 and M79) are also in the arsenal. Delta personnel are equipped with night-vision goggles, something that is entirely appopriate for a unit that is so night-oriented.

Above: *Marine equipped with M16A2 rifle and the 40mm M203 grenade launcher. The heavier M16A2 is a substantial improvement over its predecessor and began entering the Marine Corps inventory in 1984.*

Above left: *US Marine Corps amphibious exercise. The AH-1 SeaCobra helo overhead provides fire support and fire support coordination to landing forces during the amphibious assault.*

Left: *M60A1 tanks have been the mainstay of USMC armored forces for years and will remain so until the 1990s. They can carry 63 rounds of 105mm, 6,000 rounds of 7.62mm and 900 rounds of .50-cal. ammunition.*

which will man a vehicle equipped with a 0.5in HMG and the Mk19 40mm "machine-gun" (actually, an automatic grenade launcher in all but name). An improved version of the 81mm mortar is expected to be issued in 1989.

Changes are also under way in the artillery, aviation and armor capabilities of the Corps. Three target acquisition batteries are being fielded over the next two years and the current 105mm and 155mm towed howitzers are being replaced by the new M198 155mm. There has also been an increase in the number of 155mm SP weapons, with additional batteries being acquired.

Marine aviation is being modernized. The F-18 Hornet is in service, while the AV-8B version of the Harrier was deployed in 1985. Two squadrons of CH-53Es, with a lift capacity of 16 tons, became operational in 1983. Unlike the Army, the USMC intends to keep its M60A1 MBTs in service until at least the end of the decade, but has ordered the Light Armored Vehicle (LAV) for use in the Light Armored Assault Battalions (LAAB); there will be 145 LAVs in each LAAB with a total of 744 being purchased by the Corps.

Selection and training

All members of the US Armed Forces are volunteers, and those for the USMC enlist directly into the Corps. Recruits go to one of two training depots, at San Diego, Ca, and Parris Island, SC, where they undergo the famous 11-week "boot camp".

Despite its size, the USMC does not have its own officer academy, although some are accepted from the Navy academy at Annapolis. The main source of officers is through the Naval ROTC, Officers Candidate School (OCS) or the Platoon Leaders Class. All officer candidates (including those from Annapolis) must undergo a rigorous selection and training course at Quantico, Va., before being accepted for a commission.

Above: *This exercise reflects the improved capabilities being added to the USMC. The new M198 155mm towed howitzer (lower left) is beefing up the artillery, while the CH-53E (right) helps with lift.*

Left: *Artillery pieces in the Marine Corps, like this M-101A1, are classified as cannon. The M1-1A1 is a familiar sight; it has been supplied to 50 countries.*

Right: *Marines have established themselves as capable partners in Norway, where Marine Air-Ground Task Forces exercise regularly.*

Far right: *Two systems that support the amphibious assault role are the LVPT-7 (left) and the all-purpose Cadillac-Gage Commando car with 90mm gun.*

Top right: *Forage caps are the trademark of Force Reconnaissance Marines – shown here practising rapelling. This elite force within an elite force has the primary role of tactical reconnaissance.*

UNITED STATES OF AMERICA
US NAVY SEALS

UNLIKE THE other US military services, the Navy has no parent command that encompasses all its special warfare elements – which are composed of its SEAL (an acronym for *SE*a, *A*ir, and *L*and), Special Boat and SEAL Delivery Vehicle units.

SEALs, according to naval warfare publications, are expected to "conduct unconventional warfare, psychological operations, beach and coastal reconnaissance, operational deception operations, counterinsurgency operations, coastal and river interdiction, and certain special tactical intelligence collection operations, in addition to those intelligence functions normally retained for planning and conducting special operations in a hostile environment".

Commissioned in 1962 in response to presidential tasking, SEAL teams were created by the unique demands of that era, as well as increased involvement in Vietnam.

The Vietnam War period proved to be one of intense activity for SEAL units, who performed vigorously and successfully in riverine and other areas. Their missions included intelligence gathering, sabotage, counter-insurgency and other ambush activities, and the extraction of POWs from Viet Cong prison camps. They often worked with South Vietnamese Special Forces, which they helped train and organize.

Their roots are anchored in the famous underwater demolition teams (UDTs) and small boat squadrons of World War II, duties that have been absorbed into the present-day SEAL units.

To fulfill their mission, SEALs may be carried to near the shoreline by a submarine, and leave it either on the surface or while submerged. They are also trained paratroops and could reach their operational areas from land- or carrier-based aircraft. Finally, of course, they could arrive by surface vessel.

Organization

Regular US Navy Special Warfare forces (there are more in reserve) are controlled by two Naval Special Warfare Groups. NAVSPECWARGRU 1 is based at the Naval Amphibious Base, Coronado (San Diego), Calif.; group two is based at Little Creek (Norfolk), Va. There are also four small special warfare units in Italy, Puerto Rico, Scotland and the Philippines, which prepare for and control the operations of some Naval Special Warfare forces when they forward deploy.

The Navy currently has five active component SEAL teams – made up of 10 platoons – with a sixth scheduled to be commissioned in late 1988. Squads and platoons, rather than complete teams, undertake most SEAL missions.

Special Boat Squadrons are found in the Atlantic and Pacific Fleets. They provide organic, specialized support for small unit SEAL operations. The Navy's two SEAL Delivery Vehicle Teams provide a clandestine infiltration/exfiltration capability.

Selection and training

Volunteers for the Navy SEALs undergo gruelling training. It is a 15-week program of indoctrination, mental and physical toughening, and extensive instruction conducted in Coronado, Calif. Officers and enlisted men undergo identical training, with the only distinction being that officers bear the extra responsibility of class leadership. The attrition rate for the course fluctuates between 55 percent and 70 percent.

SEALs receive extensive training in combat swimmer technique, advanced demolitions, field communications and small arms handling. As well as being qualified for underwater demolition, SEALs must be qualified parachute jumpers. This expertise, combined with basic skills ranging from gunner's mate to signalman (skills acquired as part of "regular Navy service"), molds the

Left: *This Mark VII, MOD-6 Swimmer Delivery Vehicle (SDV) launches its team at sea at a depth of 35 feet (12m). Described as the modern descendent of miniature submarines and human torpedoes, their main purpose is to carry swimmers faster, farther and with less exertion than they could manage themselves. They also transport heavy equipment.*

Right: *When SEAL teams are separated from their objectives by a long distance, personnel and their swimmer delivery vehicles are delivered by other means. The submarine USS Grayback (now retired) had hangars built on deck to carry SDVs, with berths installed for 67 fully-equipped SEALs. Other specially-modified submarines have since become active.*

Below: *The inflatable boat small (IBS) is a key element in SEAL equipment, and muscle-straining IBS exercises are central to the SEAL training program. The IBS mounts a 7.5hp silent-running outboard engine and was used by the SEALs in Vietnam for a wide variety of missions.*

Navy SEAL into a combination of frogman, paratrooper and commando.

Weapons and equipment

The SEALs have in the past taken their own line on weaponry – although they use weapons common to other US special units such as the M161A rifle and the M60 general purpose machinegun.

Modern SEAL weapons include the US Navy Model 22 Type 0.9mm silenced pistol developed by Smith & Wesson especially for them. Constructed throughout of stainless steel to prevent rust in the salt-water environment, the pistol is nicknamed the "Hush-Puppy", from its designed role of killing guard dogs.

Specialized weapons and equipment used by this force include bubbleless close-circuit underwater breathing apparatus, and steerable parachutes. Special Boat Units use the 65ft (59.4m) Spectre class fast patrol boats and the Seafox, a 36ft (33m) light special warfare craft.

Uniforms

There is no special uniform for SEAL personnel: they wear standard naval uniform with their own insignia, comparable to that of the naval air arm and submariners. On operations, they wear Scuba gear appropriate to the operational environment. SEALs wear combat uniform, but wear the soft floppy "jungle-hat" rather than a helmet.

Right: *Camouflage cream liberally applied, a SEAL team member, armed with short barrel CAR-15 with special flash suppressor, prepares for action. Firearms training is thorough.*

Below: *While amphibious and underwater operations are the SEALs' specialty, each member is an elite infantryman as well and must learn covert reconnaissance skills.*

USSR & WARSAW PACT

Above: *Soviet paratroopers man a twin ZU-23 anti-aircraft weapon. They outnumber the West in conventional weapons as well as in elite forces.*

USING THE term "special purpose forces" to describe Soviet elite units does not carry with it the connotation that these forces and their missions are somehow abnormal. In fact, quite the opposite is true; these forces and their operations and tactics are part and parcel of Soviet military doctrine. The operations include airborne, heliborne, amphibious operations and unconventional warfare in the enemy rear.

The Soviet Union can claim legitimate title as pioneers of paratroop and air landing forces. In fact, in 1931 the Lenin Military District was where the first paratroop landing unit was formed. At the beginning of World War II, the USSR fielded 15 independent airborne brigades; they now have more airborne divisions than the rest of the world put together.

Because of the severe shortage of air transport during the early stages of "The Great Patriotic War" and due to the early lack of air superiority, most of the 50 Soviet airborne operations were of small scale and largely characterized by poor planning and execution. For the next 20 years, attention was centered on the problem of linking up the airborne forces operating in rear areas with advancing ground force units. Additionally, the firepower of the airborne units was increased with the addition of self-propelled assault guns, such as the ASU-57 and ASU-85.

However, it was not until the 1960s that the Soviet military began to solve the problems of employment – especially the linkup with advancing ground forces. Resolving this problem resulted in a major effort to re-equip airborne units to increase their mobility and firepower.

Airborne units are an integral part of many operations at Army and *front* levels. To allow flexibility in employment on a theater level, Soviet airborne forces are directly subordinate to the Supreme High Command. Operational control of airborne units is delegated to the Soviet General Staff for some specific operations down to the division/tactical level, with most airborne units retained under the control of the Soviet Supreme High Command for contingencies. Soviet military planners consider airborne units to be an extremely valuable resource. They are to be used judiciously, and where they would enhance the likelihood of surprise, deep penetration and rapid exploitation.

The Soviets categorize airborne missions based upon the depth and importance of objectives, plus the size of forces involved. Strategic missions (more than 310 miles/500km) are undertaken when the objectives are power projection, political and industrial centers, airfields or ports, or the isolation of one member of an enemy coalition; operational missions (up to 30 miles/50km) are undertaken when the objectives are nuclear delivery and storage sites, command posts, logistics and communications utilities, airfields, ports, critical bridges, mountain passes, or the blocking of the enemy's withdrawal; special missions (30 to 300 miles/50 to 500km) objectives are tactical nuclear delivery and storage sites, demolition, arson, and seizure of new technology.

Airborne assault forces are airlifted by military aircraft, supplemented by civilian Aeroflot airliners. Employing these airborne assault forces consists of the traditional parachute drop, landing of troops by fixed wing aircraft and possible insertion by helicopters. The Soviet airborne forces are a key asset in the Soviet Union's capability to project power rapidly, as was evident in Czechoslovakia (1968) and Afghanistan (1979), when airborne troops were quickly air landed into critical strategic objectives. The present Soviet airborne/air assault strength is formidable (between 102,000 and 107,000 men), highly mobile, and provides the means to carry the battle to the depths of NATO's rear area.

Heliborne operations

The Soviet Army has drawn upon the experience of the US Army in Vietnam in order to develop its own concept of heliborne operations since the 1960s. These heliborne assets have been in use in combat in Afghanistan since early 1980. They provide the lower level commmander with a more responsive force than airborne elements, and the training required is much less.

Typical heliborne missions are securing the opposite side for a river crossing; communications; pursuit of a withdrawing enemy; deception troop insertions; ambushes and raids; seizing critical terrain such as mountain passes, crossroads, etc.; laying and clearing mines in the enemy rear; inserting combat units in the enemy rear.

The Attack Helicopter Regiment of the Army and Air Assault Brigade/Airmobile Assault Regiment of the *front* have similar missions, but at a greater depth to the enemy's rear.

Soviet Spetsnaz operations

While airborne forces are often touted as the elite of Soviet forces, the troops of "Special Designation", or Spetsnaz, with political reliability and sophisticated training in airborne and sea insertions, sabotage, terrorism, assassinations, demolitions, intelligence gathering, and selected attack of high value deep targets, should perhaps be more properly considered the elite Soviet force.

Each Soviet Union military district or group of forces (which becomes a *front* in time of war) has its own Spetsnaz unit up to brigade size. These are often referred to in organization charts as Diversionary Brigades. While under the operational control of the *front* commander, Spetsnaz forces are ultimately subordinate to the General Staff GRU (Main Intelligence Directorate). Although the GRU is the second largest intelligence service in the world, after the KGB, it is not subordinate to the KGB. However, a Spetsnaz force may be used by the KGB for special missions as a direct assignment from the Main Intelligence Directorate.

These forces can be deployed across the borders into Western Europe prior to hostilities in small teams, wearing NATO uniforms or civilian clothes and speaking the local language. They will attempt to penetrate or destroy critical military facilities and organizations (with an overall goal of disrupting or destroying NATO forces, adding to the confusion prior to and during war).

Since personnel in Spetsnaz units are parachute qualified and skilled in communications, demolitions, and foreign weapons, they may penetrate in the early part of (or prior to) hostilities in the guise of groups of tourists, delegations, sports teams, or as crews and passengers on merchant ships, civil aircraft or commercial trucks. Additionally, some Spetsnaz units have developed a significant capability to perform underwater demolitions in Western European ports as a mission of a special Spetsnaz naval brigade.

The Soviets have consistently emphasized offensive and defensive operations spanning the military and political spectrum. The Spetsnaz forces alone are reportedly between 29,500 and 37,000 strong.

"Peacetime strategies" – including a fifth-column-style forward deployment and active strategic psychological operations, especially subversion and disinformation – are important to the USSR. Other Soviet forces that have a distinct military complexion and roles that might be considered to have a special operations flavor are the Border Guards (175,000 troops) and the Interior Army (260,000). The former, which belongs to the KGB, is charged with suppressing ethnic dissident movements in the frontier regions, and repelling the advances of foreign military units until the arrival of other elements of the Army. The latter group belongs to the Ministry of Internal Security and combats anti-state activity inside the Soviet Union.

Warsaw Pact Special Purposes Forces

The Spetsnaz forces include troops from East Germany, Czechoslovakia, Poland and the USSR. Only Poland in the Warsaw Pact countries has elite formations that are divisional in size.

The following is a summary of the units there and in other Eastern Bloc countries.

Poland. The Polish Army has a proud airborne tradition. As a result, its special purpose forces include an airborne division and a marine division. The 6th Pomeranian Air Assault Division is located outside Krakow in the Warsaw Military District. About 4,000 strong, it is not as heavily mechanized as its Soviet counterpart. It has an independent special forces battalion, formerly designated the 4101st Paratroop Battalion, which is trained in rear area scouting and sabotage.

The Air Assault Division's counterpart marine formation is the Coastal Defense Unit, which is believed to be designated 7th Luzycka Naval Assault Division. Despite its designation, it is an army, not a navy unit, and has something more than 5,000 troops assigned. Its role is to support the amphibious operations of the Soviet Baltic Fleet.

Other special military units include the Polish Navy's two battalion naval infantry (the "Blue Berets") and a number of trainer units that can handle demolitions of an offensive and defensive nature. In addition to these forces, there is a wide range of internal security forces under the Ministry of Internal Affairs and the Army Internal Service plus an even larger civilian security structure.

East Germany. There are three elements within the National People's Army that constitute the core of East German special forces: (1) An airborne battalion – the 40th (Willi Sanger) Airborne Battalion, which is stationed in the Baltic; (2) the 29th (Ernst Moritz Arndt) Regiment, based at Rugen Island, and trained for amphibious operations; and (3) a number of smaller elite groups such as a diversionary battalion and a number of combat swimmer companies in the navy (*Volksmarine*).

There is a huge internal security force in the East German Frontier Troops (50,000 strong) and the Guard Regiment, which is considered the elite of this type of East German unit and is responsible for internal security activities and the guarding of government facilities.

Czechoslovakia. This country apparently has a light airborne force stationed near Prosnice consisting of one active, one reserve, one special operations and a training battalion – plus support units. It is believed to be the successor to the 22nd Vysadkova Brigade. Internal Security is handled by the Czechoslovak border guards and the Interior Guards.

Hungary. The Hungarian People's Army has a single, 400-man airborne battalion and Interior and Frontier Guards.

Romania. A nominal member of the Warsaw Pact, Romania has the 161st Paratroop Regiment at Buzau, the 2nd and 4th Mountain Brigades at Brasov and Curtea de Arges, respectively, and a single naval infantry battalion at Giurgia. Internally, there is a 17,000-man Frontier Troops organization plus a Security Troops force of 20,000.

Bulgaria. The Bulgarian People's Army has a single airborne regiment based in the Burgas-Plovdiv region, and the Navy has three Naval Guard companies.

THE ELITE FORCES

SOVIET UNION
AIRBORNE FORCE

ACCORDING to a Soviet dictionary, an airborne assault *(Vozdushnyy Desant)* comprises "Troops airlifted to the enemy rear to conduct combat activities there. According to its scale, an airborne assault may be tactical, operational or strategic. The assault may be effected either by parachute or from landed aircraft, or by a combination of both".

The first parachute unit in the world was a group of 12 Soviet soldiers who appeared as a unit on August 2, 1930. Since then the Soviet Army has led the world in the development of parachute operations, and its parachute force has almost invariably been the largest in the world, as it is today.

The estimated range of total Soviet airborne/air assault strength is between 102,000 and 107,000 men and consists of eight 6,500-man airborne divisions, eight 2,000- to 2,600-man air assault brigades, three 1,700- to 1,850-man airmobile brigades, about 10 500-man independent air assault battalions, and 16 1,500-man Spetsnaz brigades.

The Airborne Force is the elite of the Soviet Army, and all eight parachute divisions are stationed within the USSR in peacetime, thus constituting, in effect, the High Command's strategic reserve. They are considered to be politically reliable and have always been the first elements in foreign deployments, (eg, Czechoslovakia, 1968, Afghanistan, 1979). A clear effort is made to promote an elitist spirit, with distinctive uniforms and insignia, special weapons and a hard, exciting training program.

This is the most important element of the Soviet armed forces; indeed, there are suggestions that the Airborne Force could be designated a sixth independent Armed Service (alongside the Army, Navy, Air Force, National Air Defense Force, and the Strategic Rocket Forces).

Above: *A Soviet paratrooper in his jumping gear. The D-1 parachute on his back is limited to a minimum height of 492 feet (150m) and a speed of 189 knots.*

Organization

The Airborne Force is an arm of service of the Army, but is independent of the Army chain-of-command and is directly controlled by a general at the Ministry of Defense. The divisions of the Airborne Force are all maintained at Category One in peacetime, ie, they are fully manned and equipped, and have the first choice of conscript. There is also an independent parachute regiment at Neurippen in East Germany. These airborne divisions have a peacetime strength of some 7,200 men and are fully motorized, with some 1,500 vehicles each. The Soviet Airborne Force regularly practises parachute drops on a divisional scale.

Formations are: 76th Guards at Pskov, Leningrad; 103rd Guards, Belorussia; 7th Guards, Baltic; 106th Guards, Moscow; 104th Guards, Transcaucasus; 105th Guards, Turkestan; 98th Guards, Odessa. The 105th is now fighting in Afghanistan with the 103rd Guards. An eighth unit, the 44th Guards Airborne Training Division, is stationed in the Baltic Military District.

Airlift for the airborne force is provided by the Military Transport Aviation – *Voyenno-Transportnaya Aviatsiya (VTA)* – which is operationally subordinate to the Soviet General Staff. The VTA has a fleet of some 1,700 aircraft, including Ilyushin Il-76 Candid, Antonov An-12 Cub and Antonov An-22 Cock, all of which can be used in the parachute role to airland 175 troops at a time. Some 200 An-12 sorties are needed to drop one airborne regiment, but this is well within Soviet capabilities.

The massive An-124 Ruslan (or Condor) is now in flight testing and is expected to provide long-range, heavy-lift jet transport capability some time during the late 1980s.

Weapons and equipment

The Soviet Airborne Force is so large that it has proven well worthwhile developing a series of special weapons and vehicles for it. Basic weapon is the AKS-74 5.45mm automatic rifle with a folding stock. Snipers use the standard-issue SVD Dragunov 7.62mm semi-automatic rifle, which, with its telescopic sight, is accurate out to 1,092 yards (1,000m).

First seen in a Moscow parade in November 1973, the *Boyevaya Machini Desnatnya* (BMD) small armed troop-carrying vehicle was developed specifically for the airborne role. It is also amphibious with water-jet propulsion.

Below: *A stick of Soviet paratroopers during a winter exercise. The Soviet Army has the world's largest parachute force.*

Below: *Soviet paratroopers deploy from their BMD combat vehicle. Note 7.62mm AKM assault rifles, leather helmets and one piece suits.*

Another formidable vehicle is the *Aviadesantnaya Samakhodnaia Ustanovka* (Airborne Self-Propelled Vehicle), ASU-85, first seen in 1962 and in widespread use with Soviet and other Warsaw Pact airborne units ever since. The vehicle can be dropped by parachute, but is not amphibious.

Uniforms

The red beret is the almost universal badge of the paratrooper – except in the Soviet Army, where the color of the beret is light blue, as are the shoulder-boards and collar tabs. There is a special paratrooper's cloth sleeve badge worn on both parade and field uniforms. All parachute divisions are "Guards" units and thus all men wear both the enameled Guards badge and the enameled parachute qualification badge.

Normal combat gear is a camouflaged coverall, although heavy lined jackets and trousers are worn in cold weather. A simple khaki cloth helmet is worn while jumping and on the ground, although the blue beret is also frequently worn on exercises. The parachutists' badge is a stylized parachute with an aircraft on each side; this is worn on the collar tabs, and is also used on airborne force vehicles.

The main parachute is the D-1 model, which is limited to a maximum aircraft speed of 189 knots and a minimum height of 492 feet (150m). Static line deployment is used, although a ripcord is also fitted. A reserve parachute is carried on the chest.

Right: *The BMD airborne combat vehicle is designed to be dropped by parachute and to provide mobile firepower for Soviet parachute units. It has a crew of three and carries six paratroopers in the rear. Amphibious, it has water jet propulsion.*

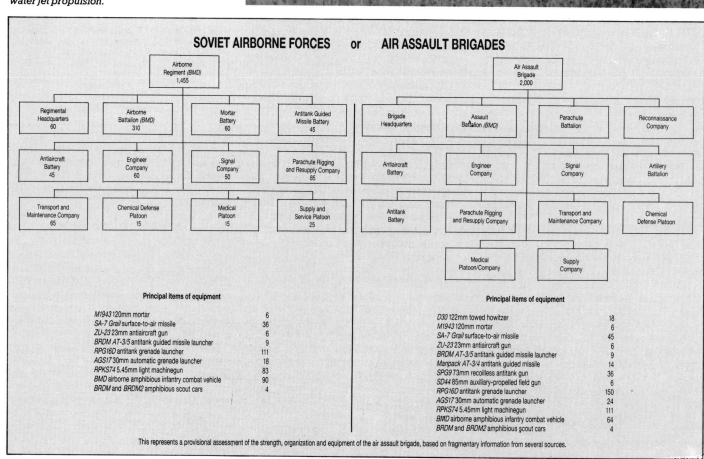

SOVIET AIRBORNE FORCES or AIR ASSAULT BRIGADES

Airborne Regiment (BMD) 1,455

- Regimental Headquarters 60
- Airborne Battalion (BMD) 310
- Mortar Battery 60
- Antitank Guided Missile Battery 45
- Antiaircraft Battery 45
- Engineer Company 60
- Signal Company 50
- Parachute Rigging and Resupply Company 85
- Transport and Maintenance Company 65
- Chemical Defense Platoon 15
- Medical Platoon 15
- Supply and Service Platoon 25

Air Assault Brigade 2,000

- Brigade Headquarters
- Assault Battalion (BMD)
- Parachute Battalion
- Reconnaissance Company
- Antiaircraft Battery
- Engineer Company
- Signal Company
- Artillery Battalion
- Antitank Battery
- Parachute Rigging and Resupply Company
- Transport and Maintenance Company
- Chemical Defense Platoon
- Medical Platoon/Company
- Supply Company

Principal items of equipment

M1943 120mm mortar	6
SA-7 Grail surface-to-air missile	36
ZU-23 23mm antiaircraft gun	6
BRDM AT-3/5 antitank guided missile launcher	9
RPG16D antitank grenade launcher	111
AGS17 30mm automatic grenade launcher	18
RPKS74 5.45mm light machinegun	83
BMD airborne amphibious infantry combat vehicle	90
BRDM and BRDM2 amphibious scout cars	4

Principal items of equipment

D30 122mm towed howitzer	18
M1943 120mm mortar	6
SA-7 Grail surface-to-air missile	45
ZU-23 23mm antiaircraft gun	6
BRDM AT-3/5 antitank guided missile launcher	9
Manpack AT-3/4 antitank guided missile	14
SPG9 73mm recoilless antitank gun	36
SD44 85mm auxiliary-propelled field gun	6
RPG16D antitank grenade launcher	150
AGS17 30mm automatic grenade launcher	24
RPKS74 5.45mm light machinegun	111
BMD airborne amphibious infantry combat vehicle	64
BRDM and BRDM2 amphibious scout cars	4

This represents a provisional assessment of the strength, organization and equipment of the air assault brigade, based on fragmentary information from several sources.

SOVIET UNION
NAVAL INFANTRY

THE FIRST 10 companies of Russian marines were raised by Peter the Great on November 16, 1705, and fought in many actions until they were disbanded following Napoleon's exile to St Helena in 1815. Temporary marine units were raised during the Crimean War (1853-56), the Russo-Japanese War (1904-05) and the Civil War (1917-22). A permanent body was not re-established until October 18, 1941, since when, apart from a low period between 1946 and 1964, the Naval Infantry has become an accepted and integral part of the Soviet armed forces, and a growing threat to the West and the Third World.

Described in Russian as *"morskaya pekhota"* (literally: "navy infantry"), there are now some 16,000 officers and men in the force, organized into five regiments. The Baltic, North Sea and Black Sea Fleets each have one assigned; there are two with the Pacific Fleet. The Soviet Infantry is graded as a "Guards" unit, and great emphasis is placed on the elite status this confers, a status reflected in special uniform and accoutrements. Like many elite forces the Soviet Naval Infantry has its own battlecry: *"Polundra"*, which roughly means "Watch out below".

Organization

Naval infantry regiments comprise three motor-rifle battalions (BTR-60PB APCs), a tank battalion (PT-76) an air-defense battalion (ZSU-23-4 and M8 Gecko), a multiple rocket-launcher company, and supporting engineer, signals and logistics units. The basic amphibious assault unit is the battalion group, and its likely composition was described in a Soviet journal as "A motorized infantry battalion detailed to operate as advanced detachment was reinforced with an artillery battery, an ATGM battery, AA, frogman and engineer platoons. It also included reconnaissance and obstacle-clearing parties, road-building teams, communications facilities, transport vehicles, and landing craft to perform transportation missions. The advanced detachment was to be supported by aviation, tactical airborne troops, support ships and mine-sweepers".

Selection and training

While some members of the Soviet Naval Infantry may be volunteers, most are conscripts, although, as befits its elite status as a "Guards" unit, it is allocated high quality men. Units and individuals are highly trained in amphibious operations and land warfare, and, like all marines, must also know something about life on board ship as well.

Physical training for the Black Beret is emphasized during routine unit training. Forty percent of the training program is devoted to wrestling, drill with the bayonet and the techniques of knife attack. The train-

Above: *Members of the Soviet Naval Infantry wear steel helmets. A five-pointed red star is often outlined on it, except during field operations when it is covered with camouflaged cloth similar to that shown here.*

ing is identical for both officer and enlisted man. Soviet marines are also required to undergo training in the Military Sports Complex and master the set of skills offered there, such as horizontal bar work; sprint in uniform; a cross country rush; a swim in uniform with assault rifle; and a longer version of the cross country rush.

Weapons and equipment

In the platoon the officer, NCOs and most marines are armed with the AKM assault rifle, while the APC driver has the AKMS folding-stock version. Each squad also has an RPK machine-gun and an RPG7V anti-tank rocket launcher. Sniper teams are armed with the highly effective SVD 7.72mm Dragunov sniper rifle.

Standard APC is the BTR-60PB, a well proven, 8-wheeled amphibious vehicle. Standard amphibious tank is the PT-76; the current version is the PT-76 Model 2 which has minor modifications to the main gun, but it would seem that a replacement for this very old vehicle must be due soon. The main advantage of the BTR-60PB and the PT-76 – of which there are 50 in service – is that they

Above: *Soviet Naval Infantry PT-76 Model 2 being unloaded from Aist class air-cushion vehicle (ACV) during a training exercise. A new ACV capable of landing elite units was seen by the West in 1986.*

Above: *Polnocny class LSTs of the Soviet Navy unload BTR 60PB APCs and a PT-76 light reconnaissance tank. The Naval Infantry would probably be "first-in" in an assault on oil-rich Mid-East nations.*

enable the leading elements of an assault landing to enter the water off the beach and swim ashore, which may be an invaluable ability in certain situations. Some 55 T-54/55 main battle tanks serve with the Soviet Naval Infantry; they are not amphibious and would land in the second wave from landing-craft direct over the beaches.

The BM-14 and BM-21 rocket launchers are used for artillery support. The ZSU-23-4 AA gun is used for air defense and is amphibious. Surprisingly, little emphasis seems to have been put on helicopters until relatively recently, although some Mil Mi-8 Hips are now being deployed for use in "vertical assault" type operations.

Uniforms

The uniform of the Soviet Naval Infantry is a combination of army and navy items, with a few unique embellishments of their own. Combat dress consists of black fatigues, with a "bush" type blouse and calf-length black leather boots. A black leather belt is also worn, with the appropriate fleet badge on the buckle. A horizontally striped blue and white T-shirt is standard with all forms of dress. The usual range of Soviet metal award brooches is worn, with all officers and men wearing the "Guards" badge. A round cloth badge with an embroidered anchor is worn on the left sleeve just above the elbow.

Various items of headgear are worn. In assault operations a black steel helmet is worn with a large five-pointed red star on the front, and a stencilled anchor inside a broken anchor on the left. On other occasions a soft black beret is worn with a small anchor badge above the left ear; the main badge is a large enamelled naval badge for officers and a small red star for NCOs and marines.

Amphibious shipping

The Soviet Naval Infantry would be of limited value without special-role shipping, and a whole range of purpose-built craft has been developed. Largest of these is the Ivan Rogov class of 14,000-ton Landing Platform Dock (LPD), of which two are now in service. Capable of carrying a complete battalion group with all its vehicles and supporting arms, the Rogov is a significant addition to Soviet global capability. Next are some 18 Ropucha class and 14 Alligator class Landing Ship Tanks (LST), both of some 4,500 tons displacement, and there are an ever-increasing number of smaller vessels. Particular investment has been made in the area of air-cushion landing craft. The Soviet Navy has a fleet of approximately 60, consisting of five classes, including the new 350-ton (estimated displacement) *Pomornik*, which may carry four PT-76 amphibious light tanks or their equivalent in its covered well deck.

Although not specifically designed for the purpose, it is clear that carriers of the Kiev and Moskva class could also be used to transport naval infantry units, and that their flight-decks would be particularly valuable for heli-borne landings.

SOVIET UNION
SPETSNAZ

Above: *Spetsnaz training is rigorous and realistic. Uniforms are similar to those of airborne troops, but can be of any force in the world. The best of these troops assemble once a year at Kirovograd and match skills.*

SPETSNAZ units are an outcome of the Soviet experiences in World War II, and appear to have started in the early 1950s, although it is only very recently that their existence has become public knowledge in the West. SPETSNAZ (Spetsialnoye Nazranie) literally means "forces at designation". Spetsnaz are the special forces of the GRU, the Soviet Military Intelligence organization; they are also known as "diversionary troops" and their units as "diversionary brigades". Spetsnaz war tasks are believed to include murder of enemy political and military leaders; attacks on enemy nuclear bases and command centres; and general attacks on military and civil targets (eg, power supplies) intended to create panic and disruption. Spetsnaz forces number some 30,000 in peacetime and serve both the Soviet Army and Navy.

Organization

It is estimated that in war the Soviets will have one independent Spetsnaz company per Army (total 41), 16 independent brigades, one Spetsnaz brigade per Fleet (total 4), one Spetsnaz regiment per Commander-in-Chief of Central Direction (equivalent to a Western "theater of operations") (total 3), plus one Spetsnaz intelligence unit per Front and Fleet (total 20). An independent Spetsnaz company consists of 9 officers, 11 warrant officers and 115 men, a much higher proportion of officers and warrant officers than in ordinary "line" units. They normally operate in up to 15 separate groups, but can come together into fewer groups for specific actions.

A Spetsnaz brigade has an HQ, an anti-VIP company (70 to 80 strong), 3 or 4 parachute battalions, a signal company and supporting units. The brigade, 1,000 to 1,300 strong, can split up into some 135 groups. The anti-VIP company is trained to find, identify and kill enemy political and military leaders, and is composed exclusively of regular troops (ie, there are no conscripts in this sub-unit).

The naval Spetsnaz brigade has an anti-VIP company, a group of midget submarines, 2 or 3 battalions of combat swimmers, a parachute battalion and supporting units. The Spetsnaz regiments are some 700 to 800 strong, split into 6 or 7 "sabotage" companies, and manned by athletes of the highest caliber, including Olympic performers.

Not surprisingly, in the eyes of Western observers, the mission and resources of Spetsnaz units are being expanded and their training accelerated. Nuclear sites are their main targets.

Selection and training

For conscript soldiers, who make up the bulk of Spetsnaz units in peacetime, the selection process starts well before they join the Army. On call-up, conscripts with Spetsnaz potential undergo a short and very intensive course, and those who show up best are sent on to another and much tougher training battalion to become sergeants. Many more sergeants

Above: *A rappelling exercise is part of the rigorous and realistic training for Spetsnaz troops. In the hand-to-hand phase of training, inmates of gulags are used and can be kicked, maimed and abused at will.*

Above right: *On a typical mission, Spetsnaz members carry a light rifle with 300 rounds of ammo, a bayonet, pistol with silencer, six hand grenades, and a lethal knife that – at a touch – propels a blade 30 feet.*

Right: *Paratroops (almost certainly Spetsnaz) on a typical Army assault course. Spetsnaz regiments reputedly include highly trained athletes, the backbone of the six or seven sabotage companies found in each regiment.*

Below: *In the aftermath of the KAL-007 airline disaster, mini-submarines (tracked), similar to those thought to be used by Spetsnaz for laying mines in Swedish waters, were seen in the area.*

are trained than there are vacancies for (those who are not selected serve as private soldiers in Spetsnaz units), thus giving an inbuilt reserve of qualified leaders.

Spetsnaz troops literally risk death during realistic training exercises. Deadly chemicals, explosive barrages and live ammunition are routinely used. Training includes infiltration techniques; reconnaissance and target location; language and customs of target nations, such as France or the UK; survival behind enemy lines; sabotage with all manner of devices; hand-to-hand combat, of course; parachute training; skiing, mountain climbing and rigorous physical conditioning.

Parachute training includes conventional drops; high-altitude, low-opening drops; and high-altitude, high-opening drops that allow Spetsnaz to drift undetected for at least 30 miles (48km) behind enemy lines.

Officers and warrant officers receive a 50 percent pay enhancement as well as parachute jumping pay. In addition, Spetsnaz qualify for military pensions earlier, since one year of service with Spetsnaz is equivalent to 18 months of regular service.

Weapons and equipment

On operations every Spetsnaz soldier would carry a 5.45mm AKS-74 rifle with some 300 to 400 rounds of ammunition, a P6 silenced pistol (or the new 5.45mm PRI automatic pistol), combat knife, six hand grenades and a light grenade launcher. Each soldier carries rations and medical kit, and each group has an R-350M radio set (with encryption and burst-transmission). The group may also carry an SA-7 SAM launcher, directional mines, explosives and other equipment appropriate to the particular mission. For those infiltrated into hostile countries prior to the outbreak of war such equipment would be smuggled in to in-place agents ready for issue when the time came. The groups could be expected to avail themselves of cars, lorries, motorcycles, etc, either provided by agents or stolen during operations.

Uniform

In order to preserve their "cover", Spetsnaz units have no special uniform or badges. In the USSR they wear the same uniform as the airborne forces and air assault troops, although (unlike the airborne forces) Spetsnaz and air assault troops do not wear the special "Guards unit" badge. In non-Soviet Warsaw Pact countries, Spetsnaz troops wear the uniform of the communications troops whose barracks they share. In Spetsnaz naval brigades the special troops wear naval infantry uniforms, except for the midget submarine crews who wear normal submariners' gear. Several sources state in a general war Spetsnaz troops would wear NATO uniforms or civilian clothes wherever the need arose.

Tactics

Spetsnaz tactical troops will be dropped by parachute deep into enemy territory at the very start of hostilities: Front brigades 310 to 620 miles (500 to 1,000km) and Army companies 62 to 310 miles (100 to 500km). This will be a massive and coordinated operation, and could well use aircraft in Aeroflot (as opposed to military) markings. The low-level-capable Antonov AN-12 transport and the long-range

Mi-6 and Mi-26 helicopters are ready to provide necessary transportation as well. Top priority targets will be nuclear-delivery means, such as missile sites, cruise-missile launchers, etc, and to cause maximum confusion as the enemy tries to deploy for war.

Spetsnaz troops with strategic tasks may well be infiltrated into target countries prior to hostilities, disguised as tourists, sports teams, cultural groups, businessmen, or members of diplomatic missions. Entry to the target country may well be by way of a third country. These groups will obviously wear civilian clothes, and will use inplace sleeper agents wherever possible as guides and sources of information, shelter and transportation. Naval Spetsnaz units will infiltrate mainly by sea, using submarines to approach close to their targets and then reaching shore by midget submarines (as Sweden is all too aware), inflatables or by swimming. Their primary targets will be naval nuclear bases, such as Britain's Royal Navy base at Faslane, Scotland, and the French base at Toulon, Southern France.

A Spetsnaz battalion is said to have been the first Soviet unit into Czechoslovakia during the "uprising" in 1968, having had the task of seizing Prague airport, thus enabling the following 103rd Guards Airborne Division to land unhindered. Spetsnaz troops have operated in Afghanistan since that country was invaded and some 4,000 fly in regularly to raid guerrilla strongholds.

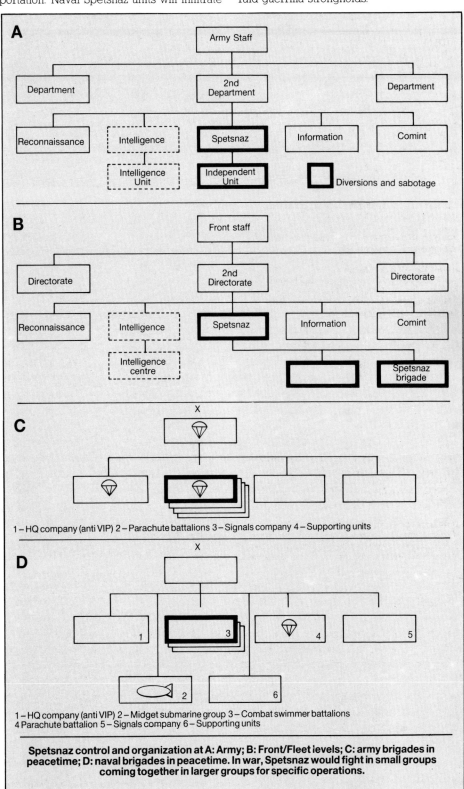

1 – HQ company (anti VIP) 2 – Parachute battalions 3 – Signals company 4 – Supporting units

1 – HQ company (anti VIP) 2 – Midget submarine group 3 – Combat swimmer battalions
4 Parachute battalion 5 – Signals company 6 – Supporting units

Spetsnaz control and organization at A: Army; B: Front/Fleet levels; C: army brigades in peacetime; D: naval brigades in peacetime. In war, Spetsnaz would fight in small groups coming together in larger groups for specific operations.

UNALIGNED NATIONS

Above: *Typifying elite forces of the "unaligned" nations, an Egyptian commando lowers himself from a hovering helicopter.*

THERE IS, perhaps, a tendency to view the world of armed forces – indeed the world itself – as red and blue. The blue represents – as it does in the symbology of wargames and elsewhere – what is loosely called the Western World. The "blue team" is made up of the United States, the United Kingdom and other NATO allies. The "red team" is represented by the Soviet Union and bloc nations of the Warsaw Pact.

How then, should the other nations of the world be accounted for – at least for purposes of this work? After all, these countries have elite forces which serve their national interests and must be taken into account.

Part of the answer lies in identifying the major elite forces in these countries and then drawing up their profiles. This has been done for elite forces of nine countries. Australia, New Zealand, India, Israel, Jordan, North Korea, South Korea, Taiwan and Thailand. This leaves the remaining nations, primarily those in Central and Latin America, Africa, the Mid-East, Far East and Oceania.

Claiming that they can all be called "Third World" won't work since this excludes Australia, Japan, Israel and others closely allied with the West. On the other side, there are Cuba, North Korea and Vietnam, close allies of the Soviets.

Using the term "nonaligned", say political scientists, won't work either, since the term carries with it the implication of a degree of formality in international relations. The term "unaligned" seems to be the best and was therefore selected to describe that great middle band of states throughout the world that are neither red nor blue.

Special operations forces in these nations – those mentioned earlier excepted – tend to be of the kind normally associated with counterinsurgency and other "stability" type operations. Given the size of most of them, indeed their individual needs, the scenario to present itself most likely would call for "cross border" action such as interdicting men and material bound for the sanctuaries of insurgents.

The orientation is much less likely to be – if it is at all – toward most special operations, which are oriented toward long-range reconnaissance, sabotage and organizing stay-behind resistance elements. Security assistance – particularly in the form of grants and training – is therefore likely to play a large role in structuring the defense forces of these nations. This is so because the great bulk of them usually have neither the resources nor the expertise to put together an effective elite force to deal with military or counter-terror matters.

The case of Mozambique is fairly typical. The British government has just given its approval to spend 1.6 million pounds (about $1.2 million) to equip and train an elite force of Mozambique soldiers to defend a railway link against South African-backed rebels. Former British special forces personnel will be used to train the new Mozambique forces.

This kind of effort is not new to the British, who have had a major influence on special operations and counterterrorist forces in many parts of the world for some time. They are very good at it. To take just a few random examples: The Special Boat Service has ties to units in Scandinavian countries who share the common problem of providing security for oil rigs; Kenya's original paratroop company trained in the UK; the SAS had a big role in building the foundations of the crack Jordanian Special Forces, as well as units in Egypt, Indonesia, Japan, the Sudan, and Bahrain. The motto of Oman's elite force, formed in the early 1980s, is "Who Dares Wins", which, of course, is the motto of the British SAS, revealing that unit's influence.

The United States is no slouch in this area, either. Chilean special forces maintain close ties to their US counterparts; SEAL badges and US parachutists' wings are found on members of the Brazilian special forces; Iranian Special Forces still wear uniform items of distinctly US origin, vestiges of earlier days; the Iraqi Special Forces Brigade was originally trained by US Special Forces, but the Soviets have had more influence in that direction of late. (Incidentally, accurate information on these forces is extremely difficult to come by; the Iraqis, for example, are so closed-mouthed about things military that they don't even publish the names of war dead.)

The red and blue characterization can extend in two directions, depending on the national interests involved. The Egyptian Commandos (slogan: "Be clandestine, daring and use surprise. Strike at night rather than in the day.") were believed to have received training in their early years from the Soviets; more recently, it comes from US forces. There are seven commando units in the Egyptian Army – about 1,000 personnel – and 250 in its special "Saiqa" unit.

On the counterterrorist front, it is countries like West Germany and France who, in addition to the US and UK, wield significant influence. It was recently reported that Ulrich K. Wegener, commander of West Germany's GSG 9, is setting up a special unit in Saudi Arabia modeled after his organization. GSG 9 has ties of one sort or another to units in Austria, Chile, Korea, Indonesia, Finland and Sweden.

French paras had considerable impact on the paratrooper unit set up in Senegal; on the counterterror front, France's crack GIGN has working arrangements with their counterparts in Saudi Arabia, Austria and in other countries.

The Soviet influence on elite forces in the unaligned nations is real, but is different in character and direction, given the closed nature of the Soviet society and the way the Soviets operate. The most direct impact they have comes from the arms they supply to other nations, which are therefore available to elite forces – or to those acting on the Soviets' behalf within the nation.

This raises the problem of measuring the influence and value of Soviet surrogates. Some measure of it may be gleaned from open data. For example, the number of Soviet forces operating in the Third World is estimated at between 22,000 and 25,000. (The US, by comparison, has 600.) This does not, of course, include the forces of Afghanistan, nor does it include surrogates such as Cuba, which has 35,000 troops in Angola alone.

Clearly, blue and red operate differently. One of the things it is imperative to recognize is the role of security assistance. Flatly stated, it has a major role in providing the expertise and resources that can be used to shape the client nation's defense posture. At a minimum, security assistance can "free up" resources for use in this direction that would not normally be available.

Moreover, since Soviet security assistance comes preponderantly in the form of weapons instead of grants and economic assistance (directly opposite to the way the US operates), the likelihood of elite forces being strengthened as a result is much higher.

A complete guide to all elite forces will not be found here – a point that bears repeating. That was not the intent; nor is it something that can reasonably be done. But the great band of unaligned nations in the middle, simply put, do not deserve to become the objects of benign neglect.

AUSTRALIA
SPECIAL AIR SERVICE

THE AUSTRALIAN SAS Regiment was formed in July 1957 as 1st SAS Company. It was the first-ever Australian special forces unit, and was clearly based upon lessons learned in the Malayan campaign, which was then winding down. In 1960, the unit was transferred into the Royal Australian Regiment, the regular infantry element of the Australian Army. On September 4, 1964, the unit became independent again, was increased in size, and became the Australian Special Air Service Regiment.

1SAS Squadron of the regiment deployed to Brunei in 1965 as part of the force countering Indonesian "confrontation", followed later by 2 SAS Squadron which went to Borneo. At virtually the same time Australia became involved in the Vietnam War and the three SAS squadrons rotated through that country from 1966 to 1971.

The Australian SAS has not deployed operationally since the end of the Vietnam War (at least as far as public knowledge is concerned). But it is of considerable interest; despite the very small size of the current Australian Army – they have only six regular battalions, for example – they still retain the SAS Regiment.

The Australian SAS developed a counter-terrorism capability in 1979 and in this capacity the Regiment has assumed responsibility for terrorist intrusions on-shore and in the case of off-shore oil rigs.

Australia also has a 350-man 1st Commando Regiment, which was raised in 1980 in Sydney. Basically comprised of reservists commanded by regular army officers, it contains elements of the former 1st Commando Company, Sydney; the 2nd Commando Company (Melbourne); and the 126 Signal Squadron (Melbourne). It is charged with conducting raids and special assault tasks.

The Australian SAS Regiment is comprised of: a headquarters; a Base Squadron; 1, 2 and 3 SAS Squadrons; a training squadron and 152 Signal Squadron. There was slight reduction with the disbandment of 2 SAS Squadron

following the Vietnam War; however, it was re-established in 1982.

Like the British SAS, the Australian SAS units; there is no recruiting direct from civilian life. Selection methods, too, are similar, but as there is no Australian marine corps there is a stronger emphasis on maritime activities.

Parachuting and rappelling are standard skills for SAS members, with other specialty training given in Scuba, small boat, mountain, HALO, assault swimmer, mountain leader, long-range mounted vehicle operations and demolitions.

Weapons

The weapons for the Australian SAS include the Browning Hi-Power, the L1A1 and M16 rifles, and the Mk5 (L34A1) sub-machine gun,

which is basically the Mk4 Sterling with silencer attached. Intended to be primarily single shot, in an emergency it can be fired fully automatic. Parker-Hale Model 82 sniper's rifles are also believed to be used. Since the Australian SAS has such wide anti-terrorist responsibilities, it also employs a diverse assortment of high-tech surveillance equipment, special ladders and other hardware.

Uniform

The Australian SAS Regiment personnel wear standard Australian Army uniform. Rather than the famous slouch-hat, however, they wear the equally famous sand-coloured beret and metal winged dagger badge of Britain's SAS. The wings, worn on the right sleeve, are also of the British SAS pattern.

INDIA
PARACHUTE BRIGADE

THE PARACHUTE units of the Indian Army are among the oldest airborne units. The first Indian parachute unit was authorized on May 15, 1941, and by October 1941 50th Indian Parachute Brigade had been formed, comprising 152nd Parachute Battalion (Indian), 151st Parachute Battalion (British) and 153rd Parachute Battalion (Gurkha).

In 1944 it was decided to form a division (44th Indian Parachute Division) and at the same time the formation of the Indian Parachute Regiment as a separate entity was authorized. The partition of the British Indian

Empire in 1947 led to the split of the parachute units between India and the newly-created Pakistan. 50th Indian Parachute Brigade was quickly involved in operations in Kashmir 1947-49.

During the 1965 Indo-Pakistan operations a special independent force of commandos was raised and on July 1, 1966, the 9th Parachute Battalion was formed to take on the task, absorbing the smaller commando force in the process. A year later part of 9th Battalion was hived off to form 10th Battalion, each with three company-sized sub-units desig-

nated "groups". In 1969 both units added the suffix "commando" to their titles, becoming 9th and 10th Commandos respectively.

Organization

The Indian Army parachute unit today is the 50th Parachute Brigade. It has parachute-trained units and sub-units of supporting arms and services – for example, artillery, engineers, signals. 9th and 10th Para-Commandos are also still part of the Indian Army order of battle, operating, as all such special forces units do, in an independent role.

Above: *Since the end of the Vietnam War, the Australian SAS has not deployed operationally. However, it was given counterterrorist responsibilities in 1979, and this responsibility was expanded to include protection for offshore gas and oil rigs one year later.*

Left: *One of the standard skills acquired by members of the Australian SAS is in handling small craft such as this Zodiac inflatable boat. In fact, special emphasis is placed on maritime skills since the country has no marine corps as a separate service.*

Right: *Australia is a country of immense size and diversity, ranging from enormous flatlands to mountainous terrain. Its elite SAS force, headquartered at Swanbourne, Perth, requires all troops to be skilled in mountain climbing – among many other specialities.*

Selection and training

All Indian paratroops and para-commandos are volunteers; some enter the regiments direct from civilian life, while others transfer in from regular army units. There is a probationary period of 30 days when the men undergo various physical and mental tests, during which many are weeded out. Those who pass are sent to the Paratroopers Training School at Agra, where five jumps, including one at night, entitle the trainee to wear the coveted wings and the maroon beret. Para-commandos undergo more specialized training to suit them for their role.

Weapons and equipment

The standard sub-machine gun of India's Army, including its paratroops, is the locally-produced version of the British L2A3 Sterling 9mm. There have been reports that the L34A1 silenced version may be in service in small numbers with the para-commandos. The current rifle is also a locally-produced version of a foreign weapon – the Belgian FN 7.62mm FAL, which is made in India at Ishapore. The light machine gun is the very popular and successful British L4A4, a 7.62mm conversion of the old 0.303in Bren.

Now at the prototype stage is a 5.56mm rifle being developed by the Indian Government's Armament and Research and Development Establishment (ARDE) at Pune. It is said to be a short, lightweight weapon suited to urban combat or for use by paratroopers and commandos.

On a normal combat jump, India paras deploy from Soviet AN-12 transports; jump rations and ammunition for three to four days are carried by jumpers.

Uniforms

The maroon (red) beret has been the headgear of the Indian Parachute Regiment since its inception on March 1, 1945. The cap-badge at that time was identical with that of the British Parachute Regiment, except that the word "INDIA" was inscribed at the base of the parachute. This badge was retained through the early years of independence and was changed to the present design – a fully opened parachute on two symbolic wings with an upright bayonet – in 1950. The para-commandos wear the red beret, but their cap-badge is a winged dagger above a scroll, similar to that of the British SAS.

There is another indication of the origins of India parachute forces in the British style camouflage and smock they wear. A leg bag sheathes rifles on operational jumps.

ISRAEL
PARATROOPS/ELITE UNITS

OF ALL THE world's elite units, none has probably seen so much or so frequent action as those of the Israeli Defense Forces (Zahal). Its paratroops, for example, were founded on 26 May, 1948 during the War of Independence. Its initial assets consisted of a dilapidated Curtiss C-46 Commando aircraft and 4,000 second-hand parachutes which had been bought as scrap to make silk shirts. The unit consisted of a mix of Israeli veterans of the British Army, the Palmach strike squadrons, resistance veterans, ghetto survivors, adventurers and some graduates of a parachute course held in Czechoslovakia.

In the early 1950s, frequent infiltration by Arab terrorists led to the formation of a small unit of high quality soldiers for reprisal operations. Known as Unit 101, it performed successfully and was amalgamated with the Paratroops, forming Unit 202. By 1955, this force was expanded into the 202nd Brigade.

Organization

Today, the Israeli Defense Forces maintain three regular paratroop brigades (the 202nd, 890th and Na'ha'l 50th), as well as three reserve brigades. It is within these formations and the infantry branch that the proliferation of bulk of the IDF's elite units has occurred.

These *sayeret* (reconnaissance) units were originally formed for border defense and were an outgrowth of regular paratroop units. They are set up according to their roles in special operations under the command of the brigade. *Sayeret Orev* is the reconnaissance anti-tank unit of the paratroops; *Sayeret Tzanhim* is the unit employed in the capacity of "shock troops"; and *Sayeret Shaldag* handles infiltration and demolition.

There are numerous other paratroop-trained units that are not connected to the paratrooper brigades. Among them are:

Sayeret Matkal. This most elite of units within the IDF is given the most important, highly classified and difficult missions. Not much is known or said about them.

Sayeret Hadruzim. An elite Druze Muslim reconnaissance unit, it serves in sensitive border areas under the IDF Northern Command.

Sayeret Golani. This reconnaissance unit is found within the Golani Brigade, a regular combat infantry brigade within the IDF. (The IDF, it should be noted, has no separate army, navy and air force. They are all branches within the IDF.) The *Sayeret Golani*, drawn from the Golani Brigade, is probably the finest reconnaissance unit in the IDF, and acts as the lead element in all operations conducted by the brigade. Its members participated in the daring rescue of hostages from Entebbe.

Sayeret Shimshon. This unit also exists within an infantry brigade, in this case the Giva'ati Brigade. This brigade, incidentally, is responsible for the marine-type amphibious operations of the IDF.

One of the most elite of units within the IDF is found in the Israeli Navy, and is known as the Naval Commandos. Acceptance into this force is even more difficult than it is into the paratroop reconnaissance units. With a 12-month training period, during which the applicant can be dropped at any point, the soldier is officially awarded Naval Commando wings and enters the operational period of his service.

Selection and training

There is a six-month basic training course for all regular paratroopers, and the training for those in the *sayeret* units is similar. The first phase of the training is geared toward physical fitness and personnel weapons proficiency. Much of the training is in the field, and includes long, harsh, fast-paced marches almost daily. Upon successful completion of this phase, the cadet is a "rifleman 3rd class".

In the two months of the second phase, the soldier is assigned his role within the unit (machine gunner, ammunition carrier, or whatever), becomes proficient in that task,

JORDAN
SPECIAL FORCES

IN JORDAN, a company of paratroopers was raised in 1963 and, having quickly proved its value, this has been expanded over the years until today the Jordanian Special Forces brigade consists of three airborne battalions. The predecessors to these units took part in numerous operations in the various Middle East wars, and have also been heavily involved during peacetime in keeping control of their troubled country. They played a leading part in the operations to suppress and finally expel the Palestine Liberation Army (PLO) commandos in 1970-71, and also retook the Inter-Continental Hotel in Amman in 1976.

Such is the reputation of the Special Forces that in 1983 US military authorities suggested that the force be expanded to two-brigade size, and be used to help cope with the security problems in the Persian Gulf. This proposal, while it recognized that Jordan's Special Forces were among the best in the Middle East, foundered on two points: first, considering that a sum of $200 million had been requested for this purpose, such a costly, huge effort of this kind would result in a special force that wasn't a special force any more, and, secondly, it would be a force that could just as easily be deployed against Israel as against another objective and, therefore, could hardly be expected to get a rousing reception in either Israel or the United States Congress.

Right: *Paratroopers in their Class "A" blouse and trousers. The wide assortment of weapons carried includes 9mm Uzi submachine guns.*

Left: *Israeli Defense Force paratroopers board a CH-53G heavy lift helicopter immediately prior to deploying to an attack in Lebanon.*

Below: *Israeli commando armed with the latest version of the Galil to enter the service, the Galil AR. He wears a ballistic infantry helmet.*

and learns to apply it. APC and helicopter training are introduced – with heavy emphasis on night fighting and urban area combat. Successful completion of this part of the course gets the soldier registered as "rifleman 5th class".

The last phase of training is at the Tel Nof Jump School. After five static line jumps, the soldier earns wings and becomes a full-fledged paratrooper. Advanced training is carried out with the units and it is at this stage that the relationship between soldier and commanding officer relaxes. In fact, officers are addressed by their first names throughout the IDF.

For the Naval Commandos, training is given in Scuba diving, infiltration, demolitions, sabotage, intelligence gathering, parachuting and HALO techniques. Medical techniques and driving skills are also taught at an intense pace.

Weapons and equipment

Like other units of the IDF, paratroopers use Israeli weapons and equipment wherever possible. These weapons are supplemented with items either purchased from Western sources or captured. The latter are usually of Eastern origin – as, for example, RPG-7 anti-tank weapons, which have been captured in great quantities and earmarked for use by the paratroopers.

The main parachute is the automatically operated EFA 672-12 (IS) type, and the small arms are Israeli. For many years, the Israeli paratroops have used the 9mm Uzi submachine gun, but this is now being replaced by the Galil assault rifle, an Israeli designed and produced 5.56mm weapon with a 35-round magazine.

Other weapons in use include the TOW anti-tank missiles, the American M16, and the FN MAG general purpose machine gun

Uniforms

IDF paratroopers wear standard Israeli uniforms and helmets. The coveted parachutists' red beret (awarded at the conclusion of training) is worn when the fiberglass combat helmet is not required. Recon paratroopers wear standard fatigues – the American OG-107 fatigue trousers are the most sought after article of clothing in the IDF inventory – as well as web'gear and other equipment while in the field.

The parachutists' badge is in silver and is worn on the left breast above campaign medals. Master parachutists' wings are awarded for 50 or more jumps and there are also free fall/HALO wings.

The olive fatigue cap has the soldier's blood type written on it. This is necessary due to the fact that the Israel Defense Force identification tag has only the soldier's name and serial number.

Organization

The three commando/paratroop battalions are organized on standard Jordanian Army lines with three companies, each with three platoons. Battalions are approximately 500 strong.

Selection and training

Members of the Jordanian Special Forces are hand-picked. They must be Bedouins with personal tribal links to King Hussein, and a proven record of undoubted loyalty. Their training is far and away the roughest in the Army – both physically and professionally. They are trained in sabotage and guerrilla operations.

In combat, they take part in elite infantry missions such as antiterrorist deployments, recce patrols, road blocks and raids. They undertake missions others may not be able or willing to.

Weapons and equipment

The three Special Forces battalions are equipped as light infantry, with weapons such as Dragon anti-tank guided missiles, 106mm recoilless rifles, mortars and small arms (M16 rifle, M60 MG, etc). Land transport is based on the usual jeeps and trucks. Air mobility is provided by the Royal Jordanian Air Force, whose transport fleet includes two squadrons with 16 Alouette III helicopters, 14 S-76 helicopters, 6 C-130B/H Hercules; 2 CN-235

transports, and two Casa C-212 Aviocars. As with the rest of the army, the Jordanian Special Forces' uniform shows both British and United States' influence. US-style leaf-pattern camouflage suits are worn and most items of personal equipment are of US origin. Parachute wings are worn on the left breast and the major visible mark is the maroon beret, but worn with the standard national cap-badge.

The Special Forces badge is a white bayonet surrounded by symbolic yellow wings and surmounted by a Hashemite crown; this is backed by a maroon shield and worn on the right upper sleeve. Bloused trousers identify members of Jordan's paratrooper units.

NEW ZEALAND
SPECIAL AIR SERVICE

THE NEW Zealand Special Air Service Squadron was formed in 1954 to join the British and Rhodesian SAS in Malaya. As in Rhodesia, the initial volunteers were taken straight from civilian life and 138 were accepted from a list of some 800. With 40 regular officers and NCOs, they were trained in New Zealand from June until November 1955 when the survivors were sent to Singapore to complete their parachute and jungle training. They soon deployed onto operations and spent 17 months out of the next two years in the jungle, killing 26 terrorists for the loss of just one of their own soldiers.

The squadron returned to New Zealand in November 1957 to be disbanded, but was resuscitated in August 1958. A troop of 30 men was sent to Korat in Thailand from May to September 1962 in support of SEATO. In 1963 the unit was redesignated 1st Ranger Squadron, New Zealand Special Air Service, and shortly afterwards the unit deployed to Borneo where it served, once again, alongside the British SAS. It also operated from time to time with Britain's SBS. 4 Troop NZSAS served in Vietnam from November 1968 to February 1971, where it served with the Australian SAS Squadron.

The unit is now stationed near Auckland, New Zealand. It has five troops, a headquarters, and a separate small training establishment. Its task is to support New Zealand defense forces in their operations and, like the SAS in the United Kingdom, has a major commitment to counter-terrorist missions. The uniform is standard New Zealand army, but badges are similar to those of the British Special Air Service.

Below: *Deployment at 2,000 feet (600m) for New Zealand SAS member. A heavy exchange program with other SAS units has aided each in their tactics and training. NZSAS also handles counterterrorist actions – not a major problem for New Zealand.*

Above: *Extensive array of weapons and equipment, which belonged to armed infiltrators who were captured by South Korean soldiers.*

Below: *Typical infiltration tunnel dug by the North Koreans, found adjacent to the DMZ. Some have been large enough to drive jeeps and other vehicles through.*

NORTH KOREA
SPECIAL PURPOSE FORCES

ONE OF THE largest elite forces in the world is fielded by the Democratic Republic of Korea (North). Known as the Special Operations Forces, there are 80,000 men in this elite force, which represents about 11 percent of the total in the North Korean People's Army.

Following the ending of overt hostilities in the Korean War, there were a number of units involved in unconventional warfare against the Republic of Korea (South). However, a single headquarters known as the VIII Special Operations Corps was established in 1969; it became the principal unit trained for special operations.

Organization

The Special Operations Forces are organized into 20 light infantry-type brigades and roughly 35 independent light infantry battalions. All units have commando/ranger and special forces-type capabilities as well as unconventional warfare-type capabilities, since Army doctrine calls for integration of these units and operations into all phases of combat operations.

Divisional light infantry battalions receive administrative and technical support from the VIII Special Purpose Corps, but are directly subordinate to the reconnaissance section of their respective division headquarters.

The light infantry brigade has approximately 3,800 men (11 percent of them officers), and is commanded by a major general or senior colonel. It is organized into a headquarters, signal company, rear services and nine light infantry battalions. These battalions have a strength of 400 men, 36 officers and 364 enlisted. Platoons within the battalions are equipped with 18 16mm mortars, 24 RPG-

Left: *Corpses of armed guerrillas caught and killed by the South Koreans. The 80,000-strong Special Operations Forces of the Democratic Republic of North Korea is considered one of the world's largest elite forces.*

Below: *Two North Korean agents (insets) captured during an attempt to land at Tadaepo, Pusan. The equipment used by North Korean Special Operations Forces varies widely, but always includes a dagger and bayonet (see left).*

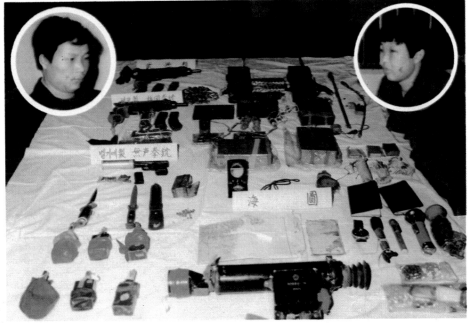

2/7s, and AT-3s and/or SA-7s.

Also important to the unconventional warfare capabilities are the training units; there are at least five Elite Training regiments known to exist under the control of the VIII Special Corps: 90th, 91st, 92nd, 93rd and 94th.

Selection and Training

The North Korean soldier is a highly disciplined and well-trained fighter. Indoctrinated against South Korea since childhood, he is likely to be conscripted between the ages of 17 and 21, and will remain in service until the age of 27. Annual training is between March and August and consists of a month-long basic training program. Once assigned to his unit, the trainee goes through further basic unit, small unit and large-scale unit training exercises.

Soldiers in the special warfare units get special emphasis on infiltration, Intelligence gathering, sabotage, underwater demolition, hand-to-hand combat and political education. Specific indoctrination and information sessions on all aspects of communist ideology are carried out on a daily basis.

Training is conducted not only during the day, but also at night. In fact, this type of training is extensive. They are also taught courses in personal survival techniques in

hostile territory; karate and knife fighting; ambush and surprise attack techniques; demolition; and communications methods. Marches over rugged terrain with a standard 88lb (40kg) pack are not uncommon.

Weapons and Equipment

Equipment is flexible and varies considerably. Common to all are a dagger and/or bayonet; pistols, including the silenced versions of the 9mm Browning automatic and the Soviet Tokarev 7.62mm automatic; the AK-47 or M16 rifle; hand grenades and demolitions; rocket launchers, either the RPG-7 or the AT-3 Sagger; and 60mm mortars. Special mission equipment can include 35mm cameras with telephoto lenses (400mm plus) and film (including infrared), plus electronic/signal intelligence equipment.

Uniforms

The light infantry, during training, are provided with the same standard uniforms as the infantry of the North Korean People's Army. However, during combat operations they can be attired in civilian clothing, South Korean Army uniforms (usually with incorrect ranks for the personnel wearing them), mottled camouflaged uniforms in summer and an all-white over garment in winter.

SOUTH KOREA
SPECIAL FORCES

Above: *The basis for all wargames in Korea is that aggressors will come over and under the DMZ. This is the scenario for joint US-ROK Special Forces teams as they parachute into their unconventional warfare areas.*

THE FORCES of the Democratic Republic of Korea (North) invaded the Republic of Korea (South) (ROK) on June 25, 1950. The resulting war pulled in the Republic of China on the side of the North, and 16 nations (including the USA) on the ROK side. An armistice (not a peace treaty) was signed on July 27, 1953, and an uneasy "peace" has continued since.

Currently stationed in South Korea is the United States 8th Army, comprising 2nd Infantry Division, 19th Support Command, at least one wing of the USAF and numerous supporting units. The ROK Army comprises five corps, with two mechanized and 19 infantry divisions, two armored brigades and a host of minor units. It also includes seven special warfare brigades.

In contrast, the army of North Korea comprises eight corps, with two armored divisions, five motorized infantry divisions, 24 infantry divisions and the usual supporting elements. Included in these massive forces in the North are no fewer than 22 Special Forces brigades. These include three commando; four reconnaissance; one river crossing regiment; three amphibious; and five airborne battalions. The North Koreans have built up sufficient forces in the central part of their territory to launch a deep and sudden attack, without help from its allies, which

would threaten Seoul, only some 28 miles (45km) south of the DMZ. Such an attack could be facilitated by the tunnels which have been dug from time to time. One such tunnel was 6.6ft (2m) square and large enough to accommodate small vehicles and light guns. The Communist Special Operations Forces brigades could use such tunnels or deploy by air or sea.

The ROK has seven special warfare brigades organized on the same lines as US special forces groups, with whom there is a close working relationship. The battalions of these brigades are often used in the ranger role for the destruction of tactical targets. These ROK special forces units are capable of using either continuous guerrilla operations from bases within enemy territory, or carrying out single operations from bases within friendly territory. The usual allocation of the special forces is one battalion to each army corps.

Selection and training

Following the usual physical and psychological tests, the volunteers undergo a hard training course which includes weapon handling skills to a very high standard and parachute training. All ROK special forces troops must also reach black belt standard in Tae-Kwon-Do or a similar martial art, and

when not on operations some four to five hours a day are spent in practice of such arts. They are also trained in tough, realistic exercises for dangerous missions along the DMZ, such as clearing North Korean tunnels. They have also been used as pursuit units when raiders have infiltrated the South. The DMZ remains a hotbed of hostile activity; incidents there have led to hundreds of deaths since the truce was signed more than 30 years ago.

Weapons and equipment

Standard sub-machine gun in use by the Korean special forces is the US-supplied 0.45 M3A1, although this must be due for replacement by a more modern and effective weapon in the near future. The rifle of the South Korean Army is the M16A1, locally manufactured, and the squad machine gun is the 7.62mm M60. The South Koreans are, however, taking steps to become more independent in the arms field and will probably produce their own small arms, also.

Uniform

Normal uniform is a camouflage combat suit. The Special Forces distinguishing mark is a black beret with the SF badge in silver. Weapons and personal equipment are all of US origin.

Pocket patches are sometimes worn for each brigade. A lion is found on the special warfare patch; an eagle on the 3rd Brigade's patch; a dragon on the 5th's; a Pegasus on the 7th's; a winged cat on a parachute on the 9th's; a bat over a lightning bolt on the 11th's; and a panther on the 13th's.

Far left: *The bitter cold winters in Korea were familiar sights on the newsreels during the 1950s. ROK Special Forces obviously find it necessary to ensure their troops are properly trained to fight effectively in such an environment.*

Above left: *Based in Seoul, the US-ROK Combined Forces Command maintains battle readiness with training exercises. These ROK Special Forces are shown in their RB15 craft on the Ham Na river during an exercise.*

Left: *Special Forces unit moves out smartly. Discipline and readiness never come naturally and must be constantly exercised. Says one ROK Special Forces officer, "One morning we will awaken to the sounds of battle."*

Above right: *Korea, according to some observers, is a land where war is a personal, imminent and continuing threat. The signs are everywhere, as witness the preparation of ROK Special Forces for such a possibility.*

Right: *Night infiltration training. ROK troops are tough, dedicated and well-disciplined – and want to keep their country free. Many US Special Forces personnel praise them highly for their skills and their tenacity.*

SOUTH AFRICA
RECONNAISSANCE COMMANDOS

AS THE military threat to the Republic of South Africa (RSA) has gathered strength over the past decade, the army of that country has had to gird itself for a lengthy campaign against a relentless, but by no means unbeatable, foe. Despite the recent accord with Mozambique the conflict will go on for years to come as the USSR, and their Cuban clients, fan the flames. The various external and internal operations have inevitably forced the South African Defense Forces to develop a number of special units, including the 32nd Battalion, which is composed almost entirely of disaffected Angolans, but the elite is undoubtedly the Reconnaissance Commando, popularly known as the "Recce Commandos" or just "Recces". (Commando is, of course, an honourable title in South African history, having been used to designate similar units in the Boer War against the British at the start of this century.)

The primary "Recce" mission is to operate deep inside enemy territory, gaining information and tracking enemy units. This is a similar task to that of the erstwhile Selous Scouts of the former Rhodesian Army, and it is likely that a number of its former members have joined South Africa's "Recces".

All "Recce" soldiers are trained parachutists, qualifying in both static and free-fall techniques, with many capable of HALO insertion. A number also receive training in seaborne operations, including underwater swimming. Tracking and survival in the bush are obviously essential, together with the usual special forces skills with explosives, radios, enemy weapons, and armed and unarmed combat. "Recces" also qualify as paramedics.

Above: *A dramatic illustration of how South African recces reach their targets. It can be on horseback, by parachute, on foot, in vehicles, by helicopter or across water.*

Selection and training

Selection courses for the "Recce Commandos" are of 42 weeks duration and are held twice a year. Unlike many other such courses, they are open not only to volunteers from the South African Army, but from the Navy and Air Force as well. The average age of those attending the course is 19, and only about 6 to 10 percent are ultimately successful. Of 700 who applied to join during a recent recruiting period, for example, only 45 were accepted. Medical and psychological tests are necessary preliminaries to attending the selection course, as is the physical test which includes: covering 20 miles (32km) in 6 hours, carrying full equipment, FN FAL rifle *and* a 70lb (32kg) sand-bag; various physical exercises (eg, 40 push-ups) within a specified time, and timed runs; swimming free-style for 50 yards (46m).

The selection course takes place in the wilds of northern Zululand, and is carried out in an operational environment. The standards set are extremely tough, and great emphasis is placed on pushing the volunteers to the limit. One of the final tests, for example, is to make the men spend one or two nights alone in the bush, with just a rifle and some ammunition to protect themselves from wild animals. The result of all this is to produce a very highly skilled, capable, and motivated soldier, who is thoroughly at home in the combat environment of today's southern Africa, either on his own or as a member of a group. In fact, South Africa's "Recces" are frequently described as "hard core professionals".

Weapons and equipment

Standard small arms are used, such as the FN 7.62mm FAL rifle (sometimes with a folding stock) and the FN MAG light machine-gun. Many soldiers carry fighting knives such as the "Warlock", a blackened stiletto designed for night raids.

Above: *South African commando in Angola. The "recces" are the elite of South Africa's defense forces, with selection and training based on that of the British SAS.*

Right: *River crossings figure extensively in warfare instruction of South Africa's recces. Another task: swim a mile underwater, attack an enemy and return to a set rendezvous.*

Uniforms

Recce commandos wear standard South African combat dress of sand-colored jacket and slacks, with high-ankled boots and a floppy "jungle-hat". The usual heavy canvas web equipment is also worn. In the field the soldiers, all of whom are white, use black camouflage paint to disguise their race at a distance.

Far left: *Weariness is evident in the face of this South African commando. The gruelling training that prepared this trooper for active operations (for which he receives extra pay) includes a run through the surf with web gear, rifle and a 60 pound bag of sand. A high degree of intelligence and motivation are also required of all commandos.*

Left: *Assembling for a bush operation designed to ferret out SWAPO guerrillas. The "skeleton" stocks make the R-4 assault rifles instantly recognizable. Recce commandos are also armed with 7.6mm FN MAG machine guns (left), which spray a lot of lethal stuff at close quarters. They also carry a blackened stilleto, rations, water, ammo pouches and first aid kits.*

Right: *A member of the South African Special Forces is "blacked up" for an operation in one of the Namibian homelands. All exposed parts of the body are covered in the same way. Recces handle special tasks, such as penetrating behind the lines, obtaining specific information and then getting out quickly.*

TAIWAN
LONG-RANGE AMPHIBIOUS RECONNAISSANCE COMMANDOS

WHEN Chiang Kai-shek and the last of the Nationalist Chinese forces were compelled to leave mainland China on December 7, 1949, they swore that one day they would return. Today that remains their stated aim despite the immense power of the Communist mainland and virtual abandonment by the USA.

The Army is very efficient and well-trained, and is currently some 290,000 strong. Their deployment is split between the main island of Taiwan, some 100 miles (160km) offshore, and the two inshore islands of Quemoy and Matsu, both of which are within artillery range of the mainland. The Quemoy garrison is some 55,000 strong and that of Matsu some 18,000. There have been several crises over this situation, particularly in 1954,

THAILAND
SPECIAL ARMY FORCES

THAILAND has long had both external and internal defense problems. Communist insurgents in Malaysia have used Southern Thailand as a sanctuary for many years, repeatedly clashing with Thai military forces. There are also tensions on the border with Burma, but the biggest problems are on the eastern border with Kampuchea (formerly Cambodia), where the Royal Thai Army finds itself face to face with the heavily equipped Vietnamese Army, the most experienced land force in Asia.

The history of RTA special forces dates back at least to 1963, when the 1st Ranger Battalion (Airborne) was reorganized and redesignated the 1st Special Forces Group (Airborne). Since then, this elite force has been expanded considerably and the various groups upgraded and redesignated as regiments.

RTA Special Forces missions are not unlike those of other similar groups elsewhere. They include the conduct of warfare behind enemy lines, psychological operations, civic action, sabotage, and "unilateral operations" against the enemy's air defense sites and command centers.

Organization

The 1st Special Forces Division was formed in 1982. It is comprised of three Special Force Fort Narai in Lopburi province. The 2nd Special Forces Division was formed in 1983 and only recently added its third Special Forces Regiment. Both units – their strength is estimated at 3,000 men – have been consolidated into a Special Warfare Command, which in turn is subordinate to Thai Army Headquarters.

Special units of the Special Warfare Command include a psychological operations battalion, a long-range reconnaissance patrol (LRRP) company, and a number of highly specialized "A" teams.

Selection and training

The RTA Special Forces are considered by many to be among the best in the region. Training is tough and realistic and the men are said to be highly motivated. Volunteers must complete both ranger and parachute schools before going to Special Forces regiments where they receive further train-

Above: *Royal Thai Special Forces soldiers in the jungle, which covers a large part of the country. The Thais have been fighting Communist guerrillas since 1950 and now face the Vietnamese.*

Right: *After a high altitude-low opening jump, a Thai Special Forces para secures his parachute. Clad in a special black uniform, he will soon join team members, who have landed within yards of each other.*

Below right: *Royal Thai Army Special Forces link up after paradrop. Training of this kind is realistic, and only the best of the "survivors" will find themselves in the Thai Special Forces.*

ing. General training is done at the RTA's Special Warfare Center at Lopburi and the regiments and is headquartered at Special Warfare School. Parachute training is conducted by the 1st Balloon Company at Camp Erawan, in the area of the headquarters of the 1st Division.

There is also a survival center, where the many specialized skills of jungle survival are taught. Great attention is paid to physical fitness, and especially to a form of martial arts based on traditional Thai boxing – which involves use of both hands and feet.

1955 and 1957; although there have been no overwhelming threats of late, the potential for trouble remains. The government on Taiwan maintains very large armed forces, which are efficient and highly trained, but are also a substantial drain on the economy.

Included in Taiwan's Army under a Special Force HQ are four special forces groups, which include the Long-Range Amphibious Reconnaissance Commandos, and para-frogmen. There are also two brigades of paratroopers. The Recce Commandos are very highly trained and are known to have been active on the mainland in the maritime provinces for many years.

There is a growing relationship – including that between special forces – among Taiwan, Israel and South Africa, which includes exchange training for special units. The countries have formed this loose alliance so they can share knowhow based on their common isolation and the fact that they all face numerically superior forces on their borders.

Standard rifle of the Taiwan Army is the M16A1, of which some 5,000 have been supplied direct from the USA. The Combined Services Arsenal at Kaohsuing has, however, produced a new rifle – designated the 5.56mm Type 65 – which is now in service with Taiwan special forces, including the Long-Range Amphibious Reconnaissance Commandos. This bears some similarities to the M16A1, although it also has features taken from the AR-18 design.

The standard sub-machine gun is the 0.45 Type 36, a locally produced version of the US M3A1. Standard light machine gun is the US M60 7.62mm, made under licence in Taiwan. Until now, the uniforms of the Taiwanese forces have been almost totally American in design and appearance.

Above: *A Thai Special Forces team member lands in a target area having used high-altitude high-opening parachute technique. Parachute infiltration is an essential skill and, to cut the cost of using aircraft in training, the Thais use a large helium-filled balloon as a jump platform. The balloon's gondola can handle six parachutists plus jumpmaster from 1,000ft, with the balloon tethered to a truck.*

Weapons and equipment

The Thai Special Forces use US equipment and weapons in the main. The basic weapon, for example, is the M16 rifle. Also used are the 7.62mm M60 general purpose machine gun and the 5.56mm H&K33 rifle, which is manufactured under license in Thailand. Like other special forces throughout the world, they also train with foreign weapons likely to be used by potential enemies.

Uniforms

The main symbol of the Special Forces is a red beret with a gold woven national army cap-badge. Working uniform is a two-piece camouflage suit, with low-visibility black embroidered rank and qualification badges.

The same uniform is worn on operations, but with a camouflaged "jungle hat". A special combat uniform of black suit and black boots is also sometimes used, topped with a black knitted balaclava helmet.

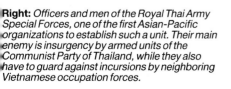

Above: *Martial art, part of physical training, is based on Thai boxing, a traditional sport that requires fitness, suppleness and courage, not to mention the use of both the hands and the feet.*

Right: *Officers and men of the Royal Thai Army Special Forces, one of the first Asian-Pacific organizations to establish such a unit. Their main enemy is insurgency by armed units of the Communist Party of Thailand, while they also have to guard against incursions by neighboring Vietnamese occupation forces.*

SECTION TWO
THE ENEMY: TERRORISM

UNITED KINGDOM: NORTHERN IRELAND   96
PALESTINE LIBERATION ORGANIZATION (PLO)   108
THE RED BRIGADES   112

THE ENEMY:
TERRORISM

DURING 10 days of terror in, Paris, the City of Light, 11 people were killed and more than 250 wounded in five separate bombings. An obscure group took "credit".

At a funk-and-soul disco in West Berlin, an early morning explosion rocked the establishment. Two US Army sergeants and a Turkish woman were killed, more than 230 injured. The US claimed indisputable evidence of involvement by Libya and retaliated with air strikes at targets in and around Tripoli and the coastal city of Benghazi.

Far from being isolated incidents, these were but two of scores of similar events that rocked civilized societies and the world at large in 1986. Reported in headlines almost daily, they are the kind of grisly activity that prompted one of the West's top military leaders to call our era one of "violent peace".

The figures bear him out. There were 897 international terrorist incidents in 1986, an increase of 9 percent over the previous year. Almost half were in the Middle East, with most of the remainder occurring in Western Europe and Latin America.

The trail of carnage includes 41,000 killed and 24,000 wounded between the years 1970 and 1984; moreover, the incidents are getting increasingly lethal. In the 1970s, 80 percent of terrorist attacks were directed against property and 20 percent against people. In the 1980s, fully half have been directed against people.

Not only is the problem growing and getting more brutal, but the odds of catching and punishing terrorists aren't that high. The Jaffee Center for Strategic Studies in Tel Aviv reports that only one out of ten terrorists is ultimately captured or killed. The inability to get at the instigators of the violent peace – for whatever reason – has been particularly frustrating for governments and the public at large, which naturally demands that "something be done about it".

But the length and breadth of terrorism's bestial arm is enormous, and this section shows how its tentacles literally wrap around the globe. Included here is a list of approximately 800 terrorist organizations in 88 separate countries – many of them interconnected. There are also profiles of terrorist organizations that typify groups which are in operation today. The Irish Republican terrorist groups operating in Northern Ireland, and the complex Palestine Liberation Organization (PLO) – together with their splinter groups – were selected because they are easily the most durable of the terrorist outfits in the twentieth century.

Italy's Red Brigades, responsible for the assassination of Premier Aldo Moro, were chosen because their roots trace directly to the ferment and unrest on the world's campuses in the late 1960s – a situation many feel nurtured the climate for today's acts of terrorism. The Brigades are essentially a communist, urban-oriented group, while "religious differences" are said to be a spur for other terrorist movements.

ALBANIA
Anti-Communist Military Council

AUSTRIA
Justice Guerilla

BELGIUM
Julien Lahaut Brigade
Revenge and Freedom

CYPRUS
Ethniki Organosis Kyprion Agoniston (EOKA-
   National Organization of Cypriot Fighters)
Ethniki Organosis Kyprion Agoniston-B (EOKA-B:
   National Organization of Cypriot Fighters-B)
National Front (Ethniki Parataxis)

FEDERAL REPUBLIC OF GERMANY
Black Cells (Schwarz Zellen)
Black Help (Schwarze Hilfe)
German Action Groups (DA)
German Empire Party (DRP)
German Socialist Student Association (SDS)
Guerrilla Diffusa (Guerrilla Dispersion-GD)
Holger Meins Commando
National Socialist Common Action Group (ANS)
People's Socialist Movement of
   Germany/Workers' Party (VSBD-PdA)
Red Army Faction (RAF)
Red Help (Rote Hilfe)
Revolutionary Cells (RZ)
Second of June Movement
Socialist Empire Party (SRP)
Socialist Patients' Collective (SPK)
Union for the Protection of the Tyrol (Tiroler
   Schutzbund)
Wehrsportgruppe Hoffman (Defense Sports Group
   Hoffman)

FRANCE
Action for the Rebirth of Corsica (ARC)
Action Front for the Liberation of the Baltic
   Countries
Andreas Baader Commando
Armed Nuclei for Popular Autonomy (NAPAP)
Association of Corsican Patriots (APC)
Autonomous Intervention Collective Against the
   Zionist Presence in France
Avengers
Basque Justice (EZ)
Breton Fight (AB)
Breton Liberation Front (FLB)
Breton Nationalist Resistance Movement (MRNB)
Charles Martel Club
Committee for Socialist Revolutionary Unity
Committee of Coordination
Communist Youth Movement, Marxist-Leninist
   (UJC-ML)
Confrontation (Faire Front)
Corsican Peasant Front for Liberation (FPCL)
Corsican Revolutionary Action (ARC)
Delta
Direct Action (AD)
Enbata Galerne
European Nationalist Fasces (FNE)

Left: *The traditional face of terrorism, exposed as Mujahadeen Commando hijackers hold to ransom 380 passengers of Iran Air 747 at Orly airport en route to Teheran. Fortunately, after hours of negotiations, the Commandos released their hostages and surrendered to French authorities, 7 July 1983.*

EUROPE

Federation for European National Action (FANE)
French National Liberation Front (FNLP)
French Revolutionary Brigades (BRF)
Group for the Defense of Europe
High School Action Committee (CAL)
Hordage (Je Tiens)
International Revolutionary Solidarity
International Solidarity
Iparretarrak (Those from the North)
Jewish Self-Defense Front
Masada Action and Defense Movement
Movement of the Youthward Brothers in War of
  the Palestinian People
New Action Front Against the Independence and
  Autonomy of Corsica (FRANCIA)
New Order (Ordre Nouveau)
Red Army Faction of Southern France
Revolutionary Communist Youth (JCR)
Secret Army Organization (OAS)
6th of March Group
Solidarity Resistance Front
Talion Law
Twenty Second March Movement
We Must Do Something
Youth Action Group

GREECE

Autonomous Resistance (Aftonomos Antistasi)
Blue Archer (Galazios Toxotis)
Fourth of August (4 Avgoustou)
National League of Greek Regular Officers
  (Ethnikos Syndesmos Ellinon Monimon
  Axiomatikon – ESEMA)
October 80 Revolutionary Organization
  (Epanastatiki Organosi 80 Oktvri)
Organization for National Recovery (Organismos
  Ethnikis Anorthosoos – OEA)
People's Revolutionary Struggle (Epanastatikos
  Laikos Agonas – ELA)
Revolutionary Nucleus (Epanastatikos Pyrenas)
Revolutionary Organization 17 November
  (Epanastatiki Organosi 17 Noemvri)

ITALY

Armed Communist Formations
Armed Proletarian Nuclei (NAP)
Armed Revolutionary Nuclei (NAR)
Autonomous Worker's Movement
Black Order (Ordine Nero – ON)
Combatants for Communism
Front Line (Prime Linea – PL)
Mussolini Action Squads (SAM)
New Order (Ordine Nuovo – ON)
October XXII Circle
Partisan Action Groups (GAP)
Permanent Struggle (Lotta Continua)
Proletarian Committee of Subversion for Better
  Justice
Proletarian Internationalism
Proletarian Justice
Proletarian Squad
Red Brigades (Brigate Rosse – BR)
Red Guerrilla
Revolutionary Action Group
Revolutionary Action Movement (MAR)

Revolutionary Fascist Nuclei (NFR)
Workers' Vanguard

NETHERLANDS

Free South Moluccan Youth Organization (VZJ)
Red Brigades
Red Help (Rode Hulp – RH)
Red Resistance Front (RVF)
Red Youth (Rode Jeugd – RJ)
Revolutionary Peoples Resistance of the
  Netherlands

PORTUGAL

Action Group for Communism
Armed Revolutionary Action (ARA)
Front for Liberation of the Azores (FLA)
Front for the Liberation of the Madeira
  Archipelago (FLAMA)

SPAIN

Anti-Fascist and Patriotic Revolutionary Front
  (Frente Revolucionario Antifascista y Patriotico –
  FRAP)
Anti-Terrorism ETA (Antiterrorismo ETA – ATE)
Apostolic Anti-Communist Alliance (Alianza
  Apostolica Anti-comunista – AAA)
Armed Struggle Organization (Organitzacio Lluita
  Armada – OLIa)
Autonomous Anti—Capitalist Commandos
  (Comandos Autonomos Anticapitalistas – CAA)
Catalan Liberation Front (Front d'Alliberament
  Catala – FAC)
First of October Anti-Fascist Resistance Group
  (Grupo de Resistencia Antifascista de Primero de
  Octubre – GRAPO)
Free Land (Terra Lliure – TL)
Freedom for the Basque Homeland (Euskadi ta
  Askatasuna – ETA)
International Revolutionary Action Groups
  (Grupos de Accion Revolutionaria
  Internacionalista – GARI)
Moroccan Patriotic Front (Frente Patriotico
  Maroqui – FPM)
Movement for the Self-Determination and
  Independence of the Canary Islands Archipelago
  (Movimiento para la Autodeterminacion e
  Independencia del Archipielago de las Canarias
  – MPAIAC)
New Force (Fuerza Nueva – FN)
Spanish Basque Battalion (Batallon Vasco
  Espanol – BVE)
Spanish National Action (Accion Nacional
  Espanola – ANE)
Warriors of Christ the King (Guerrilleros de Cristo
  Rey)

UNITED KINGDOM/IRELAND

Angry Brigade
Anti-Nazi League
Black Liberation Army
British Movement
First of May Group
Free Wales Army (MAC)
International Marxist Group (IMG)
Irish Freedom Fighters

Irish National Liberation Army (INLA)
Irish Republican Army (IRA)
Irish Republican Socialist Party (IRSP)
Keepers of Wales (Cadwyr Cymru – CC)
Loyal Citizens of Ulster (LCU)
Loyalist Association of Workers (LAW)
National Front (NF)
National Party (NP)
People's Democracy (PD)
Protestant Action Force (PAF)
Provisional Irish Republican Army (PIRA)
Radical Student Alliance (RSA)
Red Flag 74
Red Hand Commandos
Shankhill Defense Association (SDA)
Sinn Fein (Ourselves Alone)
Socialist Worker's Party (SWP)
Tartan Army
Troops Out Movement (TOM)
Ulster Defense Association (UDA)
Ulster Freedom Fighters (UFF)
Ulster Protestant Volunteers (UPV)
Ulster Volunteer Force (UVF)
Ulster Workers' Council (UWC)
Worker's Revolutionary Party (WRP)
Young Militants

YUGOSLAVIA

Cominformists
Croat Illegal Revolutionary Organization (Hrvatska
  Illegalna Revolucionarna Organizacija – HIRO)
Croat Liberation Movement (Hrvatski
  Oslobodilacki Pokret – HOP)
Croat National Congress (Hrvatsko Narodno
  Vijece – HNV)
Croat National Resistance (Hrvatski Narodni Otpor
  – HNO)
Croatian Intelligence Service
Croatian National Liberation Forces – Fighters for
  a Free Croatia
Croatian National Resistance
Croatian Revolutionary Brotherhood (Hrvatsko
  Revolucionarno Bratsvo – HRB)
Croatian Youth (Hrvatska Mladez – HM)
Drina
Fighters for a Free Croatia (Borciza Slobodnu
  Hvratsku – BSH)
Freedom for the Serbian Fatherland (SOPO)
Krizari (Crusaders)
Rebel Croat Revolutionary Organization (Utstasa
  Hvratska Revolucionarna Organizacija – UHRO)
Trotskyist Organization
United Croats of West Germany (Ujedinjeni Hvrati
  Njemaske – UHNJ)
World League of Croat Youth (Svetska Liga
  Hvratske Omladine SLHO)
Young Croatian Army for Freedom
Young Croatian Republican Army

Along those lines, it has been alleged that terrorism rears its ugly head when there are grounds for it: that is, when the government is so oppressive that terrorist groups just naturally form. It would follow that countries run along communist lines – in which people are offered the least amount of participation in society – should be most infected with the strains of "violent peace".

Quite the opposite is true. In fact, of 6,700 acts of terror recorded between 1968 and 1980, only 62 were in the East Bloc nations. Suffice it to say, that the amount of activity there is negligible and therefore terrorist organizations in those countries are not listed – except in Yugoslavia and Bulgaria, with good reason: the latter in particular is at the hub of a new phenomenon called "narco-terrorism".

The shadowy, lucrative world of narcotics is rapidly becoming a

AFRICA

ALGERIA

National Liberation Front (Front de Liberacion Nationale – FLN)
Revolutionary Committee for Unity and Action (Comite Revolutionnaire pour l'Unite et l'Action – CRUA)
Secret Army Organization (Organization de l'Armee Secrete – OAS)
Secret Organization (Organization Secrete – OS)

ANGOLA

Front for the Liberation of the Enclave of Cabinda (Frente da Libertacao do Enclave de Cabinda – FLEC)
National Front for the Liberation of Angola (Frente Nacional de Libertacao de Angola – FNLA)
National Union for the Total Independence of Angola (Uniao Nacional para a Independencia Total de Angola – UNITA)
Popular Movement for the Liberation of Angola (Movimento Popular para a Libertacao de Angola – MPLA)

CANARY ISLANDS

Canary Islands Independence Movement
Canary Islands Intelligence Service
Movement for Self-Determination and Independence for the Canary Islands

CENTRAL AFRICAN REPUBLIC

Central African Movement for National Liberation (MCLN)
Independent Reflection Group (GIRA)
Movement for the Liberation of the Central African People (MLPC)
Oubanguain Liberation Front (FLO)
Oubanguain Patriotic Front (FPO)

CHAD

Chad Armed Force (FAT)
Chad Liberation Movement (MPLT)
Chad National Liberation Front
Common Action Front (FAC)
National Patriotic Movement (MNP)
Northern Armed Forces (FAN)
Popular Armed Forces (FAP)
Popular Front for the Liberation of Chad (FPLT)

DJIBOUTI

National Independence Union (UNI)
Popular Liberation Movement
Somali Coast Liberation Front (FLCS)

EGYPT

Atonement and Holy Flight from Sin (Al Takfir Wal Hijira)
Al Djihad Conservative Organization
Al Islamiya
Al Jamiyat
Arab Egypt Liberation Front
Coptic Societies in the Near East
Egyptian National Front (ENF)
Holy War (Al-Jihad)
Muslim Brotherhood Egyptian Communist Party (ECP)

Egyptian Naitonal Front
Front for the Liberation of Egypt
Islamic Association
Libyan National League
Muslim Brotherhood
National Coalition
National Front
New Wafd Vanguard
Repentance and Holy Flight
Social Arab Nasserist Party
The Coptic Orthodox Church

ETHIOPIA

Eritrean Liberation Front (ELF)
ELF – General Command
ELF – Revolutionary Council
Eritrean Liberation Front – Popular Liberation Forces (ELF-PLF)
Eritrean People's Liberation Front (EPLF)
Ethiopian Democratic Union (EDU)
Ethiopian People's Revolutionary Party (EPRP)
Oromo National Liberation Front (ONLF)
Popular Liberation Forces (PLF)
Somali-Abo Liberation Front (SALF)
Tigre People's Liberation Front (TPLF)
Western Somali Liberation Front (WSLF)

GUINEA BISSAU

African Party for the Liberation of Ginea and Cape Verde (PAIGC)

KENYA

Mau Mau
Northern Frontier District Liberation Front (NFDLF)

LESOTHO

Basotho Congress Party (BCP)
Lesotho Liberation Army (LLA)

LIBERIA

Movement for Justice in Africa (MOJA)
Progressive Alliance for Liberia (PAL)

LIBYA

Arab Revolutionary Brigades
Libyan National Association
Libyan National Salvation Front
Libyan Baathist Party
Red October
Pan Arab Command
Warriors for Imam Moussa Sadr
7 April Libyan Organization
Martyrs of Palestine

MALAWI

Congress of Second Republic of Malawi
Malawi Freedom Movement (MAFREMO)
Socialist League of Malawi (LESOMA)

MAURITANIA

Alliance for a Democratic Mauritania
Free Man Movement
Mauritanian Democratic Union
Walfougi Front

MOROCCO

Forward Movement (Ilal Alam)
National Union of Moroccan Students
Popular Front for the Liberation of Saguia el Hamra and Rio de Oro, or Polisario Front

MOZAMBIQUE

Free African Movement
Mozambique Liberation Front (Frelimo)
Mozambique Resistance Movement (MRM, a.k.a. Mozambique National Resistance)
Revolutionary Committee of Mozambique (Coremo)
United Mozambique Front (FUMO)

NAMIBIA

South West African National Union (SWANU)
South West African People's Organization (SWAPO)

SOMALIA

Democratic Front for the Liberation of Somalia (DFLS)
Somali Democratic Salvation Front (SDSF)
Somali Liberation Front
Somali National Movement (SNM)
Somali Salvation Front (SOSAF)
Somali Worker's Party (SWP)

SOUTH AFRICA

African National Congress (ANC)
Azanian People's Organization (AZAPO)
Pan Africanist Congress (PAC)
South African Communist Party (SACP)
White Commando (Wit Kommado)

SPANISH SAHARA

Mustafa el Wali Bayyid Sayed International Brigade

SUDAN

Anya Nya
Azania Liberation Front)ALF)
Sudan African Liberation Front (SALF)
Sudan African National Union (SANU)
Sudan Communist Party (SCP)
Sudanese Socialist Popular Front (SSPF)

TUNISIA

Arab National Rally (RNA)
Islamic Progressive Movement (MIP)
Islamic Trend Movement (MTI)
Movement of Socialist Democrats (MDS)
Popular Revolutionary Movement (MPR)
Popular Unity Movement (MUP)
Progressive Nationalist Front for the Liberation of Tunisia (FNPLT)
Revolutionary Party of the Tunisian People (PRPT)
Tunisian Armed Resistance (RAT)
Tunisian Communist Party (PCT)

UGANDA

Uganda Freedom Movement (UFM)
Uganda National Liberation Front (UNLF)

major source of revenue – supplanting, at least to some degree, such "tried and true" methods as robbing banks, pulling off kidnappings and soliciting patronage from those who are enamored of the "cause".

Estimates are that Bulgaria touches at least one quarter of the heroin that reaches the United States and 80 percent of that going to West Germany. Profits from these efforts are used to put together incredibly complex arms deals under which weapons end up in the hands of terrorists.

In some cases, individual states underwrite the cost of bloodshed. According to some estimates, Libya spends between $70 million and $100 million per year to bankroll nearly 40 terrorist organizations. Other countries that sponsor terrorism include Iran, Syria, Cuba, Bulgaria and Tunisia, which gives the terrorist PLO a safe haven.

Left: *Terry Waite (right), special envoy of Britain's Archbishop of Canterbury, and Ambassador Robert Oakly (background), US Department of State anti-terrorist expert, shown with Father Lawrence Jenco following his release in July 1986 after 19 months of captivity in the hands of the Shi'ite Moslem fundamentalist group, Islamic Jihad. Having been instrumental in the release of Father Jenco and others, Terry Waite himself fell victim to the hostage-takers of Beirut, Lebanon, in 1987. At the time of going to press, his whereabouts were still unknown, despite conflicting rumours that he was being held in Teheran and that he died in captivity at the beginning of July.*

Above: *Almost universally denounced as a state terrorist, Libyan leader Mu'ammar al-Qadhafi admits to supporting terrorist movements, such as the Irish Republican Army.*

Uganda National Rescue Front (UNRF)
Uganda National Resistance Movement (UNRM)
Uganda Popular Front (UPF)
Ugandan People's Movement (UPM, or Ugandan Patriotic Movement)

WESTERN SAHARA/MOROCCO

Association of People from Sahara (AOSARIO)
People's Front for the Liberation of Saguiat al Hamra and Rio de Oro (Polisario)

ZAIRE

Council for the Liberation of Congo-Kinshasa (CLC)
Congo National Liberation Front (FLNC)
National Movement for Union and Reconciliation in Zaire (MNUR)
People's Army of the Oppressed in Zaire (APOZA)
People's Revolutionary Party (PRP)

ZIMBABWE

African National Council (ANC)
Patriotic Front (PF)
Zimbabwe African National Union (ZANU)
Zimbabwe African People's Union (ZAPU)

MIDDLE EAST

AFGHANISTAN

Afghan Nation (Afghan Mellat)
Afghan National Liberation Front
Alliance of Islamic Fighters (Hedadia Mujahideen Islami Afghanista)
Islamic Afghan Association (Jamaat-i-Islami Afghanistan)
Islamic Alliance for the Liberation of Afghanistan (IALA)
Islamic Party (Hizb-i-Islami)
Movement for the Islamic Revolution (Harakat-i-Inkalab-i-Islami)
Muslim Brotherhood (Ikwhan-i-Muslalamin)
National Islamic Front for Afghanistan (Makaz-i-Milli)
People's Democratic Party of Afghanistan (PDPA)
Teiman Atahad-Islami

BAHRAIN

Al-Sanduq Al-Husseini Society
Islamic Front for the Liberation of Bahrain
Popular Liberation Front of Aman and the Arab Gulf

IRAN

Araya
Azadegan Movement
Armed Movement for the Liberation of Iran
Arab Popular Movement of Arabistan
Baluchistan Liberation Front (BLF)
Baluchistan People's Democratic Organization (BPDO)
Baluch Pesh Merga (Baluch Volunteer Force)
Black Wednesday Brigade
Bahai Faith
Baluchi Autonomist Movement
Bahai Community
Forghan (Koran)
Forgan
Hezbollah (Party of God)
Iran Liberation Army (ILA)
Iran Liberation Movement (ILM)
Islamic Arab Front for the Liberation of Baluchistan (IAFLB)
Iranian National Front (INF)
Islamic Jihad
Kurdish Democratic Party of Iran (KDPI)
Kurdish Sunni Moslem Movement
Komaleh
Liberation Front of South Arabistan
National Front (NF)
National Front of the Iranian People (NFIP)
National Democratic Front (NDF)
National Council of Resistance for Liberty and Independence (NCR)
National Resistance Movement
Nationalist and Revolutionary Front of Iran
Organization for Marxist Leninists
Pars Group
People's Sacrificers
People's Crusaders
People's Fighters
People's Party
People's Fadayeen (Fedayeen-e-Khalq)

People's Mujahideen (Mujahideen-e-Khalq)
Peykar (Struggle)
Popular Front for the Liberation of Ahvaz (Jabhat Tahrir Ahvaz)
Razmandegan (Fighters)
Party of Equality
Group of the Martyr
Arab Political and Cultural Organization (APCO)
Turkoman Autonomists
Tudeh (Party of the Masses)
Union of Communists

IRAQ

Al-Daawa (The Call)
Dawah Party
Dissident Baathists
Democratic Party of Kurdistan (DPK)
Iraqi Communist Party (ICP)
Kurdish Democratic Party (KDP)
Kurdish Socialist Party (Bassock)
National Front for the Liberation of Iraq (NFLI)
National Democratic and Pan-Arab Front
Patriotic Union of Kurdistan (PUK)
Supreme Council of the Islamic Revolution of Iraq
Unified Kurdistan Socialist Party (UKSP)

ISRAEL/PALESTINE

Arab Liberation Front (ALF)
Abu Nidal Group
Al-Asifa
Al-Seeir
Arab Nationalist Youth Organization for the Liberation of Palestine.
Arab Revolutionary Army – Palestine Command
Democratic Front for the Liberation of Palestine (DFLP)
Black September Group
Black June Organization
Eagles of Palestine
Movement for the National Liberation of Palestine
Movement of Arab Nationalists
Nature Carta
Palestine Armed Struggle Command (PASC)
Palestine Communist Party
Palestine Front for the Liberation of Palestine
Palestine Liberation Army
Palestine Liberation Front
Palestine Liberation Organization
Palestine Action Front in Occupied Territories
Palestine National Liberation Front (Al-Fatah)
Palestine Popular Struggle Front
Popular Front for the Liberation of Palestine-General Command (PFLP-GC)
Redemption of Israel
Rejection Front
Sa'iga (Thunderbolt)

JORDAN

Arab Nationalist Movement
Force 17
Jordanian Communist Party (JCP)
Moslem Brotherhood

KUWAIT

Muslim Fundamentalists

If there are doubters about the scope and extent of terrorism and its international flavor, the massacre at Lodi Airport in Israel should help remove the blinkers. It was planned in Paris by Venezuelans and executed in Israel by terroists recruited in Japan. The arms for the massacre were supplied by an Algerian diplomat and financed by Libyan money that was funneled through a bank in Luxembourg.

The phenomenon is also regional. Tremors went through Europe recently when a so-called "Terrorist International" was announced. It was to be a loose coalition of some of the most militant of terrorist groups on the continent, incuding France's Direct Action, the German Red Army Faction, the Italian Red Brigade, the Belgian Fighting Communist Cells and the Portugese Popular Forces of the 25th of April.

That Europe is acutely sensitive to the problem is not too surprising.

SOUTH ASIA

LEBANON

Al Amal
Arab Democratic Party
Arab Liberation Party
Arab Socialist Action Party
Armenian Community
Armenian Revolutionary Federation
Al-Morabitoun Militia
Alawaite Youth
Cedar Guardians
Christian Militia
Conservative Lebanese Front or Kufur Front
Druse Progressive Socialist Party
Free Lebanese Army
Front for the Liberation of Lebanon
Fityan Ali Organization
Guardians of the Cedars of Lebanon
Hezbollah
Independent Nasserite Movement (INM)
Islamic Amal
Islamic Group
Kataeb
Lebanese National Movement
Lebanese Revolutionary Party (LRP)
Lebanese Communist Party
Lebanese Forces
Lebanese Youth Movement
Lebanese Red Brigades
Lebanese Armed Revolutionary Factions
Marada Militia
Maronite League
Marada Brigade
Movement of the Disinherited
Murabitoun
Muslim Brotherhood
Musawi
Nationalist Front
National Guards
National Liberation Militia
National Movement
National Resistance Front
Organization of Holy Struggle
Organization of Revolutionaries of the North (ORN)
Organization of the Baath Party
Organization of Communist Action
Organization of the Oppressed in the World
Permanent Congress of the Lebanese Order of Monks
Phalange, or Lebanese Phalangist Party
Pink Panther Militia
Populist Nasserite Organization
Progressive Socialist Party
Progressive Vanguards
Rawnad Al Islah Militia
Revolutionary Islamic Organization
South Lebanon Army
Syrian Social Nationalist Party
Tanzim
Towhid Tigers Militia
Union of the Forces of the Working People – Corrective Movement
Worker's League
Zahla Bloc
Zgharten Liberation Army

OMAN

Popular Front for the Liberation of Oman (PFLO)
Dhofar Liberation Front
Popular Front for the Liberation of Oman and the Arabian Gulf (PFLOAG)

QATAR

Popular Front for the Liberation of the Arabian Peninsula
Shiite Muslim Fundamentalists

SAUDI ARABIA

Baatha Party of Saudi Arabia
Communist Party of Saudi Arabia
Committee for the Defense of the Rights of Man in Saudi Arabia
El-Salaf El-Saleh (Sunnite)
Muslim Revolutionary Movement in the Arabian Peninsula
Party of Labor
Popular Front for the Liberation of the Arabian Peninsula
Shi'ite Muslim Fundamentalists
Union of the People of the Arabian Peninsula

SOUTH YEMEN

Front for the Liberation of Occupied Yemen (FLOSY)
National Democratic Front (NDF)
National Liberation Front (NLF)
Organization for the Liberation of the Occupied South (OLOS)
South Arabian League

SYRIA

Arab Communist Organization
Islamic Front in Syria
Muslim Brotherhood
National Alliance for the Liberation of Syria
National Front for the Liberation of Arab-Syria
National Salvation Command
Party of Communist Action
Vanguard of the Arab Revolution

TURKEY

Armenian Secret Army for the Liberation of Armenia (ASALA)
Federation of Turkish Revolutionary Youth (Dev Genc)
Grey Wolves (Bozkurtlar)
Idealist Clubs (Fikir Kulupler Federasyonu)
Marxist-Lenninist Armed Propaganda Unit (MLAPU)
National Salvation Party (NSP)
Nationalist Action Party (NAP)
Revolutionary Left (Dev Sol)
Revolutionary Road (Dev Yol)
Socialist Enlightenment (Sosyalist Aydinlik)
Turkish People's Liberation Army (TPLA)
Turkish People's Liberation Front (TPLF)
Turkish Worker's Party (TWP)
Turkish Worker's Peasant Party (TWPP)
Union of Turkish Nationalists (Turkiye Milliyetciler Birligi)

BANGLADESH

Communist Party of Bangladesh (CPB)
East Bengal Communist Party (EBCP)
East Bengal Communist Party Marxist-Lenninist (EBCP-ML)
East Bengal Poletarian Party, or East Bengal Workers' Movement (Purba Bangla Sharbohara – PBSP)
East Bengal Workers' Movement
East Pakistan Communist Party Marxist-Leninist (EPCP-ML)
Mukti Bahini (Freedom Fighters)
National Socialist Party (Jatyo Samajtantrik Dal – JSD)
People's Revolutionary Army (Biplopi Gono Bahini – BGB)
Revolutionary Soldiers' Association (Biplopi Shainik Sangstha – BSS)
Shanti Bahini (Peace Fighters)
Amra Bengali (We Bengals)
Anand Marg (Path of Bliss)
Dal Khalsa
Dalit Panthers
Mizo National Front (MNF)
Naga Federal Army (NFA)
Naga Nationalist Council (NNC)
Nagaland Federal Government (NFG)
Naxalites
People's Liberation Army (PLA)
Rashtriya Swayamsevak Sangh – RSS (National Self-Service Organization)
Revolutionary Army of Kuneipak (RAK)
Revolutionary Government of Manipur (RGM)
Revolutionary Youth and Students' Federation

PAKISTAN

Al-Zulfikar Movement
Baluch People's Liberation Front (BPLF)
Baluch Students' Organization (BSO)
Baluch Students' Organization – Awami (BSO-Awami)
Movement for the Restoration of Democracy (MRD)
Pakistan Liberation Army (PLA)
Parari
Popular Front for Armed Resistance (PFAR)
World Baluch Organization (WBO)

SRI LANKA

Liberation Tigers
People's Liberation Front (Janatha Vimukthi Peramuna – JVP)

Left: *One of the most notorious terrorist sights of all, as a Black September "commando" peers over the balcony at the Munich Olympic Games, 1972. Two Israeli Olympic athletes were killed at the Olympic Village, and nine were taken hostage. All perished with the terrorists in a "shoot-out" at a military airfield during the organized "escape".*

One of the most inhuman acts of terrorism that ever took place occurred at the Olympic Games in Munich in 1972; if there was a grisly benefit from the massacre, it was that West Germany's counterterrorist group, GSG 9, was formed as a direct result, strictly as a police unit under control of the Ministry of the Interior.

This unit, and others similar to it, have mushroomed. Prior to Munich, there were very few efficient counterterrorist units to be found in the world. Now there are scores – trained to the eyeballs and armed to the teeth – ready to perform their missions as required. Some are part of military formations, others are separate units attached to either police forces or other agencies of government. They exist in every major, and many minor, nations. (Some are discussed more fully in the section on elite units.)

FAR EAST

BURMA
Arakan Liberation Front (ALF)Burma Communist Party (BCP)
Chin National Organization (CNO)
Kachin Independence Organization (KIO)
Karen National Liberation Army (KNLA)
Karen National Union (KNU)
Karenni National Progressive Party (KNPP)
National Democratic United Front (NDUF)
New Mon State Party (NMSP)
Parliamentary Democratic Party (PDP)
Shan State Army (SSA)
Shan United Army (SUA)
Shan United Revolutionary Army (SURA)
United Pa-O Organization

INDONESIA
Communist Party of Indonesia (Partai Komunis Indonesia-PKI)
Delegation of the Central Committee of the PKI
Democratic Union of Timor (Uniao Democratica de Timor-UDT)
Free Aceh Movement (Gerakin Aceh Merdeka)
Free Papua Movement (Organisasi Papua Merdek-OPM)
Holy War Commando (Kommando Jihad)
Popular Democratic Association of Timorese (Associcao Popular Democratica dos Timorenses-APODETI)
Revolutionary Front for the Independence of Timor (Frente Revolucionaria Timorense de Libertacao e Independencia – FRETILIN)
Thirtieth of September Movement (Geraken September Tigapulah – Gestapu)

JAPAN
Aso Unified Red Army
Central Core (Chukaku)
East Asia Anti-Japanese Action Front (EAAJAF)
League of Communists (Bundo)
League of Revolutionary Communists (Kakkyodo)
Red Army (Sekigun)
Revolutionary Workers' Association (Kakumaru)
Zengakuren (National Union of Autonomous Committees of Japanese Students)

KAMPUCHEA (CAMBODIA)
Kampuchea National United Front for National Salvation (KNUFNS)
Khmer Issarek (Free Khmer)
Khmer People's National Liberation Armed Forces (KPLNAF)
Khmer People's National Liberation Front (KPNLF)
Khmer Rouge (Red Khmer)
Khmer Serei (Free Khmer)
National Liberation Government of Kampuchea (NLAK)
National Liberation Movement (NLM)
National Liberation Movement of Kampuchea (Moulinaka)
National United Front of Kampuchea (NUFK)

LAOS
Lao Issara (Free Laos)

Lao National Liberation Front (LNLF)
Pathet Lao (State of Laos)

MALAYSIA
Communist Party of Malaya (CPM)
Communist Party of Malaya Marxist-Leninist (CPM-ML)
Communist Party of Malaysia – Revolutionary Faction (CPM-RF)
Malayan Peoples' Army (MPA)
National Revolutionary Front (Barisan Revolusi Nasional – BRN)
North Kalimantan Communist Party (NKCP)
North Kalimantan People's Guerilla Forces (NKPGF)

OCEANIA
Kanak Liberation Party (Parti di Liberation Kanak – PALIKA)

PEOPLE'S REPUBLIC OF CHINA
Chinese Communist Party (CCP)
Kuomintang (Nationalists)
Red Guards

PHILIPPINES
April 6 Liberation Movement
Bangsa Moro Liberation Organization (BMLO)
Mindanao Independence Movement (MIM)
Moro National Liberation Front (MNLF)
New People's Army (NPA)
Patriotic Youth (Kabataang Makabayang – KM)
People's Anti-Japanese Resistance Army (Huks)
People's Liberation Army (Hukbong Mapagpalayang Bayan – HMB)

THAILAND
Asia 88
Committee for Coordinating Patriotic and Democracy-Loving Forces (CCPDF)
Communist Party of Thailand (CPT)
Free Thai Army (FTA)
National Revolutionary Front (Barison Revolusi Nasional – BRN)
Nawapol, or Nawaphon (New Force)
Pattani Islamic National Revolutionary Party (Phak Patiwat Phaochan Islam Pattani – PPPIP)
Pattani National Liberation Front (Barisan Nasional Pembebasan Pattani – BNPP)
Pattani United Liberation Organization (PULO)
Phak Mai (New Party)
Red Guard (Krathing Daeng)
Sabil-Illah (Way of God)
Thai People's Liberation Armed Forces (TPLAF)
Thailand Patriotic Front (TPF)

VIETNAM
League of the Independence of Vietnam (Viet Minh)
National Front for the Liberation of South Vietnam (Viet Cong)

NORTH AMERICA

Above: *Most terrorist attacks against the United States are targeted on overseas bases, such as the US Embassy, Beirut, 1983.*

CANADA
Quebec Liberation Front (Front de Liberacion du Quebec – FLQ)

UNITED STATES
Armed Forces of National Liberation (Fuerzas Armadas de Liberacion Nacional (FALN)
Black Panther Party (BPP)
Boricua Popular Army (Ejercito Popular de Boricua – EPB, or Los Macheteros)
Coordination of United Revolutionary Organizations (Coordination de Organizacions Revolucionarias Unidas – CORU)
DeBois Clubs
George Jackson Brigade
Jewish Defence League
Ku Klux Klan (KKK)
May 2 Movement
National Socialists White People's Party (NSWPP)
New American Movement (NAM)
New World Liberation Front (NWLF)
October League
Omega 7
Organization of Afro-American Liberty
Polar Bear Party
Revolutionary Action Movement (Movimento de Accion Revolucionaria – MAR)
Revolutionary Communist Party (RCP)
Students for a Democratic Society (SDS)
Symbionese Liberation Army (SLA)
Vencereamos (We Shall Overcome)
Weatherman

In its domestic form, dealing with terrorism properly falls within the province of the nation's police forces. When it transcends national boundaries, however, and is aided and abetted by state sponsors such as Libya's Mu'ammar al-Qadhafi (who has labeled terrorism a "noble" act), then the threat level goes up correspondingly. And with it the need to use conventional and elite units to deliver an appropriate military response.

Terrorism has been recognized for what it is in the international arena – another form of warfare. Terrorists must be considered the enemies of civilization and its values, from whatever motive they act. That is why a book on elite formations must deal with this topic; it is these units, after all, which will have a big hand in maintaining the "violent peace".

Above: *Armed police move in on Libyan terrorist "diplomats", London, 1984.*

CENTRAL/LATIN AMERICA

ARGENTINA
Argentina Anti-Communist Alliance (AAA)
Armed Forces of Liberation (AFL)
Armed Peronist Forces (FAO)
Armed Revolutionary Forces (FAR)
Montoneros
National Liberation Army (ELN)
National Liberation Movement (MLN)
People's Guerrilla Army (EGP)
People's Revolutionary Army (ERP)
Red Brigades of Worker Power (BRPO)

BOLIVIA
Bolivian Revolutionary Worker's Party (PRTB)
Movement of the Revolutionary Left (MIR)
National Liberation Army (ELN)

BRAZIL
Armed Revolutionary Vanguard (VAR)
Brazilian Revolutionary Communist Party (PCBR)
Communist Party of Brazil (PCDB)
Groups of 11 (G-11)
National Liberating Action (ALN)
National Liberation Commando (COLINA)
National Revolutionary Movement (MNR)
Peasant Leagues (Ligas Camponesas)
Popular Action (AP)
Revolutionary Movement 8 October (MR-8)
Revolutionary Popular Vanguard (VPR)
Workers' Politics (POLOP)

CHILE
Fatherland and Liberty (Patria y Libertad)
Movement of the Revolutionary Left (MIR)
People's Organized Vanguard (VOP)
White Guard (Guardia Blanca)

COLOMBIA
April 19 Movement (M-19)
Armed Revolutionary Forces of Colombia (FARC)
Communist Party of Colombia Marxist-Leninist (PPC-ML)
Group of Revolutionary Commandos – Operation Argimiro Gabaldon
Independent Revolutionary Worker's Movement (MOIR)
Invisible Ones
Military Liberation Front of Colombia
National Liberation Armed Forces
National Liberation Army (ELN)
People's Revolutionary Army – Zero Point
Popular Liberation Army (EPL)
Red Flag
Revolutionary Armed Forces of Colombia (FARC)
Revolutionary Liberal Movement (MRL)
Revolutionary Worker's Party
September 14 Worker's Self-Defense Command
United Front for Guerrilla Action
United Front for Revolutionary Action
Worker's Self-Defense Movement (MAO)
Workers', Students' and Peasants' Movement (MOEC)

COSTA RICA
Revolutionary Commandos of Solidarity
Roberto Santucho Revolutionary Group

DOMINICAN REPUBLIC
Dominican Popular Movement (MPD)
Movement of the Revolutionary Left (MIR)
Revolutionary Movement 14 June (MR-14)
Trinitarian National Liberation Movement (MLNT)
Twelfth of January Liberation Movement
United Anti-Reelection Command

EL SALVADOR
Armed Forces of National Resistance (FARN)
Communist Party of El Salvador (PCES)
Farabundo Marti Popular Forces of Liberation (FPL)
National Democratic Organization (ORDEN)
People's Armed Revolutionary Forces (FRAP)
People's Revolutionary Army (ERP)
Popular Leagues of 28 February (LP-28)
Popular Revolutionary Bloc (BPR)
Revolutionary Party of Central American Workers (PRTC)
United Popular Action Front (FAPU)
White Fighting Union (UGB)
Workers' Revolutionary Party of Central America

GUATEMALA
Guatamalan Anti-Salvadoran Liberating Action (GALGAS)
Guatemalan Labor Party (PGT)
Guatemalan Nationalist Commando
Guerrilla Army of the Poor (EGP)
National League for the Protection of Guatemala
National Liberation Movement
People's Guerrilla Army of the Poor (EGP)
Rebel Armed Forces (FAR)
Revolutionary Movement Alejandro de Leon 13 November (MR-13)
Revolutionary Organization of the People Under Arms (ORPA)
Secret Anti-Communist Army (ESA)
Twelfth of April Revolutionary Movement
Twentieth of October Front
White Hand (Mano Blanca)

HAITI
Coalition of National Liberation Brigades
Haitian Coalition

HONDURAS
Cinchonero Popular Liberation Movement (MPL)
People's Revolutionary Movement (MRP)
People's Revolutionary Union (URP)
Workers' Revolutionary Party (PRTC)

MEXICO
Armed Communist League (LCA)
Armed Vanguard of the Proletariat
Los Lacandones
Mexican People's Revolutionary Army
National Revolutionary Civic Association (ACNR)
Party of the Poor (Partido de los Pobres)
People's Armed Command
People's Liberation Army
People's Revolutionary Armed Forces (FRAP)
People's Union (Union del Pueblo)
Revolutionary Action Movement (MAR)
Twenty-Third of September Communist League
United Popular Liberation Army of America
Zapatista Urban Front (FUZ)

NICARAGUA
Nicaraguan Armed Revolutionary Forces (FARN)
Sandanistga National Liberation Front (FSLN)

PARAGUAY
Agrarian Peasant Leagues (LAC)
First of March Organization, a.k.a. Politico-Military Organization, or OPM)
Political Military Organization
Popular Colorado Movement (MoPoCo)

PERU
Armed Nationalist Movement Organization (MANO)
Condor
Front of the Revolutionary Left (FIR)
Movement of the Revolutionary left (MIR)
MTR (expansion unknown)
National Liberation Army (ELN)
Peruvian Anti-Communist Alliance (AAP)
Peruvian Communist Party – Red Flag
Revolutionary Vanguard
Shining Path (SL)
Tupac Amaru

URUGUAY
Armed Popular Front
National Liberation Movement (MLN)
Organization of the Popular Revolutionary – 33 (OPR-33)
PCU (expansion unknown)
Raul Sendic International Brigade

VENEZUELA
Armed Forces of National Liberation (FALN)
Movement of the Revolutionary Left (MIR)
Popular Revolutionary Movement (MPR)
Red Flag (Bandera Roja)
Zero Point (Punto Cero)

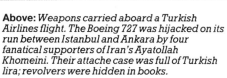

Above: *Weapons carried aboard a Turkish Airlines flight. The Boeing 727 was hijacked on its run between Istanbul and Ankara by four fanatical supporters of Iran's Ayatollah Khomeini. Their attache case was full of Turkish lira; revolvers were hidden in books.*

Right: *In April 1984, so-called Libyan "diplomats" fired from the embassy in London, killing a British policewoman. During this period Libyan assassination teams were on the prowl seeking to eliminate the opponents of Libyan leader Qadhafi.*

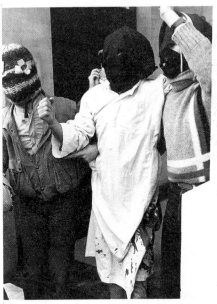

Above: *These hooded, forbidding figures are members of the Spanish ETA terrorist group of the Basque Separatist movement that carries out sabotage, assassination and kidnapping. Most of their operations are in Spain, but many have spilled over into France.*

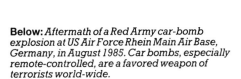

Below: *Aftermath of a Red Army car-bomb explosion at US Air Force Rhein Main Air Base, Germany, in August 1985. Car bombs, especially remote-controlled, are a favored weapon of terrorists world-wide.*

Below: *A grisly footnote on the pages of our times. Terrorists increasingly leave their political messages in blood-red letters on the sidewalks, in the skies and, most importantly, in the minds of people worldwide*

UNITED KINGDOM
NORTHERN IRELAND

Keith Maguire

THE BRITISH mainland witnessed several manifestations of both political extremism and political violence during the 1970s, but nothing that resembled the scale of these phenomena that occurred in Northern Ireland. Terrorism in Northern Ireland resulted in the highest level of killings anywhere in Western Europe, and terrorist groups and their political fronts achieved a sizeable share of the popular vote.

Over 2,500 people have been killed in Northern Ireland due to terrorism since 1969. Horrific though this number is, it is quite small compared to the estimates of more than 40,000 killed in Lebanon since 1976, or the 11,000 who disappeared in Argentina during the "dirty war" from 1976-83.

Serious intercommunal conflict broke out in Northern Ireland in August 1969, leading to the introduction of the British Army as a peace-keeping force. There was a transfer of population as individuals of one religious denomination fled from areas controlled by those of the other religious group, back into areas where their own group was the dominant one.

During the 1970s, 62 percent of the Northern Ireland population was Protestant and 38 percent was Catholic, and this cleavage was reinforced by a political division of Unionists (Loyalists) and Nationalists (Republicans). The Unionists in Northern Ireland were in a permanent majority over the Catholics, but both sides were in a double majority/double minority position. Though the Unionists saw themselves as a majority in Northern Ireland they feared absorption into the Irish Republic as they were a minority in the island as a whole.

Above: *IRA terrorists at the barricades during civil rights demonstration. Mingling with non-terrorists during riots is common.*

Both sides wanted victory over the other side and were unwilling to compromise for the overall benefit of both communities within Northern Ireland. Those moderates in each community who did advocate compromise were denounced as traitors. Terrorist groups were to receive a certain legitimacy because extremists of the same ethnic community were seen as preferable allies to moderates from the other community.

The terrorist problem has involved a three-cornered struggle between Republican groups such as (1) the Provisional Irish Republican Army (PIRA, an offshoot of the Irish Republican Army, IRA) and the Irish National Liberation Army (INLA); (2) Loyalist groups such as the Ulster Volunteer Force (UVF) and the Ulster Freedom Fighters (UFF); and (3) the security forces. There are other legal groups such as the Ulster Defence Association (UDA) and Down Orange Welfare (DOW) on the Loyalist side which have existed for a doomsday scenario should the British government ever decide to withdraw from the province. The security forces have been comprised of the Royal Ulster Constabulary (RUC) backed by the British Army and the locally recruited Ulster Defence Regiment (UDR). The strength of both the security forces and the Army has varied over the years: the number in the RUC, including reservists, is around 14,000, while the UDR can call on a further 7,000 men; currently British soldiers in the province number just over 10,000.

Irish Republican Army (IRA)

The Irish Republican Army (IRA) is an unofficial and illegal semi-military organization which was established in the Republic in 1919 to help achieve by armed force independence of the whole of Ireland from British rule. The northern part of the island is governed by the United Kingdom; the IRA has never accepted the legitimacy of the political boundaries established in 1921 and, in each decade since then, have tried to launch terrorist campaigns to force the British to withdraw from Northern Ireland. Further-

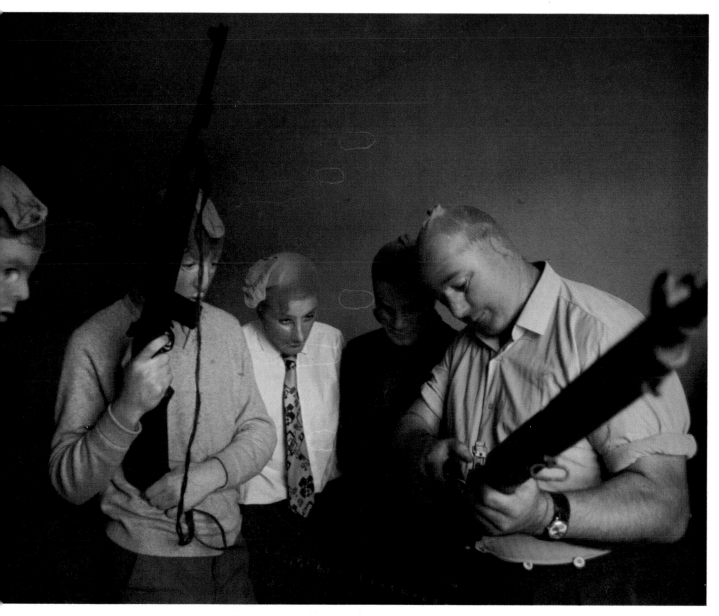

more, the IRA refused to recognize the legitimacy of the Southern Irish governments. The failure of the IRA to achieve any of their goals reflected not only the effectiveness of the police forces in Northern Ireland and in the Irish Republic but also the lack of support for the terrorist organization among the Catholic community.

The failure of IRA terrorism from 1921-61 had caused the development of two wings within the movement – the left-wing socialists (the Official IRA), and the right-wing Nationalists (who became the Provisional IRA). The former were based mainly in the south and the latter in the north and in the border counties. The latter wished to organize another guerrilla struggle to drive the Ulster Loyalists and the pro-British Catholics out of Ireland.

The wing that became the OIRA sought to move in a socialist direction and, in May 1972, declared a truce and largely withdrew from terrorist activity. However, from 1970-72 they

Above: *Provo members get checked out on use of a variety of weapons. Arms such as the Springfield 03 rifle at right are being replaced with M16s and Beretta SMGs.*

Below: *Hooded members of the INLA give a military funeral in Londonderry for Patsy O'Hara, who died from a hunger strike – the fourth INLA member to do so.*

Left: *Members of the Provisional Irish Republican Army (PIRA) in training. In the early years, marksmanship was not noteworthy. That has changed, with the sophistication of weapons, training and tactics continually improving.*

had been responsible for a number of killings and the bomb explosion at Aldershot, on the British mainland, which killed seven people.

The wing that became the PIRA in 1969 played a major role in provoking riots in the summer of that year, and it was they who began the terrorist campaign against the British Army in 1971. The PIRA escalated their attacks throughout 1971 and 1972, killing 43 British soldiers in 1971 and 103 in 1972. Northern Ireland government attempts to halt the increase in terrorism were to no avail and only led to the further discrediting of the regime at Stormont, the seat of government.

In March 1972, the British government decided to suspend the Northern Ireland government and introduce direct rule from Westminster, London. They also arranged talks with the leadership of the PIRA but they were unable to meet the demands of the terrorists. The PIRA believed that they could secure a unified Ireland by using the same tactics as had the National Liberation Front in Aden and EOKA in Cyprus. They hoped that by killing the same number of British soldiers as the National Liberation Front had done in Aden they could force the British government to withdraw from Northern Ireland before the amount of casualties caused an adverse effect on public opinion. The PIRA also hoped to draw the British government into a similar position in Northern Ireland to that which the French had been in during the Algerian War and which the United States had been in during the Vietnam War. The PIRA knew that they could not beat the British Army in the field, but reasoned that they could make the cost of the British Army remaining in the field too high politically for the British government.

The PIRA also tried to bomb the Protestants into submission because, even if the British Army had been withdrawn, the PIRA would still have to overcome the local resistance of the Loyalists. The tactics used against the Loyalists were sectarian assassinations and no-warning bomb attacks on civilian targets.

Negotiations with the British government had left the PIRA with the belief that one more push would be enough to force the British out of Northern Ireland, but the increase in sectarian killings by Loyalist terrorists and the Ulster Workers Council (UWC) strike of 1974 made them realise that the Loyalists were not beaten and that the British could afford to maintain a higher level of casualties than PIRA could inflict on them.

This realization, coupled with an increasing use of indigenous security forces in Northern Ireland, led the PIRA to try to spread the terrorist war to the British mainland. However, while they carried out some spectacular atrocities, including assassinations and bombings in 1974/75, they lacked the support for a sustained offensive on the mainland.

Most of the deaths due to terrorism in Northern Ireland have been caused by Republican terrorists, with the Loyalists responsible for a sizeable share between 1971and 1977, but for a much smaller share thereafter.

However, the ratios have not remained consistent for the duration of the troubles. From 1971-77, Loyalist terrorists were responsible for over a third of all deaths at a

time when the number of killings in the province was much higher.

This led to the combined total of deaths caused by Republican terrorists rising to 65 percent. Since 1977, the conflict has been essentially one of the PIRA and INLA fighting the security forces, with the role of the Loyalist terrorists being marginal. The peak years of the killings in 1972/3, 1975/6 and 1981 were specifically due to short-term causes.

From February 1971 until November 1971, the PIRA took the initiative in killing British soldiers and Protestant civilians. Thereafter the Loyalist terrorists carried out reprisal killings against Catholics in retaliation for any PIRA actions. The PIRA tried to make the British Army its main target but they were drawn from this policy by the actions of the Loyalists and increasingly they became involved in a sectarian struggle with the Protestant community. From 1977 onwards, the Loyalist terrorists largely withdrew from sectarian killings and so a new pattern of

violence emerged, as shown in the table.

In 1972, the escalation in the killing was due to the Loyalist fear that British government surrender to the PIRA was at hand. The Loyalists reasoned that the only way to stop the perceived surrender was to kill more Catholics than the PIRA could kill Protestants and members of the security forces. The British government truce with the PIRA in 1975 led the Loyalists to believe that British withdrawal was imminent and that they had better prepare for an all-out sectarian war.

The first steps in such a war would have been an increase in the amount of sectarian killings, especially in areas that may have been a future border. Examples of these type of killings were those carried out by the UVF in Armagh in July 1975. The peak violence in 1981 was due to the PIRA and the INLA trying to raise the overall level of terrorism as part of a strategy to turn the balance of forces in the Nationalist camp in their favor.

PIRA membership in 1970 was around 600,

Above left: *This car is stopped at what is clearly labeled "Provisional IRA Checkpoint". Both Provos are armed with M16 rifles – which is a cold comment on the easy availability of modern weapons in Northern Ireland.*

Above: *Vigilante squad in Northern Ireland, with "suspect" against the wall. In the past, enforcement of such "No Go" zones – areas that terrorists declare "off limits" to Protestants, the police and British troops – has been common.*

Right: *Planning meeting for PIRA members. Their crude weapons – note the bolt action rifles and tape – are much in evidence. British authorities estimate the current Provo active-terrorist strength at approximately 500.*

organized into brigades and battalions. By 1974, PIRA membership was around 2,500 but between 1975-77 a reorganization took place from large territorial formations into a cell system, and the number of people who were actually involved in terrorism was drastically reduced. By 1981, there were around 400 hard-core terrorists with a backup of about 1,000 other PIRA members acting in a part-time capacity in supplies, transportation and intelligence gathering.

From 1975 onwards, internal shifts took place within the leadership of the Republican movement that resulted first in the eclipse of the Southern leaders and subsequently by a generational shift with the younger Northern leaders taking over both the PIRA and its political front, Sinn Fein. The old guard seceded from the movement after the 1986 Ard Fheis (annual conference) to form a splinter group.

Tactically, the rise of the Northerners saw a switch from the indiscriminate use of terrorism to its more selective use aimed at the killing of off-duty members of the security forces or Protestant civilians living in isolated border areas. The aim of this policy was to make more areas Nationalist-dominated by making them unsafe for members of the

security forces to live in. Consequently, it was reasoned, if members of the security forces were unable to live there, and if the presence of the security forces took a lower profile, then the PIRA would be able to increase their control of the area. In this way, the PIRA hoped to make it dangerous for the security forces to live or operate in ever-greater areas of the province.

The PIRA plan to take state power in Northern Ireland is based on the use of selective terrorism and taking advantage of changes in the demographic makeup of the province. The Catholics are increasing as a percentage of the population and the PIRA reckon that if they can hold 10 percent of the popular vote, which they have on occasion, they will then be in a position to challenge for state power at a later date.

There are areas where they have strong local support, such as in West Belfast, Derry and along the border in South Armagh. It is in these areas bordering their strongholds that selective PIRA terrorism is likely to continue.

The other main Republican terrorist group is the INLA which broke away from the Official IRA in 1974. Although committed to a left-wing philosophy, their aims and policies are very similar to those of the PIRA. Lacking

the membership figures of the PIRA, the INLA have laid more emphasis on spectacular atrocities. Three attacks in particular brought the INLA to public attention; these were the assassination of British Member of Parliament Airey Neave in 1979, the bombing of the Droppin Well bar in Ballykelly in December 1982, when 17 people were killed, and the killing of 3 Protestants during an attack during a church service in Darkley in South Armagh in November 1983.

With a membership of around 50, the INLA's capacity for terrorism is much more limited than that of the PIRA. Since their formation, the INLA have been responsible for more than a hundred deaths, and in 1982 they were responsible for nearly 30 of the 97 deaths that resulted from terrorism in that year. Internal feuds, informers, and the assassination of a number of their leaders by Loyalist terrorists have reduced the capacity of this group to engage in a sustained and widespread campaign of terrorism.

The level of terrorism from Loyalist groups has usually depended on the capacity of the security forces for maintaining law and order. Terrorist violence from Loyalist groups reached its highest levels in 1972/3 in a spate of sectarian killings when it appeared that the

NUMBER OF DEATHS DUE TO TERRORISM

1969	1970	1971	1972	1973	1974	1975	1976	1977	1978	1979	1980	1981	1982	1983	1984	1985
13	25	173	467	250	216	247	297	112	81	113	76	101	97	78	64	54

YEAR

Deaths due to terrorism by agency

Security forces 12 percent	Loyalist groups 28 percent	Republican groups 59 percent	Unidentified 1 percent

Deaths from terrorism by agency from 1977 onwards

Security forces 25 percent	U.V.F. 5 percent	U.F.F. 5 percent	P.I.R.A. 55 percent	I.N.L.A. 10 percent

Terrorist groups and their political wings

	Group	Political wing
Republican	PIRA	Sinn Fein
	INLA	Irish Republican Socialist Party
	Official IRA	Workers Party
Loyalist	UDA	Ulster Loyalist Democratic Party
	UVF	Progressive Unionist Party

1987 Westminster election: percentage of the popular vote in Northern Ireland

Party	Percent
Democratic Unionist Party	11.7 percent
Ulster Unionist Party	37 percent
Alliance Party	10 percent
Social Democratic and Labour Party	21.1 percent
Workers Party	2.6 percent
Sinn Fein	11.4 percent
Popular Unionist Party	2.5 percent

Left: *Terrorists quite frequently use stocking masks to disguise their identity. Weapons are chosen for their utility and their availability – this is a US Model 1903 Springfield rifle – although much newer weapons are now in use.*

Right: *Cache of weapons uncovered in a raid on Ulster Defence Association headquarters, Belfast. This display at Royal Ulster Constabulary headquarters showed weapons including homemade Sten guns, pistols and ammunition.*

Below right: *Armory of urban conflict: collection of milk bottles, some made into "Molotov cocktails", discovered by police in the Republican section of Old Park, North Belfast. Large cans contain gasoline.*

British government had permitted the breakdown of law and order in the face of PIRA terrorism. In 1975/6, the Loyalists again believed that the only way to halt the rising tide of PIRA assassinations was by reprisal killings.

The oldest Loyalist terrorist group was the UVF whose origins went back to 1966, when a gang led by Gusty Spence killed several Catholics in the Shankill Road area of Belfast. Spence and his associates were jailed and the UVF was declared an illegal organization by the Northern Ireland government.

The Loyalists, however, feared that a campaign pursued by the Northern Ireland Civil Rights Association (NICRA) was aimed at destroying the effectiveness of the state, in order to soften it up for a further campaign of IRA terrorism similar to that of 1919-21. Loyalist hardliners fostered this belief during the mid-1960s and consequently, when Republican terrorism surfaced in the early 1970s, their electoral support increased.

Other Loyalists formed vigilante groups in order to protect their areas from attack, especially those areas that bordered Republican territory. With the outbreak of intercommunal rioting in August 1969, these groups came into confrontation with Repub-

lican rioters. However, with the onset of PIRA terrorism in 1971, these groups joined together to form the Ulster Defence Association (UDA).

The UVF reemerged to argue that PIRA terrorism should be met by counter-terrorism and it began to organize reprisal sectarian killings from November 1971 onwards. The UVF was nominally organized into brigades and battalions covering most of the Loyalist areas in Belfast, East Antrim and North Armagh. Its membership peaked in 1974 at around 5,000 but it declined steadily thereafter and was little more than 600 by 1981. The UVF had also absorbed the Red Hand Commando group, whose membership varied from 50-200 and it was involved in a number of terrorist incidents in the early 1970s.

In its early days, there was overlapping membership between the UDA and the UVF, but after 1973 membership became exclusive to one group or the other. The UDA's membership peaked at 53,000 in 1974 but declined to around 15,000 by 1981. The UDA had two wings: one based in North and West Belfast, and the rest of the organization. The former group believed in sectarian killing and was responsible for most of the assassinations of the 1972/3 period. This group became known as the Ulster Freedom Fighters and it eventually left the UDA, although some of its members retained membership in the North and West Belfast sections of the UDA.

The UDA's main purpose was to be able to defend Loyalist areas in the event of a British withdrawal from the province. Along with groups such as Down Orange Welfare and the Orange Volunteers, the UDA formed the Ulster Army Council and this body was responsible for working out contingency plans for taking over the running of Northern Ireland in the event of a British withdrawal. The Ulster Army Council was to be responsible for the transfer of Loyalists living in isolated areas behind a reduced but defendable border of an Independent Ulster. It was the Ulster Army Council that provided the manpower for the UWC strike in May 1974. The Loyalists feared that political

agreements would lead to the transfer of Northern Ireland out of the United Kingdom and into the Irish Republic. Most Unionists were opposed to such agreements and, armed with 11 out of 12 of the Northern Ireland seats at Westminster and more than 50 percent of the popular vote from the February 1974 Westminster general election, the Unionist politicians, the Ulster Army Council and a group of Loyalist industrial workers called the Ulster Workers Council planned to bring down the Northern Ireland government by means of a general strike.

Estimates of the combined strength of the Loyalist militia groups have varied from 55,000 to 100,000, but even if the lower figure is accepted then it was still a sizeable amount of manpower and it outnumbered the police and Army in the province. The British government decided against trying to break the strike and, when the Northern Ireland Executive resigned, the strike was called off.

Once the security forces got the upper hand against the Republican terrorist groups, support for Loyalist militias fell away, fueled by reports of gangsterism and internal feuding in their ranks. Groups such as Down Orange Welfare were disbanded and many Loyalist terrorists were denounced to the security forces.

After 1978, Loyalist terrorism changed direction. The UDA withdrew from carrying out sectarian killings and the UFF switched targets from Catholic civilians to those connected with Republican terrorist groups or their political fronts. The UVF (also known as the Protestant Action Force) continued to carry out sectarian killings but on a much smaller scale, especially once Lenny Murphy was killed. Murphy was the leader of the notorious Shankill butcher gang, who tortured many of their victims to death with knives and meat cleavers.

One of the main reasons for the fall in support for Loyalist terrorist groups was the British government's Ulsterization policy. The original Northern Ireland security forces comprised the RUC and the Ulster Special Constabulary ("B" Specials). These forces

Above left: *An expert from the bomb disposal squad works on a mortar that belonged to a Provisional Irish Republican Army (PIRA) terrorist. Terrorist weapons range from crude home-made mortar launchers to sophisticated delayed-action explosive devices.*

Above: *British para on duty in Northern Ireland checks out suspect. In recent years, operations by terrorists in urban areas have become increasingly risky as British intelligence has effectively penetrated IRA cells.*

Right, top and bottom: *This set of photos captures the elements of a highly controversial incident that occurred at a Sein-Fein Noraid rally on August 12, 1984. David Hegarty (at left in riot gear and holding plastic bullet gun) shot and killed a 22-year-old rioter. Controversy arose because police guidelines state that plastic bullets can only be fired from a distance of 20 yards (18m) and at targets below the waist.*

were overstretched by the civil disorders of August 1969 and so the British Army was brought in to assist.

The RUC and the "B" Specials were central targets of NICRA complaints and in an attempt to appease these critics, a number of changes were instituted. The RUC was disarmed and the "B" Specials were disbanded. The weakening of the security forces led to the escalation of PIRA terrorism in 1971, which the security forces were unable to contain. This inability to protect the Loyalist community led directly to the Loyalist terrorist violence of 1972.

Realizing that terrorist violence was getting out of control, the British government surveyed its options and embarked on what became known as the Ulsterization strategy. This involved the building up of the RUC, the RUC Reserve, the UDR, the establishment of

non-jury courts for judging terrorist cases and a reduction of the role of the British Army.

Such reduction of the role of the British Army was helped by the appointment of Kenneth Newman (later Sir Kenneth Newman) as Chief Constable of the RUC in 1976. Newman insisted on the primacy of the police in dealing with public order and terrorism. This in turn led to the RUC taking over in the front line in most areas of the province. One area where the Army was still needed was in the border country and especially in the Crossmaglen salient. In 1976, Britain's Special Air Service (SAS) was deployed in these areas in order to reduce PIRA control there. Following the killing of several PIRA activists by the SAS, the level of PIRA terrorism declined, although the border areas continued to pose problems for the security forces.

The SAS trained the RUC's elite E4a unit in

Left: *Security forces with members of the Royal Ulster Constabulary fire tear gas during a riot. Note the Saracen armored car vehicle, and the amount and variety of debris that have been hurled by the rioters.*

Below left: *Overturned vehicles serve as a shield for security forces. A principal tactic of the IRA has been to foment actions that require reserves to be called, thus providing targets for snipers.*

Below: *Sniper of Northern Ireland security force positions himself on a ledge in Belfast. Snipers are thought to have the authority to shoot well-known and armed terrorists on sight.*

counter-terrorist operations. E4a units worked as part of the Headquarters Mobile Support Units (HMSUs) and, despite some controversy over several incidents in which they were involved, they made a very effective contribution to reducing the level of Republican terrorism and in stopping the flow of recruits into terrorist organizations.

Another prong of the government counter-terrorist strategy was the use of "supergrass" trials, whereby charges would be made against a large group of terrorists based mainly on the testimony of an ex-terrorist. Large numbers of PIRA, INLA and UVF terrorists were brought before the courts because of the evidence of supergrasses, and an enormous amount of intelligence was gained as a result of terrorist defections. However, the Court of Appeal in Northern Ireland refused to accept the uncorroborated testimony of supergrass witnesses and consequently a large number of terrorists were freed.

Since 1973, the security forces in Northern Ireland have done their best to wage a counter-insurgency campaign against both Loyalist and Republican groups, while keeping to as many of the safeguards of a liberal-democracy as has been possible. Respecting the civil liberties of citizens has not been easy on account of the challenge posed by the terrorist organizations of both communities. The reduction of the number of deaths due to terrorism in Northern Ireland from 1972 levels to those of 1985 show that while the security forces have not been able to eradicate terrorism, they have largely been able to contain it.

The weapons used by terrorists in Northern Ireland have been many and varied, from "home-made" crude explosive devices to sophisticated small arms which are in service with the armed forces of many

countries.

The Loyalist terrorist groups have three main types of gun. Their greatest need is for pistols for assassinations and they have used both revolvers (such as Webleys) and automatics (such as Berettas) in even numbers. Their second need is for machine guns for terrorist attacks on pubs, clubs and any other form of social gathering. For this requirement, they have used the occasional Sterling or Schmeisser of World War II vintage but the most common weapon for this type of operation is the home-made submachine gun. These weapons do not need to be accurate in their aim or even to be very durable; they need only to be able to spray a group of people indiscriminately with bullets. The Loyalists have also a number of Armalite rifles for sniping and for a doomsday scenario, but these have little use for regular terrorist operations.

The UDA and the UVF have few external allies to help with the problem of weapons requirement. Their main source of outside help has come from their co-religionists in Scotland and their allies there have not been able to provide much which has escaped the attention of the British Special Branch.

For specific killings, the intelligence officers of the terrorist group would try to establish a pattern on the movements of the target – for example, his address, car registration, the time he leaves for work, the time that he comes home, where he drinks, where he shops and any other factors of interest. They would then select a three-man team to carry out the "hit". This would include a driver and two gunmen using a hijacked car and operating in the nearest Republican-dominated area to their home neighbourhood, so that they could return to the safety of their own area as soon as possible after the killing had been carried out.

Above: *Standard riot gear is very much in evidence, including heavy body armor, as troops move in. Despite such precautions, terrorists now come in closer and drill their shots at "soft" spots, such as the back of the neck.*

Left: *Three key elements in the painful drama that is Northern Ireland: civil police, the British Army and the ever-present civilian. The latter is a constant concern to security enforcement personnel, as this photo vividly underscores.*

Above right: *Member of the RUC patrols with his stock-retracted H&K MP5 sub-machine gun at the ready. The RUC are no more loved by the IRA than the British Army are; more than 200 have been killed since 1969.*

For random sectarian killings, a three-man team would cruise Catholic areas in search of a target, select one, shoot him and return to their own area as soon as possible, often in as little as five minutes after the killing.

Republican terrorists have required greater numbers and types of weaponry on account of the greater scope of their operations. They have needed pistols for assassinations, and Mausers and Berettas have been among those weapons used. The PIRA have also needed a large supply of high velocity rifles for sniping at the security forces, and the weapons that they have used for this have varied over the years. In the early days, AR 180s were the preferred weapons, but in later years M16s and Remington Woodmasters became available from sources in the United States.

Over 75 percent of PIRA weaponry is

either of US origin or bought in the United States, with the rest coming from the Middle East. A variety of machine guns have been used, ranging from Carl Gustavs to M60 general-purpose machineguns. The INLA by contrast have almost exclusively used Soviet weaponry, specifically the AK-47 which has come to them through their contacts with other terrorist groups such as the French Action Directe and the Italian Red Brigades. The INLA have also had links with the Popular Front For the Liberation of Palestine and have had several of their members trained in Lebanon, especially in the use of explosives.

The INLA have very few experts in this field but one of them was used in the attack to kill Airey Neave in 1979. In later years, the INLA was reluctant to expose its experts to capture and so it was inclined to use activists of a lesser quality, as can be seen from those captured in the attempt to kill Lt. Col. Batey, the former head of the SAS regiment.

By contrast, the PIRA have a much larger number of bomb makers who have acquired some expertise and these people have been saved for the spectacular attacks, while lesser personnel have been used for the majority of operations. Three types of explosive are used by the PIRA – Commercial, Co-op mix (a mixture of sodium chlorate and nitro-benzene), and Anfo which is a mixture of ammonium nitrate and fuel oil. Despite rumors that Spanish ETA, had supplied the PIRA with explosives, there has been no

evidence of the use in Northern Ireland of Goma-2, which would have been the case at some stage. Some evidence of the use of timers from other European and Middle East groups has been evident. In more recent years, the PIRA have made increasing use of McGregor remote control device to set off their bombs.

Most of the explosives of the commercial types were made by Irish Industrial Explosives in the Irish Republic but in recent years the actions of the Irish security forces have made this much more difficult for the terrorists to obtain. The ingredients for the Co-op and Anfo type of bomb are fairly easy to get and it is difficult to see what measures could be taken to limit the availability of the type of substances required for making those types of bombs.

The PIRA have also acquired Soviet-made RPG-7 rocket launchers and been able to improvise mortar attacks. Most of these have been unsuccessful and between 1973 and 1978 no members of the security forces were killed in mortar attacks. But in one hit on the police barracks in Newry in 1985, nine officers were killed. For the majority of PIRA operations, volunteers with a minimum of local training are assigned for bombings and shootings.

The PIRA's links with the Palestine Liberation Organization (PLO) date back to a meeting in 1972 at the Baddawi camp in the Lebanon. The PLO has provided explosives training to nearly 20 PIRA terrorists and has

sent several shipments of arms, but these have all been intercepted by the intelligence services, usually with the help of the Israelis in the early stages of the operation. Colonel Gaddaffi of Libya sent a one-off donation to the PIRA in 1974, but thereafter his help has been limited to verbal gestures of support and, in his interviews with the press, Gaddaffi has shown that he is very confused about the nature of Irish politics and in particular the links between legitimate Irish political parties and terrorist groups.

Terrorists from both sides of the population raise their money in the same ways but in different percentages. The PIRA raise over 25 percent of their income from thefts and armed robberies, with a further 25 percent from racketeering and the rest coming from donations from the United States. The Loyalists raise about 90 percent of their income from racketeering, but they need a lot less money than the PIRA.

The annual PIRA budget is estimated at around £4.5 million ($6.75 million), with expenditure going on the pay of terrorists (50 percent), welfare and money to their political front equally dividing the rest. The racketeering activities consist of protection, drinking clubs, co-operatives, Department of Health and Social Security frauds, European Economic Community frauds and some legitimate businesses set up with stolen money but now quite legitimate companies. The taxi services have also provided terrorists with a sizeable income.

PALESTINE LIBERATION ORGANIZATION (PLO)

OF ALL THE players on the stage of terrorism, one of the most durable is the Palestine Liberation Organization (PLO). It has been – and in some cases continues to be – an arm of the anti-Israeli cause, a Civil War threat in Jordan, a political empire in Lebanon and a scattered terrorist organization.

In reality, the PLO is an umbrella organization composed of at least eight main groups – chief among them Al Fatah, headed by Yasser Arafat, PLO chairman – and numerous factions. More than 100 governments consider the PLO the sole representative body of the Palestinians – which means it has some form of diplomatic representation in more countries than actually recognize Israel. In the West, only the United States and Israel have refused to deal with the PLO. Moreover, the PLO's budget (it has $5 billion in assets by some accounts) and infrastructure are larger than those of many third world countries.

It is common for factions within the PLO to disagree over the political direction of the movement, the tactics to be used in dealing with Israel, and even the political composition of what their vision is for the "new Palestine".

PLO members Al Fatah, Saiqa and the Popular Front for the Liberation of Palestine

represent almost 80 percent of the organization's strength and, in the Middle East scheme of things, are considered the moderates of the organization. The Democratic Front for the Liberation of Palestine, the Popular Front for the Liberation of Palestine, the Popular Front for the Liberation of Palestine-General Command, the Palestinian Popular Struggle Front, and the Arab Liberation Front are all considered the radical faction.

The major difference between the factions is that the latter demonstrate a total unwillingness to consider negotiations with Israel over the future of Palestine. This group depends largely on the support of Libya and Iraq and is, therefore, directed largely by those countries' interests.

Al Fatah, or the Palestine National Liberation Movement, is the largest faction of the PLO, and generally enjoys the support of Syria and Egypt; it receives financial backing from Saudi Arabia and some Persian Gulf States. It was set up and began to emerge in the 1950s as a nationalist movement to liberate Palestine from Israeli occupation.

When the PLO was formed in 1964. Al-Fatah and its leader, Yasser Arafat, had an arch-rival, a problem that was resolved

rather neatly in 1969 when Arafat became PLO chairman. During the Lebanese Civil War, Fatah played an important role, particularly in th negotiations that ended the fighting.

The organization participated in a number of bloody terrorist incidents, hijackings and sabotage operations against Israeli enterprises and helped provoke the Israeli invasion of Lebanon in 1982. As a result, Arafat's guerrillas found themselves in Syria, Iraq and Tunisia.

Saiqa, or Thunderbolt, is the PLO faction most closely tied to Syria, and maintains bases in that country and in Lebanon. Founded by Syrian authorities as a commando force in 1968, Saiqa reflects the socialist, pan-Arab philosophy of the Syrian Ba'ath Party.

This has frequently found the 3,000-member group at odds, to the point of armed violence, with other PLO factions. Saiqa generally acts as an instrument of Syrian policy and is said to hold more allegiance to Syria than to the PLO executive committee of even Yasser Arafat himself.

The **Popular Front for the Liberation of Palestine,** or PFLP, is the most left-wing of the PLO factions, and was formed in 1967 by the merger of the Heroes of the Return, the

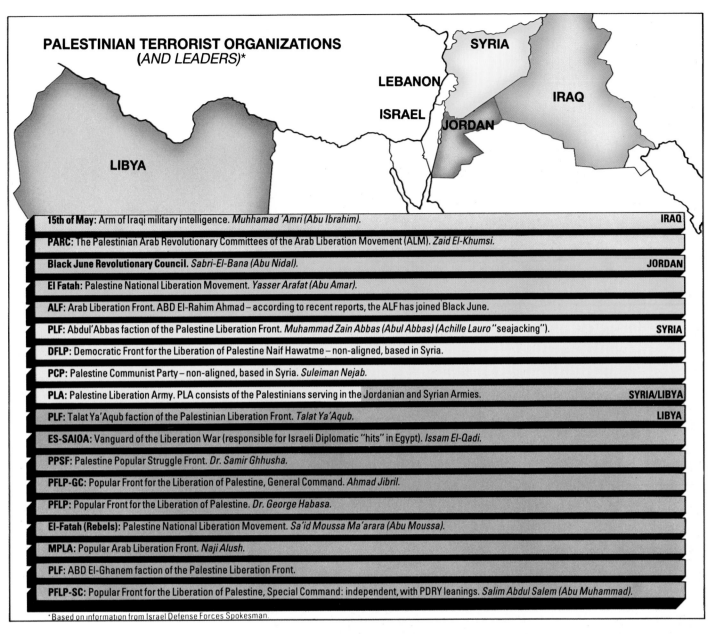

PALESTINIAN TERRORIST ORGANIZATIONS
(AND LEADERS)*

15th of May: Arm of Iraqi military intelligence. *Muhhamad 'Amri (Abu Ibrahim).*	**IRAQ**
PARC: The Palestinian Arab Revolutionary Committees of the Arab Liberation Movement (ALM). *Zaid El-Khumsi.*	
Black June Revolutionary Council. *Sabri-El-Bana (Abu Nidal).*	**JORDAN**
El Fatah: Palestine National Liberation Movement. *Yasser Arafat (Abu Amar).*	
ALF: Arab Liberation Front. ABD El-Rahim Ahmad – according to recent reports, the ALF has joined Black June.	
PLF: Abdul'Abbas faction of the Palestine Liberation Front. *Muhammad Zain Abbas (Abul Abbas) (Achille Lauro "seajacking").*	**SYRIA**
DFLP: Democratic Front for the Liberation of Palestine Naif Hawatme – non-aligned, based in Syria.	
PCP: Palestine Communist Party – non-aligned, based in Syria. *Suleiman Nejab.*	
PLA: Palestine Liberation Army. PLA consists of the Palestinians serving in the Jordanian and Syrian Armies.	**SYRIA/LIBYA**
PLF: Talat Ya'Aqub faction of the Palestinian Liberation Front. *Talat Ya'Aqub.*	**LIBYA**
ES-SAIOA: Vanguard of the Liberation War (responsible for Israeli Diplomatic "hits" in Egypt). *Issam El-Qadi.*	
PPSF: Palestine Popular Struggle Front. *Dr. Samir Ghhusha.*	
PFLP-GC: Popular Front for the Liberation of Palestine, General Command. *Ahmad Jibril.*	
PFLP: Popular Front for the Liberation of Palestine. *Dr. George Habasa.*	
El-Fatah (Rebels): Palestine National Liberation Movement. *Sa'id Moussa Ma'arara (Abu Moussa).*	
MPLA: Popular Arab Liberation Front. *Naji Alush.*	
PLF: ABD El-Ghanem faction of the Palestine Liberation Front.	
PFLP-SC: Popular Front for the Liberation of Palestine, Special Command: independent, with PDRY leanings. *Salim Abdul Salem (Abu Muhammad).*	

*Based on information from Israel Defense Forces Spokesman.

·**Above left:** *Charred wreckage of airliner at Beirut International Airport, blown up by PLO, is a grisly testimony of terrorist failure to swap the aircraft for the release of other terrorists held prisoner.*

Right: *PLO training for children – in this case bayonet practice – on the West Bank. It instills a martial spirit in the trainees. Other trainees have no weapons; two are much easier to hide.*

Palestine Liberation Front, and segments of the Arab National Movement. It has an estimated membership of 4,000 and was the first Palestinian group active in skyjacking.

Supported by Iraq, Libya and Algeria, the PFLP adopted a hard-line policy in dealing with Israel that left – and continues to leave – sharp divisions within the PLO. In September 1974, the PFLP withdrew from the PLO Executive Committee to form the "Rejection Front", which refused to negotiate or make peace with Israel or even recognize its right to exist.

Above: *PLO terrorists on patrol in the Golan Heights in Syria. The black gutra (headcloth) of the second man from rear clearly identifies him as a member of PLO. Red gutras are worn for regional identification by the Saudis and others.*

Left: *Two typically-clad Beirut street fighters at barricades at the Shatila Palestinian refugee camp. Note American web gear and the Soviet assault rifle, a widely favored weapon of terrorists.*

Right: *PLO terrorist practises with RPG-7 rocket launcher and gas mask. This clearly indicates training in USSR or Soviet bloc nation since only their military units train with and without gas masks.*

The **Popular Front for the Liberation of Palestine-General Command** was formed in 1970 after it split from the PFLP. With an estimated membership of 500, it is headed by Ahmad Jibril, a former captain in the Syrian Army. Boobytrapped packages and letter bombs were a specialty of the PFLP-GC at one time, and the organization gained a measure of notoriety, not to mention world opprobrium, when, in 1974, its members pitched the bodies of Israeli children from the top of an apartment house during a siege.

The **Democratic Front for the Liberation of Palestine** was formed by disillusioned members of the PFLP who fault the PFLP as well as the moderate Al-Fatah for bourgeois tendencies. Interestingly, the DFLP opposed

international terrorism; inside Israel, it was another matter – and the group claimed responsibility for the Ma'alot school massacre.

The rhetoric of Nayef Hawatma, the group's leader, reveals the DFLP to have as much contempt for the PFLP, Hashemite Jordan and Egypt as it has for Israel. The Syrian-based DFLP has an estimated 3,000 members and maintains relations with Cuba, the People's Republic of China and the USSR.

The **Arab Liberation Front (ALF),** led by Aba-al-Rahim, was formed in 1969 from the Iraqi Ba'ath Party and maintains close ties in that country. When the ALF was formed, the Iraqi government ordered all Al Fatah offices in Baghdad closed, to ensure that the ALF

would be the sole Iraqi representative in the PLO. Since then, the ALF has been a frequent target of the Al-Fatah, sometimes leading to armed violence. Al Fatah even organized judicial tribunals that ended in the execution of some ALF members.

PPSF, or the **Palestine Popular Struggle Front,** emerged in 1968 in Jordan. With roots in the Palestine Liberation Army's commando structure, PPSF supported the Rejection Front. Consisting of approximately 200 members, the group is led by Dr. Samir Ghusha and is currently based in Libya.

The **Palestine Liberation Front,** led by Abul Abbas, is another PLO faction with Iraqi ties worth mentioning. Formed in 1977, the PLF is a staunch member of the Rejection

Front and is an offshoot of the PFLP-GC.

Despite its internal divisions, the PLO has operated alone or in cooperation with foreign groups in 58 countries, including Israel. In 1970, following the PLO's expulsion from Jordan, Al Fatah created the Black September organization to perpetrate attacks outside Israel. The Black September name, which was linked to the massacre of Israeli athletes at the 1972 Munich Olympics, has also been adopted by other PLO factors who wish to remain anonymous.

Before the 1982 war in Lebanon, the PLO cooperated actively with foreign terrorists, supplying arms and ammunition and terrorist training at PLO camps in Arab countries.

Meanwhile, the PLO's factions received financial backing, training and supplies from the Soviet Union and other Eastern European countries, China, North Korea, Vietnam, Iran and Cuba, as well as Arab nations – Algeria, Libya, Egypt, North Yemen, South Yemen, Saudi Arabia, Iraq, Syria, Lebanon and Jordan.

The PLO dispersed

In 1982, Israel's "Peace for Galilee" operation forced the PLO to flee Beirut and Southern Lebanon, destroying its base of operations and training grounds. This expulsion drastically reduced the operational assistance and connections between the PLO and international terrorist organizations. The PLO is now dispersed among eight Arab countries and lacks a base from which it can direct and coordinate guerrilla operations across the Israeli border.

Without this base, the only method for certain PLO factions to keep the struggle going is to resort to stepped-up terrorist activity. This is particularly true since the PLO is simply unable to mount a significant military threat to Israel – due to Israeli military superiority as well as the state-based factionalism within the PLO itself.

Unless the PLO can weld itself into a unified movement, a successful political accommodation with Israel will be impossible. Terrorism will therefore remain the only acceptable method of expression for the more radical factions of the movement.

THE RED BRIGADES

WHETHER terrorism is measured in terms of incidents, the number of people involved, or even technical sophistication and brutality, Italy comes off as having one of the most serious problems on the European continent. Nearly 100 leftist terrorist organizations and nearly two dozen neo-fascist groups are found within her borders. One study claims "there are 700 to 800 terrorists living in Italy's underground and up to 10,000 persons who actively support terrorist activities".

Among them are those who support the Red Brigades *(Brigate Rosse)*, an organization identified with such practices as kneecapping, politically targeted assassinations and other forms of intimidation. The Brigades reject the established Italian Communist Party, no doubt partly because of its active role in opposing terrorism; and, in their own way, the group typifies the urban terrorist organization grounded in Marxist-Leninist ideals.

They often resort to violence to extol their political philosophy. Between the time of their formation and 1982, they were responsible for the murders of 50 people and were involved in the kidnapping of 50 more. Since 1980, they have murdered an average of four prominent people a year and have been stepping up their anti-United States and anti-NATO rhetoric, although they have yet to attack NATO targets. In March 1987 two assassins on a motorcycle shot dead Italian Air Force General Licio Giorgieri, Director of Space and Air Armaments. An ominous feature was the belief that the killing was organized jointly by the Red Brigades and other European terrorist units, including France's Action Directe, as part of a joint attempt to undermine NATO.

Some observers credit the "Cultural Revolution of 1968" with putting the imprimatur of legitimacy on the face of violence and creating the climate in which the Brigades could function effectively. Student revolutions throughout Europe at the time challenged not only the educational system of the state, but the government, family and church.

Red Brigades literature says: "Our commitment in the factories and the districts has been from the beginning that of organizing proletarian autonomy for the resistance against the counter-revolution in progress. ... Urban guerrilla warfare plays a decisive role in the action of political disarticulation of the regime and the state". These terrorists have clearly lost all faith in existing institutions and feel that "guerrilla warfare" (terrorism) provides a chance to change all they have rejected.

The intellectual founders of the Red Brigades were Renato Curcio and his wife, Margherita Cagol, who led the organization in the early 1970s. They put together a nucleus of supporters from universities, industry, the church, and the Italian Communist Party – or at least those who had become disillusioned with the Party.

Cagol was killed in a shootout in 1975 and Curcio jailed in 1976, but the nucleus that had been put together so carefully by them picked up the reins of leadership. A key

member of that group, Giorgio Semeria, had established the five-member cell structure of the organization. Only one member of the cell knew how to contact the leader in a higher level cell ... and independent pyramids of cells (known as columns) were established in Milan, Rome, Turin and Genoa.

Early brigadists received much of their inspiration from jailed intellectuals who espoused terrorism and much of their training from Uruguayan and Argentinian exiles who had taken asylum in Rome from military regimes in their native countries. These exiles – drawing upon their own experiences – were instrumental in helping establish safe houses, and taught the Brigades the need for painstaking attention to security. These precautions made them appear virtually impenetrable by the police and increased the public's fear of them.

Early Red Brigades activity was centered around Milan, where property damage, usually in the form of arson, was inflicted on prominent conservatives, businessmen, and members of the ultra-right Italian Social Movement. Their weapons were Beretta M4 and M12 sub-machine guns acquired locally; they sometimes used Czechoslovakian Skorpion sub-machine guns provided by West German terrorists.

Their activities soon expanded to the industrial cities of Turin and Genoa, and kidnapping assumed an important role, primarily for its psychological impact. The targets of kidnappings were selected methodically to ensure the pillars of Italian society came under full frontal attack: magistrates and jurors were targeted to help prevent conviction in court; journalists and editors to help prevent exposure in the media; and teachers/university professors to

help ensure that the "correct" ideology prevailed. And, finally, supporters of the Christian Democrats were targeted to influence the form of political opposition to terrorism.

Among other things, the Red Brigades were responsible for the abduction and murder of former Prime Minister Aldo Moro in 1978, the kidnapping of US Army Brigadier General James Dozier in 1981, the assassination of Leamon Hunt, director general of the Sinai Peacekeeping Forces in 1984, and the assassination of trade unionist and Christian Democrat economist Ezio Tarantelli in 1985.

Moro was put on "trial" before a "people's tribunal", which condemned him to death as an enemy of the proletariat and then demanded the release of 13 terrorists as the price of his life. The mock trial of Moro (a similar "trial" was later to be held for General Dozier) riveted national and international attention on the drama for 54 days, something an outright execution could never have hoped to accomplish. Moro's bullet-riddled body was later to be discovered in an abandoned car.

Dozier was kidnapped on December 17, 1981 and held hostage for 42 days before being rescued by Italian "Leatherheads", an elite counterterrorist force. Probably the most significant effect of the Dozier episode was that it resulted in key inroads being made into the Red Brigades. The group's influence waned considerably thereafter.

However, the Brigades – which once numbered 3,000 and apparently hit a peak in 1978 – may be getting a fresh start, as evidenced by the Giorgieri assassination. Italy's leading investigator of terrorism, Judge Imposimato had said in late 1986 that the group is finding new popularity among younger members of blue-collar families.

Left: *Bearded Renato Curcio, Red Brigade's leader, held captive with two other "Brigadists", Mantovani, left, and Bonavita, awaiting trial in Turin in 1976. Unfortunately, this was not the end of the Brigades.*

Right: *End of the trail for some Brigadists, as they are led from the Turin court to jail. The explosive Curcio had already been expelled from the proceedings after outbursts against the authorities he thought corrupt.*

Below and bottom: *Disturbing and revealing evidence of the Red Brigades' ruthless terrorism. At bottom is the body of ill-fated former prime minister Aldo Moro's bodyguard, gunned down during the kidnap.*

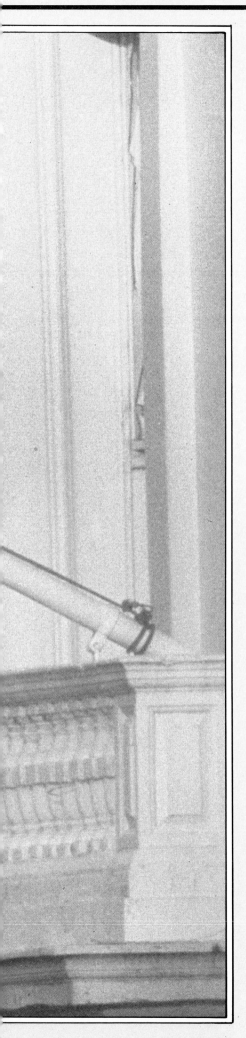

SECTION THREE
OPERATIONS: THE VISIBLE PAYOFF

RESCUE AT ENTEBBE   119
MOLUCCAN TRAIN INCIDENT   122
MOGADISHU RESCUE   125
OPERATION EAGLE CLAW   128
THE IRANIAN EMBASSY SIEGE   132
THE DOZIER RESCUE   137
WIRELESS RIDGE   140
RESCUE IN GRENADA   143
THE ACHILLE LAURO   145

OPERATIONS
THE
VISIBLE PAYOFF

NAMES LIKE Djebel el Ank, Porto Empedocle, Zerf, Cisterna and Cabanatuan have long since moved into history's more obscure pages, only to be replaced by their counterparts of the 1970s and 1980s. Those new names include Entebbe, Djibouti, Grenada, the Falklands, and others. What they share in common is that they are all operations conducted by special/elite forces. Where they differ is in locale – Tunisia, Italy, Germany and the Philippines were sites of the first group – and the conflict environment in which they were conducted. The first set of operations, for example, were conducted during all-out war (World War II).

The second set of operations is no less global in nature and reaches into three hemispheres; however, these operations were all conducted in low-intensity conflict environments. To carry the comparisons a step further, the operations in both cases cannot be viewed as unqualified successes. In World War II, Cisterna, for example, resulted in the outright defeat of US Ranger forces which were already reeling from heavy losses suffered during conventional military operations. Djibouti, Entebbe and the Train 747 (Moluccan Train Incident) operations were overall successes by any yardstick – but hostages nevertheless died as the result of assaults mounted during the operations.

The point is that much can be learned by examining the operations of elite units as they do the job they were created to handle in the first place. In the last analysis, it doesn't really matter whether those units' missions are primarily (or even exclusively) military or counterterror by nature. Operations are where the payoffs in setting up and maintaining these forces become the most visible. Like nothing else, they spotlight the importance of training, planning, proper equipment and the need for generous dashes of audacity and flexibility – among other things – in carrying them out.

This is why these operations have been included in this discussion of elite/special forces. Nine of them – which were conducted by a variety of elite units – have been selected for analysis and discussion, and their results are assessed. It could just as easily have been 100 or 200 operations, since there are truly no two missions alike; but these nine are, perhaps, as representative a group as was available. Given the usual secrecy that by necessity shrouds the typical operation, it became clear the richest yield would come from looking at recent operations about which enough was known so they could be looked at with some profit.

Incidentally, it would be a serious mistake to dwell overly long on those operations that may be perceived as something less than a ringing success. Nothing can more quickly devalue the role of special units as a force for deterrence – a role that is arguably their most significant.

There is simply no effective way this can be measured. We can never know, for example, how the fierce reputation of the Gurkhas may

Above: *Royal Netherlands Marines about to arrest South Moluccan terrorists. In the late community carried out a series of terrorist acts, for which authorities meted out stiff sentences.*

Right: *Mohammed Appas, generally known as Abul Appas. This terrorist headed the Palestine Liberation Front faction responsible for the "seajacking" of the Achille Lauro. He was released by Italian authorities.*

Below: *Egyptian Commandos stormed a hijacked Egyptian 737 on 24 November 1985. Captain Hani Gala, center, killed the hijack leader with an axe, and was injured by a terrorist bullet during the drama.*

have influenced the thinking of Argentinian commanders during the Falklands War. Nor will we ever know how the highly effective work of the Italian counterterrorist apparatus in the incident involving American Brigadier General James L. Dozier in 1982 influenced the infrastructure of the Red Brigades and their future plans.

We do know that no American generals have been kidnapped on Italian soil since. We do know that a repeat of the Iranian embassy siege – either in London or elsewhere – has not taken place since the British Special Air Service took care of that problem in 1980. We also know that the Israeli special forces have not boarded C-130s and gone continent-hopping in the last few years.

Whether this can all be attributed to operations of this kind – and, not so coincidentally, these are the very operations that are discussed in detail over the next several pages – is debatable. What isn't debatable is that there would likely be many more such incidents without the looming presence of elite units in nations worldwide.

This is why looking at these operations – and the lessons they teach – is so valuable. The prestigious Combat Studies Institute at the US Army's Command and General Staff College at Fort Leavenworth, Kansas, studied the first group of operations mentioned earlier. They were all conducted by the US Rangers and were considered representative of the types of special operations conducted in the wartime environment by that unit. The conclusion of the Institute: "Many factors determined the outcomes of the operations . . . and of these there are four that are important enough to merit special emphasis. These are surprise, the quality of opposing forces, the success of friendly forces with which the Rangers were cooperating, and popular support". Of these factors, surprise was paramount.

Compare this with another observer's summary analysis of most of the operations selected for inclusion in this book. To paraphrase his analysis: split-second timing is needed to capitalize on any advantage in time gained from the creative use of distraction. There is a need to have the cooperation of local authorities – since that can often spell the difference between life and death. Locale is important, since nothing will ever happen unless you can get to the place where you are to carry out your mission.

Certainly these basic tenets and tactics can be studied over and over again. Taken as a general rule, they are sound and they work. But it would be a great mistake to assume that what works in one situation will work one-for-one in another. The variables in each situation are just too great. The tactics used by the Special Air Service during the siege of the Iranian Embassy in London, for example, may hold out the example that flexibility is a virtue (some of the rope bought for the scaling effort came directly from a hardware store), but that hardly makes it the ideal way to approach a similar situation.

By the same reckoning, the tactics applied by the German GSG 9 to an airplane hijacking may not be adaptable to future situations of the same kind.

The lessons are there to be learned, of course. But each situation is unique, and each one addresses literally hundreds of different considerations.

Of course, that is one of the reasons the elite forces of the world have one of the most difficult jobs around and why they must have such high caliber personnel to deal with the bewildering variety of situations in which they find themselves. It can hardly be any other way.

Above: *British troops in the Falklands had not only to combat the enemy, but also a harsh climate and inhospitable terrain. Equipment had to be adapted, and precise knowledge of the strengths and limitations of weapons had to be known. British elite units (SAS, SBS Parachute Regiment, Gurkhas, and others) performed tasks involving technical expertise and much daring.*

Below: *US Marine inspects Soviet Bloc-supplied weapons in Grenada. Many thought the resistance to US invasion forces would be light and unprepared. In reality, there were well-equipped and highly trained guerrilla forces. There are lessons to be gleaned from all operations mounted by special operations forces. No two could be considered the same; Grenada was no exception.*

RESCUE AT ENTEBBE

Left: *Israeli Army Chief of Staff General Mordecai Gur at press conference in Tel Aviv on 4 July praising Israeli Commandos who rescued hostages at Entebbe. They had been held for a week by the pro-Palestine hijackers of an Air France aircraft. Seated at his left is Brigadier Dan Shomron, who led the raid.*

Below: *Hostages arrive at Lod airport following their dramatic rescue at Entebbe. It was mid-morning when the C-130 Hercules transport touched down and lowered its rear ramp to release its cargo of men, women and children into the outstretched arms of relatives and friends watched by a crowd of thousands. The ordeal was finally over.*

A T 0900 hours June 27, 1976, Air France flight AF 139 left Tel Aviv airport en route for Paris with 254 passengers and crew aboard. The A300 Airbus aircraft staged through Athens and it was on the second leg of its flight when, at 1210 hours, it was sky-jacked by a combination of Palestinian and Baader-Meinhof terrorists led by a German called Wilfried Boese. The pilot succeeded in pressing the "hijack button" as he turned for Benghazi, where, after a 6½ hour delay, the plane was refueled; it then flew on to the terrorists' destination – Entebbe in Uganda, which was under the erratic rule of "Field Marshal" Idi Amin Dada.

Amin endeavored to maintain an apparently neutral posture, but covertly he supported the terrorists in their demands that unless 53 Palestinian or other terrorist prisoners held in a number of countries were released the hostages would be shot at 1200 hours on July 1. Ugandan troops were deployed at Entebbe airport, supposedly to "keep the peace", but they in fact assisted in guarding the hostages. Amin even visited the hostages and, after he had left, the Israelis and Jews of other nationalities were segregated, although the Air France aircrew insisted on joining them.

On the morning of July 1, the Israeli government, playing for time, announced that it was willing to consider the release of Palestinian prisoners. The hijackers, increasingly confident of eventual success, responded by extending their deadline by three days. They also released all the non-Jewish hostages, who were flown to Paris, where they were debriefed by French and Israeli intelligence.

The Israeli planners had many problems. The first clearly was shortage of time: time to achieve something before the terrorists killed any of their hostages and time to set up a rescue attempt. The second was to find out just where the hostages were being held and under what conditions. Third, there was the problem of getting a rescue force to Entebbe and back. Fourth, there was the problem of

what to do with the non-Jewish hostages.

Fortunately, the problems resolved themselves one after another. The Kenya government agreed to the use of Nairobi airport, and a coup in Sudan resulted in the closure of all but one of that country's air control radars. Intelligence on Entebbe Airport and the local situation began to be processed, aided considerably by the debriefing of the released non-Jewish hostages. This eased the problem of consulting foreign governments. US sources, however, made information, including satellite photographs of Entebbe, available, and France remained involved, not only because it had been an Air France airliner that was hijacked in the first place, but also because the courageous crew insisted on staying with the Jewish hostages.

The Rescue

Lieutenant-General Mordecai Gur, Israeli chief-of-staff, considered that a raid on the airport was feasible, and at 0730 hours on July 3 Prime Minister Rabin reviewed all the facts and then gave the political go-ahead for the operation. Later that morning a full-scale dress rehearsal was held in northern Israel. Drawn from the 35th Parachute Brigade and the Golani Infantry Brigade, the 100-plus force, commanded by Brigadier-General

Dan Shomron, aged 48, performed well in an attack on a dummy layout manned by Israeli troops, and all seemed to augur well for the real thing, which was scheduled for the next day. The dress rehearsal lasted just 55 minutes from the time the aircraft landed to the time it took off again (the actual rescue was to take 53). The primary weapons selected for the raid reportedly were the MAC-10 and Galil assault rifles, the latter equipped with night sights. The force to enter the airport terminal and rescue the hostages was to be led by Lieutenant-Colonel Jonathan Netanyahu, known throughout the Israeli Army as "Yoni".

At 1600 hours that afternoon (July 3), two hours after the full Israeli cabinet had been made aware of the "go" decision, four Israeli C-130 Hercules aircraft took off for the long flight to Entebbe. The route took them down the middle of the Red Sea at high altitude in the hope that Saudi Arabian radars would treat them as unscheduled civil flights. There was, in fact, no response, so they were able to turn and fly down the Sudan-Ethiopia border and into Uganda.

Two Boeing 707s were also involved, leaving two hours after the slower C-130s. One was a flying command post fitted with special communications; it caught up with the

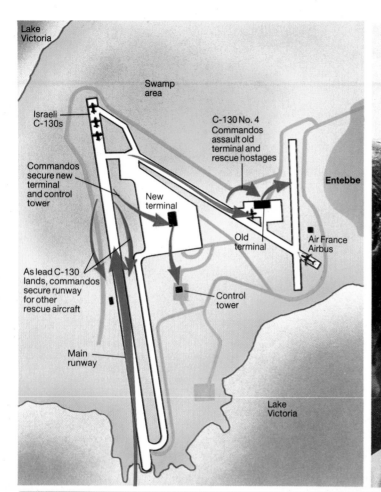

Above: *Scenes of unrestrained jubilation marked the arrival of the Israeli commandos after their arrival at Lod airport. It was marred only by the loss of assault team leader Lt. Colonel Jonathan (Yoni) Netanyahu.*

Above left/left: *Speed and deception were keys to success at Entebbe. Heavily armed jeeps and a Mercedes (left) disguised as Uganda dictator Idi Amin's personal limousine were used to fool the Ugandan airport guards. The Hercules No. 1 and 2 aircraft (with the command group) set down several minutes apart and deployed troops; Hercules No. 3 carried reserve troops and touched down on the main runway after lighting was extinguished; the role of Hercules No. 4, which had further reserve forces, was to taxi to the old terminal and pick up rescued passengers.*

four C-130s near Entebbe and remained in the area throughout the operation with Major Generals Benny Peled and Yekutiel Adam aboard. The other 707, fitted out as an emergency hospital, went straight to Nairobi, arriving just before midnight; it then waited, its medical staff ready for any wounded from the operation across the border in Uganda.

The four C-130s arrived at Entebbe without incident and landed at precisely 0001 hours. The first aircraft landed close to the control-tower, disgorging its paratroops in a Mercedes car and three Land Rovers while still moving. The men charged into the tower and succeeded in preventing the controllers from switching off the landing lights; even so

emergency lights were deployed, just in case. These were not needed and the second and third aircraft taxied up to the terminal where the hostages were being held and discharged their paratroopers straight into action. The fourth C-130 joined the first near the control tower.

The main Israeli squad brushed aside the ineffective resistance from the Ugandan Army guards and charged into the terminal building. The second group destroyed Ugandan Air Force MiG fighters to prevent pursuit when the raiders took off again and also as a noisy and obvious diversion.

The third group went to the perimeter to cover the approach road, since it was known

that the Ugandan Army had a number of Soviet-built T-54 tanks and Czech OT-64 armored personnel carriers some 20 miles (32km) away in the capital, Kampala. Had this force appeared, it could have had a major effect as the Israelis had no heavy weapons. The fourth group was made up of 33 doctors who, being Israelis, were also well-trained soldiers and brought down covering fire from the area of the C-130s.

With Shomron in control in the tower and satisfied that the first phase had been successful, it was now "Yoni" Netanyahu's turn to lead the crucial assault on the terminal building to rescue the hostages. The terrorist leader, Boese, behaved with surprising in-

decision, first aiming at the hostages and then changing his mind, going outside, loosing off a few rounds at the Israelis and then heading back for the lounge; as he returned he was shot and killed. His fellow German, Gabrielle Tiedemann, was also killed outside the building.

The Israeli soldiers rushed into the lounge where the hostages were being held, shouting at everyone to get down on the floor; in the confusion, three of the hostages were shot by stray bullets, an almost inevitable consequence in such a situation. While some of the soldiers rushed upstairs to kill the two terrorists remaining there, the hostages were shepherded out to the waiting C-130s. At this point "Yoni" Netanyahu emerged from the terminal to supervise the loading and was killed by one shot from a Ugandan soldier in a nearby building, a sad loss.

At 0045 hours the defensive outposts were called in as the first C-130 roared off into the night with its load of rescued hostages on their way to Nairobi, with the fourth and last leaving at 0054.

Apart from the loss of Colonel Netanyahu, three Israeli rescuers were wounded. Three hostages were killed in the rescue, while a fourth, Mrs Dora Bloch, who had been taken off to a local hospital earlier, was murdered by the Ugandans in revenge for the raid. On the other side, in addition to the terrorists, there were 20 Ugandans killed and more than 100 wounded.

The whole operation was a brilliant success, mounted on short notice and in a most unexpected direction. It confirmed the Israeli reputation for quick and determined "ad hoc" actions, conducted with great dedication and skill. The Ugandans could not be described

as substantial foes, but the terrorists had obviously been trained for their task. Interestingly, it later became known that Colonel Ulrich Wegener of GSG 9 was with the Israelis on the operation, possibly because of the known presence of the two Germans with the terrorists.

The first rescue attempt of its type – unless one considers the US raid on Son Tay Prison in Vietnam, which the Israelis reportedly used as a model – the Entebbe rescue caught the terrorists and Ugandans completely off guard. After Entebbe, terrorists had at least to take into account the possibility that a rescue mission could be carried out in hostile territory over great distances.

Top: *After the Israeli assault teams returned to Lod airport on July 4, they received grateful thanks from the nations. The spectacular and successful hostage rescue was put into place and executed within one week.*

Above: *Aerial view of the Air France aircraft which was hijacked with 12 crew and 254 passengers aboard, on the runway at Entebbe airport. The air terminal (left background) is where the passenger hostages were held until freed by Israeli commandos.*

MOLUCCAN TRAIN INCIDENT

THROUGHOUT the Netherlands in the 1970s, repeated terrorist incidents by South Moluccans grabbed headlines. The incidents were used by the terrorists to press demands that the Dutch government support independence for their homeland – the Moluccan Islands, now a part of Indonesia, but formerly a Dutch colonial possession. (They were at one time known as the Spice Islands.) The radicals spearheading the terrorist activity were generally the Dutch-born children of Moluccan natives, and had begun forming guerrilla squads in the late 1960s and accumulating arsenals of weapons.

Violence included the killing of a policeman in 1973 when South Moluccans seized the Indonesian embassy in The Hague; the following year, South Moluccans stormed and damaged The Hague Palace itself; and in 1976, they killed three hostages during a train hijacking.

But on May 23, 1977, two groups of South Moluccan terrorists launched their most spectacular attack yet in the opening phase of what was to become a three-week drama. The groups simultaneously hijacked a Dutch train and occupied an elementary school in a northern part of the Netherlands.

The raid began when two terrorists pulled an emergency cord to stop express train 747 as it traveled between Assen and Groningen. Five masked gunmen rushed aboard, herding 49 hostages into the first-class compartments.

Minutes later and a few miles away, seven terrorists invaded an elementary school, forcing 110 hostages into the main classroom. Of the 110 hostages, 106 were released unharmed a few days later after a virus struck the children.

In addition to demanding assistance in their independence efforts, the Moluccans insisted that they, as well as 21 other South Moluccans jailed for various assaults (including the planned kidnapping of Queen Juliana) be allowed to leave the country. Dutch officials handling the situation steadfastly refused to meet the terrorist demands, but continued to negotiate with them. There was a reluctance to use force, despite the previous train seizure only 18 months earlier.

However, the order for the June 10 rescue assault came only after negotiations dragged on for three weeks with no progress . . . and

as the Dutch public grew increasingly impatient and bitter over the stalemate. What was to follow was later characterized, appropriately enough, as a switch from psychology to technology.

Execution

Even though the Dutch government was reluctant to use force, contingency plans had been put in place from the start. To break the dual siege, it was determined that a dual attack would be required. If either the train or the school were taken individually, the terrorists at the remaining location seemed certain to exact vengeance on the hostages in their custody.

Throughout the siege, the specially picked Royal Dutch Marines, and civilian and military police had been rehearsing assaults on an empty train at the nearby Gilze Rijin Air Force Base. Eight combat swimmers had approached the train by way of a canal that ran within 15 yards (5m) of the tracks and had put sensitive bugging devices in place.

Special radar that could detect the heat differences in hot and cold surfaces had also been put in place; this allowed the Marines to monitor the movements of the terrorists through the metal in their weapons. Other sophisticated devices were used so that the Marines would know where the terrorists and hostages were likely to be should the "go" decision be made for the assault.

When it came, Marines wearing night-vision goggles approached the train, and launched what was to be a 20-minute attack. Six F-104 Starfighter aircraft immediately flew in criss-cross patterns just a few feet above the train, kicking in their afterburners in an attempt to distract the terrorists and encourage the hostages to keep their heads down. As the jets roared overhead, a force of Marine and police sharpshooters raced across a 100-yard (30m) field and opened up with their weapons on areas of the train where the terrorists normally slept. Shortly before 0500, the assault force blew the doors off with framing charges and went in with Uzis blazing.

Six of the nine terrorists were killed during the assault; two hostages who had panicked and stood up as bullets blazed about were killed also. Seven other hostages, two Dutch Marines and one terrorist were wounded.

Above: *A menacing rifle barrel protrudes from a window of the school house near Assen, Holland, where six South Moluccan terrorists seized teachers and 105 schoolchildren and held them hostage for three days.*

Above: *One of several terrorism incidents that plagued Dutch authorities in the 1970s. Like most others, these acts of terrorism involved support of a political cause, that of Dutch-born children of Moluccan natives living in the Netherlands, who have demanded independence of their homelands, the Moluccas, from Indonesia which took over sovereignty of the group of islands from the Netherlands in 1949. Here, Dutch Marines stand guard outside the besieged administration building in Drenthe Province, in the North of Holland. The Marines freed 70 hostages held by three Moluccan terrorists in the incident which occurred about a year after the train-and-schoolhouse siege of 1977.*

Left: *Three years earlier, on 8 December 1975, Moluccan terrorists seized the Indonesian Consulate in Amsterdam. Here a masked and hooded terrorist armed with a submachine gun forces one of the hostages to retrieve food left for them by the authorities.*

Right: *The end of yet another Moluccan terrorist incident, again involving hostages on a hijacked train, in late 1975. It took 12 days of negotiation before the 24 hostages were released.*

Simultaneously with the assault on the train, Marines assaulted the school at Bovensmilde, rushing the building with armored personnel carriers from all four sides, one of them bursting through a wall. The 10-minute attack met no resistance; four terrorists were captured (three were asleep in their underwear) and the four hostages rescued unharmed.

Assessment

The assault demonstrated that the Dutch would resort to force if necessary to counter terrorism. This was particularly important to the government since the belief had been prevalent among South Moluccans that force would not be used, no matter how hard the Dutch were pushed. Perhaps another salutory effect of the split-second, high-tech and successful attack was that it helped temper some of the derogatory remarks directed at long-haired Dutch troops by their more conventional colleagues from other European nations.

Another point was eventually driven home: terrorism would not go unpunished in the courts either. Seven of the terrorists, aged 18 to 28, received prison terms ranging from six to nine years, while another received a one-year term for helping plan the dual seizure.

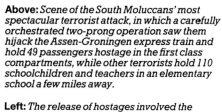

Above: *Scene of the South Moluccans' most spectacular terrorist attack, in which a carefully orchestrated two-prong operation saw them hijack the Assen-Groningen express train and hold 49 passengers hostage in the first class compartments, while other terrorists hold 110 schoolchildren and teachers in an elementary school a few miles away.*

Left: *The release of hostages involved the coordinated efforts of Marines frogmen/commandos, Air Force F-104s flying low across the train as a diversionary tactic before the commandos smashed their way in, civilian and military police "sharpshooters", and of course the intelligence services.*

Below: *Calm before the storm. The express train seen just before the Marines raided, using shaped charge explosives to gain entry. Six of the nine terrorists were killed and, despite the accidental deaths of two hostages and injuries to other hostages and rescuers, the operation was considered a success.*

MOGADISHU RESCUE

ON OCTOBER 13, 1977, a Lufthansa 737 airliner en route from Palam in the Balearic Islands to Germany was hijacked by terrorists over the French Mediterranean coast. On board the aircraft were five aircrew (two pilots, three stewardesses), 86 passengers and four terrorists, two of them women. The hijackers' leader called himself "Captain Mahmoud", and was subsequently identified as a notorious international terrorist, Zohair Youssef Akache. He ordered the aircraft captain to fly to Fiucimino Airport in Rome, where the airliner was refueled.

From Rome, the airliner set off eastwards and landed at Larnaca in Cyprus at 2038. Here, "Mahmoud" demanded that the aircraft be refueled again, or he would blow it up, the first of many threats to use explosives. After refueling, the airliner took off and overflew various Middle East countries. Permission to land at Beirut was denied and the runways were blocked, so it was taken on to Bahrein in the Persian Gulf where the same thing happened. It was flown on to Dubai where, despite being refused permission to land, the crew were forced to do so for lack of fuel.

At one point at Dubai the airliner lost power and the temperature inside rose to over 120°F (49°C); many of the passengers, some of them quite elderly, became very distressed. While here, the crew managed surreptitiously to signal that there were four hijackers.

Then on Sunday, October 16, the airliner suddenly took off, only 40 minutes before the first deadline for blowing it up. It was refused permission to land in Oman and arrived over Aden airport with sufficient fuel for another ten minutes' flying; despite warnings from air traffic control, the aircraft was brought down safely on the taxi track.

Pilot executed

By now conditions inside the aircraft were very bad, and "Mahmoud" was acting in an increasingly unpredictable and unstable manner. Jürgen Schumann, the pilot, was allowed to leave the airliner to check the under-carriage and disappeared for a few minutes. When he returned he was taken to the first-class cabin and made to kneel on the floor; "Mahmoud" then shot him in the head, killing him instantly, directly as a result of Schumann's earlier, successful effort to feed information about the terrorists to authorities.

The next morning the co-pilot, Jürgen Vietor, took off and flew the airliner to Mogadishu, the capital of Somalia. There, German government spokesmen contacted the hijackers and said that they were prepared to release 11 terrorists held in jail and fly them to Mogadishu; "Mahmoud" postponed his deadline to 0245 hours the next morning (October 18).

Above: *The hijacked Lufthansa 737 seemingly deserted under the hot sun at Mogadishu. Inside, tension was mounting as conditions worsened, and the terrorist leader became more agitated and unpredictable.*

Below: *Somalian soldiers keep watch on the aircraft from a safe distance, fearful of pre-empting the rescue attempt.*

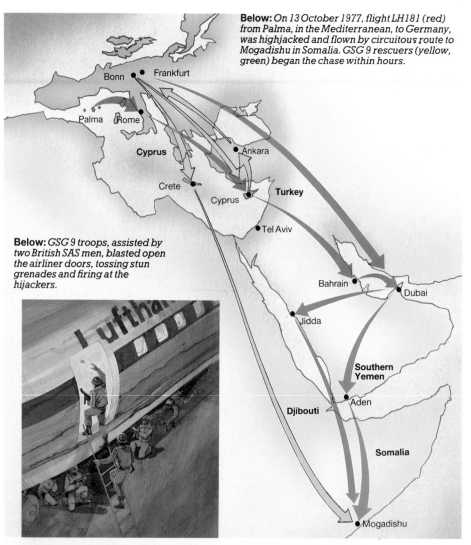

Below: *On 13 October 1977, flight LH181 (red) from Palma, in the Mediterranean, to Germany, was highjacked and flown by circuitous route to Mogadishu in Somalia. GSG 9 rescuers (yellow, green) began the chase within hours.*

Bonn
Frankfurt
Palma
Rome
Cyprus
Ankara
Crete
Cyprus
Turkey
Tel Aviv
Bahrain
Dubai
Jidda
Southern Yemen
Aden
Djibouti
Somalia
Mogadishu

Below: *GSG 9 troops, assisted by two British SAS men, blasted open the airliner doors, tossing stun grenades and firing at the hijackers.*

The rescue

A 30-strong contingent from GSG 9 was in the air within hours of the hijacking and arrived in Cyprus just as the Boeing 737 was taking off. Following a brief discussion with the Cypriot police, the GSG 9 aircraft took off again and returned, via Ankara, to Frankfurt. Meanwhile, a second aircraft containing Hans-Jürgen Wischnewski, West German Minister of State, psychologist Wolfgang Salewski, and another 30-strong group from GSG 9, led by their commander Ulrich Wegener, had left West Germany and gone to Dubai. From there they went to Mogadishu, where they were given permission to land.

In Mogadishu, Wischnewski took over discussions with the hijackers. As the 1600 hours deadline approached and it was clear that "Mahmoud" would in all probability carry out his threat to blow up the aircraft, the German Minister said that the 11 prisoners would be released. "Mahmoud" gave them until 0245 hours the following morning to produce the 11 at Mogadishu. At 2000 hours the first group from GSG 9 who had gone to Cyprus and then returned to Germany arrived in Mogadishu and the rescue briefings began.

At 0205 hours, just 40 minutes before the deadline, Somali troops lit a diversionary fire ahead of the aircraft. Two hijackers went to the cockpit to try to assess its significance, whereupon the tower contacted them by radio and started to discuss the conditions of the exchange. They said it would commence in the near future, when the aircraft arrived from Germany with the released prisoners on board.

At 0207 precisely the emergency doors

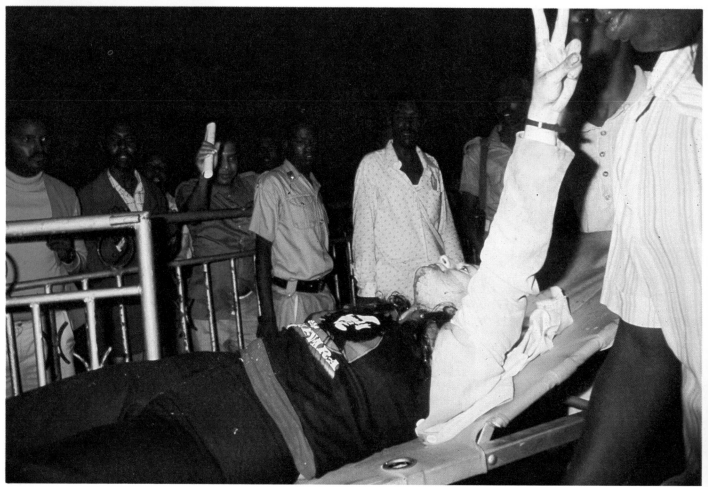

over the aircraft wings were blown open and members of the rescue party tossed in some "stun grenades". The men of GSG 9, with two British SAS men lent by the British government, had reached the aircraft and climbed onto the wings completely undetected; the hijackers (and the hostages) were taken by surprise.

The men of GSG 9 rushed into the aircraft shouting to the hostages to keep down on the floor, and opened fire on the hijackers. "Mahmoud" was fatally wounded in the first few seconds, but managed to throw two hand-grenades before he died; fortunately their effects were cushioned because they rolled beneath seats. One of the women terrorists died also and the second man was wounded inside the aircraft but died outside it a few minutes later. The second woman, Suhaila Sayeh, was wounded but did not die. Meanwhile the passengers were herded off the aircraft through the doors and emergency exits; three hostages had been wounded, but none killed.

The operation ended at 0212 hours and was entirely successful. GSG 9 had proved itself and received a well-merited heroes' welcome when they returned to Germany.

Mogadishu was, at the very least, a tribute to the intensive physical and mental training given by the GSG 9, as well as to that unit's attention to technological backup, examples being the special rubber-coated-alloy assault ladders used, and the stun grenades. At its best, it formed a new standard for rescue operations in that no hostages were killed during the assault – unlike at Djibouti and Entebbe which, though outstandingly successful in their own right, had resulted in at least one death.

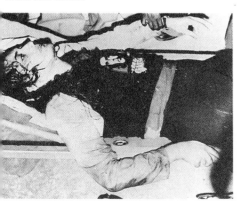

Left/far left: *Gravely wounded, Suhaila Sayeh, the only survivor of four Red Army Faction hijackers, is carried away on a litter, still defiant. None of the passengers was seriously hurt.*

Above and below: *GSG 9 anti-terrorist troops arrive back at Frankfurt to an ecstatic reception after their entirely successful rescue operation. Forgotten was Germany's humiliation of the Munich Olympics terrorist attack; the nation's crack anti-terrorist unit, organized by the Federal Border Police, had proven itself capable of combating terrorist action against West German lives and property wherever it might occur. They have not been forced to react so publicly since Mogadishu.*

Below: *The body of Jurgen Schumann, pilot of the Lufthansa 737, is carried from the aircraft. He was cruelly executed at Aden by hijack leader "Mahmoud" for passing along information about the terrorists over the radio.*

OPERATION EAGLE CLAW*

O N NOVEMBER 4, 1979, a group of Iranian "students" poured into the US Embassy compound in Teheran and seized 53 occupants. They were to hold them hostage for 444 days.

From the earliest days of the crisis one of the options under constant review and development was a military rescue, although both diplomatic and military endeavors were constantly bedeviled by the continuing chaos in Iran, the uncertain ever-changing intentions of the captors, and the vacillating position of the Iranian leadership. An unchanging factor was the remoteness of Teheran from available US bases. The plan that was eventually decided upon centred on Colonel Charlie Beckwith and the elite Delta force, although it obviously involved many more both resources directly and indirectly. The overall codename was "Operation Eagle Claw", its helicopter element "Operation Evening Light".

The plan was complicated mainly by the problems of time and space, and comprised some preliminary moves and a three-phase operation.

Preliminary moves

In the preliminary moves Delta was to fly, via Germany and Egypt, to Masirah airfield in Oman. There they would transfer to C-130s and, flying at very low level to avoid radar, cross the Gulf of Oman and southern Iran to land at Desert One, a remote site in the Dasht-e-Karir Salt Desert, 265 nautical miles (490km) south east of Teheran. Meanwhile, eight US Navy RH-53D helicopters, which had been deployed some weeks earlier via Diego Garcia would take off from the carrier USS *Nimitz* and, flown (also at very low level) by US Marine Corps crews, join up with the main party at Desert One.

Phase I: Insertion

At Desert One the plan was for the six C-130s

Above: *The senior military member of the hostages held in Iran for 144 days, US Colonel Schaefer, attending a special memorial service for the eight servicemen killed in the attempt to rescue him and fellow hostages on 24 April 1980. Unsuccessful though the mission was, America's message to hostage-takers was clear.*

(three troop carriers; three to refuel the helicopters) to land and await the helicopters, which were scheduled to arrive some 30 minutes later. Because Desert One was beside a road (judged to be little used), a 12-strong Road Watch Team was the first to deploy to intercept and detain any passing Iranians.

When they had refueled, the helicopters were to load the assault team and fly on towards Teheran, dropping off the men at a landing-zone and then proceeding to their helicopter hide some 15 miles (24km) to the north. The assault group was to be met by two agents at the landing zone and guided by them to a remote wadi, some 5 miles (8km) away. Helicopters and men would then rest in their hides through the day.

Phase IIA: The rescue

After last light one agent would take the 12 drivers/translators to collect six Mercedes trucks, while the other agent would take Colonel Beckwith on a route reconnaissance. At 2030 hours the complete unit would embus at the hide and drive to Teheran, the actual rescue operation starting between 2300 and 2400 hours. Having disposed of the guards and released the hostages, it was planned to call in the helicopters, either to the embassy compound if an LZ could be cleared (the "students" had erected poles to prevent a surprise landing) or, if this was impracticable, to a nearby football stadium. Once all the hostages were clear the assault party would be taken out by helicopter, the White Element (see table) being the last out.

Phase II: Rescue at the Foreign Ministry

Concurrently with Phase IIA the 13-man special team would assault the Foreign Ministry, rescue the hostages there, and take them to an adjacent park where they would all be picked up by a helicopter.

Phase III: Extraction

While the action was taking place in Teheran, a Ranger contingent would seize Manzarieh airfield, some 35 miles (56km) to the south, and several C-141 turbojet transports would fly in. Once everyone had been evacuated from Teheran to Manzarieh they would be flown out in the C-141s, the Rangers leaving last. All surviving helicopters would be abandoned at Manzarieh.

Contingency plans

Various contingencies were foreseen and plans made accordingly; for example, in the event that not enough helicopters were available to lift everyone out of Teheran in one lift. One critically important condition had been agreed throughout the planning, name-

*Note: this entry was prepared by the Editor.

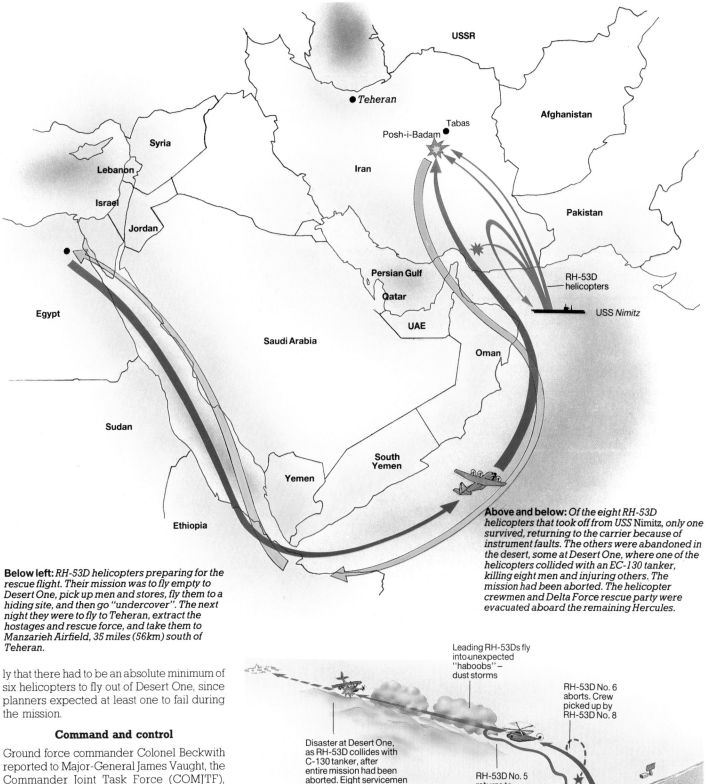

Below left: *RH-53D helicopters preparing for the rescue flight. Their mission was to fly empty to Desert One, pick up men and stores, fly them to a hiding site, and then go "undercover". The next night they were to fly to Teheran, extract the hostages and rescue force, and take them to Manzarieh Airfield, 35 miles (56km) south of Teheran.*

Above and below: *Of the eight RH-53D helicopters that took off from USS* Nimitz, *only one survived, returning to the carrier because of instrument faults. The others were abandoned in the desert, some at Desert One, where one of the helicopters collided with an EC-130 tanker, killing eight men and injuring others. The mission had been aborted. The helicopter crewmen and Delta Force rescue party were evacuated aboard the remaining Hercules.*

Leading RH-53Ds fly into unexpected "haboobs" – dust storms

RH-53D No. 6 aborts. Crew picked up by RH-53D No. 8

Disaster at Desert One, as RH-53D collides with C-130 tanker, after entire mission had been aborted. Eight servicemen are killed. Remaining servicemen, including Delta Force, flown to Masirah airfield, Oman.

RH-53D No. 5 returns to Nimitz, aborting mission

ly that there had to be an absolute minimum of six helicopters to fly out of Desert One, since planners expected at least one to fail during the mission.

Command and control

Ground force commander Colonel Beckwith reported to Major-General James Vaught, the Commander Joint Task Force (COMJTF), who was at Wadi Kena airfield in Egypt; they were linked by portable satellite systems. General Vaught had a similar link back to Washington, DC, where General David Jones, then Chairman of the Joint Chiefs of Staff, was in session with President Jimmy Carter throughout the critical hours of the operation. In a last-minute change of plans, Air Force Colonel James Kyle was appointed commander at Desert One.

Execution

The C-141 airlift of the ground party went according to plan, as did the C-130 flights to Desert One. The first aircraft, carrying Colonels Beckwith and Kyle, Blue Element and the Road Watch Team, landed safely and the Road Watch Team deployed, immedi-

ately having to stop a bus containing 45 people who were detained under guard.

Minutes later two more vehicles appeared from the south; the first, a petrol tanker, was hit by an anti-tank rocket and burst into flames, but the driver escaped in the second vehicle which drove off at high speed. The first C-130 then took off, leaving those on the ground briefly on their own. The second C-130 then came in and unloaded and, after the remaining four C-130s had landed, took off

again for Masirah. The four C-130s and the ground party then waited for the helicopters – and waited . . .

The eight helicopters were, quite literally, the key to the operation. They had taken off from USS Nimitz) some 50 miles off the Iranian coast) at 1905 hours (local), as scheduled, and headed north for Desert One. At about 2145 hours helicopter No. 6 indicated an impending catastrophic blade failure, one of the two really critical problems requiring an abort.

The crew landed, confirmed the problem, removed sensitive documents and were then picked up by helicopter No. 8 which then followed the others some minutes behind.

About one hour later the leading RH-53Ds ran into a very severe and totally unexpected dust storm; all emerged from this, flew on for an hour and then encountered a second and even worse dust storm. (What they encountered was a *haboob*, a meteorological phenomenon in which gusts generated by thunderstorms kick up masses of dust many miles away. In Iran, where the dust is extremely fine, a *haboob* can linger in the air for hours.)

The helicopter force commander – Major Seiffert, USMC – had earlier lost his inertial navigation system and, entirely blinded, flew back out of the first dust storm and landed, accompanied by helicopter No. 2. Major Seiffert had a secure radio link to COMJTF, who told him that the weather at Desert One was clear; consequently, after some 20 minutes on the ground both aircraft took off again and followed the others to Desert One.

Meanwhile, helicopter No. 5 suffered several problems, including the loss of its gyro, a burnout of its tactical navigation system, and a radar receiver failure. With no artificial horizon or heading, and with mountains ahead, he was compelled to abort, and barely made it back to the *Nimitz*, thus leaving six helicopters to continue the mission.

The first helicopter (No. 3) cleared the dust storm some 30nm (56km) from Desert One and, using the burning Iranian petrol tanker as a beacon, landed some 50 minutes late. The remaining aircraft straggled in over the next half-an-hour, all coming from different directions (except Nos. 1 and 2, which were together). The crews were shaken by their experience, but the helicopters were quickly moved to their tanker C-130s, refueling

began, and the assault party started to board their designated aircraft.

Colonel Beckwith was fretting on the ground, 90 minutes behind schedule, when he was informed that helicopter No. 2 had had a partial hydraulic failure during the flight; the pilot had continued on to Desert One in the hope of effecting repairs, but these proved impossible. The decision to call the whole thing off was quickly reached. There was no problem in aborting at this stage, even though the rescue team had never practised an abort order. The only minor complication was that helicopter No. 4, which had been on the ground longest, needed to top up with fuel before setting off to the *Nimitz*. Only one C-130 had enough fuel left and to clear a space for No. 4 helicopter No. 3 took off and banked to the left, but, because of the height (5,000ft/1,525m) and its weight (42,000lb/19,050kg), it could not maintain the hover and banked right into the C-130.

The effect was instantaneous and disastrous: both aircraft exploded, debris flew around and ammunition began to cook off. Five USAF aircrewmen in the C-130 and three Marines in the RH-53D died, but 64 Delta men inside the C-130 escaped quickly from the aircraft and rescued the loadmaster. The decision was then made to abandon the remaining helicopters and the whole party returned to Masirah in the three C-130s.

In hindsight, it can always be said mission planners should have done more, that 10 helicopters should have been sent instead of eight, that much more should have been known about *haboobs*, and so on. But the Chief of Naval Operations, Adm. Thomas Hayward, summed it up rather cogently in an interview shortly after the attempted rescue. "There had to be some mistakes made," he conceded. But, in the end, the mission was affected at least as much by an incredible string of misfortunes.

Above and right: *RH-53D Sea Stallion helicopters. They are being readied for operation Eagle Claw in the hangar and above the deck of the aircraft carrier USS* Nimitz. *The helicopters have good range and payload and were the key to the success of the mission, as well as the ultimate cause of its failure. Lack of proper preparation, non-availability of spares – and the apparent hopelessness of the mission – have all been blamed for this failure.*

Below: *C-130 aircraft of the type used during operation Eagle Claw in the attempt to rescue American hostages held in Teheran. One of the aircraft's missions was to fly a Ranger company into Manzerieh, secure the airfield and to help the rescuers and hostages to be extracted.*

Below right: *Five members of the USAF first Special Operations Wing and three Marines were killed in the Desert One collision during operation Eagle Claw. Memorial services were held at Hurlburt Field, Florida. At least five other US servicemen were injured and flown back to Kelly Air Force Base, Texas.*

Below left: *Iranians inspect abandoned equipment left by US forces near a deserted air force base some 185 miles (300km) north of Teheran. The mission was ultimately cancelled when several of the necessary eight RH-53D helicopters developed a number of problems.*

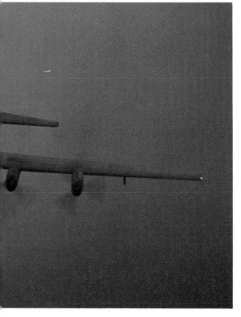

THE IRANIAN EMBASSY SIEGE

THE SIEGE of the Iranian Embassy in London in April-May 1980 caught the imagination of the world and brought the SAS into the limelight because the denouement took place before the gathered press photographers and TV. The eerie, black-clad figures, their efficiency and the success and sheer drama of the event established the SAS a public reputation and created an expectation of success which will endure for many years.

The Iranian Embassy at No. 16 Princes Gate, London, opposite Hyde Park, was taken over at 1130 hours Wednesday April 30 by six terrorists armed with three 9mm automatic pistols, one 0.38in revolver, two 9mm submachine guns and a number of Chinese-made hand grenades. There were six men directly involved: Oan, the leader (27 years old), and five others, all in their early twenties. They were all from Arabistan, an area of Iran some 400 miles (643km) from Teheran, which had long resisted the rule of the Aryan northerners. Most had supported Ayatollah Khomeini's takeover from the Shah, only to find him as ruthless a suppressor of minorities as his predecessor. The terrorists represented a group entitled the Democratic Revolutionary Movement for the Liberation of Arabistan (DRMLA), a Marxist-Leninist group based in Libya, whose cause was regional autonomy (not independence) for Arabistan.

The occupants of the embassy at the time of the takeover numbered 29: four British and 22 Iranian men and women, three of whom escaped during the early minutes. The terrorists' demands were initially that 91 prisoners in Arabistan be released by the Iranian authorities. The deadline was set for 1200 hours Thursday May 1, and during that night the terrorists had the first of many contacts with the London police and the media.

One sick Iranian woman was released late on Wednesday night and a sick Englishman the following morning. The first deadline was postponed when the police transmitted a message from the terrorists to the press, and a second deadline (1400 hours) passed without a move from either side.

By Friday morning there had been numerous contacts between the terrorists and the police, some direct and some through intermediaries, but by now specific threats were being made against the lives of the hostages. Negotiations continued throughout Saturday and a major advance was achieved when the terrorists agreed to release two hostages in return for a broadcast on the radio of a statement of their aims. One hostage was released in the early evening and after the statement had been broadcast word for word another was released. The atmosphere in the embassy became almost euphoric, helped by a good meal sent in by the police.

Above: *Witnessed on television screens throughout the world, the siege at the Iranian Embassy in London ended abruptly in explosions, flames and gunfire on 5 May, 1980, when British Special Air Service commandos stormed the building. In a rescue raid that lasted just a few minutes, five of the six terrorists were killed, and all hostages survived.*

Throughout Sunday the British government discussed the situation with various Arab ambassadors, but no agreement could be reached on a possible role for them in reaching a resolution to the crisis. In the embassy the major event in an anti-climatic day was the release of an Iranian hostage who had become ill. On Monday the terrorists were noticeably more nervous and a shouted discussion between two British hostages and the police at noon did little to ease the tension. At about 1330, Oan's patience apparently snapped and he shot Abbas Lavasani, one of the Embassy staff, in the course of a telephone discussion with the police. This was the turning point.

Any doubts about whether anyone had actually been killed were resolved just after 1900 when the dead body was pushed through the front door of the Embassy.

SAS soldiers had visited the scene on the first day of the siege, and thereafter they stood by in an Army barracks some two miles away. The police had obviously tried their best to identify just where the hostages and their captors were and what they were all

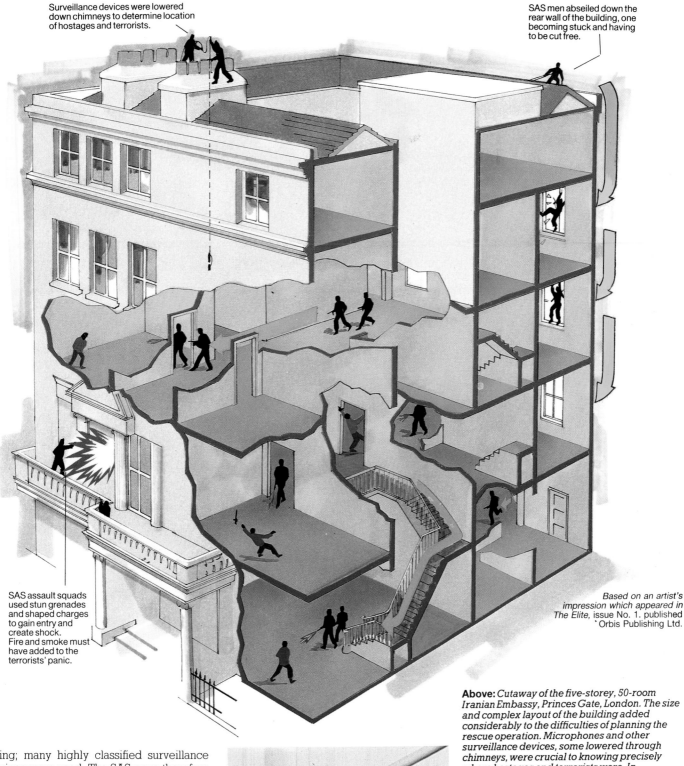

Surveillance devices were lowered down chimneys to determine location of hostages and terrorists.

SAS men abseiled down the rear wall of the building, one becoming stuck and having to be cut free.

SAS assault squads used stun grenades and shaped charges to gain entry and create shock. Fire and smoke must have added to the terrorists' panic.

Based on an artist's impression which appeared in The Elite, issue No. 1. published Orbis Publishing Ltd.

Above: *Cutaway of the five-storey, 50-room Iranian Embassy, Princes Gate, London. The size and complex layout of the building added considerably to the difficulties of planning the rescue operation. Microphones and other surveillance devices, some lowered through chimneys, were crucial to knowing precisely where hostages and terrorists were. In synchronized assaults at front and back, the SAS men scaled down the outside walls and over balconies from adjoining buildings, using stun grenades and other explosives for maximum shock, and ran from room to room firing with lethal accuracy at the terrorists.*

doing; many highly classified surveillance devices were used. The SAS were therefore as ready as it was possible to be in the circumstances when, in accordance with British legal practice, the police formally asked the military to deal with the situation.

The rescue

The plan was to use just 12 men in three teams of the customary four-man SAS groups; two teams were to take the rear, descending by rope from the roof, one team to reach the ground and the second the first-floor balcony. Both would then break in using either frame-charges or brute force. Team three was to be at the front, crossing from a balcony at No. 15 Princes Gate to No. 16. Once inside all three teams were to rush to reach the hostages before they could be harmed.

Left: *Black-clad SAS man climbs over the balcony at the front of the embassy, armed with H&K MP5 submachine gun. His progress would have been covered by another squad at street level, and the terrorists themselves would have seen him had they been watching television at the time!*

Everything that could be done to heighten the impact of the attack was done. The 12 SAS men were dressed from head to foot in black, even including rubber anti-gas respirators, and looked extremely menacing. They would gain entrance using 4ft×2ft (1.2×0.6m) frame charges, followed by stun grenades ("flash-bangs"). Teargas would also be used. The combination of explosions, noise, smoke, speed of action and the appearance of the men was intended to strike confusion and dread into the minds of the terrorists – and it succeeded brilliantly.

The SAS men had, naturally, pored over the plans of the 50-room building in minute detail and had also spent many hours studying the photographs of the hostages. But, in the end – as every soldier knows – all the training and planning have to be translated into action.

At 1926 hours precisely the men of the rear attack force stepped over the edge of the roof and abseiled down. The first two went down each rope successfully, but one of the third pair became stuck, a hazard known to abseilers everywhere. In the front, SAS men appeared on the balcony of No. 15 and climbed over to the embassy, giving the world's press and the public an image which will last for years.

Above: *Part of the SAS frontal assault force on the balcony of the embassy building. The grave danger these commandos, and the hostages, were in was prime-time TV viewing for millions. The rescue occurred on May Day holiday, and the "armchair drama" was more compulsive viewing than any adventure film could have been. But it was no vacation for those actively engaged. As soon as the assault began, terrorists started shooting hostages, wounding some, but not killing any. The only surviving terrorist hid among the hostages, but was recognized and taken into custody.*

Left: *Two SAS servicemen, in civilian clothes but with balaclava helmets, give cover from outside the wall of the embassy. They are aiming 9mm high-power Browning pistols, but have a rifle and tear gas launcher ready at their feet.*

Right: *The SAS had long been legendary, but photos like this gave the service a totally new public image. The all-black outfit, including serviceable "overalls" undoubtedly over bullet-proof vests, black hoods with standard respirator, special-grip boots and favored H&K MP5 submachine gun, is a shock to the enemy. And terrorists also got a message from the SAS performance – these crack troops shoot to kill.*

Above and right: *SAS assault teams moments before blasting into the front windows of the embassy. No photos have been publicly released of the action inside the building. While this incident enhanced their worldwide image, the SAS shun publicity, preferring to carry out operations clandestinely both to maintain high chances of success through surprise, and also to safeguard the identities of individual servicemen.*

Simultaneously, police spoke to the terrorists on the telephone and distracted their attention at the critical moment the SAS burst in. Stun grenades exploded, lights went out and all was noise and apparent confusion. Some parts of the embassy caught fire and the SAS man hanging on the rope at the rear was cut free and dropped onto a balcony – a risk preferable to that of being roasted alive.

The SAS men swept through the embassy. Two terrorists were quickly shot and killed. One started shooting the hostages in an upstairs room, but stopped after causing a few wounds. Within minutes five of the six gunmen were dead, with the sixth sheltering among the newly freed hostages. All survivors were rushed downstairs into the garden, where the remaining terrorist was identified and arrested.

The entire operation took eleven minutes from start to finish. While the SAS is the last organization in the world to seek out publicity, its well-heralded assault had at least two effects: first, it reinforced the message to potential terrorists that their activities could be dealt with in a severe, if effective, manner; and, secondly, it gave the British public a healthy shot of national pride.

THE DOZIER RESCUE

THE CAUSE and mystique of Italy's Red Brigades terrorists received a crushing blow with the successful rescue of US Brigadier General James L Dozier in January 1982. The lightning-like (90 seconds) rescue effort was conducted by one of Italy's elite anti-terrorist units – the *Nucleo Operativo Centrale di Sicurezza* also known as "Leatherheads" because of the leather helmets they wear.

Dozier, highest-ranking US military officer at NATO's Southern Command in Verona, had been kidnapped from his apartment on December 17, 1981, by members of the Red Brigades. His kidnappers had carried him off in a steamer trunk, driving him from Verona to Padua, a university town 48 miles (77km) to the east. He was then trundled up to a second floor apartment in a run-down residential area of the town. The general was manacled to a camp bed under a blue pup tent – where he was to spend most of the next 42 days – a measure designed to prevent him from ever describing his surroundings.

Dozier's captors announced that he had been taken to a "people's prison" and that he would be submitted to "proletarian justice". In a communique, Dozier, a decorated veteran with a Silver Star, Bronze Star and Purple Heart for service with the 11th Armored Cavalry Regiment in Vietnam, was accused of service as "an assassin and hero of the American massacres in Vietnam". The captors later released a five-page transcript of Dozier's "interrogation", based mostly on

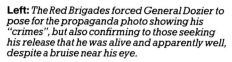

Left: *The Red Brigades forced General Dozier to pose for the propaganda photo showing his "crimes", but also confirming to those seeking his release that he was alive and apparently well, despite a bruise near his eye.*

Below: *In his more familiar trim uniform, General Dozier gives evidence in Verona at the trial of his Red Brigades captors.*

Above: *Tired and unshaven, but doubtless relieved, General Dozier is escorted to safety after his release from 42 days of captivity in the hands of the Red Brigades in a second-floor apartment at No. 2 Via Pindemonte, in a run-down area of Padua. His captives called it a "people's prison", rented by Emanuela Fascella, 20-year-old history student daughter of a local physician. She was arrested with other Red Brigadists.*

personal records taken from his apartment during the kidnapping.

The scope of the search launched for Dozier exceeded even that in 1978 for former Italian Prime Minister Aldo Moro, who was executed by the Red Brigades after 54 days of captivity. Some 6,000 Italian lawmen were deployed, supported by American and European antiterrorist experts. Dozens of terrorist suspects were uncovered, weapons ranging from handguns to surface-to-air missiles seized, and thousands of Brigades

strategy papers and documents confiscated.

In central Rome the search netted two guerrillas who were apparently on the verge of another major kidnapping. Police stormed three Red Brigades headquarters in the Eternal City, capturing a key theorist. Five suspected terrorists were arrested north of the city.

Each step unraveled more leads concerning Dozier's whereabouts. Tip-offs were thoroughly investigated, no matter how trivial they seemed at first blush. And, finally, the search narrowed to an apartment building on Via Pindemonte, a residential street in Padua.

Detectives pinned down the location about 12 hours before the leatherhead commandos launched their raid. An assault at night was ruled out for fear that Dozier wouldn't be recognized in the dark and could become the victim of a deadly crossfire.

Execution of the rescue

The activity leading up to the assault, reasoned the commandos, might alert the Brigades to the efforts, so the squad timed its mission for execution during the city's midday bustle. At dawn, about 80 plainclothes officers dressed as scruffy young men began to filter into Via Pindemonte. Around 1130 hours, as a construction crew with a bulldozer provided a noisy cover, they quickly cleared the area to prevent pedestrians from being hurt should a shootout follow.

As the area was being cleared, a small green removals van carrying the rescue squad pulled up to the apartment building. Ten masked commandos dressed in black

Above: *The general, manacled to his bed in the tent, was about to be shot by a terrorist when a Leatherhead commando rifle-butted the brigadist to the ground. Dozier's life had been under threat before, but never had death been so close . . .*

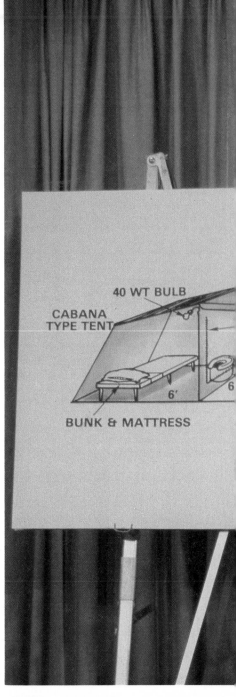

40 WT BULB

CABANA TYPE TENT

6' 6

BUNK & MATTRESS

and cradling M12s (lightweight short-barreled burp guns) leapt out. One blocked the exit from a supermarket on the apartment building's ground floor; the others raced to the second floor toward the dingy apartment where the Red Brigades were located.

The first of five Brigades members was surprised in the hall and dispatched with a karate chop to the forehead. Yet another Brigades member immediately rushed to the room where Dozier was located and leveled a pistol at him. But before he could shoot, an Italian commando took him to the floor with a swing of his rifle butt. The remaining three *brigatisti.* surrendered without resistance, with not a shot having been fired during the entire operation. Dozier was rescued unhurt on January 28, 1982, some 42 days after he had been snatched from his apartment.

Assessment

The rescue effort established Italy's leatherheads as an anti-terrorist force to be reckoned with, and revealed valuable information about the operations and tactics of the Red Brigades. Not since 1975 had a Red Brigades kidnap victim been rescued alive.

An American official commented: "It was a textbook operation. They cracked the (Red Brigades) column, the people talked, and they followed up on every single lead. They did it right and it worked."

The momentum of the search itself continued after Dozier's release. Italian police continued to arrest terrorist suspects around Verona and uncovered numerous safe houses between that city and Venice.

Momentum of another kind was provided by General Dozier himself. According to an Italian police official, he provided highly valuable information on the tactics and operations of the Red Brigades, information of the type that could very well prove vital in further efforts to combat terrorist groups.

Certainly, the Red Brigades were "wounded" by the Dozier rescue and the general rounding-up of actual *brigatisti* and their supporters. At the time of the kidnapping, it was estimated that there were 400 active members and some 10,000 active above-ground

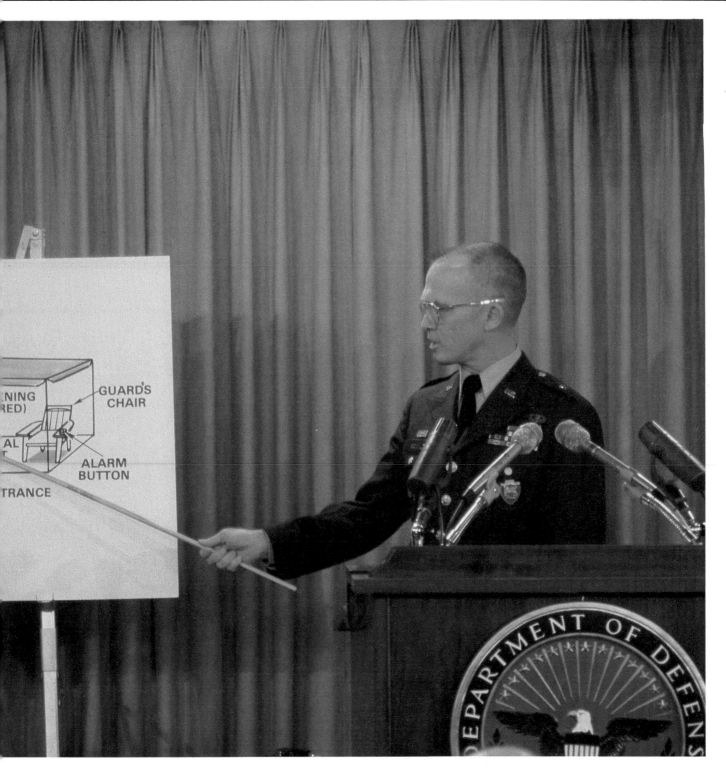

GUARD'S
CHAIR

NING
RED)

AL

ALARM
BUTTON

TRANCE

Above: *General Dozier at his famous news conference describes the tent in which he was kept captive for 42 days. After the first few days his guards stopped wearing hoods or blindfolding him to conceal their identities. Dozier interpreted this as a sign that he had been sentenced to die.*

Left, far left: *The search for General Dozier was characterized by its intensity and thoroughness, even outstripping the efforts to find Aldo Moro, former Italian Premier. It was a massive, coordinated operation conducted by police (seen here checking vehicles at highway road blocks), international and internal intelligence services, and elite commando units.*

supporters. They were well-funded from the proceeds of bank robberies and other criminal acts, besides apparent support from outside Italy.

The Red Brigades had suffered many setbacks before, partly as a result of the Italian Government offering light sentences to members who were prepared to "squeal". In 1978, when Aldo Moro, former premier was abducted and murdered, there had been almost 2,400 acts of political violence. By 1980 the number of terrorist incidents had almost halved, and arrests of suspected terrorists reached more than 1,000.

The Italian security forces, including *testi di cuoi*, or Leatherheads, had vastly improved their organization, training and weaponry by the time of the Dozier kidnapping and rescue. The Italian authorities had established the *Nucleo Operativo Centrale di*

Sicurezza (NOCS) elite Leatherheads commando squad, apparently using as a model the British SAS and West German GSG 9. In their training much emphasis is placed on knowing the enemy and their tactics, expertise in sophisticated surveillance equipment and methods, and swift, silent assault missions. There is rivalry within the Italian security forces, however, with some police feeling slighted at the introduction of a new commando squad. If this resentment results in an unwillingness to cooperate fully, such as by less than full exchange of intelligence, any future rescue or other counter-terrorist operation could be hampered.

And there is fear that a new breed of Red Brigades has taken over from the old, so the authorities are not complacent; they are determined to stamp out acts of terrorism with equal ruthlessness.

WIRELESS RIDGE

THE BATTALION attack by the British 2nd Battalion, The Parachute Regiment (2 Para), on Wireless Ridge, on June 13-14 during the Falklands War in 1982, is an excellent example of an action by a highly trained, fit and experienced infantry unit. This action is of particular interest because 2 Para were the only battalion in the Falklands War to carry out two battalion attacks, and thus the only one to be able to put into practice the lessons learned, in their case at high cost, at Goose Green on May 28.

On June 11, 2 Para was moved by helicopter from Fitzroy on the south coast to a lying-up position west of Mount Kent. At 2300 hours the battalion set off on foot to an assembly area on a hill to the North of Mount Kent, ready to support either 3 Para in their attack on Mount Longdon or 45 Commando Royal Marines, whose mission was to take the position known as Two Sisters. Both attacks were successful, leaving 3 Para, 45 Commando and 42 Commando firmly established.

On June 12, 2 Para moved forward some 9 miles (15km), skirting Mount Longdon on its north-western side, to an assembly area in the lee of a steep escarpment which offered some cover from the sporadic artillery shelling. Orders were received in mid-afternoon for an attack on Wireless Ridge that night, but this was later postponed to the following night.

On June 13 Argentinian Skyhawk attack aircraft flew in low from the West. Intense fire from the ground prevented this attack from being pressed home, but a number of moves in preparation for the forthcoming British battalion action were delayed, especially the registration of targets by the artillery and mortars.

At Goose Green 2 Para had been very short of fire support. In this battle, however, they were to have two batteries of 105mm light guns in direct support, the mortars of both 2 and 3 Para, naval gunfire support from ships within range, as well as the battalion's own machine gun and MILAN anti-tank missile platoons. Last, but by no means least, a troop of two Scimitar (1×30mm cannon) and two Scorpion (1×76mm gun) light tanks of The Blues and Royals were an integral part of 2 Para's battle plan.

The battalion moved out at last light (2030 hours local). As they moved to the forming-up places (where the troops shake out into battle formations), the sort of report a commanding officer dreads was received: Intelligence had just discovered a minefield in front of A and B Companies' objective. At this stage, however, there was no alternative but to go ahead.

The artillery supporting fire started at 0015 hours on June 14 and D Company crossed the start-line at 0045 hours. D Company reached its first objective with little trouble, finding that the enemy had withdrawn, leaving a few dead in their slit trenches. While D Company reorganized, enemy 155mm airburst fire began to fall on their position. Meanwhile, A and B Companies began their advance, B Company through the minefield.

Some sporadic fire came from a few trenches, but was quickly silenced, and 17 Argentine prisoners were taken and a number killed in this phase of the battle – the remainder fled. Several radios (still switched on), telephones and a mass of cable suggested that the position had included a battalion headquarters, As A and B Companies started to dig in, accurate and fairly intense enemy artillery bombardment

Left: *During the Falklands campaign, much of the fighting revolved around taking the high ground – obviously successfully here by British Paras – which was often fiercely defended by Argentinian troops.*

Above and right: *Faces of war in the Falklands as (above) troopers rest during a lull in the fighting, and (right) men of 3 Para duck as a shell comes in. The wounded men they were tending died as this picture was taken.*

Below: *A support company being briefed before moving out on the assault on Wireless Ridge. A model is being used to explain the mission plan.*

began, which was to continue for some nine hours.

Following the success of A and B Companies, D Company crossed its second start line at the West end of the main ridge, while the light tanks and the machine guns moved to a flank to give covering fire. The ridge itself was a long spire broken in the middle, with each section some 900 yards (300m) in length. The first feature was taken unopposed and there was then a short delay while the British artillery readjusted to its targets for the next phase. During this time the second feature was kept under heavy fire by the light tanks, the machine guns and the MILAN missile being used in a direct-fire artillery role!

Just as the attack was about to start, the commanding officer received a new piece of intelligence, that instead of one enemy company at the other end of the ridge there were two! This was hardly likely to impress the Paras who by this stage of the campaign had established a considerable moral ascendency over the Argentines, but in the early minutes of this final phase of the battle D Company received some casualties as the enemy fought back with unexpected vigor, withdrawing one bunker at a time. As the Paras poured onto the position, however, the enemy suddenly broke and ran, being continuously harassed off the position by the machine guns of the British Scorpions and Scimitars, and chased by the exhilarated Paras.

As D Company began to reorganize they, too, came under artillery fire, as well as remarkably effective small arms fire from Tumbledown Mountain and Mount William to the South, which had not yet been captured by 5 Infantry Brigade. The enemy could be heard trying to regroup in the darkness below the ridge, and to the south in the area of Moody Brook.

At daybreak a rather brave, but somewhat pathetic enemy counterattack developed from the area of Moody Brook, which seems to have been some sort of final gesture. It petered out under a hail of artillery, small arms and machine gun fire.

This seems to have been the signal to many Argentines that the game was up, and shortly afterwards ever-increasing numbers of disheartened and disillusioned Argentine soldiers were observed streaming off Mount William, Tumbledown and Sapper Hill to seek short-lived refuge in Port Stanley.

A and B Companies of 2 Para were now brought forward onto Wireless Ridge, and the battalion's night attack was successfully concluded. The paras had lost three dead and 11 wounded. Lack of time and opportunity precluded counting the Argentine casualties, but it has been estimated that, of an original strength of some 500, up to 100 may have been killed, 17 were captured, and the remainder fled.

The taking of Wireless Ridge illustrates the standards achieved by a crack unit. In this night battle, it defeated a force of equal strength, which was well prepared and dug in and occupied a dominant feature. No. 2 Para had learned the lessons of Goose Green well. They had also given the lie to the allegation that parachute units lack "staying power". It is, perhaps, unfortunate that the battle of Goose Green, deservedly famous, has overshadowed this later minor classic at Wireless Ridge.

Below: *It took British forces 10 hours to secure Wireless Ridge, forcing the collapse of the complete Argentinian Army. The value of fire support had been learned at Goose Green. The attack on Wireless Ridge was preceded by extensive bombardment to soften up defenders.*

Above: *Blindfolded by his tunic, a captured Argentinian officer is led away for interrogation. The men of Britain's Parachute Regiment proved too tough and well-organized for the Argentinians, and immensely courageous against a numerically superior foe.*

Below: *An Argentinian conscript, still wearing the British jersey he looted from the Moody Brook barracks after the Argentinian invasion, is led away by a trooper of 3 Para. When Wireless Ridge had been taken, the Paras replaced their helmets with the familiar red berets.*

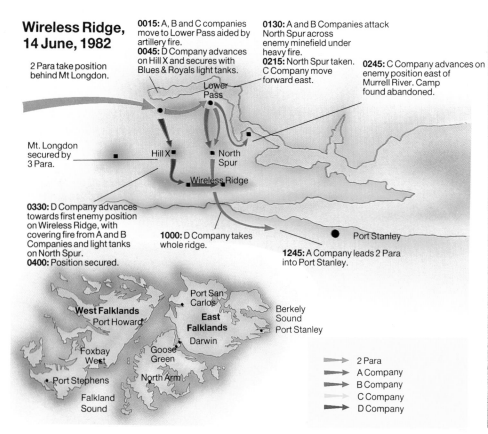

Wireless Ridge, 14 June, 1982

2 Para take position behind Mt Longdon.

0015: A, B and C companies move to Lower Pass aided by artillery fire.
0045: D Company advances on Hill X and secures with Blues & Royals light tanks.

0130: A and B Companies attack North Spur across enemy minefield under heavy fire.
0215: North Spur taken. C Company move forward east.

0245: C Company advances on enemy position east of Murrell River. Camp found abandoned.

Lower Pass

Mt. Longdon secured by 3 Para.

Hill X

North Spur

Wireless Ridge

0330: D Company advances towards first enemy position on Wireless Ridge, with covering fire from A and B Companies and light tanks on North Spur.
0400: Position secured.

1000: D Company takes whole ridge.

Port Stanley

1245: A Company leads 2 Para into Port Stanley.

Port San Carlos

West Falklands
Port Howard

East Falklands
Darwin

Berkely Sound
Port Stanley

Foxbay West

Goose Green

Port Stephens

North Arm

Falkland Sound

➡ 2 Para
➡ A Company
➡ B Company
➡ C Company
➡ D Company

RESCUE IN GRENADA

FOLLOWING the end of the Vietnam War, American forces tried to keep a low profile on the international scene. Two rescue operations were attempted in efforts to secure the release of the crew of the *Mayaguez* and the Iranian embassy hostages. US troops also took part in various peace-keeping forces such as those in the Sinai and in Beirut. However, major use of force was eschewed for both international and domestic reasons.

But in October 1983 President Ronald Reagan, at the request of the six-member Organization of Eastern Caribbean States, sent troops to the island of Grenada "to restore peace, order and respect for human rights; to evacuate those who wish to leave; and to help the Grenadians re-establish governmental institutions". On October 19, Grenada's Prime Minister. Maurice Bishop and several Cabinet members and labor leaders had been murdered by former military associates. A 16-man Revolutionary Military Council, headed by Army Chief General Hudson Austin and Deputy Prime Minister Bernard Coard, took power. The council imposed a 24-hour curfew, warning that violators would be shot on sight, and closed the Port Salines airfield.

US Intelligence reported Soviet/Cuban backing for the revolutionary regime, with Cubans establishing new fortifications, arms caches and military communications on the island. President Reagan viewed Grenada as "a Soviet-Cuban colony being readied as a major military bastion to export and undermine democracy". Of particular concern was the position of some 1,000 US citizens, especially the 600-odd young Americans at the True Blue Medical School near the Port Salines airfield. The prospect of these youngsters being held hostage by the

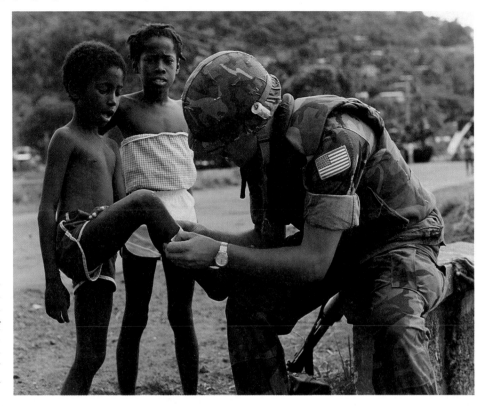

Marxist government was serious and would have provided a far worse crisis than even that of the Iranian embassy staff. For their part, the Eastern Caribbean States saw the violence and disintegration of political institutions on the island as an unprecedented threat to peace and security in the region.

Information on the resisting troops and their disposition in Grenada seems to have been fairly sparse, but the US forces had three immediate objectives within the overall mission of capturing the island and restoring

Above: *A child receives medical attention during Operation Urgent Fury, the rescue operation by US Forces on Grenada. The short campaign started on 25 October, 1983, and was completed on 2 November.*

Below: *American medical students head toward homeward-bound aircraft at Point Salines. The US/multi-national operation rescued 622 American and 87 foreign students in Grenada.*

a democratic government. These three tasks were the freeing of the 600 medical students, the release of the governor (Sir Paul Scoones) and the defeat of the Cuban troops on the island.

US Navy SEALS were responsible for capturing the governor's residence, and Marines for the Pearls Airport on the island's east coast. The crucial task was, however, the taking of Port Salines airfield, which was being constructed and guarded by Cubans. This task was given to the Rangers.

Execution

The assault by the 24th Marine Amphibious Unit on Pearls Airport began at 0500 hours (local) on October 25, while H-hour for the Rangers was 0536. This was the first major combat operation for the two participating Ranger units – the Fort Stewart, Georgia-based 1st Ranger Battalion, and the Fort Lewis, Washington-based 2nd. The Rangers left the staging airfield on Barbados in the early hours aboard MC-130E Hercules aircraft of 8th Special Operations Squadron, 1st Special Operations Wing, USAF, based at Hurlburt Field in Florida. (The lead planes carried members of the 1st Battalion, with the 2nd following closely behind.) These aircraft were accompanied by AC-130 Hercules gunships (the famous "Spectres" of the Vietnam War) of 16th Special Operations Squadron.

As they came in over Port Salines, searchlights were suddenly switched on, which quickly found the lumbering C-130s and enabled the anti-aircraft guns to open up on the aircraft and descending parachutists. The AC-130s were quickly called into action and silenced most of the Cuban guns. Among the lead elements in the assault was a 12-man team from the 317th Tactical Airlift Wing responsible for combat control of the drop, and these were quickly inside the air traffic control building.

On the ground, the Rangers, told to expect some 500 Cubans (350 "workers" and a "small" military advisory team) found themselves under attack from some 600 well armed professional soldiers. The Cubans were armed with mortars and machine guns, and had at least six armored personnel carriers. A brisk battle developed in which the Rangers quickly gained the upper hand, and by 0700 they were in complete control. The runway was cleared of obstacles (boulders, vehicles, pipes) and at 0715 the first C-130 of the second wave was able to land with reinforcements.

The Rangers then moved out, heading for the medical campus; brushing aside snipers and scattered resistance, they reached their objective by 0830 hours and were greeted by some very relieved students. The campus was secured by 0850, although the other medical school at Grand Anse was not liberated until the following day.

Assessment

The liberation effort accomplished what it set out to do. The booty of the effort confirmed US intelligence reports that the USSR and Cuba were turning Grenada into a military base in the Western hemisphere. The long-term implications of this were that the island could eventually have become a staging area for the subversion of nearby countries; it would

also have considerable value as a transit point for troops and supplies moving from Cuba to Africa and from Europe and Libya to Central America.

Captured documents indicated that the USSR and North Korea, as well as Cuba, had made secret treaties with the Grenada Revolutionary Military Council, and had agreed to provide the leadership with more than $37.8 million in artillery, anti-aircraft weapons, armored personnel carriers, small arms, and

ammunition. The Soviet Union had tried hard to keep these arrangements secret. In fact, it wasn't until 18 months after the arms shipments began that they established diplomatic ties with Grenada.

The convincing list of documents found in the aftermath of Grenada included a roster of Grenada's militia; a summary of Political Bureau meetings; a top-secret report from a Grenadian double agent who attempted to infiltrate the CIA operation in Barbados;

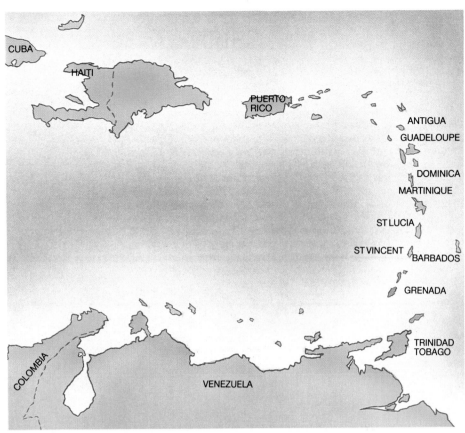

Above: *After the battle, an MC-130E stands ready for cargo loading at Point Salines airfield. MC-130Es dropped the first wave of US airborne assault troops.*

Left: *Many large caches of weapons and ammunition were discovered at locations all over Grenada. Some labelled "Cuban Economic Office" contained 7.62mm ammunition.*

Above: *Grenada is a tiny island in the Caribbean but the US was determined that it would not become another Cuba. A six-member organization of Eastern Caribbean States – with Grenada abstaining – decided on 21 October 1983, to intervene with force.*

Below: *Details of many of the operational points for operation Urgent Fury. Some 400 Marines and Rangers landed at Pearls Airport. Caligny barracks was a Cuban training camp; 550 Ranger landed at Point Salines while SEALs struck at the government house.*

Below: *A Cuban prisoner is taken into holding area for interrogation. More than 1,100 Cubans and Grenadians were captured.*

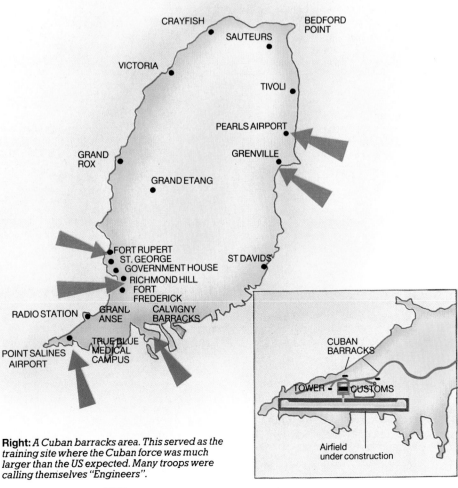

rosters and correspondence concerning the training of Grenadian troops in the USSR, Cuba and Vietnam; and a training agreement between Grenada and Nicaragua. In all, there was more than enough documentary evidence to still the voices of those who criticized the operation from a political standpoint. From yet another standpoint, the military one, it was a success – and one in which US special forces acquitted themselves well.

Right: *A Cuban barracks area. This served as the training site where the Cuban force was much larger than the US expected. Many troops were calling themselves "Engineers".*

ACHILLE LAURO INCIDENT

THE SAGA of the *Achille Lauro* began when four Palestinian guerrillas, armed with Soviet-made machine guns and brandishing hand grenades, took 80 passengers and 340 crewmembers hostage aboard the Italian cruise liner in October 1985. They threatened to kill the passengers, beginning with the Americans, then moving on to Jews and British citizens, if their demands for the release of 50 Palestinians held in Israel were not met.

What followed were 51 hours of threats and violence. Walls and ceilings were sprayed with bullets. The terrorists pulled pins from grenades and tossed them in the air. Gasoline bombs were placed in various parts of the liner. Ultimately, the grisly scenario led to the execution of Leon Klinghoffer, a 69-year-old handicapped American, murdered in his wheelchair.

As these events were unfolding, the *Achille Lauro* wandered along the north coast of Africa seeking haven. Ultimately, the cruiseliner anchored off Port Said, Egypt, and the seajackers – after negotiations with Palestinian, Italian and Egyptian officials went ashore.

Americans, predictably, were demanding that the "seajackers" be brought to justice, and Egyptian President Hosni Mubarak announced they had already left Egypt – allegedly under terms of an agreement struck before the murder of Klinghoffer was known. US intelligence, however, indicated that the four hijackers were still in Egypt and that neither that country nor the PLO had quite figured out what to do with them. This delay provided the United States with an opportunity to shape a plan to help deal with the emerging situation.

Execution

The US Navy aircraft carrier, USS *Saratoga*, was cruising off Albania and was called into action just two hours before the mission. The Italian government, later to play a key role in dealing with the terrorists, was not notified until after the mission had begun.

The plan involved calling in the *Saratoga's* aircraft to surprise the terrorists who would be flying over the Mediterranean, and forcing the Egyptian aircraft carrying the terrorists to land in Sicily.

Intelligence sources had in fact confirmed that the hijackers were still in Egypt, and that they planned to fly to Algiers aboard an Egyptair Boeing 737. Just 45 minutes after the 737 took off from Al Maza Air Base, northeast of Cairo, it was intercepted.

Awaiting it were E-2C Hawkeye radar aircraft, F-14 Tomcat fighters and EA-6B Prowler electronic warfare aircraft. At first, the F-14s trailed the 737 with no lights on and with cockpits darkened. When they prepared to intercept, they turned on their lights and surrounded the airliner.

The Egyptair pilot desperately tried to radio Cairo for instructions, but his communications had been jammed by the EA-6B aircraft. The pilot, recognizing his position, eventually agreed to follow American orders.

The formation approached Sigonella Air Base, a NATO installation on Sicily's densely populated eastern coast. However, Italian air traffic controllers refused the 737 permission to enter their airspace. It was only after the Egyptian pilot declared an in-flight emergency that clearance was finally received.

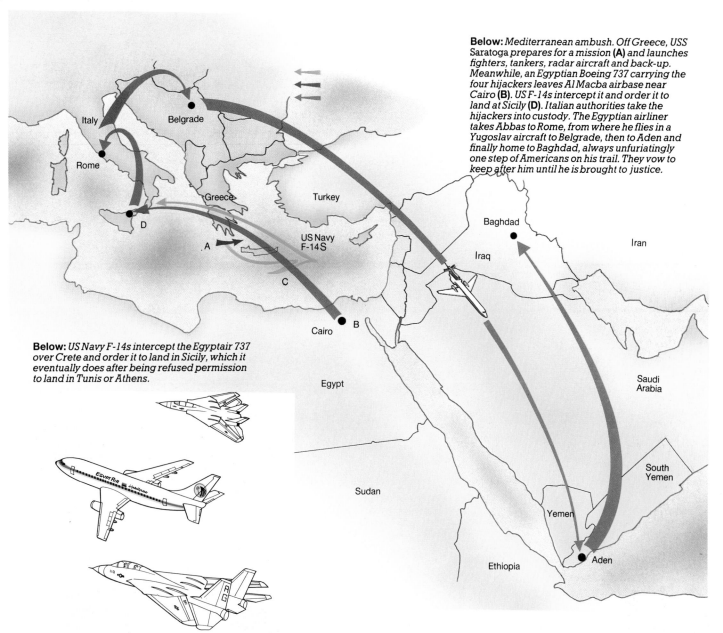

Below: *Mediterranean ambush. Off Greece, USS Saratoga prepares for a mission (A) and launches fighters, tankers, radar aircraft and back-up. Meanwhile, an Egyptian Boeing 737 carrying the four hijackers leaves Al Macba airbase near Cairo (B). US F-14s intercept it and order it to land at Sicily (D). Italian authorities take the hijackers into custody. The Egyptian airliner takes Abbas to Rome, from where he flies in a Yugoslav aircraft to Belgrade, then to Aden and finally home to Baghdad, always unfuriatingly one step of Americans on his trail. They vow to keep after him until he is brought to justice.*

Below: *US Navy F-14s intercept the Egyptair 737 over Crete and order it to land in Sicily, which it eventually does after being refused permission to land in Tunis or Athens.*

Above left: *The aging Italian cruise liner Achille Lauro was seized by a handful of Palestinian terrorists in October 1985. An American victim, Leon Kalinghoffer, was brutally murdered during the incident.*

Right: *Abdel Atif Fatyer, one of the four Palestinian terrorists who seajacked the cruise ship Achille Lauro, is detained in a cage under the close scrutiny of the Italian* carabinieri. *Italian law forbids the death penalty, but prisoners can be held for up to six years while the case is built against them.*

At left: *Achille Lauro under guard in Israel after the incident.*

One F-14 led the 737 into Sigonella while three others stayed in formation up to the traffic pattern. Following the lead F-14, the 737 taxied to an isolated corner of the base, where it was immediately surrounded by Italian *carabinieri*. Its passengers were taken into custody.

Not only were the four hijackers aboard, but also Abul Abbas, a high-ranking aide to PLO Chairman Yasir Arafat. Abbas was not only the suspected mastermind behind the *Achille Lauro* incident, but the person who was instrumental in getting the terrorists off the liner when it finally docked in Egypt. Abbas later slipped out of Italy before he could be prosecuted. Because an American citizen was killed during the "seajacking", US chagrin at the escape of Abbas was great, creating diplomatic difficulties between Italy and the United States.

Assessment

In the eyes of many observers, the operation demonstrated that high technology can indeed work well in a counterterrorist situation. It was considered a triumph of electronics and communications carried out on short notice under cover of darkness and at high speeds.

To this day, a definitive account of all the high tech that went into the operation has not been made available. However, it worked and the United States clearly demonstrated that it had the resolve to back its threats to strike back at terrorists who attacked American citizens. What really counted was that terrorists who took the law into their own hands for whatever motive were ultimately brought before the bar of justice.

SECTION FOUR
WEAPONS AND EQUIPMENT

AMMUNITION   158
PISTOLS   166
RIFLES   168
ANTI-RIOT WEAPONS   181
SHOTGUNS   186
SUBMACHINE GUNS   190
MACHINE GUNS   202
MISSILES & GRENADE LAUNCHERS   204
VEHICLES   210
AIRCRAFT   214

WEAPONS AND EQUIPMENT

ANSWERING the question of which weapons are used by elite forces in the free world and the Soviet bloc really turns on whether you're in the market for an encyclopedia or something as straight-forward as a representative sampling of those most commonly used. The latter proved to be an infinitely preferable option here, since there is an awesomely wide variety of weapons in such use. For example, many people don't know that the actual number of calibers has actually *increased* since the end of World War II – despite what might have been heard about "standardization" efforts.

There are a number of reasons for this, but let's take just one example. When US forces left Vietnam in 1975, they left behind no fewer than 1,100 aircraft, 400 naval vessels, 50,000 motor vehicles, 800,000 M16 rifles, tens of millions of rounds of ammunition, hundreds of tons of bombs, plus several thousand tons of explosives – including every bomber's friend, C-4 plastic.

Much of this material has been sold, given and otherwise distributed throughout the world and either used as received or, in some cases, modified to suit the buyer. While this example is certainly among the more dramatic available, it can be repeated many times over in different locations and with different parties.

There is much in the way of new weapons and equipment used by elite forces that simply can't be discussed. We know, for example, that the British Special Air Service has an Operational Research Wing that gives them access to the most state-of-the-art weapons, surveillance devices, communications equipment, protective clothing, transporta-tion and survival equipment. It was not until the siege at the Iranian Embassy in London, for example, that the public at large knew about their all-black fighting rig and their use of the Heckler & Koch MP5 sub-machine gun.

But, whatever weapon and gear selected, the first criterion is always, "What is needed to accomplish the particular mission?" If the job is to clear hallways, for example, the weapon is likely to be a shotgun, a P7 pistol or sub-machine gun instead of an M16. If the situation is one involving terrorists with multiple hostages in adjacent rooms, the choice might even narrow down to the ammunition.

In this case, kinetic energy rounds that "evaporate" the target might be the option. Glaser safety slugs disintegrate on impact and enhance hydrostatic shock in the body; though the casing of the round is weakened, it can pierce internal walls, thus doing possible harm to friendlies. Of course, although it will penetrate light body armor it will not penetrate heavy body armor – another consideration when planning the mission and selecting the weapons to be used.

The first demand for weapons is absolute reliability. They must work right the first time . . . and every time. The small arms of elite forces are a compromise on the following parameters: reliability, as stated; small size; fully automatic operation; the ability to be pointed quickly

Left: *US Army Ranger – identifiable by his black beret and cap badge – sights an M16A1 rifle during a training exercise. Ranger battalions, because of their mission, are the most lightly equipped infantry troops in the Army.*

Above: *Members of the French counter-terrorist unit GIGN display the awesome range of weapons they need for their mission. Trooper holds H&K MP5 SMG at left bottom; at the bottom right, another cradles an FRF-1 sniping rifle.*

Left: *The skill and equipment needed by counter-terror groups are demonstrated by this elite forces member. The black uniform, abseiling equipment and H&K MP5 submachine gun are being used to practise training for building entry.*

Below: *Training with explosives and riot equipment for the crack GIGN counter-terror unit. The assault team is ready to move into the room after an explosion has been set off by other team members.*

(balance). Essentially, special forces are looking for as small a weapon as possible which still offers reliability and pointing capability. These are the attributes of the free world's mainstay sub-machine guns, the H&K MP5 and Uzi, and the Soviet bloc's Skorpion, which have all the parameters to a certain degree, rather than some. They share the virtues of being compact and capable of firing heavy bullets at a rapid rate at short range. The silenced version of the Sterling L34 is used, but doesn't enjoy universal popularity because of its horizontal magazine, though its reliability and extreme quietness are plus factors.

Another consideration for personal weapons is minimum weight and maximum firepower – which helps explain the popularity of the M16 rifle among elite forces.

When it comes to pistols, it is almost a matter of personal taste. While some special forces personnel select their own weapons, more often compatibility with other members' weapons is the deciding factor in the issuing of weapons for the situation in hand.

Technology has had an impact all its own on the pistol, and will

Above: *Browning high-power automatic pistol, but this one's a bit special – it can be stowed back into its stock.*

Left and below: *Parker-Hale Mode 85 sniper rifle shown on bipod (left) and in the hands of camouflaged soldier. This model is highly accurate and sturdy; its stock is ambidextrous and adjustable for length. Among other options, the Model 85 can be fitted with an L1 Starlight scope*

doubtless have more. Much has been heard, for example, about the Glock 17, a 9mm pistol invented and manufactured in Austria. Made in part of hardened plastic, it is accurate, reliable and, according to some accounts, frighteningly easy for a terrorist to smuggle past airport security. Tests conducted by the Federal Aviation Administration in the United States have shown that it is as detectable as other weapons – but that hasn't lessened Libya's interest in purchasing them.

Ammunition is obviously a vital factor in the consideration of equipping elite forces. The requirements, features, uses and important (and some unusual) types of small arms ammunition are discussed in some detail in the pages which follow.

When moving into the area of heavier weapons – those you'd expect to find in your standard military arsenal – the choices narrow down considerably. Machine guns, anti-tank weapons and mortars used by elite forces are whatever happens to be standard issue because these are fully tested weapons and there are very few alternatives to them; it also makes logistical sense.

Above and above right: *Accuracy International's PM bolt action 7.62mm NATO rifle with a free-floating stainless steel barrel. It has a box magazine which will hold up to 12 rounds. Accuracy is excellent at ranges of 655 yards (600m) or even more. The standard scope size is the Schmidt Bender 6×42, although the model shown above right has a Leupold Stephens 16×M1 Ultrascope.*

Left: *The V261 Scorpion submachine gun. Short, ugly and deadly, this Czechoslovakian-manufactured weapon system is in great favor with terrorists, particularly in Western Europe.*

Below: *Firing the FR-F2 repeating rifle from the prone position with weapon resting on a bipod. It is designed for rifle ammunition with all NATO 7.62mm cartridges.*

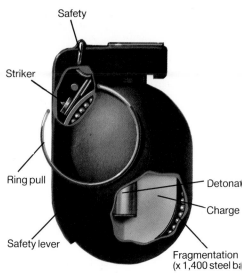

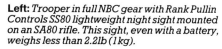

Safety

Striker

Ring pull

Safety lever

Detona...

Charge

Fragmentation
(x 1,400 steel b...

Above: *The MISAR MU-50G controlled-effect grenade which can be thrown or fired (from FRANCHI Spas 12). It has high penetration, but is safe for users 22 yards (20m) away.*

Left: *Trooper in full NBC gear with Rank Pullin Controls SS80 lightweight night sight mounted on an SA80 rifle. This sight, even with a battery, weighs less than 2.2lb (1kg).*

Above: *The Sub-skimmer with assault craft and mini submarine. When the mini submarine has to submerge its side tubes are pumped flat; this allows it to proceed on electric power at a cruising speed of 3.7km per hour for four hours.*

As one of the members of the Weather Underground in the United States put it (he was talking about an assault rifle, but the principle is the same): "It wouldn't make much sense to arm with the AK-47 because ammo is hard to come by, and think of the hassle you'd get trying to buy it in thousand-round lots!" Indeed!

Then there are aircraft with specialized electronics, transports and gunships as well as helicopters for quick insertion and retrieval, that have to be considered. Body armor would easily fill a catalog. So would knives, which are obviously kept simple, sharp and well maintained. Examples of some that are good tools as well as fighting knives are the Khukri, K-Bar or Camillus, and the Parkerized Tanto.

Ground transport systems, kayaks and boats are also important, along with skimmers that carry special forces at high speeds in sea conditions that would bar other craft from operating. Representative of boats in use by elite forces are the Rigid Raider of Britain's Special Boat Service and the Seafox used by the US Navy's SEALs.

Grenades used by elite forces would fill a catalog as well. But even today the make of the stun grenades used by the SAS at the Iranian Embassy siege has never been revealed, although there are a number of logical choices on the market that suggest themselves. This only underscores the complexity – indeed, the near futility – of any effort at cataloging here.

Below: *New elements that can be found in the kit of a British Special Air Service commando. On top is a flare that can be used in emergencies, and an all-purpose knife is shown with its carrying case.*

As for exotic electronic equipment, electro-optical capabilities and other high technology equipment … "nobody talks". This makes a good deal of sense since the counterterrorist business is brutal enough without alerting the enemy to your capabilities.

Terrorists, on the other hand, rarely have sophisticated equipment developed specifically for their own use, nor do they usually have the training to use it. They normally adapt existing resources to the job at hand. Thus, for example, attacks have been carried out with mortars constructed from steel pipes secured by wires to a girder and mounted on an angle-iron frame, with the projectiles for the mortar packed with explosive and triggered electronically.

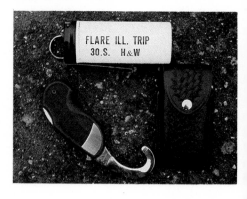

FLARE ILL. TRIP
30.S. H&W

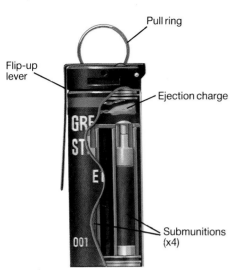

Pull ring

Flip-up lever

Ejection charge

Submunitions (x4)

Above: *Haley & Weller E182 Multi-burst stun grenade, a disorientation grenade employing high candela and decibel levels. It weighs just over ½lb (250g).*

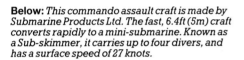

Below: *This commando assault craft is made by Submarine Products Ltd. The fast, 6.4ft (5m) craft converts rapidly to a mini-submarine. Known as a Sub-skimmer, it carries up to four divers, and has a surface speed of 27 knots.*

Above: *Simulated exercise of elite force unit members preparing assault with a Haley & Weller stun grenade. The grenade's noise and flash temporarily stun opponents. It is used primarily in hostage release situations.*

Right: *Nautiraid two-man canoe with paddles plugged in fore and aft. British SBS members used craft such as these in the Falklands campaign, to get to shore on clandestine intelligence-gathering missions.*

Below and inset: *The Seawolf amphibious aircraft which can be adapted for several special operations missions. Its capability to operate from water or land enhances its value.*

Left: *In order to meet the needs of counter-terror teams, especially in hostage-rescue situations, a number of rapid-opening systems have been developed, containing explosive charges in strip form, a primer and detonator. This is the Haley & Weller Dartcord system, which can be used to blow precision holes through doors, steel and brickwork. It has a chevron cross-section designed to produce the maximum cutting effect.*

Right: *The British radio-controlled Wheelbarrow was introduced to deal with unexploded bombs, for instance in a car, without endangering bomb disposal personnel. In position, it examines the problem on a TV monitor and the operator explodes the bomb accordingly. Its value has been demonstrated in Northern Ireland time and time again.*

Left: *The LMT Radio Professionnelle RB12A ground surveillance radar operates by remote control to detect people (1.2 miles/2km) or vehicles (2.5 miles/4km), and determines their bearing and range using a solid state transmitter.*

Right: *Modern detection device. During trials of a British Aerospace Cargo Surveillance System, contents of a 20ft (6m) standard container were X-rayed. The linear accelerator picked up eight hand-gun images in a wooden box.*

Below: *The LMT/RP (Thomson-CSF) Rasit 3190B is a long-range (out to 18.6 miles/30km) ground surveillance radar used to acquire, detect, localize and recognize moving targets, on or near the ground and under all weather conditions. It can be mounted on a wide-variety of military vehicles.*

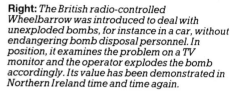

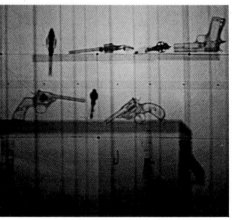

The term in the trade for this kind of activity is IED – for improvised explosive device – and it is used to describe anything from bombs made on the kitchen table to suitcases and briefcases which are themselves bombs, and any other jerry-built device that can be used by a terrorist.

This doesn't mean other small, readily concealable weapons and optical and electronic devices are not available to terrorists if they know the right sources. But then counterterrorist units have access to modern technology in a much more direct fashion and they use it. Everybody is familiar with the electronic baggage scan at the airport; other devices, perhaps less familiar to the public, are electro-optical equipment for examining the mail, and electronic "sniffers" for identifying explosives.

Other equipment is also becoming better known. The fiber optic borescope, for example, is something that is particularly useful in siege-type operations. It enables security forces to "see" through walls and doors through a very small hole, drilled probably during a diversionary tactic.

And coming from the drawing boards is "two way armor", where those under siege can fire their weapons from the inside, exploding the armor in a lethal pattern at the attacker ... while remaining protected themselves. Sensing devices are used to detect the presence, or absense, of heat, which helps reveal the positions of those inside a building.

There are special security cars and exotic body armor for just about any circumstance. Remotely-controlled robots can locate, defuse or destroy explosive devices. These originated with the British "Wheelbarrow", which was developed in response to the increasingly sophisticated bombs of the Provisional Irish Republican Army.

And there are all manner of stun grenades to disorient targets for brief but critical seconds. In fact, they were used to good effect during the assault on the hijacked Lufthansa airliner at Mogadishu in October 1977.

And one mustn't forget specially-shaped framing charges that blow in windows and door with pinpoint precision; nor the plastic anti-riot rounds (they aren't really rubber bullets, even though they are known as such to the public) that induce severe bruising and shock.

It's easy to see why the only true option available here was to describe in the following directory a representative sampling of more than 50 weapons and special equipment used by elite forces.

Below right: *The Matra Manurhin Defense Disrupter Gun, shown here on a light bipod, is designed to neutralize improvized explosive devices through partial demolition with 30mm ammunition. It is fired with 24V of electricity and weighs 5.5lb (2.5kg). It could save the lives of traditional bomb disposal squads.*

This entry was written by Peter Eliot

COMBAT ammunition can be divided into three separate categories; military, police and special forces. Each category has a distinctly different set of parameters it must fulfill.

First military. Both the Geneva and Hague Conventions make specific mention as to the type of ammunition allowed in a conflict between nations. The apparent reason behind these rules is a humane desire to inflict as little injury as possible. In fact, the more cynical among us tend to point out that a man who is killed on the battlefield can be ignored by his companions, but a wounded man would normally mean that at least two other active participants of the battle would be neutralized while they attempt to evacuate the casualty, plus an estimated seven rear-echelon people needed to transport and hospitalize the man afterward. If all of this can be achieved with just one sub-standard shot, why bother to kill?!

The standard military criterion is based on *reliability* in all climatic conditions. In guns which are often badly maintained and which are (in the case of NATO or other multi-nation armed forces) weapons other than that for which the the one the round was specifically made, the only suitable round to fulfill this criterion is ball. This is a fully jacketed, round-nosed or spire-pointed bullet with sufficient power and weight to operate in a variety of weapon types.

The second category of combat round, designed for the police, has a very different set of rules. While not intended for international usage, the advice of official British experts is taken seriously the world over, not least that of the Working Party of the British

Home Office on firearms who have specified what in their opinion the ideal police round would be. Their conclusions are based on sound information and are in general terms excellent. The major problem, which caused the actual recommendations to be slightly flawed (in my opinion), is the relatively low level of training given to police officers both in the UK and around the world generally. This means that the danger to innocent bystanders has a higher emphasis than the neutralization of the threat. This is to be applauded, but not if it allows the criminal to kill or injure police or civilians *after* being shot.

The Home Office criteria are as follows:
1. Maximum speed of incapacitation.
2. Minimum penetration.
3. Minimum richochet.
4. Minimum lead pollution.
5. Non-expansion in the human body.

Numbers 1 to 3 are all good tactical considerations in an urban conflict situation with the possibility of an innocent passerby being endangered. Point number 4 is simply a training consideration, but point number 5 is where the problems start. Simply stated, maximum speed of incapacitation and non-expansion in the human body are exact opposites. To achieve one you must lose the other, except in absolutely ideal laboratory conditions.

I suspect that the stated opinion of a very senior British police officer involved in firearms has a lot to do with this final criteria. He said when asked why the police were being issued poor ammunition, ". . . since Waldorf [mistakenly shot by police in 1985 – Ed.] we have shot ten people, none of whom were

armed with a firearm, one had a knife, a couple had imitation firearms and the rest were unarmed, and none of these people died. I would prefer that a police officer died, than have the terrible problem of attempting to deal with the situation caused by the death of an innocent bystander." As statistically 87 percent of people shot with normal ammunition survive, one can understand his view point. The problem is that as top US small arms tactician Jeff Cooper once said, "If you're going to shoot someone, shoot them with something effective; if not they will get annoyed and shoot you back."

The problem seems to be that tactically reality has been suborned to political and moral expediency.

Most European nations have similar restraints, in fact, one Northern European country police force has a directive specifically stating that "A felon should be incapacitated with firearms by shooting him in the legs"!

Special forces ammunition has, as you would expect, the least political and moral restrictions of all ammunition types. The paramount consideration is stopping power. The operation which special forces personnel are normally involved in would be close range reactive combat where the immediate neutralization of the enemy is paramount. It would be likely that further hostages or innocent bystanders could be killed if the enemy is not stopped immediately (not to mention the cost of replacing the special forces operative who came second!). In normal warfare small arms play an extremely small part in the battle. First would come the artillery and/or bombing raid, then the

7.62 for scale

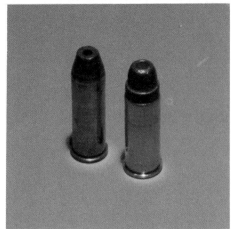

Above: *Two of the standard "stoppers", also incorrectly called "dum dums". Left, a .41 MAG conical semi-jacketed hollow point; right, a .44SP lead round-nose hollow point.*

Left: *Smg rounds used by elite forces for both training and operations. Top row, standard ball rounds in 9mm, 9mm short and 32 ACP. Second row, 9mm SPLAT, three experimental SPLAT bullets; .45 ACP "exploder". Bottom line, 9mm sub-sonic; 9mm GECO plastic; 9mm THV; and 9mm Glazer.*

Right: *Two "exploders": .45 ACP and .357 mag projectiles, with small explosive core which detonates on contact to increase energy.*

7.62 for scale

Above: *Revolver ammunition, both normal and specialist rounds, used by elite forces in training or operations. Top line, left to right, .44 Magnum semi-jacket soft point; .357 Magnum conical armour-piercing; .38SP Equalloy, .38SP Plus P (high velocity police load); .38SP SPLAT (synthetic plastic ammunition for training); .38SP THV; .357 Mag conical soft point. Line two, long rifle .22 used in training for simulated urban warfare; .38SP GECO plastic; Two .38SP rubber bullets (used to shoot trainers during exercises); Experimental SPLAT (top); Equalloy (bottom); .38 Hydro-Shock; .38 PTFE (experimental CQB anti-personnel round); THV-type bullets, .44SP (top); .44 MAG (bottom). Bottom line, .41 Magnum semi-jacketed hollow point; .38SP 158cr round nose; .44 Magnum lead semi-wad cutter .38SP+P; .44 Magnum conical steel semi-jacketed soft point; .44SP lead hollow point; .22 short.*

mortars and heavy machine guns, and finally the infantry goes in with normally a three-to-one numerical advantage.

Special forces tend to go in cold, often outnumbered by their target, and without the "softening up" beforehand. In these circumstances special forces need "state of the art" training and equipment, which includes the most effective ammunition possible.

Unfortunately almost all modern high-tech weapons suitable for close quarter battle (CQB) operations are 9mm. This would seem to be acceptable, as statistically more people are killed by 9mm than by any other calibre in modern warfare. The problem is, however, that although 9mm kills it doesn't stop. One of the more excessive examples of 9mm's lack of stopping power was written up in an American training manual. It quoted a police incident where two officers engaged a felon with Smith and Wesson M59 9mm pistols and after shooting him 33 times he stopped! They had both been forced to reload.

New 9mm "stopping" rounds

Because of this and innumerable similar incidents all over the world, the major ammunition manufacturing nations have all produced ammunition which is designed to make the 9mm into a stopping round. To achieve this the first attempt was to produce a higher velocity, thin-jacketed hollow point bullet. One of the first of these was the American Super Vel. This round had some successes but was very high pressure and tended to misfeed in standard weapons.

There are basic ballistic problems inherent in 9mm which the ammunition manufacturers were trying to overcome. The 9mm round was designed with one basic factor in mind: it had to operate in a reciprocating machine. This meant that a smooth, tapered round with no sharp angles or other blemishes had to be used. It had to be small enough to fit into the butt of a pistol, but powerful enough to operate a sub-machine gun; the 9mm parabellum was all of these things. The problem is that, because of the necessary bullet configuration in shape, weight and velocity, the 9mm round tends to shoot straight through your intended target and on toward the next county!

This means that in gross terms if a projectile has, say, 100 foot pounds of energy and it exits the target with a retaining energy of 40 foot pounds, it has only dumped 60 foot pounds into the target. Add to this the shape of the bullet causing minimal damage and, as the 60 foot pounds are transferred over an average of 12in, this gives the rather unimpressive figure of 5 foot pounds per cubic inch. The figures are rounded up to produce a simple picture, but in fact the actual percentages of retained energy for 9mm are as stated.

Stopping power can be enhanced by five methods. First by enlarging the projectile. Obviously, the larger the diameter of the bullet the more damage it will do. This option is not possible, as 9mm is the caliber and any increase requires either a retrograde step back to .45 ACP (ie, a Thompson or Ingram), or it would mean having to build a gun around the mythical "perfect caliber"! Both of these solutions would have serious resupply problems in the field.

The second possible answer is to use a bullet with good wound channel capabilities. Former American small arms ammo developer Elmer Kieth developed the semi-wad cutter bullet for precisely this reason. Instead of the wound channel simply closing behind the bullet, a core is cut out which causes the subject to lose blood much more quickly, and the damage to major organs is usually more severe. The major problem with this approach is an unacceptably high percentage of failures to feed.

Third, hollow- or soft-point bullets can be used. These are designed to expand on impact, which increases the diameter of the projectile sufficiently to cause it to stop in the body, dumping all of its energy. Or, if it passes right through, the increased size will ensure that most of the energy is transferred, which will cause a corresponding increase in damage to body tissue.

This system is utilized in almost all rifle rounds used for hunting purposes and is totally effective. The problem with pistol caliber is that the velocity is too low to guarantee bullet deformation, as 1,500 foot pounds is the threshold point for the expansion of jacketed lead bullets and this is normally unobtainable in standard pistols/SMGs using these bullets. Lightweight, high-velocity hollow points have been tried but their main problem is if you make the jacket weak enough to rupture effectively on soft targets, a wallet or any item of military kit could break up the bullet before it can do any damage.

Fourth we have frangibility (bullet breakup). Some high-velocity hollow points have been known to break up on impact, but unfortunately this effect depends on which area of the body the projectile hits. Even under the best conditions the energy can be dissipated on cover rather than the target. In fact, the .223 rifle round, which has a relatively thin jacket, has been known to break up on small twigs and long grass! The best of frangibility is where a high energy bullet hits a bone which causes secondary fragmentation and a high energy transfer.

Finally we have the "Plus P". Basically, here the velocity is increased and the weight decreased to achieve a higher kinetic energy. This is the most effective of the original methods used to increase stopping power, since the lighter bullet tended to slow down quicker, which often caused it to stop in the body, transferring all of its energy. The successes gained by the application of kinetic energy rather than momentum caused the ballistic experts to attempt to define the perfect stopping round. The parameters were as follows:

1. Totally reliable.
2. High energy dump.
3. No shoot-through.
4. Ability to defeat basic body armor.
5. Low recoil.
6. No richochet.

At first glance these requirements seem almost unobtainable, and they certainly are if standard bullet design is used. However, after sufficient research almost anything is possible, and that is the case here. There are so many types of what are now called "fourth generation rounds" available that one is almost spoilt for choice. These rounds can be

Above: *Four Glaser safety rounds, probably the best known of all 4th generation rounds, used b many elite forces for the "soft kill" option (no shoot through). From left to right, 7.62mm (.308in) for close range/sniping; .44 Magnum; .3 Special; and 9mm.*

Right: *The French THV rounds seen here with t experimental AET bullets of similar design are probably the best examples of 4th generation ammunition made to date. Note the pronounced reverse ogive. Left to right, .38 special THV; .44 MAG bullet; 9mm THV; .44 SP bullet.*

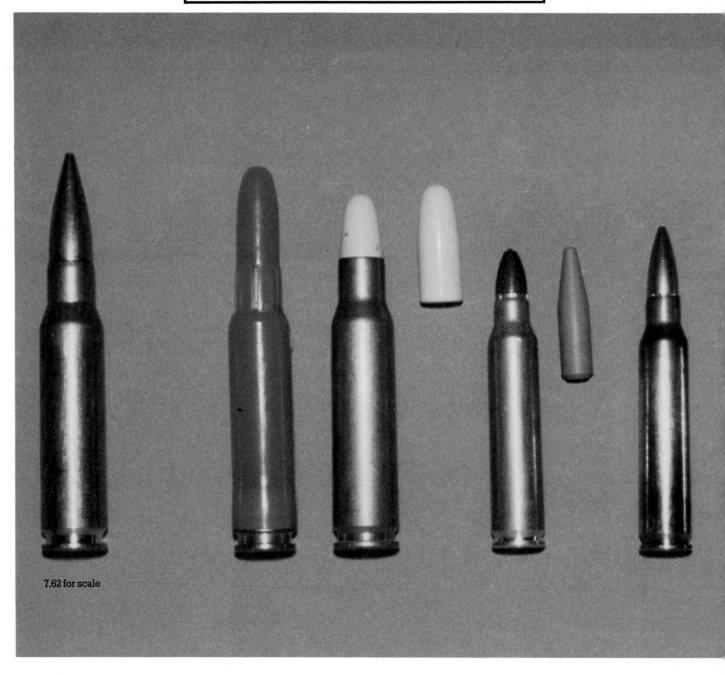

7.62 for scale

divided into two main categories, the first is Frangibility. The second is AET (Accelerated Energy Transfer) Profile.

There are three contenders in the first category. The first, Glaser Safety Slug, is well established and has an enviable reputation when it comes to stopping power. As we said earlier, 87 percent of people shot with small arms survive, yet to date over 90 percent of the people shot with Glaser have died! This is a phenomenal increase in stopping power, and is achieved by utilizing the bullet's energy in the most efficient way possible.

The construction of the bullet is the secret; but it could be likened to a shotgun charge encapsulated in a thin cupronickel jacket with a plastic cap at the front to seal the shot in. This is fired at, depending on the calibre, about 1,800fps. When it hits an uneven surface, or a semi-liquid medium, the cap ruptures, spilling the No. 12 shot out of the bullet. As a sphere has the largest surface area of any object of a given size, the shot gives up its energy into the target eight times faster than if the bullet had stayed intact. This speed of energy transfer causes massive systemic

shock and stops the subject almost instantly.

Glaser has three problem areas, however. The first is its cost. At between $3 and $4.5 (£2 and £3) per round, you can't afford to practise a lot. Secondly, if you hit a hostage or noncombatant, they are dead. There is no chance to say sorry. More important though, is, if the hostile is hiding behind a hostage, you have no ability to shoot through the hostage to engage the hostile. Finally, and most important, the round is totally defeated by any form of angled cover. Even an internal softwood door causes the bullet to break up if hit at anything less than 80 per cent from true.

There is, however, a special round which is black-tipped, as against the blue for the standard round. This is designed for police and military use, and has some body-armor and angle-penetration capabilities, but we have not been able to test this as yet.

The second round in this category is called "Spartan", which is made in Britain as a training round. It is designed to break up on impact with a steel back stop, and not to over-penetrate or travel too far. These characteristics are achieved by producing a

bullet made from lead dust and polymer mix, which is pressure-moulded into the required shape. This idea was first started with the .22 short Gallery ammunition which is still used in funfairs the world over.

Some of this "training" ammunition was sent to one of the UK's special forces units and they immediately realized its true potential. Basically, the human body is made of two very hard substances, bone and high water content tissue. Bone is obviously hard but flesh seems soft. Consider the properties of water: it is incompressible, which is why it is used in hydraulics. If a high-velocity round hits water (ie, a person) the water cannot move out of the way quickly enough for the bullet, and it cannot be compressed. Something has to give, and the bullet which is designed to break up does exactly that!

This round is still in its development stage, but it looks promising. The only problem inherent to its design concept is that it will never fulfill all of the "fourth generation" criteria as the velocity cannot be pushed up high enough due to its lead content making the weight too high.

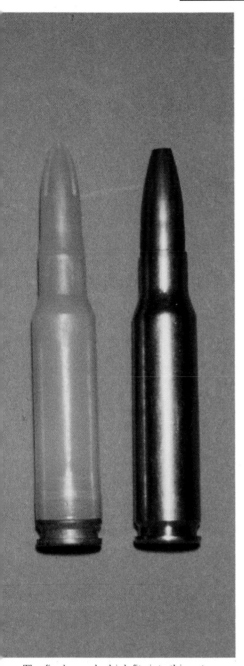

Left: *Elite forces have an advantage over standard military or police units in that they can use both state-of-the-art weapons and ammunition. When engaged in any non-war conflict (where the Geneva and Hague conventions have no standing) they can use whatever round is best suited to the situation. Here are a few. Left to right: 7.62 plastic training; 7.62 Equalloy and an Equalloy bullet; 5.56 frangable training; 5.56 experimental SPLAT bullet; 5.56 standard ball; 5.56 soft point; 7.62 blank; and 7.62 Glaser.*

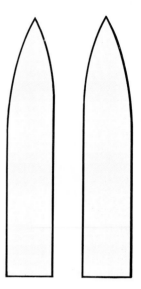

Right: *Cross section of the German contender in the 4th generation stakes: 9mm ammunition GECO action or (BAT) with its hollow core, designed to tumble on impact.*

The final round which fits into this category was a direct development of the "Spartan" round. One of the design team from the British Research and Development Centre in Enfield looked at the requirements for a true "fourth generation" round and took the basic concept of "Spartan" and improved it to fit most, if not quite all, of the requirements.

The new round is called "Splat". As with "Spartan", it is a metal-and-polymer mix bullet. But it has two important differences. First, the metal content both in volume and in weight is designed to produce in excess of 1,800fps and certain break-up in the human body. Second, the profile of this bullet is designed to allow it to penetrate soft-to-medium cover *without* breaking up until it exits the far side. This is an enormous advance over both "Glaser" and the "Spartan" rounds.

It has two other distinct advantages over these rounds. It will retail at approximately the same low price as standard ball, and it is non-lead. This is important for training in non-range areas, since lead pollution is a serious hazard for both the military and police who shoot regularly.

The AET Profile round is the second type of the "fourth generation" round. The first effective round of this type was developed for .38 revolvers, and basically a hollow base wad cutter was loaded into the case upside down! As you can imagine, the expansion properties of such a bullet were high, to say the least.

In an attempt to improve the penetration by controlling the rate of expansion and enhancing the strength of the projectile, a steel pin was swaged into the center of the hollow. This tended to have the interesting effect of producing two projectiles – one lead, which expanded and stopped quickly, and the other steel, which punched through the target. This had an extra advantage in that the steel pin tended to defeat some body armor.

In recent years the round has been produced in many other calibers, both for revolvers and automatics, including the 9mm. The only problem we know of to date is reliability. The weapon has to receive specialist gunsmithing (barrel porting) to accept this round for total reliability, which is an unacceptable condition for military use.

It took 10 years or more to produce the next AET round, and when it came out it was the start of a flood. The list is extensive: Geco action; CBX; Equalloy; KTW; THV. This is just a cross-section of the numerous specialist rounds available to date. Within this group of rounds, there are three basic systems of energy transfer.

The first type, which is made in Germany, is "Geco action", or "Geco BAT" as it is known in the USA. This is a totally hollow bullet with a plastic core. When the round is fired the core is displaced, falling away from the bullet within a short distance from the barrel. When the bullet hits the target, its construction causes it to tumble. This has the desired effects of causing high tissue damage, and permitting the bullet to be retained within the body. This ensures a high-energy transfer. The only problem noted to date is a failure to penetrate angled cover.

The second type of AET round, "Equalloy", is made in England. At the moment it is designed only for revolvers but it has a definitive application in the anti-hijack role on aircraft, so is worthy of discussion here.

The bullet, made from an aluminum alloy, is extremely lightweight. To allow it to and weighs only 0000 grains. To allow it to attain sufficient velocity in the weapon, the bearing surface of the bullet is almost twice as long as a standard round. A nylon coating is used to ensure a good seal and to stop the aluminum from depositing in the barrel. On test 2,050fps was recorded, but it was still possible to get the bullet to stop in 3.5in of Swedish soap (human tissue substitute)!

The third type of AET Profile round is "THV". This is a totally new concept, which we consider to be as close to the "perfect round" as possible. The ballistic phenomenon used is a "reverse ogive", where the forward section of the bullet protrudes beyond the case. This profile causes the cutting area in contact with the target to be concave rather than convex. This has an effect on the body similar to that of a belly flop to a diver. As discussed earlier, hydraulic effect can be used to transfer energy in the target, so long as the velocity is high enough. With this projectile, not only is the velocity high enough at 2,500fps, but it also has the effect of transferring energy over a 90 degrees angle throughout the bullet's path.

Add to this, that the construction allows good armor piercing, relatively low richochet (by comparison with standard ammunition), low recoil, good stopping power and to date no problems on functioning, and you have a near-perfect special forces round.

A number of special forces units around the world use shotguns for some tactical situations, normally for house clearing and similar close range operations. The American SEALs use the Winchester Marine, and Remington 870 has been seen in use by a variety of forces across Europe and America.

There are two main reasons why the manually operated, small-magazine-capacity, bulky shotgun is often used rather than a compact SMG or pistol. First, stopping power. SG or 0.0. buck has 9 .33 cal. soft lead balls in each cartridge, each travelling at approximately 1,300fps (395m/sec)! This can be likened to a nine-round burst from a submachine gun being delivered at the same instant.

The overpowering reason is variety: a

Below: *Cutaway a 12-gauge CS Ferret gas cartridge. Note fin stabilisers and fracture grooves at front of the projectile.*

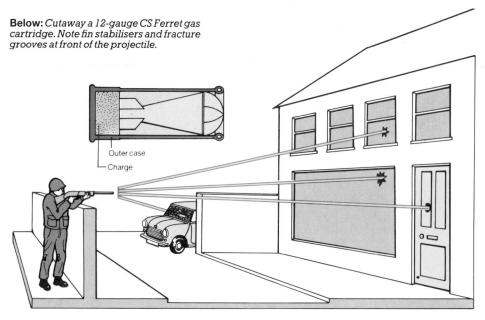

Outer case
Charge

Above: *The CS Ferret gas cartridge is capable of being fired from any 12 gauge shotgun and is accurate at 100 yards (90m) although has little penetrating ability at the range. However, at 25 yards (29m) the projectile is capable of penetrating wooden doors or glass.*

standard 12 bore/gauge shotgun can shoot a vast number of different cartridges ranging from birdshot to grenades. Perhaps this short list will explain the characteristics of the following cartridges will help to explain:

Lethal cartridges

Birdshot (close range, will not penetrate internal walls).

Small buckshot – AAA, BB – close to medium range, 16/50ft (5/15m), will not kill non-combatants outside operational area.

Large buckshot – SSG, SG, LG (w = 000, 000, 0 Buck) – medium to long range, 50, 130ft (15, 40m), some penetration of hard cover, excellent stopping power out to 100ft (30m). Gives a spread of approximately 1in per yard (25mm per meter) of range.

Rifled slug – Medium to long range, 50/165ft (15/50m). Very high penetration of hard cover, excellent stopping power. Must be point aimed.

TC armor-piercing slug – All of the characteristics of rifled slug, plus ability to penetrate *all* soft body armor and most light armored vehicles.

B.R.I. slug – gives rifle-like accuracy and

therefore extends the combat range to 655ft (200m) plus.

HE slug (high explosive) – Gives the ability to neutralize a room or car at 330ft (100m) plus.

Non-lethal – Tactical cartridges

Hatton round – A type of slug specially developed to blow hinges off doors without injuring the occupants of the room.

CS Ferret – Used to fill a room or car with CS gas.

Flares – Signalling purposes.

Incendiary – Diversionary fires, destroying vehicles, etc.

Rubber ball – Riot control, long range.

Rubber SG – Riot control, medium range.

Plastic birdshot – Riot control, close range.

With this amount of choice, the operative can arm himself to suit the scenario, taking into account all of the tactical requirements for the specific set of circumstances he has to deal with.

The major problem of the shotgun is the bulk and shape of the ammunition. The area taken by 50 rounds of 12 bore is approximately the same as 600 rounds of 9mm. Secondly, elite forces can only use a manually

Above: *This photograph gives a reasonable idea of the selection of shotgun cartridges available to the military or police special forces. The array is by no means complete, but shows a good cross section. Top row, in pairs, SG (00 Buck); Anglia slug; Brenekr slug; BRI slug. Second row, first three are shotgun grenades; Hatton slug; Tungsten AP slug; Fiochi slug; Nike tracer; 12-gauge blank, and 12-gauge plastic birdshot and rubber ball (both for training). Bottom row is a line of various production and experimental rifle slugs. Note that numbers one, three and five are all experimental tungsten penetrators.*

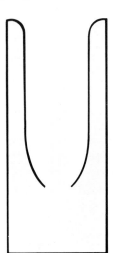

Above: *The Hydro-shock bullet; main projectile is lead; pin core is made of steel.*

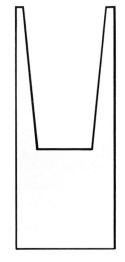

Above: *.38 hollow base wadcutter, the bullet on which the Hydro-Shock was based.*

operated shotgun, rather than a semi or fully automatic version. This is due to the shape of the cartridges and the relatively low pressure produced, being insufficient to cause a gas blow back system to operate reliably each time.

7.62 for scale

Left: *Some of the more interesting shotgun cartridges. From the left, the first round is the CS Ferret, a standard size cartridge which will fit any 12-gauge. The next three items are an Argentinian shotgun grenade liberated in the Falklands. This particular system employs colour coded cables for different ranges. The grenade is rear initiating. Next, the BRI slug, a .50 bullet giving the shotgunner rifle-like accuracy beyond 200 yards (180m). The Hatton round, next, is a British slug designed specifically for smashing door hinges, at which it is singularly effective. Finally, the SPAS penetrator; this tungsten carbide discarding sabot slug is capable of defeating the side armor on a light armored personnel carrier!*

HECKLER & KOCH 9mm P7M8 PISTOL

Origin:
Federal Republic of Germany.
Type:
Pistol.
Dimensions:
Length 6.8in (171mm); height
5.1in (128mm); barrel 4.2in
(105mm).
Weights:
Filled magazine 2lb 1oz (950g);
without magazine 1lb 1oz
(780g).
Caliber:
9mm × 19 Parabellum.
Feed:
8-round box magazine.
Muzzle velocity:
1,155f/s (350m/s).

Heckler and Koch's P7 has the most radically new design of recent German service pistols. Its gas-retarded blowback operating mechanism is the same idea that was used in the World War II German *Volk-sturmgewehr* (VG1-5) and in an experimental Swiss self-loading pistol developed during that same era. Cocking the P7 is accomplished by squeezing the cocking lever, which runs the full length of the forward portion of the pistol grip, instead of the conventional double action trigger.

The P7M8 is one of two distinct versions of the P7K3 pistol, the other being the P7M13. The former holds 8 rounds in the magazine, the latter 13 – meaning there are minor changes in the frame. The P7M8 pistol is a recoil-operated weapon with a gas-retarded inertia bolt. The grip and slide are made of high-grade steel and case hardened. The fixed barrel is firmly pressed into the hardened steel grip. The barrel's polygonal profile and chamber are manufactured in one process by the cold forging method. The sight radius of 5.7in (147mm) is especially long; the height of the sight line above the firing hand is only about 1.25in (32mm).

The handy shape of the grip and the well balanced center of gravity with the very small distance of barrel axis and firing hand – only about ½in (15mm) – result in positive behavior of the weapon when it is fired. The grip has an ergonomically ideal angle of 110 degrees to the barrel. When the operator aims the pistol, he will instinctively use the pistol as an extension of his arm and point it at the target.

The magazine is placed almost vertically to the barrel. This guarantees optimum feed of the cartridges from the magazine to the chamber, so that jams are less likely.

The pistol is currently in use with West German Army and police units, as well as with military and police forces in other nations.

Top: *GSG 9 member covers his partner with P7 M8 during "arrest" training. Note the improvized hood.*

Above: *The P7 M13. The only difference between this and the P7 M8 is the magazine capacity (13 rounds instead of 8). A major problem is that the pistol grip is too large for the average-sized hand.*

Left: *The P7 M8 field-stripped. Note the unique squeeze cocking system on the front of the pistol grip, and the fixed barrel, enhancing accuracy by its positive locking.*

Right: *This view of the P7 shows the distinctive sighting system which consists of three dots. The sight picture can be quickly picked up in most light conditions and is designed for a speedy combat shot.*

HECKLER & KOCH 9mm P9S PISTOL

Origin:
Federal Republic of Germany.
Type:
Self-loading pistol.
Dimensions:
Pistol length 7.68in (192mm);
barrel length 4.08in (102mm).
Weights:
9mm pistol (empty) 1.9lb
(0.88kg), (loaded) 2.34lb
(1.065kg); magazine (empty)
0.16lb (0.074kg), (loaded) 0.40lb
(0.18kg).
45 ACP (empty) 1.65lb (0.75kg),
(loaded) 2.2lb (1.01kg);
magazine (empty) 0.147lb
(0.067kg), (loaded) 0.48lb
(0.22kg).
Cartridge:
9mm × 19 Parabellum and .45
ACP.
Feed:
9-round box magazine (.45 ACP,
7 rounds).
Muzzle velocity:
386ft/sec (351m/s), and 286ft/sec
(260m/s) in .45 ACP.

In the late 1960s, Heckler & Koch
of Oberndorf-Neckar, Federal
Republic of Germany, began to
take a hard look at military pistols. By 1972 the company had
announced its P9S, which adapted the roller-locked bolt of its
G3 rifle to the configuration of a
reliable delayed blowback system of operation.

There seems to be little doubt
that the P9S can be considered
the first in a true new generation
of military handguns; its roots
clearly lay in the need during the
1970s for a modern pistol for use
in counterterrorist operations,
which were on the increase,
especially in Western Europe.

The P9S has a concealed double-action hammer, with an indicator pin which protrudes when
the hammer is cocked, and a
hammer decocking lever in the
right front of the butt grip. After
inserting a magazine and loading the chamber in normal fashion, the hammer can be safely
lowered by pressing down on
the decocking lever, squeezing
the trigger and then gently allowing the lever to ride up and
lower the hammer.

The trigger is released and
the safety catch applied, with the
result that the pistol can now be
holstered and carried in safety.
To fire, all that is needed is to
release the safety and pull the
trigger; alternatively, the decocking lever can be pressed
down to cock the hammer and
allow a single-action first shot for
accuracy, should time permit
this.

The P9S pistol has polygonal
rifling, which – it is claimed –
helps reduce the deformation of
the bullet, thus increasing the
muzzle velocity. A lack of corners at the bottom of the grooves
means less accumulation of fouling and an improvement in both
accuracy and the ease of maintenance.

The P9S was adopted by the
West German Border Police,
which has responsibility for the
crack GSG 9 forces. It has also
been adopted by various unnamed armies and several police forces in many countries. It is
available in the United States in
.45 caliber and in special long-barreled target versions.

Above: *The 9-round H&K P9S 9mm pistol. A loaded magazine can be inserted into the pistol grip when the safety is on, and the catch then engages. To chamber a round a slide is pulled back and released. This cocks the hammer, and a pin protrudes from the rear of the slide when this is fully forward. The extractor stands proud when the cartridge is chambered; pin and extractor can be seen by day and felt by night.*

5.56mm FA MAS RIFLE

Origin:
France.

Type:
Selective fire rifle.

Dimensions:
Without bayonet 30.28in (757mm); barrel 19.51in (488mm).

Weights:
Without magazine, sling or bipod 7.94lb (3.61kg); magazine, .33lb (0.15kg) empty; .99lb (0.45kg) loaded with 25 rounds; bipod, .374lb (0.17kg).

Cartridge:
5.56mm × 45mm NATO: M193-type ammunition.

Effective range:
330yd (300m).

Muzzle velocity:
3,168f/s (960m/s).

Rate of fire:
(cyclic) 900-1,000 rounds/minute.

The FA MAS (Fusil Automatique, Manufacture d'Armes de St. Etienne) is France's newest service rifle and has proven to be a highly effective and generally well-conceived piece of ordnance for general service and special forces use. First introduced in 1973 (and subsequently modified), the rifle was placed into production in 1979. Delivery of the first complement of 148,000 rifles was completed in 1983.

Firing from the closed-bolt position, the method of operation is by means of delayed blowback, the system having been adopted from the French AA52 general purpose machine gun. A black plastic lower handguard, pinned to the barrel and receiver, extends to the magazine well and cannot be removed.

Because it has a "bullpup" configuration, the trigger mechanism and pistol grip have been mounted to the lower handguard, forward of the magazine well. The pistol grip is ergonomically designed, with three finger grooves and a storage trap that contains a bottle of lubricant. The sheet metal trigger guard can be pulled away from the rear retaining pin and rotated for firing with gloves under arctic conditions, an obvious advantage to mountain forces. The trigger is connected to a long, thin strip of sheet metal which rides in a slot on the right side of the receiver and reaches the hammer mechanism.

To remove a magazine, a spring-loaded plastic catch must be pressed back. Magazines are inserted by pushing them straight into the well.

Among the interesting features of the FA MAS are optional right- or left-side ejection and three-round burst mode as an alternative to single shot or fully automatic. With its high cyclic rate (900-1,000rpm), the three-shot burst mode is a real boon in controlling the weapon. Each weapon is equipped with an ambidextrous web sling. The foresight is mounted on a column pinned to the barrel; the rearsight is also on a column, above the return spring cylinder.

Versions of the FA MAS have scopes integrated into the carrying handles, as are short barreled models with 16.5in (405mm) barrels. A new carrying handle that will accept any

Above: *FA MAS Bullpup assault rifle, free-standing on its bipod and magazine. This weapon is well suited to special forces operations due to its compact size and massive fire power. But a major problem is the ejection ports position, which causes problems when the rifle is fired from the hip or from the medial combat position.*

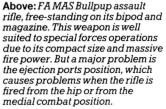

Left: *A telescopic sight mounted directly onto the FA MAS carrying handle. The accessory is not designed to make the weapon into a sniper's rifle but is to allow elite forces and specialist police officers to clearly identify their targets when hostages or non-combatants are in the kill zone. Note the prone position adopted.*

NATO STANAG scope is under development. The weapon is widely used among elite troops such as France's naval infantry, Foreign Legion and paratroops.

A short version – the FA MAS Commando – is another variation available and is intended for use by commando and similar special forces. The barrel has been shortened to 16.2in (405mm), but in other respects is the same as the service weapon.

Right: *The FA MAS field stripped for general cleaning. Although of unusual design, the basic construction is the same as most other modern assault rifles and machineguns. The major differences are the position of the trigger group and the recoil system. Note the exposed sights on the frame.*

Above and center right: *The FA MAS is an extremely compact weapon as you can see in the far right picture. But its design causes some problems in the field. The tall bipod and magazine height lift the weapon higher in the prone position than most other weapons; this produces a high firing profile. Also, the bipod position gives only a small arc of fire.*

Right: *French trooper wading a river with his assault rifle and Bergen. One of the obvious advantages of this weapon is its length. It is about 12in (305mm) shorter than most of its contemporaries, an important advantage when house clearing, or parachuting or when the weapon has to be concealed to get to the operational theater.*

G3SG/1 SNIPER RIFLE

Origin:
Federal Republic of Germany.
Type:
Sniping rifle.
Dimensions:
Length, fixed butt 42.2in
(1,025mm); retractable butt
33.6in (840mm); barrel 18.0in
(450mm).
Weight:
Unloaded, with sight 12.2lb
(5.54kg).
Cartridge:
7.62mm×51 NATO.
Feed
20 round box magazine.
Range:
656 yards (600m).
Rifling:
4 grooves r/h one turn in 12.2in
(305mm).

Muzzle velocity:
2,560-2,625ft/sec (780-800m/sec).
Rate of fire:
(cyclic) 500-600rpm; (auto)
100rpm.

It was much of the work on assault rifles such as the Stg 45(M) during World War II that supplied the design information for the Heckler & Koch G3. After a development phase in Spain with the weapon (using an unusually long 7.92mm bullet), further development work was transferred to Heckler & Koch in Stuttgart. The G3 replaced the FN FAL rifle in the Bundeswehr in 1959.

Current models make extensive use of plastic and stampings; only the barrel and bolt components are machined. Designed for semi- and fully-automatic fire, the weapon has a three-position selector/safety lever above the pistol grip on the left side.

A standard feature of the rifle, which enhances accuracy, is the roller delayed blowback action, which requires no gas to be bled off, and no piston either. Since there are no fittings attached to the barrel, there is nothing to interfere with the barrel's harmonic variable.

Retaining the G3's iron sights, the SG/1 modification allows for the use of the same quick release scope mount that clamps to its parent. The glass in the mount is the Zeiss diavari 1.5-6X scope, which features excellent clarity and good light gathering.

The G3SG/1 uses a modified trigger which features a "set" lever behind the trigger itself, the use of which reduces the pull to 2.75 pounds (1.247kg). One other area in which the G3SG1 is different from its parent is that the buttstock is fitted with a detachable comb which allows for up to an inch (25.4mm) of variation for proper eye-to-scope orientation.

The G3 is in service with the armed forces of at least 12 countries; the G3SG/1 sniper rifle is in use with the Federal Republic of Germany's crack GSG 9 counter-terrorist unit, the Italian carabinieri, and other police forces.

HECKLER & KOCH PSG1

Origin:
Federal Republic of Germany.
Type:
Sniper rifle.
Dimensions:
Length 46.7in (1,210mm); barrel
25.6in (650mm).
Weights:
Without magazine 17.85lb (8.1kg);
magazine empty 9.88oz (276g).
Cartridge:
7.62mm×51.
Feed:
5- or 20-round magazine.

A new member of the Group I series of Heckler & Koch rifles, the *Prazisionsschutzengewehr* (High-precision Marksman's Rifle) PSG 1 is under development only for police and service sniper use. It is a semi-automatic, single-shot weapon using H&K's roller-locked bolt system.

The semi-automatic PSG1 is based on the G3 military assault rifle, which has been proven in service with 50 nations. It is fitted with a polygon bored heavy barrel, and the trigger, fitted with an adjustable trigger shoe, is normally set to break at 3.3lb (1.49kg). A special low-noise bolt-closing device is fitted, and the stock has an adjustable comb and butt pad that allow fitting to individual shooters. A bipod attaches directly to the stock,

eliminating variations in zero because of the differing pressures exerted on the barrel.

The PSG1 is topped with the state-of-the-art Hensoldt 6×42 scope with LED-enhanced manual reticle. The scope-mounted activator produces a helpful red dot for approximately 30 seconds, plenty of time to get off that critical shot; moreover it mounts directly to the PSG1's permanent base.

Windage and elevation adjustment is by moving lens, six settings from 110 to 655yd (100 to 600m), and there is fine adjustment facility to compensate for any mounting offset angle.

Below: *The newest member of the Group I series of H&K rifles, the PSG 1, is designed for use under exceptional operational conditions. It takes a sniper with excellent training.*

Below: *Standard G3 rifles which put the mean point of impact correctly and produce minimum groups are modified to become G3SG/1 sniping rifles.*

Below: *The PSG 1 sniping rifle, with its special system for silent and positive bolt closing, was developed for police and service work. It comes with many accessories, including a transport case with two 20-round magazines; two 5-round magazines; plastic cleaning rod; and a high precision tripod. Further accessories include a magazine filling and emptying device and a carrying sling. The PSG 1 incorporates the famous Heckler and Koch roller-locked bolt system and other standard features.*

Left: *One of the more convenient features of the PSG 1 is a butt stock that can be adjusted to fit the firer's shoulder. The butt stock not only features adjustable length, but a pivotted butt cap and a vertically-adjustable cheek piece. With tripod and magazine, the PSG 1 weighs 20.5lb (9.31 kg).*

5.56mm & 7.62mm GALIL ASSAULT RIFLE

Origin:
Israel.

Type:
Assault rifle.

Dimensions:
Length, stock extended, 5.56 model 38.6in (979mm), 7.62 model 41.3in (1,050mm); stock folded, 5.56 model 29.2in (742mm), 7.62 model 31.9in (810mm). Barrel, 5.56 model 18.1in (460mm), 7.62 model 21in (533mm).

Weight:
5.56 model 8.6lb (3.9kg); 7.62 model 8.7lb (3.95kg).

Caliber:
5.56 model .223; 7.62 model .308.

Max effective range:
5.56 model 550yd (500m); 7.62 model 660yd (600m).

Muzzle velocity:
5.56 model 3,230ft/sec (980m/sec); 7.62 model 2,800ft/sec (850m/sec).

Rate of fire:
Both models 650 rounds/minute.

Despite the fact that Israel's Galil assault rifle has a rich, battle-tested heritage, it was only first issued in 1973. Actually, it is the system of the Galil with the heritage, since it is actually that of the AK-47 Kalashnikov, the most widely distributed and used of all assault rifles.

Credit for the rifle's development is given to an Israeli ordnance officer with the surname of Galili, along with Israel Military Industries. They realized that by using the full-scale Finish Valmet M-60/62 receiver and a stout but not-too-heavy barrel, the system would serve both the 5.56 NATO cartridge and the 7.62 NATO round as well.

The operating system is a rotating bolt gas system and, with the exception of the stamped steel breech cover, the Galil is fully machined. The forearm is wood, lined with Dural, and has ample clearance around the barrel for heat dissipation. When extended, the buttstock has a positive latching system which prevents wobble by wedging the hinge end's tapered latching lugs into corresponding slots.

These are released by the simple expedient of squeezing with the right hand and folding the stock outward. The bipod folds and rotates into a slot on the underside of the forearm, where the legs then spread apart by spring tension to latch into retaining slots.

The ambidextrous safety switch on the left side is a small lever, but its reciprocal right-side member also acts as an ejection port cover. The magazine is held by a catch in front of the trigger guard. To operate, the lever is taken off "safe" and the cocking handle pulled to the rear. When released, the carrier is driven forward and the top round pushed from the magazine into the chamber.

The bolt comes to a halt and the cam pin (engaged in a slot in the carrier) rotates the bolt, which forces the cartridge forward, whereupon the extractor slips over the rim and the gun is ready to be fired.

The system used for the trigger and firing mechanism is that employed in the M1 Garand rifle, the AK series and many others. Some 35 rounds are held in the 5.56 magazine and that for the 7.62 holds 25 rounds, but 50-round magazines have been produced for it.

Sights for the Galil are folding "L" rear with two peeps, one for 330 yards (300m), and a second for 550 yards (500m). Unique to the system is its set of folding night sights which use tritium for illumination. For close quarter work at night or in a dark jungle, these sights are undetectable

The Galil was adopted by South Africa after incorporating certain preferred modifications (such as carbon plastic stock instead of steel tubing to better fit terrain needs) and is called the R-4 (Rifle 4). It has also proved itself in South West Africa and Angolan operations.

Below: *Israel Defense Force soldier armed with a 5.56mm Galil. Large capacity magazine causes a high prone position to be adopted, reducing the firer's accuracy and increasing threat from return fire.*

Above: *The 5.56mm Galil is a mechanically sound, strongly constructed weapon. Note the layout of the controls; the selector switch located above the pistol grip is designed so that it is the reverse of almost all other Free World weapons, with "safety" not "fire" being engaged by the natural forward push of the thumb.*

Left: *7.62mm Galil section light machine gun. This weapon fills the gap between the assault rifle and the belt-feed medium machine gun. Designed to give light, and medium range suppressive fire, also due to its heavier caliber, it gives better penetration of lightly armored vehicles. Note the straight magazine.*

Above: *IDF troops in a typical Middle East operation. The Galil is one of a very small number of 5.56mm rifles which will operate effectively in the conditions found in this type of terrain. Note the M60 tank with two 30 cals on the turret.*

Left: *Israel paratroopers covering their comrades during an assault on PLO terrorist positions. Clearly seen are their Galil assault rifles, versatile weapons which were developed using tried and tested Eastern European technology allied to Israeli ingenuity.*

5.56mm AR 70/223 BERETTA

Origin:
Italy.
Type:
Rifle.
Dimensions:
Length (overall), AR 70 39.8in (995mm), SC 70 38.4in (960mm); (butt folded), SC 70 29.4in (736mm); barrel, AR 70 18.0in (450mm), SC 70 18.0in (450mm).
Weights:
Empty, AR 70 8.4lb (3.8kg), SC 70 8.1lb (3.7kg); full magazine, AR 70 9.1lb (4.15kg), SC 70 9.2lb (4.2kg).
Cartridge:
.223 (5.56mm×45mm).
Rifling:
4 grooves r/h, 1 turn in 12.2in (304mm).
Feed:
30-round magazine.
Grenade:
40mm.
Muzzle velocity:
3,135f/s (950m/s).
Rate of fire:
(cyclic) 650rpm.

Beretta started work in 1968 to replace their 7.62mm BM 59 rifle, in service with the Italian Army, with an updated product. The project for a replacement was directed from the beginning by Vitorio Valle, head of the research and development department and P C Beretta, the company's general manager.

They evaluated the Stoner 63, M16A1, FN CAL and the Kalashinikov, hoping to come up with a blend of the best features, which they could then combine with their own innovations. The basic design was put in final form by 1970 – giving the weapon its name, Beretta Model 70.

The 70-series weapons fire from the closed-bolt position and are gas operated; there is no gas regulator. Since the gas port has been placed close to the muzzle end of the barrel, the system needs a 14in (355mm) piston. With the gas system located in the conventional position above the barrel, the magazine must feed from the bottom; however, balance and handling are enhanced by this location.

The trigger system is simple and clean. Semiautomatic fire is obtained by the usual disconnector between the trigger and sear. Upper and lower receiver bodies are sheet metal stampings, and guide rails and ejector are welded and riveted to the upper receiver shell. The hold open system which retains the bolt group in the rearward position after the magazine has been emptied is almost identical to the one used on the M16.

There are two easily interchangeable buttstock configurations. A high-impact rigid plastic stock with a steel butt plate is used on the assault rifle (AR 70) model. The buttstock in the folding stock version (the SC 70 or Special Troops Carbine) is fabricated from tubular steel with an aluminium butt plate and plastic sleeve over the top tube.

In addition to Italian elite forces, special forces of South Africa use the AR 70.

7.62mm BM59 RIFLE SERIES

Far left: *The AR70 is a lightweight 5.56mm weapon capable of firing single-shot or automatic. Italy's San Marco Marines were the first to receive it.*

Bottom: *COMSUBIN commando with the shortened SC70.*

Below: *Note the barrel length of this SC70 Short, the smallest of the Beretta family, with a 16in (464mm) barrel. It is used for close quarter battle and paratrooper ops.*

Origin:
Italy.
Type:
Rifle.
Dimensions:
Length 43.8in (1,095mm); barrel 19.6in (490mm).
Weight:
10.1lb (4.6kg).
Feed:
20-round detachable box magazine.
Caliber:
7.62mm.
Rifling:
4 grooves r/h.
Effective range:
660yd (600m).
Muzzle velocity:
2,716f/s (823m/s).
Rate of fire:
(cyclic) 800rpm.

This is the standard rifle manufactured by Pietro Beretta and is based upon the mechanism of the US M1 Garand rifle with an M14 magazine system, which the company made in large quantities for NATO use after World War II.

There is a light machine gun version of the BM59, as well as three other versions. These three include the standard BM59, the alpine rifle and the paratroop rifle. In all versions, it is a gas-operated, selective-fire weapon, with the gas regulator of the two position spindle type. In addition, all current versions include the following features: a winter trigger; a cartridge-clip guide for loading magazines; a bipod; a bolt stop that keeps the bolt open after firing the last round; a two-position selector for semi- or fully-automatic fire; a safety catch in front of the trigger guard; and a grenade launcher tri-compensator (this is detachable in the paratroop version).

The BM59 will fire any anti-personnel or anti-tank grenade with a boom having an inside diameter of 22mm. It has a fully adjusted aperture rearsight and a protected post foresight. The main difference between the standard version and the paratroop (BM59 Mark Ital Para) and alpine (Mark Ital TA) versions is in the stock. The latter two versions have collapsible folding stocks and plastic pistol grips. There is no forward pistol grip, which could be useful.

Above: *The BM59 is one of the few battle rifles still in use that actually looks and shoots like a rifle! Balance is superb, and when scoped it makes an excellent sniper rifle.*

Below: *The BM59 Paracudisti was made for airborne troops, shown with both a folding stock and detachable grenade launcher. Its 800rpm makes it a somewhat uncontrollable weapon on auto.*

Bottom: *The BM59 Alpini is the same as the Paracudisti except that the grenade launcher is fixed. Note the very high bipod (which gives a high firing position) and folding stock.*

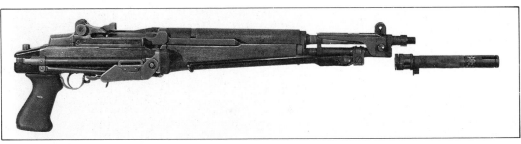

5.45mm AK-74 and AKS-74 ASSAULT RIFLES

Origin:
Soviet Union.
Type:
Assault rifles.
Dimensions:
Length (AK-74) 37in (930mm); (AKS-74, with butt folded) 28in (690mm); barrel 16in (40mm).
Weight:
(unloaded) (AK-74/AKS-74) 7.9lb (3.6kg).
Rifling:
4 grooves r/h; 1 turn in 7.8in (196mm).
Cartridge:
5.45mm × 39.
Feed:
30 round plastic box magazine.
Effective range:
495yd (450m).
Muzzle velocity:
2,970ft/sec (900m/s).
Rate of fire:
(cyclic) 650rds/minute.

As indicated by its designation, the AK-74 assault rifle was developed in 1974 and probably entered service around 1977. The folding stock AKS-74, sometimes referred to as the AKD, was first seen with Soviet airborne troops in the Red Square Parade in Moscow on November 7, 1977.

The AK-74 is basically an AKM rechambered and rebored to fire a 5.45mm cartridge. Externally, it has the same general appearance as the AKM, with two notable differences: the AK-74 has a distinctive, two-port muzzle brake (giving it a slightly greater overall length than the AKM), and a smooth plastic magazine which is slightly shorter and is curved to a lesser extent than the grooved metal AKM. It uses the same type bayonet as the AK series weapons. The folding stock version, designated AKS-74, has a Y-shaped tubular stock with an extremely narrow buttplate, as opposed to the T-shaped, stamped-metal buttstock of the AKMS.

The muzzle brake on the AK-74 uses a fluidic device to minimize recoil and muzzle climb. Although the AK-74 is somewhat heavier than the AKM when empty, its loaded weight is slightly less, primarily because of the plastic magazine and its smaller caliber ammunition, which can inflict a particularly nasty wound. There are reports the AKS now has a Soviet version of the US M203 grenade launcher.

Among limitations of the rifle are that the gas cylinder is in a vulnerable position and, if dented, may cause weapon malfunction, and that the reddish-brown or orange color of the plastic magazine does not lend itself to camouflage.

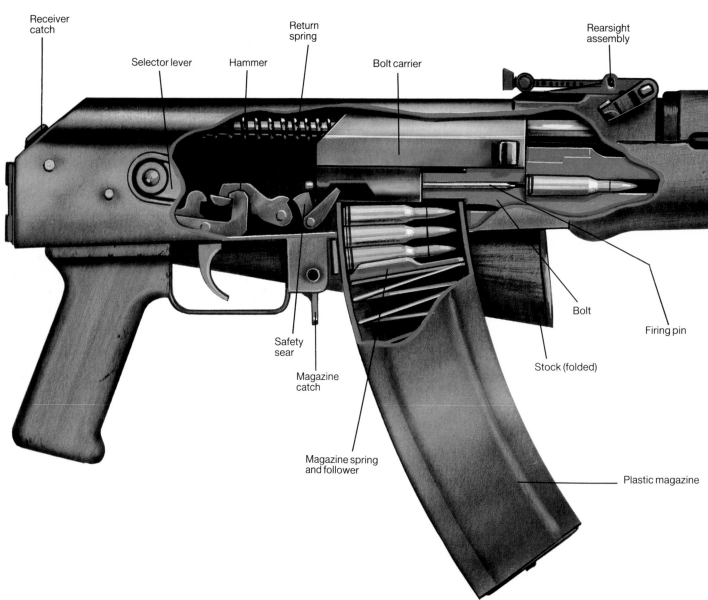

Receiver catch

Selector lever

Hammer

Return spring

Bolt carrier

Rearsight assembly

Safety sear

Magazine catch

Magazine spring and follower

Bolt

Firing pin

Stock (folded)

Plastic magazine

Above: *Troopers carrying the AK-74 in a Red Square Parade. It is almost the same as the AKM/AK-47, except for the caliber. Note the new flash eliminators.*

Above: *The AKMS is identifiable by its plastic magazine and forward folding stock. Unlike the AK-74, it has the same muzzle brake as the AK-47.*

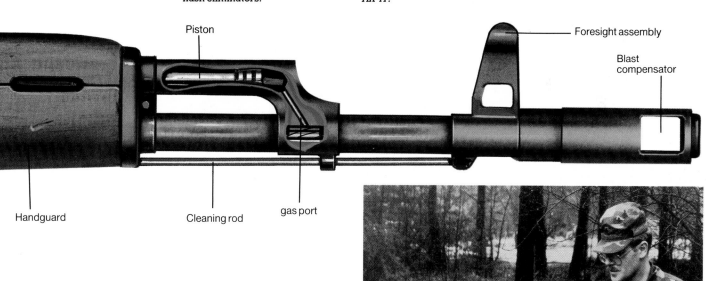

Piston

Foresight assembly

Blast compensator

Handguard

Cleaning rod

gas port

Right: *US Special Forces training with the AK-74. All elite forces find it useful to know how to operate foreign weapons (allies' and enemies'), especially behind the lines if their own weapons should fail.*

7.62mm AK-47 and AKM ASSAULT RIFLES

Origin:
Soviet Union.
Type:
Assault rifle.
Dimensions:
(AK-47): butt extended 34.8in (869mm); butt folded 30in (699mm); barrel 16.6in (414mm); (AKM): length 35in (876mm); barrel 16.6in (414mm).
Weights:
(AK-47) 9.5lb (4.3kg); (AKM) 6.9lb (3.15kg).
Cartridge:
7.62mm×39 M1943.
Feed:
30 round detachable box magazine.
Effective range:
330yd (300m).
Muzzle velocity:
(AK-47) 2,343ft/sec (710m/sec); (AKM) 2,360ft/sec (715m/sec).
Rate of fire:
(cyclic) 600rpm.

The Soviet Army has always understood the value of sheer volume of fire, particularly if it could be produced by not very highly trained troops firing simple weapons. During World War II, they had seen and been impressed by the German MP44. When the war was over, they set out – with the assistance of German designers – to produce a similar weapon.

This led to the Avtomat-Kalashnikova assault rifle. Although designed in 1947 and thus referred to as the AK-47, the AK was actually adopted in 1949 and entered service in 1951. The AK was the basic infantry weapon of the Soviet Army until the introduction of the AKM, which was developed in 1959 and entered service in 1961. All 7.62 Kalashnikov assault weapons are highly

dependable weapons. They produce a high volume of fire and are simple to maintain. The AK-47 is accurate and sufficiently heavy to shoot well in automatic at the ranges likely to be required in modern war – up to 330 yards (300m) – without undue vibration.

Produced in greater quantity than any other modern small arm, the AK-47 and AKM can fairly be said to have set a new standard in infantry weapons. The original AK-47 came with a wooden stock or (for AFV crews, paratroopers and motorcyclists) a folding metal stock. It owed much to German design and uses a short cartridge firing a stubby bullet. A gas-operated weapon with rotating bolt (which is often chrome-plated), it can readily be used by troops all over the world, of any standard of education, and gives extremely reliable results under the most adverse conditions. Versions with various designations have been produced in at least five countries, and it is used in at least 35 armies.

The curved magazine and silhouette are hallmarks of terrorists and guerrillas in Lebanon, Syria, South Yemen, Mozambique, Angola, Rhodesia and Central America.

The present standard Soviet infantry small arm is the AKM, an amazingly light weapon that makes extensive use of metal stampings and plastic, and has a cyclic-rate reducer, compensator and other improvements. Both rifles can be fitted with luminous sights or the NSP-2 infrared sight and a bayonet, which doubles as a saw and an insulated wire cutter.

Right: *The AK-47 is simply the best weapon ever to exist in the terrorist armory. Robust, simple and accurate, it uses a cartridge many accept as being the best mid-range round in the world. The distinctive sound of its full auto fire causes Free World soldiers to dive instantly for cover.*

Below: *An unusual version of the AKM. The normal distinguishing feature is its angled gas deflector, but here a standard AK-47 type barrel is fitted. Note also the distinctive banana-shaped magazine on this weapon held by a serious-looking Soviet soldier in dress uniform.*

7.62mm DRAGUNOV (SVD) SNIPER RIFLE

Origin:
Soviet Union.
Type:
Rifle.
Dimensions:
Length 48.25in (1,227mm).
Weight:
(with POS-1 sight) (empty) 9.4lb (4.3kg); (loaded) 10.5lb (4.78kg).
Cartridge:
7.62×54mm rimmed.
Maximum range: 1,420yd (1,300m).
Muzzle velocity:
2,725ft/sec (830m/sec).
Rate of fire:
(semi-automatic) 30rds/minute.

The SVD was developed in 1965 and entered service in 1967. It is the standard Soviet sniper weapon. One squad in each motorized rifle platoon has an SVD, and selected riflemen receive regular, centralized sniper training. Largely due to its open buttstock, the SVD is lighter than older sniper rifles.

Both the bolt mechanism and the gas recovery system are similar to those of the AK and AKM assault rifles; however, because of the difference in cartridges, parts of it are not interchangeable with these

weapons. The most distinguishing features of the SVD are the open buttstock, which is fitted with a cheek pad for ease in sighting, and the telescopic sight mounted over the receiver.

It has a combination flash suppressor/compensator and may mount the standard AKM bayonet. Four magazines, a cleaning kit, and an extra battery and lamp for the telescopic sight are issued with the weapon.

Only light and heavy ball-type ammunition can be fired with accuracy, which is one of the limitations of the SVD. Even

Above: *The Dragunov was one of the first dedicated sniper rifles to be based on a semi-auto action. Most other countries still use bolt action.*

though it is equipped with a bayonet, the rifle is not an ideal weapon for close combat because it can fire only in the semi-automatic mode. Its weight and length also limit its maneuverability.

Right: *Both weapons shown are used by Communist Bloc and Communist-backed forces. Above is the AKM, below the SKS (Semi-automatic Karbine Simonov). Both fire the 7.62×39mm round produced by the USSR and PRC. Though the SKS was produced in similar volume to the AK series, it appears popular only with Chinese-backed groups.*

Below: *The Soviet AK-47. A major advantage of this weapon is its cartridge. The round pushes a 123 grain bullet at 2,330fps (710mps). This is powerful enough to be effective, but the recoil is low enough to allow full auto to be controllable. Note how the folding stock becomes part of the fore end when closed.*

The Soviet Army has always set great store by sniping and in World War II men were specially trained to spot German officers by their badges of rank and then shoot them.

Right: *The telescopic sight used on the Dragunov sniper rifle. It is a detachable, non variable 4 power scope with an extension tube fixed to the rear to give the correct eye relief. The weapon has limitations, but is praised by snipers.*

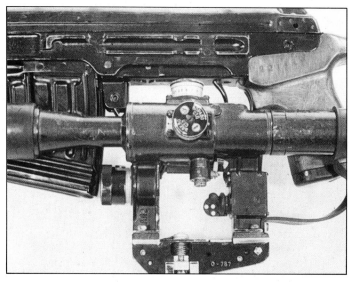

5.56mm COLT COMMANDO

Origin:
United States.
Type:
Assault rifle/sub-machine gun.
Dimensions:
Length (butt extended) 31.5in (787mm), (butt telescoped) 28.4in (711mm); barrel 10.2in (254mm).
Weight:
(with sling and loaded) 7.1lb (3.23kg).
Cartridge:
5.56mm.
Feed:
Magazine
Rifling:
4 groove r/h.
Effective range:
55 yards (200m)
Muzzle velocity:
3,049ft/sec (924m/sec)
Rate of fire:
(cyclic) 700-800rpm.

The Colt Commando is essentially a shorter and handier version of the AR-15 and was developed for use in Vietnam for battle at close quarters. Mechanically, it is identical to the AR-15, but with a much shorter barrel than the 21in (533mm) barrel of the rifle. This reduced the muzzle velocity slightly and had a serious effect on accuracy at longer ranges; it also caused considerable muzzle flash, which made it necessary to incorporate a 4in (100 mm) flash hider which can be unscrewed if necessary.

The Colt Commando has a telescopic butt which can be pulled out when it is required to fire from the shoulder, and in spite of the limitations on accuracy imposed by the shorter barrel, the weapon proved useful in Vietnam. It features selective fire and a holding-open device and is actuated by the same direct gas action.

Designed as a survival weapon, it filled the sub-machine gun role so well that it was issued to US Special Operations Forces. It is also believed to be in limited use by the British SAS.

Above: *USAF SOF members with Colt Commandos during Operation Reforger. The 7th Special Operations Squadron is the only such Air Force unit on the Continent; almost self-sufficient, it trains regularly with personnel of Western European nations.*

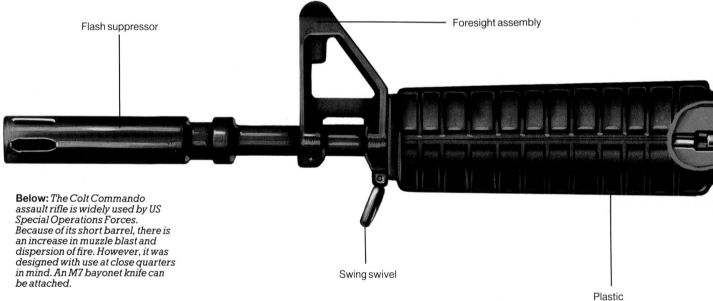

Flash suppressor

Foresight assembly

Below: *The Colt Commando assault rifle is widely used by US Special Operations Forces. Because of its short barrel, there is an increase in muzzle blast and dispersion of fire. However, it was designed with use at close quarters in mind. An M7 bayonet knife can be attached.*

Swing swivel

Plastic handguard

Top: *Special Operations training at the John F. Kennedy Special Warfare Center and School, Fort Bragg, North Carolina. Personnel are thoroughly familiarized with both foreign-made and all US weapons during training.*

Above: *The Colt Commando was originally developed for use in Vietnam, where some of the terrain conditions resemble those in which these members of the 1st Special Operations Squadron, Hurlburt Field, Florida, are operating.*

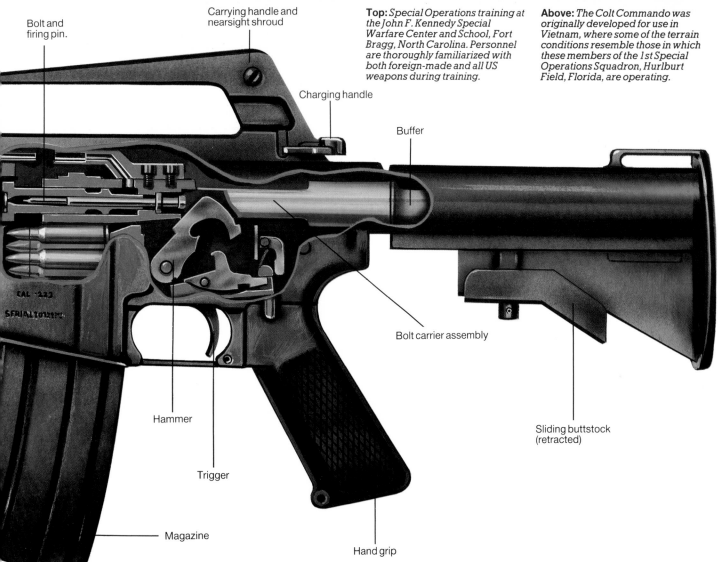

Bolt and firing pin.

Carrying handle and nearsight shroud

Charging handle

Buffer

Bolt carrier assembly

Hammer

Trigger

Magazine

Hand grip

Sliding buttstock (retracted)

M16A1/A2

Origin:
United States.
Type:
Rifle.
Dimensions:
Length overall (with flash suppressor) 38.9in (990mm); M16A2 40.0in (1,000mm); barrel 19.8in (508mm).
Weights:
M16A1 7.0lb (3.18kg); M16A2 7.5lb (3.4kg); with standard 30-round magazine 8.2lb (3.72kg); sling 5.3oz (182g).
Caliber:
5.56mm.
Feed:
20- and 30-round box magazine.
Maximum effective range:
300yds (274m).
Muzzle velocity:
3,280f/s (1,000m/s).
Rate of fire:
700-950rpm (cyclic); 150-200rpm (auto); 45-65rpm (semi-automatic).

The M16 (previously the AR-15), designed by Eugene Stoner, was a development of the earlier 7.62mm AR-10 assault rifle. It was first adopted for use in Vietnam. When first used in combat, numerous faults became apparent, most of them traceable to a lack of training and poor maintenance. Since then the M16 has replaced the 7.62mm M14 as the standard rifle of the United States forces.

Millions have been manufactured, most by Colt Firearms. The weapon was also made under license in Singapore, the Republic of Korea and the Philippines. The M16A2 has been adopted in Canada, which will build 80,000 under license, but with full-automatic capability in place of the burst-control option. Twenty-one armies use the M16.

The weapon is gas-operated and the user can select either full-automatic or semi-automatic. Both 20- and 30-round magazines can be fitted, as can a bipod, bayonet, telescope and night sight. The weapon can also be fitted with the M203 40mm grenade launcher, and this fires a variety of 40mm grenades to a maximum range of 382 yards (350m). The M203 has now replaced the M79 grenade launcher.

The Commando sub-machine gun model of the M16 is a special version with a shorter barrel, flash suppressor and a telescopic sight, reducing the overall length of the weapon to 27.9in (710mm). It is in use with US Special Operations Forces. The

M231 is a special model which can be fired from within the M2 Bradley Infantry Fighting Vehicle.

There has been consistent dissatisfaction with the M16A1 in the US Army, and even more so in the other main user – the US Marine Corps. One of the major complaints is its lack of effectiveness at ranges above 340 yards (300m), which has come to a head with the increased emphasis on desert warfare. This, combined with the high average age of current stocks, led to a major review in 1981. As a result, the M16A2 is a rifle that is actually a throwback to the 1950s; it is a weapon that has finally come full circle to where it should have begun in the first place. It entered inventories in 1987.

The barrel of the M16A2 is heavier, with a thicker profile. It weighs 8.15lb (3.69kg) with sling and empty 30-round magazine compared to the 7.9lb (3.58kg) of the M16A1. Other major changes include a three-round burst device, intended to cut down ammunition waste from the full-automatic operation on the A1; a new rear sight with a windage knob; a square-edged front sight post to give better target definition; a buttstock and handguard made of stronger materials; a flash suppressor that doubles as a muzzle compensator; and a wedge-shaped projection at the rear of the ejection port to deflect hot brass away from the face of the left-handed shooter.

Most importantly, the requirements for a longer-range weapon have been met by rebarreling to use the new NATO 5.56mm round more effectively. The longer, heavier bullets of these rounds are fully stabilized by the M162A's barrel, which is rifled with a twist of one turn in seven inches (one in 177mm). This improves the maximum effective range to about 550 yards (500m).

Above right: *A US Marine with M16 in training. Both 20- and 30-round magazines can be fitted to the M16, as can a bipod, bayonet, telescope and night sight.*

Right: *The M16, here in the capable hands of US Marines, has been used in 21 armies throughout the world. It is made under license in South Korea, Singapore and the Philippines.*

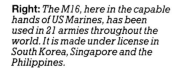

Above: *A "product improved" M16A2 has only started being distributed in the US. A modified version of it has been adopted for use by the Canadian forces. Requirement for longer range over the M16A1 has been met by rebarreling the rifle to use NATO 5.56mm ammunition more effectively.*

Right: *Green Berets on field exercise with M16s at the ready. In addition to providing these special forces with improved adjustable sights over these weapons, the new M16A2 barrel improves the maximum effective range of the rifle to about 550yd (500m) compared to 510yd (460m) of the current round.*

Below: *The M16 painted on the wall, as well as the very real weapon in the hands of this IRA terrorist (the word "Provo" is painted on the wall beside him), is clear testimony that modern weapons – no matter the country of origin – can be bought by terrorists.*

Above: *Walking past a bridgelayer is a US Army sniper armed with M21, with neither suppressor nor scope fitted. The other soldier has an M3A1 sub-machine gun.*

7.62mm M21 RIFLE

Origin:
United States.
Type:
Sniping rifle.
Dimensions:
Length (overall) 44in (1,120mm);
barrel 22in (559mm).
Weight:
(Full, with magazine) 14.5lb
(6.6kg).
Caliber:
7.62mm (NATO).
Feed:
Magazine.
Muzzle velocity:
2,800f/s (850m/s).

The M21 is the US Army's current sniping rifle, and is a variant of the M14, the standard Army rifle. The M21 is in effect an accurized M14, differing in that the barrel is gauged and selected to ensure correct specification tolerances. Spread of fire, with a ten-round group, must not exceed 6in (150mm) at 985ft (300m).

The weapon has a walnut stock impregnated with an epoxy resin. The receiver is individually fitted to the stock using a glass fiber compound, and

the firing mechanism is carefully hand-fitted and polished to improve operation and minimize carbon build-up. Trigger pull is light at between 4.4 and 4.7lb (2 and 2.15kg).

A suppressor would be fitted to the muzzle, reducing the velocity of emerging gases (but not velocity of the bullet), and thereby "silencing" the rifle, making it difficult to locate the firer.

The telescope used has a variable magnification from X3 to X9.

ARWEN 37

Origin:
United Kingdom.
Type:
Anti-riot weapon.
Dimensions:
Adjustable length – 29.9in
(760mm) to 33.1in (840mm).
Weights:
6.8lb (3.1kg) empty; 8.4lb (3.8kg)
loaded.
Caliber:
37mm.
Ammunition:
(Type AR1) baton, range 65 to
330ft (20-100m); (Type AR2)
multi-source irritant smoke,
range 280 to 310ft (85-95m);
(Type AR3) baton with discrete
dose of CS irritant, range 7 to
165ft (2-50m); (Type AR4) multi-
source screening smoke, range
280 to 310ft (85-95m); (Type
AR5): non-pyrotechnic
barricade-penetrating irritant.
Rate of fire:
60 rounds/minute; sustained rate
of 12 aimed shots/minute.

In 1977, the British Ministry of Defence drafted a requirement for a multi-shot weapon for use in Northern Ireland. By 1979, the Royal Small Arms Factory Enfield (now Royal Small Arms Limited) had produced three candidates. The first was a pump-action weapon with a four-shot capacity; the second was a revolver action weapon with a five-shot capacity; and the third was a self-loading weapon, fitted with a box magazine. In addition to the weapons, a prototype baton round was also developed.

Following trials of the prototypes, it was decided in early 1981 that a final mockup development would be produced . . . which incorporated the barrel and revolving action of prototype two with the trigger/pistol grip and stock of prototype three. There were other modifications and developments, but

the resulting anti-riot weapon was designated the Arwen 37.

The caliber was selected because it is the optimum size for the required energy/velocity combination. It is equipped with a rifled twist of 1-in-21in (1-in-540mm) for optimum accuracy. The pistol grip and trigger housing contain an integral ambidextrous safety lever. The weapon, as an additional safety feature, is fully cocked only when the first pressure is fully taken up. Upon release of the trigger, the action returns to the uncocked state.

The trigger is designed for operation by both index and middle fingers. Taking up the second pressure on the trigger and releasing it fires the weapon and revolves the feeding mechanism, bringing the next round into line with the breech. Recoil is not heavy. The revolving feed mechanism is easily removed for cleaning. The Arwen 37 is loaded through the open port on the right side, and this loading aperture also acts as an ejection port for ejecting cartridges automatically.

Its sights are presently of the folding aperture type, though it is planned to replace this with a single optical sight with integral reticule illumination. Two variants of the Arwen 37 have been produced; it is not fitted with a stock and has a shorter barrel than the Arwen 37.

The Arwen 37V has been developed for use in armored vehicles and is fitted with an optical sight on an extended stem. Its barrel is of a slightly different exterior configuration to the Arwen 37, and it is also not fitted with a stock.

In any of its different configuration, Arwen provides police or paramilitary forces with a highly effective and flexible method for containing situations involving riots and civil disobedience.

Above left: *The Arwen 37 five-load riot-control weapon, with butt adjustable to six positions, and operable left- or right-handed.*

Above and inset: *The Arwen 37's ammunition includes non-lethal body-blow AR1 (range out to 330ft/100m), irritant gas AR2 (range 280-310ft/85-95m), body blow plus*

irritant gas AR3 (range from 6 to 165ft/2-50m), plus smokescreen, barricade penetration and high explosive rounds all useful to counterterrorist forces.

MARK XII-C PEPPER FOG TEAR GAS/FOG GENERATOR

Origin:
United States.
Type:
Tear gas/fog generator.
Dimensions:
53.4in (1,34omm) × 13.6in (340mm) × 9.8in (245mm).
Weight:
17.6lb (8kg) empty; 27.06lb (12.3kg) when fully charged.

This resonant pulse jet device can produce approximately 100,000 cubic feet (2,831 cubic meters) of irritant or inert training gas in a period of 26 seconds. It can hold enough agent to generate smoke for 20 minutes. The Pepper Fog can be used with CN, CS or special CS – and it is used by police and military forces throughout the world.

Below: *The Pepper Fog gas generator, made by Smith and Wesson for riot control and military purposes, is a relatively lightweight unit, which can easily be re-charged in the field. It has its own self-contained power unit, ensuring free mobility of the operative, who can be on foot or vehicle-mounted.*

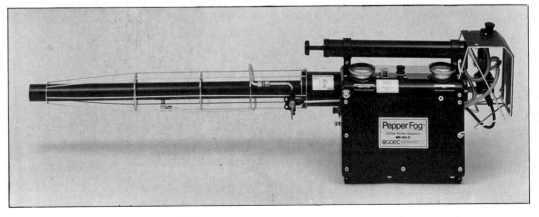

ARMSEL STRIKER

Origin:
South Africa.
Type:
Semi-automatic shotgun.
Gauge:
12 gauge, 2¾in (70mm).
Dimensions:
Length: 20in (500mm) with butt folded; 31.2in (78cm) with stock extended. Barrel: 11.8in (300mm).
Weight:
9.25lb (4.2kg) unloaded.
Practical range:
165 to 120ft (50 to 70m).
Rate of fire:
12 rounds/3 seconds.

The "Striker" shotgun – second name "The Protector" – is the invention of a Rhodesian farmer, who developed it as a counter-terrorist weapon for use in the Rhodesian bushwar (1972-80).

At the conclusion of the Rhodesian bush campaign, the "Striker" found a home in South Africa and is now manufactured in Johannesburg and a potential military, security and anti-terrorist weapon. It does not conform to any standard shotgun configuration; its windup coil spring-driven 12-round drum magazine is actuated by a two-phase double-action trigger-indexing setup.

Because of its great controllability, it can be fired with one hand like a pistol with complete control for repeat shots. The "Striker's" balance sits between the hands via twin pistol grips, which are of fiberglass-rein-forced polycarbonate. The safety button is at the top of the rear pistol grip just to the rear of the trigger, and runs from side to side at 90 degrees to the center line.

This safety is trigger locking, but a built-in feature prevents it from firing even if dropped. This is because the chambers of the magazine are out of alignment with the barrel and the firing pin until the double-action trigger is pulled through its primary stage.

Its unchoked barrel has a practical range of 55 to just over 75 yards (50 to 70m), but the "Striker" is also listed as dangerous when used with buckshot or slugs to just beyond 545 yards (500m). Recoil and muzzle rise are relatively negligible in both one – and two-handed firing; the optional sight for the gun also aids in accuracy. The sight is a small (5.5in/140mm) and light (4.5oz/127g) day or night sight mounted like a telescope sight with windage and elevation adjustments.

It is now sold mainly as a home defense and police/security guard gun. According to accounts, while a number of mining concerns in South Africa have bought the "Striker" for security forces, both the British SAS and the Royal Marines' SBS are considering its purchase.

Right: *The remarkable Armsel Striker "clockwork" shotgun, designed to fire shot or slug loads, with or without the stock folded.*

SPAS FRANCHI 12

Right: *The SPAS Franchi 12 riot shotgun will fire a variety of rounds, from buckshot and solid slug to small pellets and tear gas rounds.*

Origin:
Italy.
Type:
Shotgun.
Dimensions:
Length 37.2in (930mm); (stock folded) 28.4in (710mm); barrel 18.4in (460mm).

DAEWOO USAS-12

Origin:
Republic of Korea.
Type:
Automatic shotgun.
Dimensions:
Length overall 38in (960,5mm); barrel 18.25in (460.3mm).
Weight:
10lb (4.5kg).
Caliber:
12-gauge, 2¾in.
Magazine capacity:
12 round box or 28-round drum.

This system is relatively new, its design having been approved with modifications in late 1985. The USAS-12 is a gas-operated, full-automatic weapon. At first, the manufacturers, Daewoo Precision Industries, were not familiar with shotguns and this resulted in several engineering problems, which have now been largely overcome. In the prototype, for example, the extractor grabbed about 3 degrees of the case rim; the production model grabs about 17 degrees.

The weapon borrows elements from many sources. The cocking handle, for example, is in almost exactly the same position to that in the H&K type firearms; the carry handle is similar to an AR-15 and in fact takes any AR-15 scope mount.

There is a semi/full-auto selector switch, and separate button type safety in back of the trigger similar to that found in Remington shotguns. The adjustable gas regulator allows the introduction of more pressure as the weapon gets dirtier in the field, thus lessening the possibility of failure.

This weapon has the potential, in the eyes of some, to be a serious gun for a variety of special applications (production guns have been arriving only with the past year).

Below: *The USAS-12 has counter-insurgency, rear and remote area, counterterrorist applications with special operations forces, including US Navy SEALs.*

Weight:
9.2lb (4.2kg).
Caliber:
12 bore.
Rate of fire:
250rpm (theoretical); 24-30rpm (practical).

This Special Purpose Automatic Shotgun (Spas) was first produced in October 1979 by the firm of Luigi Franchi. Its decision was based on the perception that a specific riot shotgun was needed, that shotguns then in use were largely modified sport models, and that a military/police weapon in this area was needed.

The gun itself has a skeleton butt and a special device enabling it to be fired with one

hand if the occasioon dictates. Short barreled and semi-automatic, the receiver is composed of light alloy and other parts (barrel and gas cylinder) are chromed to resist corrosion.

Automatic action of the shotgun permits it to fire about four shots a second. Using standard buckshot rounds, it can put 48 pellets a second on a target at almost 44 yards (40m). It uses a wide range of ammunition: buck-

shot, solid slug, small pellets and tear gas rounds. With a grenade launcher fitted to the muzzle, it can fire grenades out to a maximum range of nearly 165 yards (150m). A special scattering device also fits on the muzzle and produces an instantaneous spread of pellets.

The Model 12 differs but slightly from the Model 11, with the main differences being in the fore-end and the improved and strengthened folding stock.

ITHACA 37

Origin:
United States.
Type:
Slide action repeater shotgun.
Dimensions:
Length 18.8 to 20in (470-508mm).
Weights:
6.5 to 7lb (2.94-3.06kg).
Caliber:
12-gauge, 2¾in.
Feed:
5- or 8-shot tubular magazine.

This shotgun is the famed basic "Featherlight" Model 37 pump action repeater manufactured by the Ithaca Gun Company of Ithaca, New York. It is a weapon that is uniquely free of stamped steel components, even to the trigger group.

The solid steel receiver does not have the usual ejection port on the right because it pops empty shells straight out of the bottom. Its unique action is centered around a dual-duty shell carrier that lifts live shells up to feed straight into the chamber.

Its pistol grip affords greater control while firing from the shoulder, and makes it practical to fire from a hip position.

The type of barrel in Ithaca's "Deerslayer" model (a trademark of the company to indicate precision-bored cylindrical barrels for general hunting uses) has been fitted to a combat shotgun. The objective is to provide a weapon capable of firing rifle slugs with optimum accuracy as well as being capable of handling the usual loadings.

A number of short-barrelled cylinder-bored configurations have been put in use by military and police forces in the US.

Above: *The Ithaca Model 37 pump action is probably the most commonly issued shotgun in America. Its light weight, fast action and 18in (525mm) barrel make it ideal as a police weapon. The extractor system will not accept European rimmed cartridges.*

Right: *The Model 37 Stakeout is simply the standard 37 with stock removed, pistol grip added with the barrel and the magazine shortened. In this chopped version, the weapon holds only 5 rounds (4 in magazine and 1 in chamber), but this is normally sufficient.*

MOSSBERG 500 ATP8

Origin:
United States.
Type:
Shotgun.
Dimensions:
Length, ATP8 40.3in (1009mm), ATP8 (pistol grip) 30.9in (762mm); barrel, ATP8 20.3in (308mm), ATP8 (pistol grip) 20.3in (508mm).
Weights:
ATP8 6.7lb (3.06kg), ATP8 (pistol grip) 6.1lb (2.72kg).
Caliber:
12-gauge, 2¾ or 3in.
Magazine capacity:
8.

The basic series of the Mossberg 500 shotguns are specially modified for police and military use. They have been described by some, as have other shotguns, as "reloadable Claymoores".

There are two main types – the six-shot and eight-shot models – but it is the latter which is used by elite forces. Its design is such as to ensure maximum reliability in use. It has an aluminum receiver for good balance and light weight. A cylinder-bored barrel, which is proof-tested to full magnum loads, provides optimum dispersion patterns and permits firing of a variety of ammunition.

The shotgun has twin extractors and the slide mechanism has twin guide bars that help prevent twisting or jamming during rapid operation. A recent addition is that the muzzle has been formed into a muzzle brake by cutting slots in the upper surface. Gas can then be expelled in such a way as to exert downward force, thus permitting easier pointing. In its pistol grip form, the Mossberg ATP8 is extremely compact and can thus be stowed more easily inside vehicles.

There is an almost infinite variety of options available.

Below: *The Mossberg 500 ATP8 as part of the 500 series is the most reliable pump-action shotgun design issued. The stock angle and generous-sized fore end make three aimed shots a second possible! The loading system is also 60 percent faster than any other, the shell carrier being receded into the block.*

Above and right: *The 500 ATP8 being carried at the ready (above) and in firing position (right). A common fallacy with modern firearms is that they should be fired from the hip. In fact, over 80 percent of all firearms training given to special forces personnel involves obtaining a flash sight picture at minimum.*

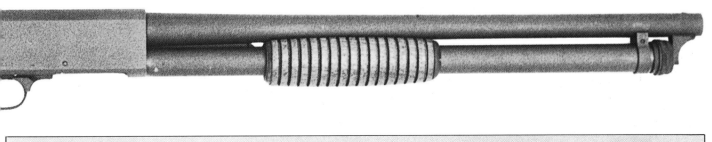

MADSEN MODEL 53

Origin:
Denmark.

Type:
Sub-machine gun.

Dimensions:
Length (stock extended) 31.8in (794mm); (stock folded) 21.1in (528mm); barrel 8.0in (198mm).

Weight:
(empty) 7.0lb (3.2kg).

Cartridge:
9mm parabellum.

Feed:
32-round box.

Rifling:
4 groove r/h.

Muzzle velocity:
1,287ft/sec (390m/sec).

Rate of fire:
(cyclic) 550rpm.

The first sub-machine gun to be made in Denmark was a type of Finnish Suomi, made under license by the Danish Madsen Industrial Syndicate in 1940. Production continued throughout World War II, with the gun being used by the Danes, the Germans and the Finns.

This same syndicate has made all Danish sub-machine guns since then. The first weapon of the present series was the Model 1946, and the Danes, profiting from wartime advances in mass production, made sure it was designed in such a way as to be able to take advantage of these improved techniques. One of the most unusual sub-machine guns ever designed and produced, the Model 53 is designed to lend itself to high speed production at extremely low cost.

The main body, including the pistol grip, is made from two side pieces, hinged together at the rear so that the weapon can easily be opened for repair, cleaning or inspection. It does, however, have the disadvantage that the springs are liable to fall out unless care is taken. The Madsen works on the normal blowback system and will fire single rounds or bursts.

One of its unusual features is a grip safety behind the magazine housing which (with the magazine itself) acts as a forward hand grip. Unless this safety is in, the gun will not function, which makes it impossible to fire it one-handed. The tubular metal stock is on a pivot and folds onto the right side of the weapon.

The Model 53 is in use with Danish police forces and in some South American and Southeast Asian countries. It is made under license in Brazil in .45 calibre. Many of the design and manufacturing features lend themselves to ready application to other small arms designs.

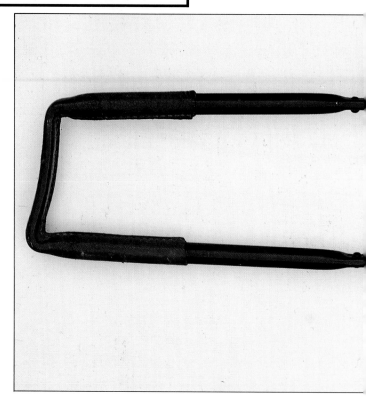

Above: *Madsen Model 53, shown here with the shoulder stock extended, is fine for normal battle and security situations. Its grip safety system makes one-handed firing impossible, a serious problem if it is necessary to both rappel and fire at the same time.*

Right: *The Madsen in its unique stripping and cleaning configuration. The weapon opens on the same hinge bolts the stock folds on. With the exception of the Brazilian copy made under licence in .45 ACP, no other weapon uses this system of disassembly.*

9mm MAT49

Origin:
France.

Type:
Sub-machine gun.

Dimensions:
Length (stock extended) 28.8in (720mm); (stock folded) 20.2in (460mm); barrel 9.1in (228mm).

Weights:
(unloaded) 7.9lb (3.6kg); (loaded) 9.2lb (4.2kg).

Cartridge:
9mm parabellum.

Feed:
32- or 20-round box magazine.

Rifling:
4 grooves l/h.

Muzzle velocity:
1,287ft/sec (390m/sec).

Rate of fire:
(cyclic) 600rpm.

The M1949 sub-machine gun, which was built by Tulle (Manufacture d'Armes de Tulle), has a good reputation among French troops. First adopted by the French Army in 1949, it saw considerable service in Indochina and Algeria. A large number of

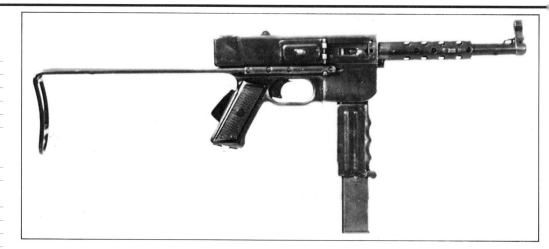

these weapons, incidentally, were captured in Indochina and later converted to the Soviet 7.76mm Type P round, and the cyclic rate was increased to 900 rounds per minute. These weapons can be recognized by their longer barrel and 35-round magazine.

Of conventional blowback design, the MAT49 has several unusual, but useful, features. The magazine housing (with magazine attached), for example, may be folded forward and clipped under the barrel – and has only to be swung back and down to be used instantly. Combined with a telescopic steel stock, this feature makes the weapon particularly usable by parachute troops. A pistol-grip squeeze safety is fitted, and this prevents accidental discharge by dropping. The ejection port cover helps keep dirt out of the internal mechanism of the gun.

The weapon is used by French forces and the armies of many former French colonies.

Above: *The steeply canted pistol grip and large fore grip on the MAT49 give excellent full auto control when fired from the hip, which made this weapon a favorite with the French for house clearing and similar operations where shouldering a weapon was found to be too slow.*

Right: *The MAT49 with the stock forward. Note that although the overall length is reduced, the stock is still at least 25 percent of the overall length.*

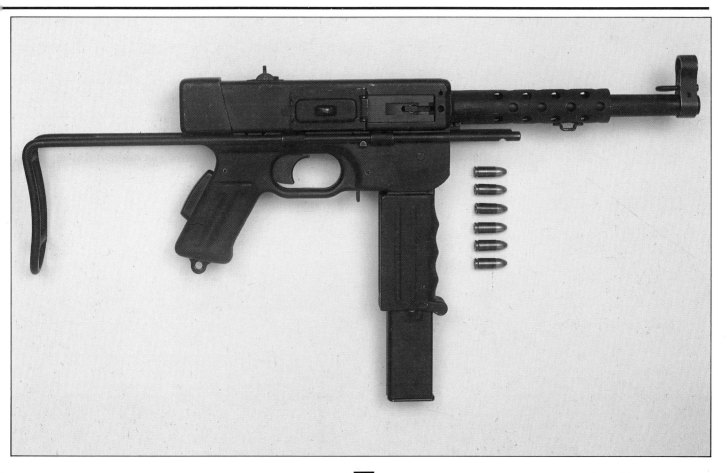

HECKLER & KOCH MP5

Origin:
Federal Republic of Germany.
Type:
Sub-machine gun.
Dimensions:
Barrel (MP5A2) 9in (225mm), (MP5A3) 9in (225mm), (MP5SD1) 6in (146mm), (MP5SD2) 6in (146mm), (MP5SD3) 6in (146mm), (MP5K) 5in (115mm); overall length (MP5A2) 26.8in (680mm), (MP5A3) 19.3in (490mm), (MP5SD1) 21.7in (550mm), (MP5SD2) 30.4in (780mm), (MP5SD3) 24in (610mm), (MP5K) 12.8in (325mm).
Weights:
(MP5A2) 5.6lb (2.5kg), (MP5A3) 6.3lb (2.9kg), (MP5SD1) 6.2lb (2.9kg), (MP5SD2) 6.8lb (3.1kg), (MP5SD3) 7.5lb (3.4kg), (MP5K) 4.4lb (2kg).
Caliber:
9mm×19.
Feed:
10/15/30 round box magazine.
Muzzle velocity:
1,320f/s (400m/s).

Rate of fire:
(MP5A2) 750rpm, (MP5A3) 750rpm, (MP5SD1)650rpm, (MP5SD2) 650rpm, (MP5SD3) 650rpm, (MP5K) 840rpm.
Sights:
Rear, four operative rotating barrel; front, hooded blade, non-adjustable.

Since its introduction in the 1960s, Heckler & Koch's MP5 has enjoyed a reputation as a weapon sophisticated enough to satisfy the requirements of the world's most elite military units – the British SAS for example. Using the same roller delayed blowback operating principle as its bigger brothers the G3 and G41, the MP5 features good handling qualities coupled with parts that are interchangeable with those in a wide range of heavier assault weapons.

The MP5 fires in one of three modes: semi-auto, full-auto or three-round burst – all of which are controlled by the trigger mechanism. Similar to the FN

Above: *The H&K MP5 SD (suppressed) is used by special forces not because it is totally silent (which it is not) but because in a fluid close quarter fight the low noise level and reduced muzzle blast makes the trooper hard to find by aggressors.*

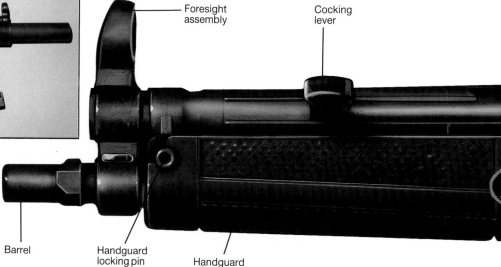

Foresight assembly

Cocking lever

Barrel

Handguard locking pin

Handguard

Chambered round

Left: *The MP5 SD with a powerful laser lock system, a combination of an almost silent, fully automatic smg capable of firing full power ammunition, and a sighting system which can instantly tell the firer where the burst is going to strike without him having to shoulder the weapon. An excellent close quarter battle weapon pack.*

FAL's trigger, the H&K's safety acts as its fire selector.

Three-shot bursts are accomplished through a small ratchet "counting mechanism" interacting with the sear. Each time the bolt cycles to the rear, the ratchet advances one notch until the third cycle allows reengagement of the sear or the trigger is released, circumventing the "counter" and ending the cycle before three shots are fired.

These arms have great appeal to Third World countries, not only for their reliability and maintainability but also for their ease of manufacture. The receiver, constructed of stamped sheet steel in 19 operations (several combined), is attached to the polygonal rifled barrel by a trunnion which is spot welded to the receiver and pinned to the barrel. The trigger housing, buttstock and fore-end are high impact plastic. H&K utilizes metal stampings and welded sub group parts.

The MP5 has an impressive list of accessories. These include: a magazine loader; a .22 cal. conversion kit; a blank firing device; a muzzle-mounted tear gas grenade launcher; and various optical devices. The MP5 has various configurations. The MP5A2 has a fixed buttstock and the MP5A3 features a retractable stock – they are interchangeable.

The MP5K was introduced in 1976 and is designed for special operations; the barrel is shorter, a vertical foregrip added and the rear-sight apertures replaced with open notches. There is no butt-stock, only a receiver cap.

The MP5SD is a silenced weapon and identical to the MP5A2/A3 with regard to functioning principle and bolt system. MP5SD1 is the weapon with receiver cap; SD2, weapon with a fixed stock; and SD3, weapon with retractable stock. The primary feature of the silenced version is that it fires below the speed of sound, thus preventing bullet blast.

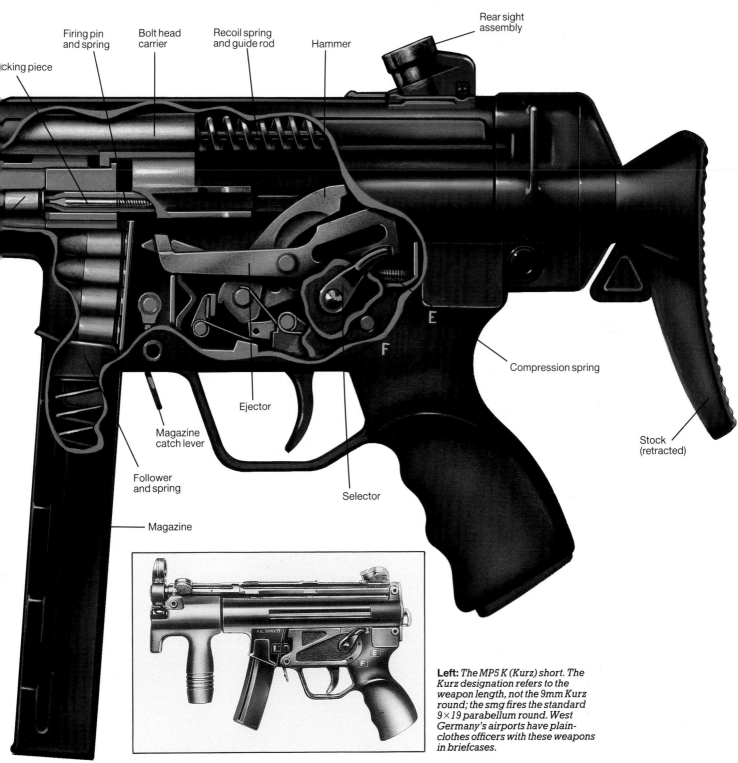

Firing pin and spring · Bolt head carrier · Recoil spring and guide rod · Hammer · Rear sight assembly · ...cking piece · Compression spring · Magazine catch lever · Ejector · Stock (retracted) · Follower and spring · Selector · Magazine

Left: *The MP5 K (Kurz) short. The Kurz designation refers to the weapon length, not the 9mm Kurz round; the smg fires the standard 9×19 parabellum round. West Germany's airports have plainclothes officers with these weapons in briefcases.*

UZI SUB-MACHINE GUN

Origin:
Israel.
Type:
Sub-machine gun.
Dimensions:
Length 25.2in (640mm).
Weight:
7.7lb (3.5kg).
Caliber:
9mm and .45 cal.
Rifling:
4 groove r/h (9mm); 6 groove l/h (.45 cal.).
Feed:
25/32/40 round box (9mm); 16 round (.45 cal.).
Muzzle velocity:
1,280f/s (390m/s).
Rate of fire:
Cyclic 600rpm (9mm); cyclic 500rpm (.45 cal.).
Sights:
Flip, 110-219yd (100-200m).

At midnight on 14 May 1948, the British mandate over Palestine ceased, and the Jewish State of Israel was declared. On the very next day the new state was invaded by its Arab neighbors. Nearly eight months of war followed, at the end of which Israel had not only defended her own territory successfully, but had also occupied some of that belonging to her attackers. In spite of her success, however, it was clear that she needed a reliable weapon which she could make from her own resources in sufficient numbers to arm the bulk of her population. A young army major named Uziel Gal, an arms expert, designed and produced that new sub-machine gun, the Uzi – which is one of the most prolific SMGs in the western world today.

Gal based his design on the Czechoslovakian postwar 9mm Models 23 and 25 sub-machine guns, a major departure from prewar and wartime designs. Early sub-machine guns were not known for accuracy. To achieve this, designers at Uhersky Brod, one of Czechoslovakia's chief arms factories, developed a concept wherein the bolt actually telescoped the rear end of the barrel, enclosing the cartridge. Major Gal kept this and another clever Czech design as well: the magazine was inserted through the pistol grip. This meant that the bolt face/breech was at the point of balance, but also just forward of the shoulder axis for more accurate point-fire from the hip.

The Uzi is a simple blowback design. The bolt is cocked by

drawing it to the rear. The sear rotates up to engage and hold it open. The trigger mechanism is also simple. A coil spring is used to tension the sear; pulling the trigger to the rear allows the sear to move down and rotate out of engagement with the bolt. The bolt's own coil spring drives it forward, stripping a cartridge from the magazine, chambering it and firing it as the striker in the bolt face impacts the primer. The momentum generated by the exploding cartridge then drives the bolt to the rear, extracting and ejecting the fired case – until it comes up against the bolt stop. Its spring then drives it forward again in a repeat cycle.

In all the years that Major Gal's 9mm Uzi has been in production, there have only been two signi-

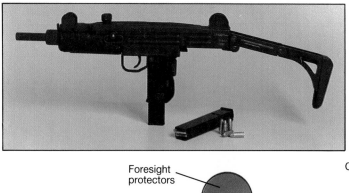

Left: *The Uzi smg with shoulder stock extended. Note the drop angle between the axis of the weapon and the butt plate, to give the firer a sight picture when the weapon is shouldered, but also causing it to climb in full auto.*

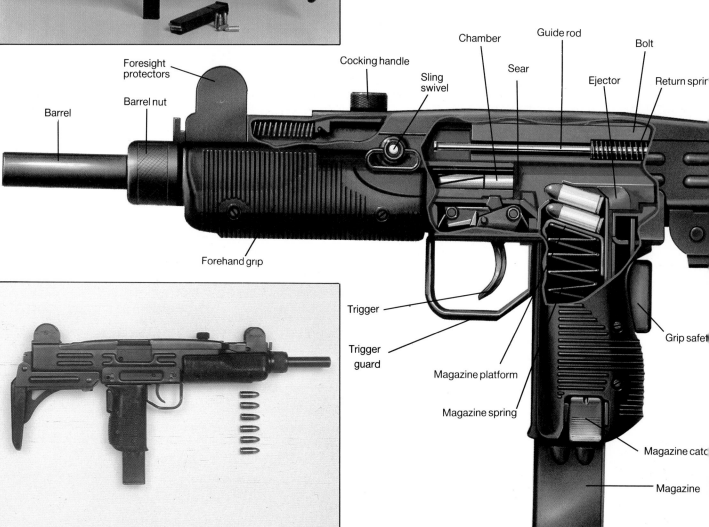

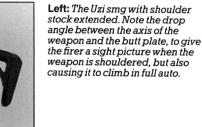

Barrel

Foresight protectors

Barrel nut

Cocking handle

Sling swivel

Chamber

Sear

Guide rod

Bolt

Ejector

Return spring

Forehand grip

Trigger

Trigger guard

Magazine platform

Magazine spring

Grip safety

Magazine catch

Magazine

9mm MINI-UZI/MICRO-UZI

ficant changes made. A grip safety, which blocks the trigger unless depressed, has been added, and the Uzi is now available in .45 Automatic Colt Pistol Cartridge.

In addition to Israeli forces, the Uzi is in use in Belgium, the Federal Republic of Germany, Iran, the Netherlands, Thailand, Venezuela and other countries. It has been ordered in the hundreds of thousands and is probably the most widely used sub-machine gun in the western world. Optional attachments include a short bayonet and a barrel-mounted searchlight. A grenade launcher may be screwed to the front of the receiver in place of the barrel locking-nut. Two 32-round magazines if clipped together increase fire capacity.

Origin:	
Israel.	
Type:	
Sub-machine gun.	
Dimensions:	
Stock folded 14.2in (360mm); stock extended 23.7in (600mm); barrel 7.75in (197mm).	
Weight:	
5.9lb (2.7kg).	
Cartridge:	
9mm and +P 9mm.	
Feed:	
20/25/32 round box.	
Rifling:	
4 groove r/h.	
Effective range:	
165yd (150m).	
Rate of fire:	
950rpm.	

Israel Military Industries has produced a smaller version of its famous sub-machine gun and designated it the Mini-Uzi. In operation it exactly resembles its larger "parent", differing only in size, weight and firing characteristics. It will accept a 20-round magazine for its 9mm Parabellum pistol ammunition, as well as 25- and 32-round magazines.

It can easily be concealed under ordinary clothing, and carried in the minimum vehicle space, which makes the Mini-Uzi particularly useful for security and law enforcement personnel and in commando operations. It can be fired full- or semi-automatic from the hip or, with stock extended, from the shoulder, and is said to maintain the high standards of reliability and accuracy set by the Uzi.

There are three models – open bolt, closed bolt, or heavy bolt – to meet specific requirements. The heavy bolt model offers a reduced rate of fire (750rmp) for situations requiring easier control.

Even newer is the smallest Uzi ever offered, which is designed to be used when the situation requires maximum concealment without sacrificing 9mm firepower. This new Micro-Uzi is less than 10in (254mm) long with shoulder stock folded and has a 1,200rpm rate of fire.

Backsight protectors

Butt (folded)

Above: *The Mini-Uzi, with its wire folding stock extended. Note the better stock angle.*

Below: *One-handed firing of the Mini-Uzi, made easier because the weight is centralized over the pistol grip. Inset is the Micro-Uzi.*

STEN GUN

Origin:
United Kingdom.
Type:
Sub-machine gun.
Dimensions:
Length overall, MkII 30.5in (762mm), MkIIS 34.3in (857mm), MkIII 30.5in (762mm), MkV 30.5in (762mm), MkVI 34.3in (857mm); barrel MkII 7.9in (197mm), MkIIS 3.7in (91.4mm), MkIII 7.9in (197mm), MkV 8.0in (198mm); MkVI 3.8in (95mm).
Weights:
(loaded) MkII 7.6lb (3.44kg), MkIIS 9.1lb (4.14kg), MkIII 8.4lb (3.82kg), MkV 10.0lb (4.54kg), MkVI 10.9lb (4.96kg).
Caliber:
9mm parabellum.
Rifling:
6 grooves r/h, one turn in 10.2in (254mm); Mk II has two grooves.
Muzzle velocity:
1,205f/s (366m/s); MkIIS and VI, 1,007f/s (304m/s).
Rate of fire:
(cyclic) 550rpm.

By 1941, Great Britain and the Commonwealth were engaged in raising and equipping new armies. In addition, there were urgent demands for supplies and replacements for North and East Africa where British and Colonial troops were operating against the Italians. This dictated an urgent requirement for a simple, home-produced sub-machine gun, and by the middle of 1941 a weapon had not only been designed but was in limited production and undergoing user trials. This was the famous Sten, which took its name from the initial letters of the surnames of the two people most closely concerned with its development – Major R V Shepherd, a director of the Birmingham Small Arms Company and H S Turpin, the principal designer, allied to the first two letters of Enfield, the location of the Royal Small Arms factory where it was first produced.

As soon as the few inevitable weaknesses revealed by the trials had been rectified, the Sten gun went into large-scale production and in its various forms provided an invaluable source of additional automatic fire power

9mm STERLING L2A3

Origin:
United Kingdom.
Type:
Sub-machine gun.
Dimensions:
Length (stock extended) 28in (690mm); (stock folded) 19in (483mm); barrel 7.9in (198mm).
Weights:
(empty) 6.0lb (2.72kg); (loaded) 7.6lb (3.47kg).
Cartridge:
9mm parabellum.
Feed:
34-round box magazine.
Rifling:
6 groove r/h.
Muzzle velocity:
1,287ft/sec (390m/sec).
Rate of fire:
(cyclic) 550rpm.

Designed by a team headed by G W Patchett of the Sterling Engineering Co, England, the Sterling began life at the end of World War II, as, not surprisingly, the "Patchett". It took the same magazine as the Sten and Lanchester sub-machine guns, but the design was much more efficient and effective than that found in either of its predecessors. The gun underwent some modifications and was formally adopted by the British forces in 1954.

Well made and finished, the gun is of normal blowback mechanism, but is unusual in having a ribbed bolt which cuts away dirt and fouling as it accumulates and forces it out of the receiver. This allows the gun to function well under the most adverse conditions. The magazine, which sticks out of the left side of the action (similar to the Sten), holds 34 rounds, although a 10-round version is also available.

Sights include a rear flip-type aperture that graduates to 110 and 220 yards (100 and 200m), and a narrow blade (almost a post) front. The gun is capable of selective fire, either semi-automatic or fully automatic. It is also fitted for a blade bayonet.

Some 90 nations use the Sterling in addition to Britain, India, Canada and New Zealand. The weapon was particularly useful to British special forces in the Falklands War and in Northern Ireland. Sterlings were also a favorite weapon for use in the Mau Mau uprisings in Kenya. A special forces operator who has used the Sterling in operations has commented, "It flows like syrup when fired. It is a nice field sub-machine gun, simple, reliable and easy to control". Many of these weapons have also been found in terrorist arsenals.

to the British forces.

The Sten worked on a simple blow-back system using a heavy bolt with a coiled return spring. In spite of its simple concept the first models made were still relatively elaborate, with a cone-shaped flash hider and a rather crude forward pistol grip which could be folded up underneath the barrel when not in use. It could fire either single shots or bursts, the change lever being a circular stud above the trigger. It also had some woodwork at the fore-end and as a bracer at the small of the butt.

So few of the Mark I versions were produced, however, that they can be disregarded for all practical purposes; only 2,000 copies of the Mark IV were produced in two models (A and B), and it can be disregarded as well.

The Sten Mark II differs only in externals from the Mark I. The barrel and barrel jacket were shortened, the design on the bolt handle altered, and a simplified buttstock issued. The second pattern (Mark IIS) has a shorter barrel, silencer, a lighter bolt and a shorter recoil spring.

Mark III does not have the detachable barrel of the other models and is probably the most cheaply made of the Sten guns. Its receiver and barrel jacket are made of a single welded steel tube, with the housing of the magazine welded to the receiver. The Mark V has a number of features that were not in the earlier models; among them are wooden pistol grip and stock, a front sight with protective ears, and lugs on the barrel for bayonets. The Mark VI is the Mark V fitted with a shortened barrel and a silencer.

Sten guns were manufactured in millions and, in fact, were used extensively by the underground in Occupied Europe during World War II. Later models are still widely used throughout the world, but they are no longer standard weapons in the UK. Built in the UK, Canada and New Zealand, it seems likely that the Sten gun will be encountered for years to come in the hands of irregulars around the globe.

Left: *The Sten Mk II is still used by irregulars and even badly trained "resistance" fighters since it is possible to cannibalise parts to repair the simple guns in the field.*

Right: *Top to bottom, Sten Mk I No. 2 Mk II; Sten Mk II, standard issue weapon; Sten Mk III, similar to the Mk II but with a fixed barrel; Sten Mk V, deluxe model with wooden furniture.*

Above: *Modern-day answer to the Sten is the Sterling L2A3, again tried-and-tested simplicity, seen here with its stock extended and very distinctive curved 34-round magazine detached.*

Left: *A British para armed with a Sterling, in an urban conflict area. The weapon's profile allows the firer to go prone without the mag getting in the way.*

Right: *Sterling L2A3 with its stock folded. The lack of concealability is a problem, the grip and magazine being 90° out of alignment with each other.*

9mm L34A1 STERLING SILENCED SUB MACHINE GUN

Origin:
United Kingdom.
Type:
Sub-machine gun.
Dimensions:
Stock extended 34.6in (864mm);
stock folded 26.4in (660mm);
barrel 7.9in (198mm).
Weights:
Empty 8lb (3.6kg); loaded 9.5lb
(4.3kg).

Caliber:
9mm parabellum.
Feed:
34-round box magazine.
Rifling:
6 grooves r/h.
Muzzle velocity:
Approximately 1,200ft/sec
(360m/sec).
Rate of fire:
(cyclic) 550rpm.

This is the silenced version of the L2A3 (see related entry) and is called the L34A1. It is somewhat longer than the L2A3 and tops the Mk 4 version's weight, unloaded, by almost two pounds (1kg). Many of its parts are interchangeable with those of the L2A3, thus keeping down replacement costs and ensuring availability.

The barrel jacket is covered by a silencer casing, with front and rear supports. The barrel has 72 radial holes drilled through it, which permits propellant gas to escape, thus reducing the muzzle velocity of the bullet. The barrel has a metal wrap and diffuser tube; the extension tube goes beyond the silencer casing and barrel.

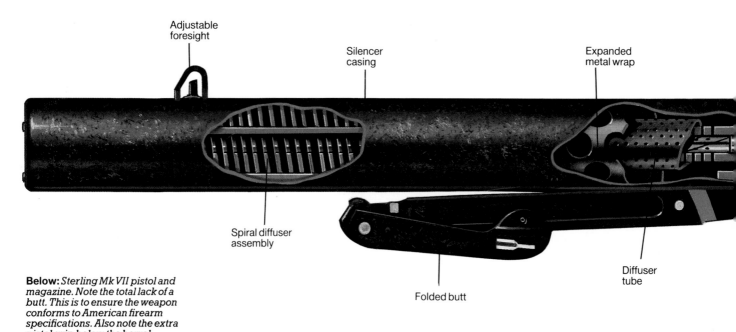

Adjustable foresight · Silencer casing · Expanded metal wrap · Spiral diffuser assembly · Folded butt · Diffuser tube

Below: *Sterling Mk VII pistol and magazine. Note the total lack of a butt. This is to ensure the weapon conforms to American firearm specifications. Also note the extra pistol grip below the barrel.*

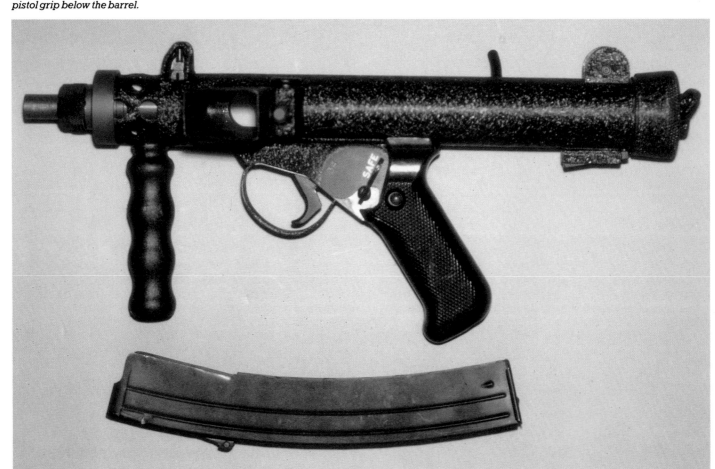

A spiral diffuser beyond the barrel is a series of discs, which has a hole through its center that allows passage of the round. Gas follows the round closely and is deflected back by the end cap; it mingles with the gases coming forward – with the result that the gas velocity leaving the weapon is low.

The silenced Sterling is used by the British Army, and versions by many other countries, and terrorist groups.

Above: *Sterling Mk VII. This is a closed bolt semi-auto weapon which would be properly described as a pistol! It is often used by civilian security units for close protection in vehicles.*

Return spring handle

Return spring

Return spring locking mechanism

Trigger assembly

Below and bottom: *The L34A1 Sterling is an extremely efficient, dedicated silenced weapon, normally fired semi-auto but capable of withstanding prolonged automatic fire with full power ammunition.*

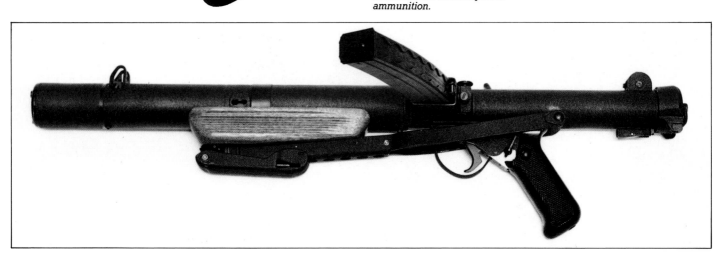

INGRAM MODELS 10/11

Origin:
United States.
Type:
Sub-machine gun.
Dimensions:
Length (no stock), Model 10 10.5in (267mm), Model 11 8.7in (222mm); (telescoped) Model 10 10.6in (269mm), Model 11 9.8in (248mm); (extended) Model 10 21.6in (548mm), Model 11 18.1in (460mm). Barrel, Model 10 5.75in (146mm), Model 11 5.1in (129mm). Suppressor, Model 10 11.5in (291mm), Model 11 8.8in (224mm).
Cartridge:
Model 10, .45 ACP; Model 11, 9mm Short (.380 ACP) or 9mm Parabellum.
Muzzle velocity:
Model 10, 924f/s (280m/s); Model 11, 967f/s (293m/s).
Rate of fire:
(cyclic) Model 10, 1,100 rounds/minute; Model 11, 1,200 rounds/minute.

This weapon is named after its inventor, Gordon B. Ingram, a practical man with clear views of what a good sub-machine gun should be. He designed a series of them after having fought in World War II, and all his wea-

pons were simple, reliable, and relatively cheap to make.

In 1946 he produced his first version (the M5), but it was not the best of times to try and sell a new sub-machine gun since the world was full of surplus weapons. Undaunted, Ingram worked on a new model for two years . . . and in 1949 set up a firm known as the Police Ordnance Company in partnership with some fellow veterans. The result was Model 6, which came in two types: one in .38in caliber, which looked like a Thompson, and another in .45in caliber, both of which sold reasonably well to police departments and in South America.

By 1959, Ingram had produced his Models 7 through 9, all of which were sufficiently successful to encourage him to go on with the series. In 1969, he went to work for a firm specializing in suppressors and during the next year this firm spun off a subsidiary. Now established, he began to design weapons entirely different from the earlier versions – and Models 10 and 11 soon appeared.

They are virtually identical except for size. Their general appearance is similar in a general way to the early Webley automatic pistols; they work on blowback, but have wraparound bolts which make it possible to keep the weapon short and improve control at full automatic fire. The cocking handle, which is on the top, is equally convenient for right- or left-handed firers; it has a slot cut in the center so as not to interfere with the line of sight. The magazine fits into the pistol grip and the gun has a retractable butt.

The whole thing is made of stampings, with the exception of the barrel, and even the bolt is made of sheet metal and filled with lead. Models 10 and 11 are both fitted with suppressors, which reduce sound considerably. The modern-pattern Ingram – out of production for a while, but just recently returned to manufacture – is the primary standard arm of Portugal, Saudi Arabia and US special units. It has been sold to six other nations as well. Its chief virtue is power (to .45 ACP if desired) in a concealable package.

M3A1 SUB-MACHINE GUN

Origin:
United States.
Type:
Sub-machine gun.
Dimensions:
Stock extended 30.8in (757mm); stock retracted 23.2in (579mm); barrel 8.0in (203mm).
Weights:
(without magazine, sling, oil bottle) 7.6lb (3.47kg); full 9.9lb (4.52kg).
Cartridge:
.45 ACP.
Feed:
30 round box magazine.
Rifling:
4 grooves r/h.
Muzzle velocity:
924ft/sec (280m/sec).
Rate of fire:
(cyclic) 450rpm.

In 1941 the Small Arms Development Branch of the US Army Ordnance Corps set out to develop a sub-machine gun in accordance with guidelines proposed by the various combat arms. The intention was to produce a weapon which could be mass-produced at low cost and by modern methods. Perform-

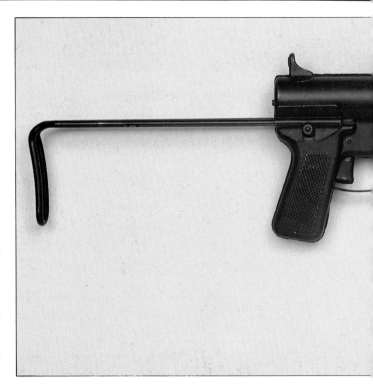

ance was to be at least comparable to that of the British Sten gun.

Development work progressed so quickly that prototypes were successfully tested well beore the end of 1942; the new weapon was accepted as standard under the designation M3.

It was a utilitarian locking arm, made as far as practicable from stampings and with little machining, except for the barrel and bolt. It worked by blowback and had no provision for firing single rounds, but this was acceptable because of its low cyclic rate. The stock was of retractable wire and the caliber was .45, although conversion to 9mm was not difficult. It bore a strong resemblance to the ordinary "grease gun", the source of its famous nickname.

Large-scale use revealed trouble with the bolt retracting handle and attempts to simplify the system resulted in the M3A1. Like its predecessor, the new gun was made by modern methods and generally reliable. It worked, as before, by blowback, but had no cocking handle, a process that was achieved by inserting the finger into a slot cut in the receiver by which the bolt could be withdrawn.

The bolt, which had no integral firing pin, worked on guide rods which saved complicated finishing of the inside of the receiver and which gave smooth functioning with little interruption from dirt. An oil container was built into the pistol grip, and a small bracket added to the rear of the retractable butt acted as a magazine filler. It used a box magazine, which was not alto-

Above left and far right: *Ingram sub-machine guns are small enough to have been dubbed sub-machine pistols when seen without their suppressors. A large number of these efficient assassination weapons have got into the hands of terrorists.*

Above: *Ingram Model 10/11 both with and without suppressor. Note the leather sleeve on the barrel of the suppressor; this has the dual purpose of protecting the firer's hand from heat and reducing vibration, thereby reducing the noise of the weapon firing.*

gether reliable in dirty or dusty conditios until the addition of an easily removed plastic cover eliminated the problem.

The Thompson – described as "a spring, a wire and a prayer" – was never popular in the US Army. It was relegated to use with the reserve forces in 1957. The M3A1 can still, however, be found in use in South America, Southeast Asia, and the IRA has been known to have them at their disposal. Stocks of the weapon were also uncovered by US invasion forces in Grenada.

Above left: *The M3A1 was extensively used by the OSS during World War II. Its .45 ACP has over double the stopping power of 9mm, which was the caliber of all British and European sub-machine guns at the time.*

Above: *A M3A1 grease gun in the hands of an apparently surrendering Viet Cong soldier. The South Vietnamese regulars who have captured him don't seem to think a man with a loaded smg is dangerous! No wonder they lost.*

7.62mm L7A1 AND L7A2 MACHINE GUN

Origin:
United Kingdom.
Type:
General-purpose machine gun.
Dimensions:
Length overall 49.3in (1,232mm); barrel (with flash suppressor) 23.9in (597mm).
Weights:
With light barrel 23.9lb (10.9kg); barrel 6.0lb (2.73kg).
Caliber:
7.62mm×51.
Feed:
Belt.
Effective range:
On bipod 880yds (800m); on tripod 1,540yds (1,400m).
Muzzle velocity:
2,765f/s (838m/s).
Rate of fire:
(cyclic) 750-1,000rpm.

At the close of World War II, the British Army had the Vickers Mark I machine gun as its sustained fire weapon and the Bren as its section light machine gun. They both used a .303 inch cartridge.

Following introduction of the NATO 7.62mm round, the opportunity was available to select a modernized general-purpose machine gun. The Belgian *Mitrailleuse d'Appui General* (MAG) was chosen after many trials, and built under license at the Royal Small Arms Factory, Enfield as the L7A1.

A few changes have been made in its design, particularly in the barrel. I addition, a tripod has been developed to permit the weapon to be used in the sustained fire role. Although almost identical to the MAG in its significant characteristics, minor changes have been made to accommodate British manufacturing methods and material specifications. The L7A2 has an attachment for a 50-round belt box on the left side of the receiver, double pawls and a double bent sear with the slide machined to match.

The weapon was developed using the best points of weapons that had already proved themselves. Both the piston and the bolt are derived from the Browning automatic rifle. Its feed mechanism is nearly one-for-one with that of the German MG42 of World War II, an earlier counterpart of the MAG in the sense that both guns were widely adaptable.

Belt-fed, the system is used as a light medium machine gun. The barrel is quick-detachable. The gun may be fired if this quick-detachable stock is removed, and the fitting of a back plate will help prevent fouling due to dirt.

If the machinegun is used in the sustained fire role on a tripod, a dial sight (as used on the British 81mm mortar) can be utilized for indirect firing.

It is a popular weapon, and, while production is now complete, has been purchased in its various forms by some 20 countries, remaining in service with the British, Belgian, Dutch and some Commonwealth forces.

Left: *British troops use the L7A2 on a NATO exercise. In the sustained fire role, the gun would be mounted on the L4A1 tripod, and the butt could be removed. The mounting has its own recoil buffer unit, and features which permit all-round traverse, elevation and depression.*

Left: *Preparing for war: British paras train with the L7A2 aboard ship on their way to the Falklands. The weapon is a compromise, and although popular is thought too heavy and cumbersome for the light role, and somewhat lacking the true sustained fire capacity.*

M60 MACHINE GUN

Origin:
United States.
Type:
General purpose machine gun.
Dimensions:
Gun (overall) 44.2in (1,105mm);
barrel 22.4in (560mm).
Weights:
Gun 23.1lb (10.51kg); barrel 8.2lb
(3.74kg) (includes bipod and gas
cylinder).
Cartridge:
7.62mm×51mm.
Effective range:
Bipod 1,100yd (1,000m); tripod
1,980yd (1,800m).
Muzzle velocity:
2,820f/s (855m/s).
Rate of fire:
(cyclic) 4550 rounds/minute.

The M60 is the standard GPMG of the US Army and has now replaced the older 0.30 Browning machine gun. Production commenced in 1959.

The weapon is gas-operated, air-cooled and is normally used with a 100-round belt of ammunition. To avoid overheating the barrel is normally changed after 500 rounds have been fired. Its fore sight is of the fixed blade type and its rear sight is of the U-notch type and is graduated from about 656ft to 3,937ft (200 to 1,200m) in about 328ft (100m) steps. The weapon is provided with a stock, carrying handle and a built-in bipod. The M60 can also be used on an M122 tripod mount, M4 pedestal mount and M142 gun mount for vehicles. Other versions include the M60C remote for helicopters, M60D pintle mount for vehicles and helicopters and the M60E2 internal model for AFVs.

The original M60 was not a complete success, perhaps because too much was expected of a general purpose gun. This inevitably results in a system that is too heavy for the light role and too light for the heavy. However, the M60 was used extensively in Vietnam and, partly because of the practical experience obtained there by regular and special forces, was improved considerably and issued as the M60E1. It is still the standard general purpose machine gun in the US Army; it is used by Delta and can be found in service in the armed forces of Australia, El Salvador, the Republic of Korea and Taiwan.

Above: *Armed with a 7.62mm M60 machine gun, a soldier of 1st/502nd Inf., 101st Airborne Div., US Army, debusses in the Sinai Desert, Egypt, as part of the Multi-national Force.*

Below: *US Army troops train in urban warfare. Soldier in the foreground mans the M60 machine gun, backed up by trooper with M203 grenade launcher.*

RPG-7V AT ROCKET LAUNCHER

Origin:
Soviet Union
Type:
Rocket launcher.
Dimensions:
Length 38.5ft (990mm).
Caliber of tube:
40mm.
Caliber of projectile:
85mm.
Weights:
Launcher 15.0lb (7kg); grenade 4.95lb (2.25kg).
Effective range:
328yd (300m), moving target; 550yd (500m), stationary.
Mass of projectile:
4.95lb (2.25kg).
Muzzle velocity:
984ft/sec (300m/sec).

The standard anti-armor weapon of Soviet infantry, the RPG-7 replaced an earlier weapon derived from the World War II German Panzerfaust which merely fired a hollow-charge projectile from a shoulder-rested tube. The original, and heavier, version of this weapon was introduced in 1962 and was known simply as the RPG-7. The RPG-7V is the current variant and made its appearance in 1968.

RPG-7V fires a projectile which, a few metres beyond the muzzle, ignites an internal rocket to give shorter flight-time, flatter trajectory and better accuracy. The HEAT or HE warhead has improved fuzing, the HEAT round penetrating to 12.6in (320mm) of armor. The PGO-7 and PGO-7V optical sights are frequently supplemented by the NSP-2 (IR) night sight. There is also a special folding version used by airborne troops designated RPG-7D.

This launcher is standard issue for Soviet Union and Warsaw Pact forces – as well as forces in North Korea, North Vietnam, and other satellite countries. There is also a light version of the launcher – the RPG-7D – which can be divided in two for ease of transportation. This version is used mainly by airborne troops in the Warsaw Pact countries

Even in the hands of unskilled and illiterate troops, it is known to be highly effective against bunkers and buildings, troops, vehicles of all types, and even helicopters when properly employed. Like many other Soviet weapons, the RPG-7V is widely distributed to a variety of guerrilla and subversive organizations and it is hardly possible to see a photograph or telecast concerning small internal conflicts without being able to pick them out, slung casually from the bearer's shoulder with the body of a rocket protruding menacingly from the top. A few have appeared in Ulster in the hands of the Provisional IRA, but do not seem to have been used with any great success.

Recent reports from Afghanistan indicate that a new disposable, single-shot, man-portable anti-tank weapon has entered service. Designated RPG-16, it is either 73mm or 75mm caliber and has an effective range of 328 yards (300m).

Right: *Soviet training photo of RPG 7V. Note that the weapon is muzzle-loaded, unlike all other shoulder-fired anti-tank weapons in service.*

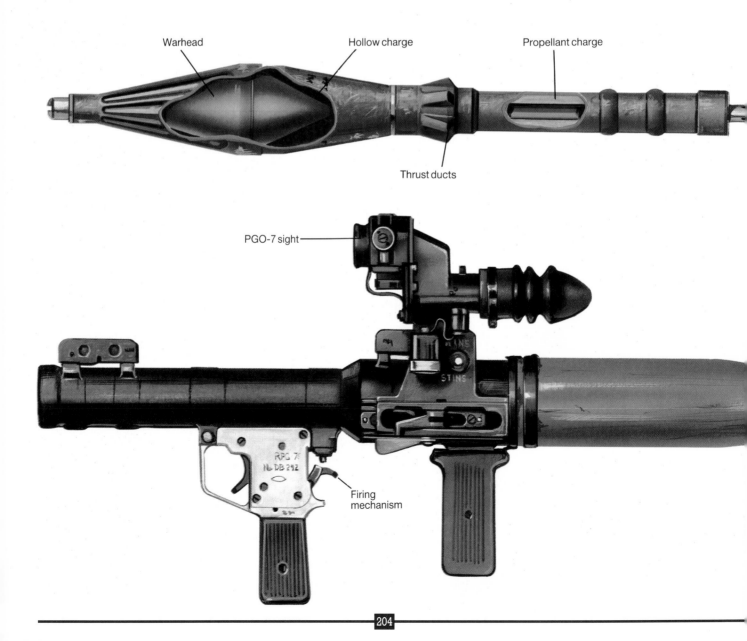

Warhead   Hollow charge   Propellant charge

Thrust ducts

PGO-7 sight

Firing mechanism

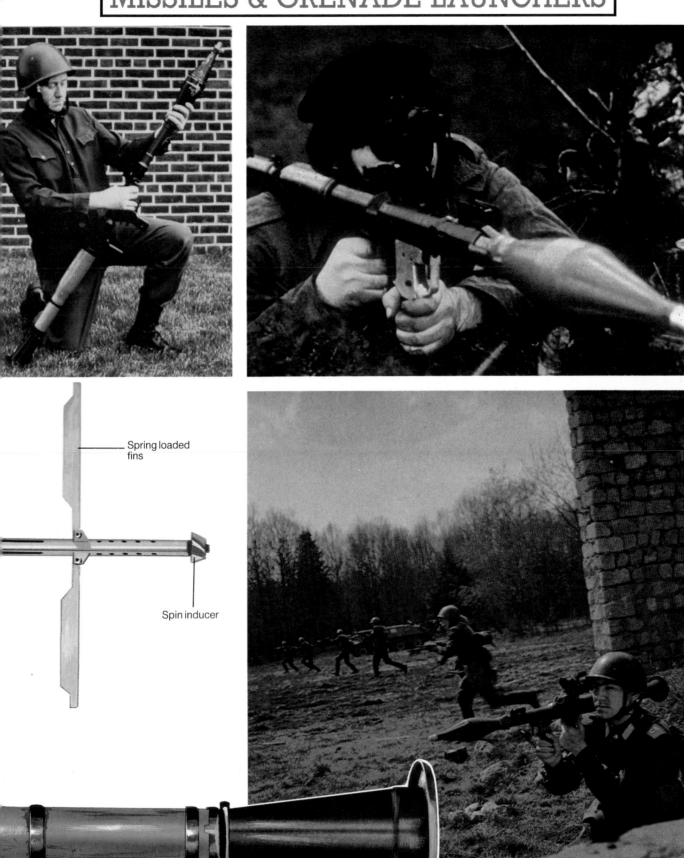

Spring loaded
fins

Spin inducer

Top right: *An IRA man with an RPG 7V. Most terrorist groups use this weapon instead of bombs against hard targets. (The IRA are known to have RPG 7D versions.)*

Right: *Soviet troops, having deployed from a BMP APC, in a section attack with RPG 7 on the flank to engage enemy tanks or hard targets.*

LAW80 LIGHT ANTI-TANK WEAPON

Origin:
United Kingdom
Type:
Portable anti-tank weapon.
Dimensions:
Length 3.3ft (1m) folded; 4.95ft
(1.5m) extended; caliber 3.7in
(94mm).
Weights:
Carry 21.1lb (9.6kg); shoulder
19.3lb (8.8kg).
Penetration:
Greater than 2.4in (600mm) of
armor.
Range:
22-500yd (20-500m).

The LAW80 is a one-shot, low cost, disposable, short-range anti-tank weapon system. It is designed to permit the operator to engage main battle tanks over short ranges with the high probability of a hit.

It is stored and transported holding 24 launchers and issued directly to the user; it is fully man-portable with personal weapons and pack with carrying handle and shoulder sling.

A sporting rifle is used with the system, which contains five rounds –any one of which can be fired without revealing position. The 9mm ammunition used is matched ballistically to the main projectile marked by a tracer and by a flash head to record a hit on a hard target. The operator can select and fire the main projectile at any time. The five rounds are considered enough for two engagements.

The LAW80 sight has its own sliding protective cover. End caps provide sealing for the tubes against immersion, despite the fact that the projectile itself is sealed. After removal of the end caps, the HEAT projectile is extended rearwards from the outer tube. The launch tube is automatically locked into position and the sight erected.

The gunner then only has to select "arm" on a lever to use the trigger to fire either the spotting rifle or the projectile. A non-electric system made up of a percussion cap in the launcher connected by a flash tube to the rocket igniter fires the projectile.

A HEAT warhead and its flying unit make up the forward part of the projectile, and there is a double ogive nose switch which also provides a maximum standoff distance from the target. At the rear of the projectile the composite aluminum and filament wound motor case has an extruded vane propellant. Four fins are mounted on the rear of the motor.

The weapon is not only used by infantry, but by Britain's Royal Marines as well. Some special operations personnel claim the LAW80 is used as anything but an anti-tank weapon; they describe it as a "super bullet", and as a device that comes under the heading of an "attention-getter" for tanks.

Above: *European elite forces, especially, can be expected to be armed with LAW80, a close-quarter battle weapon, with accurate and high hit and kill probability.*

M203 40mm GRENADE LAUNCHER

Origin:
United States.
Type:
Grenade launcher.
Dimensions:
Launcher length 15.8in (394mm);
barrel length 12.2in (305mm).
Weights:
3.0lb unloaded (approx. 1.36kg);
3.6lb loaded (approx. 1.63kg);
9.7oz ammunition (277g); 11lb
loaded (5kg) (with M161A1 and
M203).
Caliber:
40mm.
Effective range:
Area targets 385yd (350m); point
targets 165yd (150m).
Trigger pull:
4.8lb (2.2kg).
Muzzle velocity:
234f/s (71m/s).

The successor to the M79 grenade launcher, the M203 was developed by the AAI Corporation at the direction of the US Army. A lightweight, single shot, breechloaded, pump action, shoulder-fired weapon, it is attached to either the M16 or M16A1/2 rifle. It is mounted below the barrel of the rifle and has its own trigger assembly and sighting arrangements.

The M203 fires the same variety of low-velocity (260fps/76m/s at the muzzle) grenades as its predecessor. This includes high explosive, high-explosive airburst, buckshot, a dual purpose round that can penetrate light armor, and a wide range of smoke, illuminating and riot-control ammunition. These launchers are the only small arms capable of dealing with light armored vehicles.

Two sighting systems are used with the M203. The primary sight consists of an aperture and post system, and has ranges marked on a quadrant scale. The secondary sight is a folding, graduated lead sight mounted on the forestock and uses the foresight of the rifle as a front aiming reference.

M203s are used by United States special forces, including Delta, Rangers, and the SEALs, as well as by foreign forces.

Below: *The M203 attaches directly to the M16A1 or A2, with two screws, and without modification to the rifle – in five minutes.*

Below: *Harness is removed, launch tube is extended, striker spring to be cocked and, ready to fire . . .*

Above: *Carrying configuration of LAW80.*

Left: *US Army trooper training with the M203 in West Germany. The high-strength aluminum barrel slides forward in the receiver to accept a round of ammunition, and slides backward automatically to lock in the closed position, ready to fire. The battle sight is adjustable for ranges 165 to 820 feet (50 to 250m), mounted on the hand-guard. A quadrant sight mounted on the handle is adjustable for 165 to 1,310ft (50 to 400m).*

Below: *The M203 grenade launcher is a single-shot 40mm weapon which, with the M16 rifle, creates a versatile combination capable of firing both 5.56mm rifle ammunition and the whole range of 40mm high explosive and special purpose ammo – anti-personnel, armor-piercing, buckshot, tear gas, and others. One warning given is that 40mm high velocity ammunition should never be used with the M203 launcher.*

DRAGON M47

Origin:
United States.
Type:
Medium anti-tank/assault
weapon.
Dimensions:
Launcher length 46.2in
(1,154mm); missile length 29.8in
(744mm); missile body diameter
4.5in (113mm); fin span 13in
(330mm).
Weights:
Weapon (carry) 32.1lb (14.6kg);
weapon (ready to fire) 30.3lb
(13.8kg); missile 13.6lb (6.2kg).
Flight speed:
Approximately 230mph
(370km/h).
Propulsion:
Gas-launched, then by side-
thruster solid propellant motors.
Warhead
Linear-shaped charge, 5.4lb
(2.45kg).
Lethality:
3ft (0.92m) reinforced concrete.

Dragon is sealed in a glass-fiber launch tube with a fat rear end containing the launch charge. The operator attaches this to his tracker, comprised of telescopic sight, IR sensor and electronics box. When the missile is fired, its three curved fins flick open and start the missile spinning.

The operator holds the sight on the target and the tracker automatically commands the missile to the line of sight by firing appropriate pairs of side thrusters. The launch tube is thrown away and a fresh one attached to the tracker.

All planned quantities of the Dragon have been bought for the US Army, which has it deployed throughout the world, and also by the US Marine Corps, which has started an improvement program to develop a better tracking unit and round. The Army is participating in this

effort and plans to retrofit 20,000 existing warheads with the new missile.

There are many experts who feel the Dragon is so faulty that it isn't worth improving. In fact, the Army has begun research on the Advanced Antitank Weapon System-Medium program that is designed ultimately to replace the Dragon. The improvement plan is meant to extend the life of the current weapon until its replacement enters service in the mid-1990s.

Right: *Members of B. Co., 3rd Bn., 187th Bde., 101st Airborne Div., one back-packing the Dragon AT missile system.*

Far right: *Dragon's interest to special forces lies in its light weight, particularly desirable for use in airborne and airmobile operations.*

STINGER, FIM-92A

Origin:
United States.
Type:
Man-portable air-defense
missile.
Dimensions:
Missile length 60in (1,524mm);
body diameter 2.75in (69.8mm).
Weights:
Launch 24lb (10.9kg); package
35lb (15.8kg).
Propulsion:
Atlantic Research.
Guidance:
Optical aiming, IR homing.
Range:
In excess of 3.1 miles (5km).
Flight speed:
About Mach 2.
Warhead:
High explosive.

This successor to the Redeye missile first went to the field in Europe in 1982. Stinger has a much improved infrared guidance system over the Redeye that permits effective attack from all angles, whereas Redeye was limited to a stern chase. Stinger also has greater resistance to countermeasures and incorporates an IFF system for positive identification of hostile aircraft. The IFF device, about the size of the average canteen, is attached to the firer's belt. It is issued as a certified round of ammunition in a disposable sealed lauching tube, which is attached to the gripstock tracking unit contain-

ing the missile's controls and pre-launch electronics.

To improve its effectiveness and cope with ECM of the future, an advanced seeker called Stinger POST (for passive optical seeker technique) is being developed. It was introduced on the production line with the fiscal 1983 buy. This version operates in both the ultraviolet spectrum as well as the infrared. The improved missile reached the field in fiscal 1987.

Stingers are being used by the anti-Soviet forces in Afghanistan with, by all accounts, deadly effect. The Soviets are now fighting that war at greater and safer distances . . . fearing this weapon in the hands of the mujahideen.

Right: *Looking every bit the Infantryman 2000, this Airborne trooper tries out Stinger, lightweight, simple and deadly. Special forces usefulness is obvious. It is hoped that the missile system won't find itself in the hands of terrorists.*

Far right: *Training with Stinger. Though the student has turned his cap back-to-front, it is quite clear from the other picture that it seems unnecessary, since the system is designed for use by helmeted and begoggled troops. There are plans for aircraft- and vehicle-mounted versions.*

ASU-85 AIRBORNE ASSAULT GUN

Origin:
Soviet Union
Type:
Air-portable, self-propelled
anti-tank gun.
Dimensions:
Gun horizontal (ahead) 28ft
(8.49m); hull 19.8ft (6.0m); width
6.2ft (2.7m); height 4.6ft (2.1m).
Combat weight:
14.00 tons (15,500kg)
Engine:
V-6 six-in-line water-cooled
diesel developing 240hp.
Crew:
Four.
Armament:
D-70 85mm gun; 7.62mm SGM
medium machine gun (coaxial);
12.7mm DShKM (roof mounted)
heavy machine gun.
Range:
161 miles (260km).
Speed:
27.9mph (45km/h).
Armor:
Up to 1.6in (40mm).

One of the major requirements for an airborne force is to have its own fire support available "on-the-spot" and as soon as possible after the initial landings. The Soviet Army has paid particular attention to this requirement, producing a range of small, light and yet highly effective fire support vehicles such as the BMD and the ASU-85. ASU is the acronym of *Aviadezantnaya Samochodnaya Ustanovka* and the 85 refers to the size of the gun.

Much heavier and tougher than the earlier ASU-57, this formidable vehicle became possible with the advent of the Mi-6 Hook and Mi-10 Harke helicopters, and – for fixed-wing dropping – high-capacity, multichute and retrorocket systems. The ASU-85 was first seen in 1962, and is widely used by the Soviet, Polish and East German airborne divisions.

The chassis is based on the ubiquitous PT-76, but is not amphibious. The gun has 12 degree traverse. It fires AHPE and HVAP projectiles, which are more powerful than the "normal" 85mm field, anti-aircraft and tank guns, at a muzzle velocity of 3,280ft/sec (1,000m/sec).

It is believed that the ASU-85 is fitted with an NBC system. It also has various night-vision devices, although these are still of the active infra-red type; other target-acquisition and ranging aids may well have been retrofitted, however, in more recent programs, thus upgrading the value of these neat and effective vehicles.

This assault gun vehicle is not designed for parachuting and is normally be airlanded, usually by the An-12 transport. The ASU-85 remains in widespread use, though it is now being replaced by a new airborne assault gun; the possible designation MZA.

Above: *Soviet paratroops deploy from their ASU-85. More of an assault gun than an anti-tank gun, 18 of the NBC-fitted vehicles are found in each Airborne Division ASU battalion.*

BMD AIR-PORTABLE FIRE SUPPORT VEHICLE

Origin:
Soviet Union.
Type:
Fire support vehicle.
Dimensions:
Length overall 17.82ft (5.4m);
width overall 8.86ft (2.55m);
height from 5.34ft (1.62m) to 6.5ft
(1.77m).
Engine:
Type 5D-20 V-6 diesel
developing 240hp.
Armament:
Turret identical to BMP, with
73mm low-pressure smooth-
bore gun with auto-loading from
30-round magazine; 7.62mm PKT
co-axial, and "Sagger" missile on
launch rail. In addition, two
7.62mm PKT in mounts on front
corners of hull.
Speed:
43mph (80km/h) on land, 6mph
(10km/h) in water.
Range:
198 miles (320km).
Armor:
(hull) .6in (15mm); (turret) .92in
(25mm).

Two of the major requirements of a parachute-landed force are the ability to move small groups of men rapidly around the battlefield, and as strong an anti-tank defense as possible. The BMD is a very neat attempt to answer the first of these, and to add a reasonable contribution to the second. First seen in the November 1973 parade in Red Square,

this trim little air-droppable fire support vehicle is yet another of the "quart-in-a-pot" designs which seem to flow from the Soviet State arsenals. Though such aircraft as the Antonov An-22 (NATO codename "Cock") could easily carry the BMP APC, it was judged that the same capability could be built into a smaller and lighter APC capable of being airlifted in greater numbers, and more readily dropped by parachute. It is issued on a scale of 330 per division to Soviet Airborne Rifle Divisions – three command versions at divisional headquarters and three airborne regiments with 109 each.

At first styled "M 1970" in the West, the correct Soviet designation is "Boevaya Mashina Desantnaya" (BMD) – for Airborne Combatt Vehicle. The vehicle has a crew of 3, and carries six parachute soldiers in open seats in the back. It is armed with the same turret as the much larger BMP, mounting a 73mm low-pressure gun, a 7.62mm coaxial machine gun, and a "Sagger" ATGW on a launcher rail. One remarkable feature is the mounting of two fixed machine guns in the front corners of the hull. It is also fully amphibious, using hydrojet propulsion. It is truly remarkable to design all this capability into such a light vehicle.

BMDs spearheaded the Soviet invasion of Afghanistan and would be used in any major airborne operation. Its roles include bold reconnaissance immediately following a landing, rapid movement away from the DZs (especially to capture key targets), direct support of infantry assaults, and anti-tank defense. It is believed that Soviet BMD airborne infantry combat vehicles are equipped with "Beeper" devices that allow the crew to locate individual systems in the drop zone.

Right: *A BMD load of ground forces and paratroopers race across the battlefield, supported by the vehicle. Early fire support is vital to the success of a paratrooper operation; many have failed for lack of it.*

Below: *The compact design of the BMD is clearly shown. Soviet designers are particularly skillful at packaging great capability into small vehicles; this type has no equivalent in the West.*

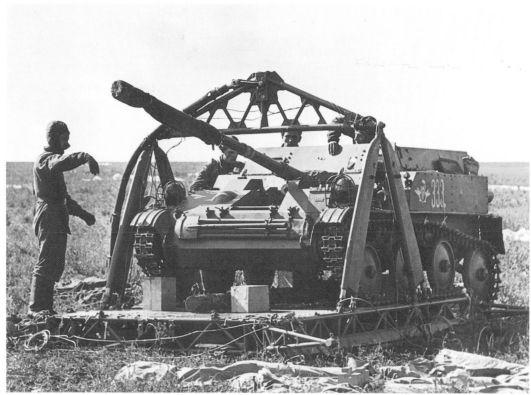

Right: *Preparing an ASU-85 for drive away. Its APHE round will penetrate 4in (102mm) of armor at 1,093 yards (1,000m). The penetration capability of the HVAP is 5in (130mm) at the same range.*

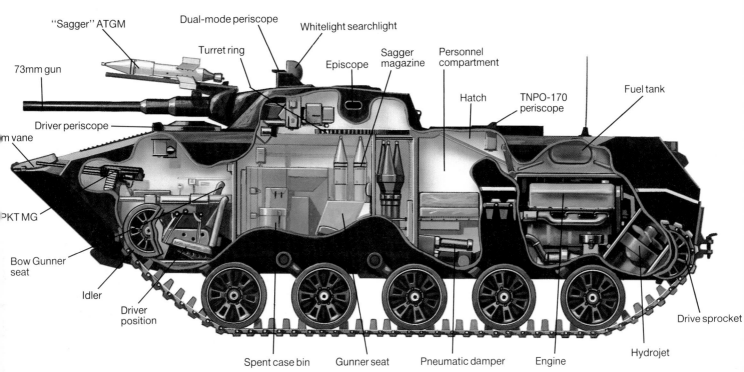

"Sagger" ATGM

Dual-mode periscope

Whitelight searchlight

Turret ring

Episcope

Sagger magazine

Personnel compartment

73mm gun

Hatch

TNPO-170 periscope

Fuel tank

Driver periscope

m vane

PKT MG

Bow Gunner seat

Idler

Driver position

Spent case bin

Gunner seat

Pneumatic damper

Engine

Hydrojet

Drive sprocket

Land Rover

Origin:
United Kingdom.

Type:
Remote area patrol vehicle.

Available designs:
(all less cabs), One Ten V8 HCPU; One Ten 2.5 HCPU; One Ten pickup; Nine pickup.

Armament:
Single NATO 7.62mm general-purpose machine gun; twin NATO 7.62mm general-purpose machine gun; single M60 7.62mm general-purpose machine gun; .50 cal. Browning machine gun; 7.62mm chain gun; other weapons on application.

Range:
500 miles (with three man crew).

Orders have been recently placed for a fully armored APC – it will be used to handle internal security tasks in Northern Ireland – that is based on the Land Rover 110 chassis. Orders have also come in from the Middle East for another vehicle based on the same chassis whose lineage can be traced back to the design of the vehicle for the 22 Special Air Service Regiment and known widely as the "Pink Panther" long range patrol land Rover. While those being supplied to the Middle East differ somewhat from the SAS Model, they are the basis for Glover Webb Ltd's new remote area

patrol vehicle.

The variations, of course, come as no surprise. Glover Webb has already manufactured more than 500 desert patrol conversions, with the new 110 model of the Land Rover simply being the latest.

The new model has an open top design and many roles, including border patrol, escort duties, surveillance and long range desert fighting in the tradition of SAS Jeeps of World War II. Armored protection can be mounted in front of the three-man crew – and elsewhere if required. Its V8 engine is linked to a five speed transmission and a permanent four-wheel drive.

A netting camouflage roll ready for use is strapped to the front end of the hood and the side. This allows the vehicle to be covered in a short period of time.

The commander's seat next to the driver is slightly raised and has a 7.62mm general-purpose machine gun mounting. An adjustable rear gun pedestal allows crews to make the most use of the terrain to hide the vehicle, and leaves the gun just high enough to provide adequate cover. Ammunition for the front mounted weapon is contained in four boxes between the driver and the commander. Up to 10

boxes can be accommodated in the rear, and stowage for three rifles is located on the left of the body bulkhead.

Because of the specialist nature of long range patrol/attack work, many detailed changes are made by the manufacture to suit individual needs. The highly maneuverable vehicle is capable of dealing with difficult terrain; it is also air transportable in a C-130 Hercules with minimum adjustment and can also be slung beneath a medium-lift helicopter.

Above right: *Long-range recce version of the Land Rover, a development of the well-proven, rugged, four-wheel drive vehicle. Note the rear-mounted anti-aircraft gun, 7.62 machine gun in the commander's position, and launchers for flares, smoke grenades, etc., at the front.*

Right: *Simplified version, with machine gun on central pivot at the rear, and masses of fuel cans behind the driver, for extra range.*

Far right: *Twin-mounted machine guns show high-elevation on this vehicle, which also has long-range communications kit. All Land Rovers can be transported by air.*

HUMMER VEHICLE

Origin:
United States

Type:
High mobility, multi-purpose wheeled vehicle.

Dimensions:
Length 15.1ft (4.57m); width 7.1ft (2.15m); height 5.8ft (1.75m).

Weights:
(empty) 4,959lb (2,254kg); (fully loaded) 7,459lb (3,379kg).

Engine:
V8 6.2 liter diesel.

Range:
350 miles (565km).

Speed:
65mph (105km/h) (maximum).

Modern armies are very dependent upon wheeled vehicles of all types, and perhaps the most important of these is the field car, which is exemplified in the US Army by the ubiquitous Jeep and in the British Army by the Land Rover. The quantity of vehicles needed is enormous, and the importance of the Hummer can be gauged from the fact

that some 40,000 will be bought by the US Army, with a further 11,000 going to the USAF and 14,000 to the USMC.

A "drive-off" was held in 1982 for the three competitors for this lucrative contract, the winner being American Motors General Division. The first production HMMWV's were delivered in 1985.

The Hummer is intended by the US Army to replace several vehicles: the early model M151 quarter-ton Jeep; M274 half-ton Mule; M8780 1¼-ton pick-up truck; M561 Gama Goat articulated utility vehicle; and M792 1¼-ton ambulance. The Hummer has four road wheels driven through geared hubs, enabling the vehicle to be no more than 5ft 8in (1.75m) high and thus bettering the design requirement of 6ft (1.82m). Considerable attention has been paid to a comfortable ride and to weight saving. Among the most thoroughly examined of vehicles to enter the

armed forces of the United States, a total of 450 tests were used to analyze each part.

The vehicle's body is extruded aluminum, which serves two purposes. First, it solves the problem of corrosion and, secondly, it makes the vehicle light enough to be carried in a transport aircraft or slung-load by helicopter. Two can be carried by a CH-47 Chinook, one under either the UH-60A Huey or CH-53 Jolly Green Giant. As many as 15 can be carried in the C-5A/B Galaxy.

The Hummer is currently available in 15 different configurations for the cargo/troop carrier, armament carrier, ambulance and command/communication missions. All variants are expected to be equipped with the same type of chassis, engine and transmission. Overall, there will be a total of 44 interchangeable parts, something that will obviously simplify logistics and maintenance.

Left: *The HMMWV fitted out with tank-busting TOW missile system. HMMWV stands for High-Mobility, Multipurpose Wheeled Vehicle, and the vehicle is called Hummer for short. It is a 1 ¼-ton general-purpose replacement for several vehicles including the universally popular Jeep, Mule and Gamma Goat.*

Below: *Stinger Missile Carrier version of the Hummer. It carries a two-man crew and bears its own parallel weaponry. This variation stows two complete anti-aircraft missile systems, permitting target engagement in less than 10 seconds. There are also recce, fire support, comms and command and control versions.*

ANTONOV An-12

Origin:
Soviet Union.

Type:
(BP) heavy airlift transport, ("Cub-B") Elint, ("Cub-C") ECM.

Engines:
Four 4,190ehp Ivchyenko AI-20M single-shaft turboprops.

Dimensions:
Span 124ft 8in (38.0m); length (normal), 108ft 7¼in (33.1m); height 34ft 6½in (10.53m); wing area 1,310sq ft (121.7m²).

Weights:
Empty (basic) 61,730lb (28t); maximum payload 44,090lb (20t); loaded 121,475lb (55.1t); maximum loaded 134,480lb (61t).

Performance:
Maximum speed (BP, normal weight, medium altitude), 419 knots (777km/h); maximum cruising speed 362 knots (670km/h); economical cruise 317 knots (587km/h); minimum flying speed 88 knots (163km/h); takeoff run (normal weight paved runway) 2,295ft (700m); initial climb 1,970ft (600m)/min; service ceiling 33,460ft (10.2km); range (maximum payload) 2,236 miles (3,600km), (maximum fuel) 3,542 miles (5,700km).

Armament:
(BP) tail turret with two NR-23 guns, (other variants) none.

More than 900 An-12s were built for military and civil use. Production ended in the Soviet Union in 1973. This aircraft (which has the NATO reporting name "Cub"), exactly comparable to the C-130

Hercules, was derived from the civil An-10 Ukraina of 1957 by redesigning the rear fuselage to incorporate a full-width rear ramp and loading doors and a tail turret. Curiously, the standard rear door comprises left and right halves which fold up internally, and a rear door hinged upward at the rear. Thus, provision is made for loading from trucks or for paradropping loads in flight, but not for easy loading of any kind of vehicle for which purpose a separate detachable ramp must be carried and fastened in place after the aircraft is parked.

The larger circular-section fuselage is pressurized and air-conditioned, and the engines drive large alternators feeding heater pads on the leading edges, on the engine inlets, propellers and windscreens to provide ice protection.

The main cargo hold is 44ft 3½in (13.5m) long and has a maximum width of 11ft 5¾in (3.5m), and the floor is stressed to accept loads of up to 307lb/sq ft (1.5t/m²). Cargo can be positioned with the aid of a hoist running on a fore-and-aft gantry with a capacity of 5,071lb (2.3t).

In the paratroop role, 100 soldiers can be seated on small folding seats along the walls and down the centre and despatched in less than one minute through the rear aperture with doors folded upward. Vehicles can include the PT-76 amphibi-

ous tank and derivatives, BTR-60, BMP, ASU-85 SP gun, ZSU-23/4 AA vehicle and various SAM launcher vehicles. The landing gear is designed for use on unpaved surfaces.

Though supplemented by the Il-76, at least 500 of the original 900 An-12 BPS remain in service. Many have a new main radar with a larger aerial. A small number have been converted into Elint (electronic intelligence) platforms to detect, monitor, record and analyse electronic signals from NATO ships, aircraft and surface forces.

The ECM (electronic countermeasures) model, called "Cub-C", is a more extensive rebuild with the turret replaced by a large dielectric rear radome. It has several high-power jammers including canoe type aerial fairings on the underside of the fuselage ahead of and behind the main-gear fairings, and bulged rear ramp/doors. About 30 of this version are serving in a strategic capacity.

An-12s are also operated by the air forces of Algeria, the People's Republic of China, Czechoslovakia, Ethiopia, India, Iraq, the Malagasy Republic, Poland and Yugoslavia.

Below: *One of a formation of aircraft engaged in a paratroop exercise. Some 400 "Cubs" are still in service, but are being replaced at the rate of 30 a year.*

Origin:
Soviet Union.

Type:
Heavy cargo airlift transport.

Engines:
Four 15,000shp Kuznetsov NK-12MA turboprops.

Dimensions:
Span 211ft 4in (64.4m), length 190ft 0in (57.92m), height 41ft 1½in (12.53m), wing area 3,713sq ft (345m²).

Weights:
Empty (equipped) 251,323lb (114t); maximum payload 176,367lb (80t); loaded 551,150lb (250t).

Performance:
Maximum speed (medium altitudes), 400 knots (736km/h);

Above: *This An-22 is unusual in that it has a plain glazed nose devoid of any radar. The only radome is under the large fairing for the right main landing gear. Until the Condor, it was the only Soviet aircraft for bulky/heavy loads.*

ANTONOV An-26

Origin:
Soviet Union.

Type:
Short-range airlift transport.

Engines:
Two 2,820ehp Ivchyenko AI-24T single-shaft turboprops plus one 1,765lb (800kg) thrust RU-19A-300 auxiliary turbojet in right nacelle.

Dimensions:
Span 95ft 9½in (29.2m); length 78ft 1in (23.8m); wing area 807.1 sq ft (74.98m²).

Weights:
Empty 33,113lb (15,020kg); payload (normal) 9,921lb (4.5t), (maximum) 12,125lb (5.5t); loaded (normal) 50,706lb (23t), (maximum) 52,911lb (24t).

ANTONOV An-22 ANTHEUS

high-speed cruise, 370 knots (682km/h); take-off run, 4,260ft (1.3km); landing run (minimum), 2,625ft (800m); range with maximum fuel and 99,200lb (45t) payload, 6,804 miles (10,950km); range with maximum payload, 3,110 miles (5,000km).

Armament:
None.

Unlike most Soviet transports, the An-22 had to be designed with an exceptionally high wing loading (nearly 150lb/sq ft, $0.75t/m^2$), but that did not stop Antonov from achieving quite

short field lengths and landing gear able to operate from unpaved strips.

The main gear comprises three tandem pairs of levered-suspension wheels on each side of the aircraft, each attached to a fuselage ring frame picking up one of the three wing spars. Tyre pressures are adjustable in flight. For a change the vast cargo compartment is fully pressurized, yet has an integral ramp for loading vehicles.

Dimensions of the main old are: length 108ft 3in (33.0m); maximum width and height, both

14ft 5in (4.4m). The floor is of titanium. Heavy cargo can be hoisted and positioned by two 5,511lb (2.5t) winches traveling on four gantries along the length of the roof of the hold, extending to the rear along the underside of the aft-hinged rearmost door (aft of the ramp) where the winches overhang the ground or a truck. Normal flight crew numbers five or six, who can enter via doors in the forward part of each main landing gear fairing, leading to a stairway to the main hold and a forward stairway to the flight-deck level where there is also

seating for 28 or 29 passengers.

No fewer than 27 world records were set by An-22, including a string of records to heights up to 25,748ft (7,848m) with a cargo of metal blocks weighing 221,443lb (100,445kg). About 55 remain in service and they are the only Soviet aircraft capable of airlifting tanks as large as the T-62. They have been used for many notable military airlifts to such countries as Libya, Morocco, Somalia, Vietnam and Peru, and have also been prominent in major maneuvers with Warsaw Pact forces.

Right: The "Curl" short-range transport; it has a rear ramp door and can handle up to 12,125lb (5,500kg) of bulky cargo, including light vehicles. A conversion kit can rapidly re-equip the interior for 24 stretchers.

Performance:
Maximum speed 291 knots (540km/h) at 19,685ft (6km); high-speed cruise at same height 237 knots (440km/h); normal cruise at 22,965ft (7km), 230 knots (425km/h); initial climb (normal weight, with jet), 1,575ft (480m)/min; service ceiling 24,600ft (7.5km); takeoff to 50ft (15m) (paved runway), 4,068ft (1.24km), landing from 50ft (15m), 5,709ft (1.74km); range (max payload, no reserves), 683 miles (1,100km), (max fuel, no reserves), 1,584 miles (2,550km).

Armament:
None.

First seen in public at the Paris

Air Show in 1969, this derivative of the An-24RT has a redesigned rear fuselage with a much more useful full-width rear ramp/door of Antonov's own invention. Though constructed like a normal loading ramp for vehicles, it can be disconnected from its normal hinges at the front and swung down on left/right sets of parallel arms to lie horizontally under the fuselage. This facilitates direct loading from trucks or conveyors, and can also be done in the air (the door being faired in by inclined strakes along each side of the fuselage) to allow air-dropping of stores. When closed, the door forms the underside of the wide beaver-

tail rear fuselage in the usual way, closing between large left/right underfins which improve airflow and directional stability and incorporate tail bumpers.

The fuselage underskin is a sandwich of duralumin and (outermost) titanium to resist damage from operations from rough unpaved surfaces, and there is local reinforcement elsewhere to resist damage from flung stones. Airframe is that of the An-24 but restressed for higher weights, and the systems are generally similar though there are ten (instead of four) flexible cells for fuel in the center section increasing mass to 12,125lb (5,500kg).

Flight crew is five as before, but with the addition of radar (not often fitted to the An-24), a large airdrop observation blister on the left side, airdrop sight and loadmaster/dispatcher station at the rear on the right. Small vehicles can be driven on board, and in the casevac role 24 stretcher (litter) patients can be accommodated, with attendant. In the troop or paratroop role up to 40 tip-up wall seats are used.

About 100 An-26 are believed to serve with the VTA and possibly as many again with other arms, a few being of the new An-26B type with improved equipment for stowing and securing three cargo pallets.

MIL Mi-8

Origin:
Soviet Union.
Type:
Medium transport helicopter.
Dimensions:
Main rotor diameter 69ft 10in (21.3m); tail rotor diameter 12ft 10in (3.9m); length overall 82ft 9in (25.2m); fuselage width 8ft 3in (2.5m); overall height 18ft 6in (5.7m).
Powerplant:
Two 1,267kW (1,700shp) Isotov TV-2-117A turboshafts.
Weights:
Empty 16,007lb (7,260kg); takeoff 24,470lb (11,100kg)
Performance:
Max speed 140 knots (260km/h); max cruising speed 122 knots (225km/h); range 289 miles (465km); service ceiling 14,760ft (4,500m).
Armament:
Various, see below.

The Mi-8 (NATO reporting name "Hip") appeared in public for the first time in 1961 during the Soviet Aviation Day display, and the Hip C version around 1964. More recently, the heavily armored Hip E and F versions have entered the Soviet inventory. Thousands of aircraft have been produced, including four new specialized military versions – with an estimated 1,615 supporting Soviet armies in the field.

This system exists in a variety of forms, some of which carry extremely heavy weapon loads. The Hip C, E and F have a five-blade main rotor and three-blade tail rotor. The fuselage is a conventional all-metal, semi-monocoque structure, with tri-cycle landing gear and external fuel tanks. There is a jettisonable main passenger door at the front port side of the cabin and large clamshell freight-landing doors at the rear. The Hip is equipped with a winch and hook for external loads.

The military Hip C has small circular windows rather than the large square windows found in the civil version. It may fit optional twin racks outboard of the fuel tanks on each side of the fuselage for a variety of external weapon stores.

Armament may include eight 16-shot 57mm rocket pods or other weapons. Aside from external stores, the Hip C also mount a light machine gun in the side door, and each window in the transport section is equipped with a support bracket to allow firing of assault rifles at ground targets from the air.

The Hip E has been labeled the world's most heavily armed helicopter. Its armament can include a 12.7mm nose machine gun, six 32-shot 57mm rocket pods (or four 250kg bombs or two 500kg bombs) – and four Swatter anti-tank guided missiles. The F version is the export model on which the missiles are changed to six Saggers.

The Mi-8 Hip is used primarily as an assault transport and general cargo transport helicopter (Hip C). But it also performs in armed support and anti-tank roles (E/F). The aircraft are standard equipment in attack helicopter regiments, along with Mi-24 Hinds, and frontline transport helicopter regiments, with Mi-6 Hooks.

Above: *The Mi-24 Hind D with a chin-mounted four-barrelled Gatling gun which provides heavy support as has been proved repeatedly in Afghanistan. Its wings can also be fitted with AT-6 Spiral anti-tank missiles and gun pods.*

Left: *The Mi-8, the military version of which can be identified by its circular windows. More powerful than a Sea King or a Black Hawk, all versions have provision for flights at night and in bad weather.*

Right: *Largest and most powerful helicopter in the world, the Mi-26 can quickly be loaded by way of the rear doors. More than 100 seats can be clipped to the floor.*

MIL Mi-24

Origin:
Soviet Union.
Type:
Attack helicopter.
Dimensions:
Main rotor diameter 55ft 9in (17m); tail rotor diameter 12ft 10in (3.9m); overall length (excluding rotors and guns) 60ft 9in (18.5m), (rotors turning) 68ft 10in (21m); height 24ft 4in (6.5m).
Weight:
(max takeoff) 24,250lb (11,000kg).
Powerplant:
(late versions) two TV3-117 turboshaft engines developing 2,200shp.
Performance:
Speed 173 knots (320km/h); range 99 miles (160km).
Armament:
Various, see below.

This helicopter (NATO reporting name "Hind") was first seen in 1974, although it had probably already been in existence for two years by that time, and was already deployed in at least two units on the NATO/Warsaw Pact border. The Hind exists in three versions, all of which share the same basic airframe, powerplant, and rotor system.

The Hind A has auxiliary wings, the undersides of which have four pylons for weapon stores, which may include four 32-shot 57mm rocket pods, or four 250kg bombs, or two 500kg bombs. Besides the four inboard pylons, two wingtip pylons have launch rails for a total of four AT-2 Swatter anti-tank guided missiles.

The Hind A also carries a swivel-mounted, single barrel 12.7mm machine gun in the nose of the cockpit, which features bulletproof, flat, antiglint windows. The rail rotor is on the starboard side on earlier models, but on the port side in later Hind As.

The D version carries the same wing armaments, but the front of the fuselage has been completely redesigned for a primary gunship role. A chin turret under the nose mounts a four-barrel, 12.7mm Gatling-type machine gun, which has a wide range of movement in both azimuth and elevation, and is also reported to be radar-directed. A sensor pack protruding below the chin turret probably houses radar and low-light-level TV. Many small antennae and blisters have been added.

The Hind E is essentially the same as the D, except that it carries four AT-6 Spiral anti-tank guide missiles. Both the D and E feature structural hardening due to the substitution of steel and titanium in critical components.

The Mi-24 combines the functions of scout, transport and attack helicopters. Its capabilities include tactical airborne assaults, close air support, anti-armor operations and anti-helicopter operations.

One of the most important helicopters in the Soviet inventory, it is known as the Soviets' "flying tank". It is the single most hated and feared weapon in the war in Afghanistan, according to some observers, and is apparently one of the primary means of delivering suspected poison gas in that country. Total estimated Hind strength is over 1,000.

MIL Mi-26

Origin:
Soviet Union.
Type:
Heavy lift helicopter.
Dimensions:
Main rotor diameter 105ft (32m); tail rotor diameter 24ft 11in (7.6m); overall length (rotors turning) 131ft 3in (40m).
Weight:
(max takeoff) 123,450lb (56,000kg).
Powerplant:
Two D-136 free turbine turboshaft engines developing 11,400shp.
Performance:
Max level speed 159 knots (297km/h); range 497 miles (800km).

The Mi-26 Halo was identified in 1978 and was first seen in public at the Paris Air Show in June 1981. It has been operational since 1982 and is replacing the Mi-6 Hook in transport helicopter regiments. At its reported engine horsepower, the Halo A may be able to fly the increased loads at speeds comparable to the Hook.

It retains the single main rotor/tail rotor configuration and the clamshell rear loading doors of the Hook. The main features of the Halo A are the eight-blade main rotor (the Hook had six) and the large twin turboshaft engines (compared with the Hook's twin 5,420shp engines). It has a cabin height of 10.33ft (3.15m) – larger than that of the An-12 Cub fixed wing transport.

The Halo A has a four man crew (pilot, copilot, navigator and engineer), and its internal cargo payload of 44,000lb (20,000kg) can be carried a distance of about 500 miles (800km). The cargo area is large enough to carry more than 100 troops, two BMDs or one BMP. The avionics package gives all-weather flight capability.

The Mi-26 has been committed to Afghanistan, where its lift carrying capabilities allow the Soviets to resupply by air, rather than by using road convoys (which can be ambushed).

AIRCRAFT

LOCKHEED AC-130 SPECTRE and MC-130 COMBAT TALON

Origin:
United States.

Type:
Gunship/ special operations aircraft.

Dimensions:
Wing span 132ft 7in (40m); length (Spectre) 97ft 9in (30m), (Combat Talon) 100ft 10in (31m); height 38ft 6in (12m).

Weight:
(maximum gross takeoff) 155,000lb (69,750kg).

Powerplant:
4 Allison T-56-A-15 engines.

Horsepower:
(Spectre) 4,910 or (Combat Talon) 4,200 equivalent shaft horsepower each.

Range:
Beyond 2,000 miles (3,200km) without refueling.

Speed:
More than 300mph (482km/h, 260 knots); (Combat Talon, on airdrop operations) 144mph (230km/h, 125 knots) for personnel, 150-288mph (240-461km/h, 130-250 knots) for equipment.

Ceiling:
(Combat Talon) 30,000ft (9,000m).

Armament:
(Spectre) two 20mm Vulcan cannons, one 40mm Bofors cannon, and one 105mm US Army howitzer.

Crew:
(Spectre) 5 officers/9 enlisted personnel; (Combat Talon) 6 officers/5 enlisted personnel.

The AC-130H Spectre gunship – the most common model in use with US Special Operations Forces – is a modified C-130 "H" model aircraft configured with a side-firing weapon system. The addition of an air refueling capability allows the gunship to respond to any location in the world in a minimum time.

AC-130s perform numerous combat roles, including close air support, interdiction, armed reconnaissance, and air base defense. They are equipped with infrared and low-light-level television detection systems, or sensors, and a computerized fire control system. They were used in Grenada to provide massive, surgically accurate firepower in support of friendly ground forces. Among the critical targets destroyed by the gunships were anti-aircraft artillery sites, armored personnel carriers and numerous enemy positions. In peacetime, the highly sophisticated aircraft has been used extensively for night search and rescue missions because of its unique detection systems.

AC-130As are in service with the US Air Force Reserve's 711 Special Operations Squadron, Eglin Air Force Base, Fla., and AC-130Hs are with the 1st Special Operations Wing, Hurlburt Field, Fla. The Air Force is expected to buy additional C-130H airframes from the manufacturer for conversion to gunships. The gunship fleet – including active and reserve units – is expected to expand to 22 aircraft by 1992. Its fiscal 1988 budget request includes procurement funds for five AC-130U models. They are expected to have extended range and to be uniquely equipped with integrated avionics

SIKORSKY MH-53H/J PAVE LOW

Origin:
United States.

Type:
Multipurpose helicopter

Dimensions:
Rotor (diameter) 72ft 3in (22m); rotors extended 88ft 2in (27m); height (to top of tail rotor) 24ft 11in (7.6m).

Weight:
(maximum gross takeoff) 42,000lb (18,900kg).

Powerplant:
Two T64-GE-7A turboshaft engines.

Horsepower:
3,936 maximum hp each engine.

Range:
600 miles (965km) without refueling

Speed:
196mph (315km/h, 170 knots).

Armament:
Three 7.62mm Miniguns or three .50 caliber machine guns.

Crew:
Six.

The MH-53H/J Pave Low helicopter is a twin-turbine engine, single rotor, heavy-lift helicopter used for airlift support of special operations missions and is capable of carrying 38 combat-equipped troops. It is equipped with a retractable air refueling probe, external hoist, two jettisonable auxiliary fuel tanks and armor plating.

Various versions of the helicopter have been used in numerous special operations, search and rescue, recovery and space program support missions over the years. The Pave Low version of the helicopter was first assigned to the 1st Special Operations Wing, Hurlburt Field, Fla., in May 1980 to enhance airlift capability for the wing's special operations missions. This version is reckoned the most sophisticated in the free world.

The MH-53H is equipped with a night/adverse weather capability through its terrain following/terrain avoidance/ground mapping radar, forward looking infrared radar (FLIR), a Doppler navigation system and an inertial navigation system that is normally found on the B-52 bomber.

In its combat rescue and recovery role, it is equipped with armor plating and self-sealing fuel tanks. An automatic flight control system allows the crew to operate under difficult conditions; in fact, it can hover at a height of 250 feet (76m) to extend a rescue cable.

There are presently nine Pave Low helicopters in the Air Force inventory, with 19 scheduled to be in service by fiscal 1988. It was formerly designated HH-53H, but that has been changed to MH-53/H/J to reflect more accurately its multipurpose role. Within five years, the special operations fleet of this aircraft is expected to grow to 41.

Left: *Combat Talon flies low level maneuvers over the Arizona Desert. The aircraft is assigned to the 8th Special Operations Squadron, which is based at Hurlburt Field, Florida. The Combat Talon is a special operations version of the C-130E and has special avionics, ECM and other devices that suit it for low-level operations.*

Right: *Close up of the MC-130 clearly showing the bulged nose and prongs. Combat Talon I aircraft (MC-130Es) are equipped for low-level and deep-penetration tactical missions by the 1st, 7th and 8th Special Operations Squadrons. By 1992, the inventory is expected to have 24 newer Combat Talon IIs (the "H" versions), with uprated T56-A-15 turboprop engines, redesigned outer wing, updated avionics and other improvements.*

systems and defensive electronic suites that will provide capability in night and adverse weather, as well as in hostile or defended areas.

The Combat Talon is a C-130E modified for special operations activities. It is equipped with the Fulton Surface-to-Air Recovery (STAR) system, specialized aerial delivery equipment, secure communications, sophisticated navigation equipment, electronic warfare and aerial refueling systems, and is also used in psychological warfare and aerial reconnaissance roles.

The Fulton STAR system is a safe, rapid method of recovering a downed aircrew member from either land or water. This is accomplished with a helium-filled balloon, a 525ft (160m) nylon lift line and a protective suit worn by the person to be rescued. The aircraft intercepts the lift line while traveling at 150mph (240km/h). The person is lifted off the ground – experiencing less shock than that caused by the opening of a parachute – and is pulled behind the aircraft. The aircrew, using a winch, reels the person aboard. Two people

or a 500lb (227kg) package can be recovered in one intercept.

Specialized aerial delivery equipment on the MC-130 includes onboard radar and computers. This special system enables the crew to locate small drop zones and deliver equipment with great accuracy in unfamiliar terrain day or night. Aircraft modifications permit relatively high-speed aerial deliveries, at an altitude down to 50ft (15m), which result in safer infiltration of and exfiltration from hostile areas by Army Special Forces and Navy SEALs.

The current force of 14 Combat Talons is assigned to the 8th Special Operations Squadron of the Air Force's 1st Special Operations Wing, Hurlburt Field, Fla. This squadron also trains aircrew members for other special operations units located – along with other special operations aircraft – in West Germany and the Philippines.

Because of the current emphasis in the United States on support for special operations, the fleet of MC-130E/Hs is expected to expand to 38 over the next five years.

Left: *An MH-53 Pave Low helicopter from the 1st Special Operations Wing being refueled by an HC-130 Hercules aircraft. They perform missions similar to that of the Combat Talon and provide the primary exfiltration capability for the United States' extensive Special Operations Forces.*

Above: *Overhead view of the "Pave Low". Equipment includes a stabilized FLIR installation mounted below the refueling boom, an inertial navigation system, Doppler, and the computer-projected map display and radar from the A-7D, with the radar installed in an offset "thimble" below the nose.*

INDEX

Page numbers in **bold** type refer to subjects mentioned in captions to illustrations

A

A-4 Skyhawk, aircraft, 56
A-6 Intruder, aircraft, 56
A-7D, radar, **219**
AAAD Airborne Anti-Armor
  Defense, 55
AAI Corporation, 206
AC-130, aircraft, 48
  Hercules, 144
  Spectre, 218
AC-130A Spectre, gunships, 48
AC-130H, gunships, 48
AC-130U, gunships, 48
ACP, bullets, **158, 159**
ACV, Aist class, **68**
AET Accelerated Energy
  Transfer, 162
AET, bullets, **161**, 163
AH-1 Cobra, helicopters, 55
AH-1 Sea Cobra, helicopters,
  56, **57**
AK-47, rifles, 79, 107, 172, 178-9,
  178, 179
AK-74, rifles, 176-7, **176-7**
AKD, rifles, 176
AKM, rifles, **66**, 67, 178-9, **178,
  179**
AKMS, rifles, 67, **177**
AKS-74, rifles, 66, 71, 176-7,
  176-7
ALF Arab Liberation Front, 110
AML-90, armored cars, 38
AMX-13, tanks, 38
AN PRC6, radio, **30**
An-124 Ruslan (Condor),
  aircraft, 66
An-12 Cub, aircraft, 66, 71, 214,
  214
An-22 Antheus (Cock), aircraft,
  66, 210, 214-15, **214**
An-26, aircraft, 214-15
ARDE Armament Research
  and Development
  Establishment, 75
ASU Aviadezantnaya
  Samochodnaya
  Ustanovka, 67, 210
ASU-57, guns, 63
ASU-85, airborne assault gun,
  63, 210, **211**
AT-3 Sagger, rocket launchers,
  79
AT-6 Spiral, missiles, 217
AV-8, aircraft, 56
AV-8B Harrier, aircraft, 58
Aba-al-Rahim, 110
Abbas, Abul, 110, 147
Abrams, General Creighton, 54
Accuracy International PM,
  rifles, **153**
Achille Lauro, **117**
Aijack, 146-7
Action Directe, 112
Adam, Major General Yekutiel,
  120
Aeroflot, 63, 71
Afghanistan, 63, 71, 208, 210
Agusta 109, helicopters, 47
Air Assault Brigade, Soviet
  Union, 64
Air France, 119
Airborne assault gun, ASU-85,
  210, **211**
Airborne Force, Soviet Union,
  65-6
Airborne Regiment, Canada,
  26, 27, **27**
Airborne Rifles Divisions,
  Soviet Union, 210
Airborne Self-Propelled
  Vehicle, 67
Aircraft, 214-19
  A-4 Skyhawk, 56
  A-6 Intruder, 56
  AC-130, 48
  AC-130 Hercules, 144
  AC-130 Spectre, 218
  An-12 Cub, 66, 71, 214, **214**
  An-22 Antheus (Cock), 66,
    210, 214-15, **214**
  An-26, 214-15
  An-124 Ruslan (Condor), 66
  Antheus An-22, 66, 210,
    214-15, **214**
  AV-8, 56
  AV-8B Harrier, 58

Aviocar C-212, 77
Boeing 707 119-20
C-5 Galaxy, 55
C-46 Commando, 76
C-130 Hercules, 48, 55, **119**
C-130B/H Hercules, 77
C-141 Starlifter, 55, 128, 129,
  130
C-160 Transall, **30**
C-212 Aviocar, 77
Candid Il-76, 66
CN-235, 77
Cock An-22, 66, 210, **214**,
  214-15
Combat Talon MC-130, 48,
  218, **218-19**
Commando C-46, 76
Condor An-124, 66
Cub An-12, 66, 71, 214, **214**
E-2C Hawkeye, 146
EA-6B Prowler, 146
F-4 Phantom, 56
F-14 Tomcat, 146, 147, **147**
F-18 Hornet, 56, 58
F-104 Starfighter, 122
Galaxy C-5, 55
Harrier AV-8B, 58
Hawkeye E-2C, 146
HC-130 Hercules, **219**
Hercules AC-130, 144
Hercules C-130, 48, 55, 119,
  119
Hercules C-130B/H, 77
Hercules HC-130, **219**
Hercules MC-130E, 144, **145**
Hornet F-18, 56, 58
Il-76 Candid, 66
Intruder A-6, 56
KC-130, 56
MC-130 Combat Talon, 218,
  218-19
MC-130E Combat Talon, 48
MC-130E Hercules, 144, **145**
MC-130H Combat Talon II,
  48
Phantom F-4, 56
Prowler EA-6B, 146
Ruslan An-124, 66
Seawolf amphibious aircraft,
  155
Skyhawk A-4, 56
Soviet Union, 214-17
Spectre AC-130, 218
Starfighter F-104, 122
Starlifter C-141, 55, 128, 129,
  130
Tomcat F-14, 146, 147, **147**
Transall C-160, **30**
United States, 218-19
Airmobile Assault Regiment,
  Soviet Union, 64
Akache, Zohair Youssef, 125,
  127
Al Fatah, 108
Allied Command European
  Mobile Force (Land), 34
Alouette III, helicopters, 77
Alpine Raiding Company,
  Greece, 24
Alpine Troops, Italy, 34-5
Alpini, Italy, 34-5
Amin, Idi, 119
Ammunition (and see bullets,
  cartridges, grenades,
  missiles), 158-65
  Home Office criteria, 158
  SPLAT, **159**
Amphibious Unit, United States
  Marine Corps, 22
Anglia slug, cartridges, **165**
Antheus An-22, aircraft, 66, 210,
  214-15, **214**
Anti-aircraft guns,
  ZSU-23-4, 69
  ZU-23, 69
Anti-riot weapons, 184-5
  Arwen 37, 184-5, **185**
United Kingdom, 184-5
  United States, 185
Anti-tank weapons,
  Dragon, 54, 77, 208, **208-9**
  LAW80, 206, **206-7**
  RPG-16, 204
  RPG-7, 77, 79, **111**
  TOW, 55, 77
Appas, Abul, **117**
Arab Liberation Front (ALF),
  110
Arab National Movement, 109
Arabistan, 132
Arafat, Yasser, 108, 147
Armalite M16, rifles (and see
  M16), 43
Armament Research and
  Development
  Establishment, 75
Armored cars,

AML-90, 38
  Saracen, **104**
Armored personnel carriers,
  BTR-60PB, 67, **68**
  M-3, 38
  OT-64, 120
Armored reconnaissance
  vehicles, M551 Sheridan,
  55
Armsel Striker, shotguns, 186-7,
  187
Arwen 37, anti-riot weapon,
  184-5, **185**
Astray, Lt Col Jose Millan, 38
Attack Helicopter Regiment,
  Soviet Union, 64
Austin, General Hudson, 143
Australia, Special Air Service,
  46, 74
Aviadezantnaya
  Samochodnaya
  Ustanovka, ASU, 67, 210
Aviocar C-212, aircraft, 77
Avon Rubber, diving suits, **43**

B

B Specials, Northern Ireland,
  102
BBE Special Assistance Unit,
  Netherlands, 24
BEP Bataillon Etranger de
  Parachutistes, France, 28
BM59, rifles, 175, **175**
BM59 Mark Ital, rifles, 34
BM59 Paracudisti, rifles, 37, **37**,
  175
BM-14, rocket launchers, 69
BM-21, rocket launchers, 69
BMD Boyevaya Machina
  Desantnaya, 66, **66**, **67**,
  210
  fire support vehicle, 210,
  210-1
BRI slug, cartridges, 164, **165**
BTR-60PB, armored personnel
  carrier, 67, **68**
Ball, bullets, **162**
Bataillon Etranger de
  Parachutistes, France, 28
Batey, Lt Col, 107
Beckwith, Colonel Charlie A,
  56, 128, 129, 130
Beirut, **108**, **110**
Belgium, 23
  1st Parachute Batallion, 46
  Escadron Special
    d'Intervention, 23
  Paracommando Regiment,
    23
  Special Intervention
    Squadron, 23
Beretta,
  pistols,
    92S, **36**
    Corto (.380 ACP), 37
  rifles,
    AR70/223, 174, **174**
    BM59 Mark Ital TA, 34
    SC70, 174, **174**
  sub-machine guns,
    M4, 112
    Model 12, 36, **36**
    Model 38/49, 34
Bigeard, General Marcel, 31
Birdshot, cartridges, 164, **165**
Birmingham Small Arms
  Company, 196
Bishop, Maurice, 143
Black Berets, Soviet Union, **68**
Black Hawk UH-60,
  helicopters, 55
Black September, 32, 111
Blanks,
  bullets, **162**
  cartridges, **165**
Bloch, Mrs Dora, 121
Blue Berets, Poland, 64
Boats (and see canoes),
  Gemini, 43
  Kestrel, 43
  Klepper Mark 13, 43
  Rigid Raider, 43, 154
  Seafox, 62, 154
  Spectre, 62
  Zodiac, **75**
Boeing 707, aircraft, 119-20
Boese, Wilfried, 119, 121
Boevaya Mashina Desantnaya,
  fire support vehicle, 66,
  66, **67**, 210, **210-11**
Bofors, cannon, 218
Border Guards, Soviet Union,
  64
Border Police, West Germany,
  167

Bovensmilde (Netherlands),
  school seige, 124
Brenekr slug, cartridges, **165**
Brigate Rosse, 112-13
Browning,
  pistols, 47, 79, **134, 152**
  rifles, 74
Buckshot, cartridges, 164
Bulgaria, Bulgarian People's
  Army, 64
Bullets (and see ammunition,
  cartridges),
  .22, **159**
  .38 hollow base wadcutter,
    164
  .38SP 158Cr, **159**
  .38SP Equalloy, **159**
  .357 Mag, **159**
  .41 Magnum, **158, 159**
  .44 Magnum, **159, 161**
  .44 SP, **158, 159, 161**
  ACP, **158, 159**
  AET, **161**
  AET Profile, 163
  ball, **162**
  blanks, **162**
  CBX, 163
  dum-dums, **158**
  Equalloy, **159, 162**, 163
  fourth generation rounds,
    160-2, **161**
  frangible training, **162**
  GECO, 163, **163**
  plastic, **158**
  Glaser, **158, 161, 162**, 162-3
  hollow, 160
  Hydro-Shock, **159, 164**
  KTW, 163
  PTFE, **159**
  rubber bullets, **159**
  semi-wad cutter, 160
  soft-point, 160, **162**
  Spartan, 162-3
  SPLAT, **158, 159, 162**, 163
  Super Vel, 160
  THV, **158, 159, 161**, 163
Bullpup, FA MAS, rifle, 30,
  168-9
Bundesgrenzschutz, Germany
  (Federal Republic), 32
Burp guns, 138

C

C1A1, rifles, 27
C-7A, rifles, **27**
C-5 Galaxy, aircraft, 55
C-46 Commando, aircraft, 76
C-130 Hercules, aircraft, 48, 55,
  119, 120, 128, 129, **130**
C-130B/H Hercules, aircraft, 77
C-141 Starlifter, aircraft, 55, 128,
  129, **130**
C-160 Transall, aircraft, **30**
C-212 Aviocar, aircraft, 77
C1A1, rifles, 27
CAR-15, rifles, 54, 57, **62**
CBX, bullets, 163
CDS Container Delivery
  System, 55
CETME Model 68, rifles, 38, **38**
CH-35, helicopters, 56
CH-46, helicopters, 56
CH-53E, helicopters, 58, **58**
CH-53G, helicopters, **76**
CIDG Civil Irregular Defense
  Groups, United States, 49
CN-235, aircraft, 77
COMJTF Commander Joint
  Task Force, 129
COMSUBIN Commando
  Raggruppamento
  Subacqui ed Incursori,
  Italy, 35-6
CQB Close Quarter Battle, 160
CS Ferret gas, cartridges, **164**,
  164, **165**
Cadillac-Gage, commando car,
  59
Cagol, Margherita, 112
Camillus, knives, 154
Canada, 26-7
  Airborne Regiment, 26, 27,
    27
  Devil's Brigade, 26
  Horse Artillery, 26
  Hussars, 26
  Mobile Command, 26
  Royal Canadian Regiment,
    26
  Special Service Force, 26-7,
    27
Candid Il-76, 66
Cannon,
  Bofors, 218
  M101A1, **58**
  Scimitar, 140

Vulcan, 218
Canoes (and see boats),
  Klepper, **42**
  Nautiraid, **155**
Cargo Surveillance System, **157**
Carter, President Jimmy, 129
Cartridges (and see
  ammunition, bullets),
  Anglia slug, **165**
  birdshot, 164, **165**
  blanks, **165**
  Brenekr slug, **165**
  BRI slug, 164, **165**
  buckshot, 164
  CS Ferret gas, **164**, 164, **165**
  Fiochi slug, **165**
  flares, 164
  Hatton, 164, **165**
  HE slug, 164
  incendiary, 164
  Nike tracer, **165**
  rifled slug, 164
  rubber, 164
  SG, **165**
  SPAS penetrator, **165**
  TC armor piercing, 164
  Tungsten AP slug, **165**
Coard, Bernard, 143
Coastal Defence Unit, Poland,
  64
Cobra AH-1, helicopters, 55
Cock An-22, aircraft, 66, 210,
  214, 214-15
Colt .45, pistols, 57
Colt Commando, rifles, 53, 180,
  180-1
Combat Studies Institute, 118
Combat Talon MC-130, aircraft,
  218, **218-19**
Combat Talon MC-130E,
  aircraft, 48
Combat Talon II MC-130H,
  aircraft, 48
Commando C-46, aircraft, 76
Commando car, Cadillac-
  Gage, **59**
Commando Raggruppamento
  Subacqui ed Incursori
  (COMSUBIN), Italy, 35-6
Condor An-124, aircraft, 66
Coronado, California, **20**
Corpo de Fuzilieros, Portugal,
  25
Crossbows, **29**
Crowe, Admiral William J. Jr,
  22
Cub An-12, aircraft, 66, 214, **214**
Cuba, and Grenada, 144-5
Curcio, Renato, 112, **112**
Czechoslovakia, 22nd
  Vysadkova Brigade, 64

D

D-1, parachutes, **66**, 67
DFLP Democratic Front for the
  Liberation of Palestine,
  110
DOW Down Orange Welfare,
  Northern Ireland, 96, 102
DRMLA Democratic
  Revolutionary Movement
  for the Liberation of
  Arabistan, 132
Daewoo Precision Industries,
  187
Daewoo USAS-12, shotguns,
  187, **187**
Darby's Rangers, United States,
  54
Dartcord, **156**
Deerslayer, shotguns, 188
Delta Force, United States,
  128-31
Democratic Front for the
  Liberation of Palestine
  (DFLP), 110
Democratic Revolutionary
  Movement for the
  Liberation of Arabistan
  (DRMLA), 132
Denmark, 23
  Fromandskorpset, 23
  Special Reconnaissance
    Company
    (Jaegerkorps), 23
  sub-machine guns, 190-1
Desert One, Iran, 128, 129-30
Devils Brigade, Canada, 26
Diving suits, Avon Rubber, **43**
Djibouti, 116
Donovan, General 'Wild Bill',
  49
Doppler navigation system,
  218, **219**
Down Orange Welfare (DOW),

Northern Ireland, 96, 102
Dozier, General James L, 112, 117, 137-9, **137-9**
Dragon, anti-tank weapons, 55, 77, 208, **208- 9**
Dragunov, rifles, 178-9, **178**, **179**
Dum dum, bullets, **158**

E

E-2C Hawkeye, aircraft, 146
EA-6B Prowler, aircraft, 146
ECIA, mortars, 38
ECM Electronic Counter Measures, 214
EFA 672-12 (IS), parachutes, 77
ESI Escadron Special d'Intervention, Belgium, 23
Egypt, 146
Egyptair, 146-7
Elint, electronic intelligence, 214
Elite Units, Israel, 76
Entebbe, 116, 119-21, **121**
Equalloy, bullets, **159**, **162**, 163
Escadron Special d'Intervention (ESI), Belgium, 23
Exploders, **159**

F

F-104 Starfighter, aircraft, 122
F-14 Tomcat, aircraft, 146, 147, **147**
F-18 Hornet, aircraft, 56, 58
F-4 Phantom, aircraft, 56
FA MAS Fusil Automatique, Manufacture d'Armes de St Etienne, 168
rifles, 168, **168-9**
FAL, rifles, 82
FIM-92A Stinger, missiles, 208, **208-9**
FLIR Forward Looking Infra-Red, 218, **219**
FN FAL, rifles, 75
FN MAG, machine-guns, 77, 82, **83**
FR-F2, rifles, **153**
FRF-1, rifles, **151**
Falkland Islands, 43, 116, **118**
Falklands War, 45, 140-3
Fascella, Emanuela, **137**
Featherlight, shotguns, 188
Fernspahkompanie, Germany (Federal Republic), 32
Ferret CS gas. cartridges, 164, **164**, **165**
Fiochi slug, cartridges, **165**
Fire support vehicle, BMD, 66, **66**, **67**, 210, **210-1**
Flares, cartridges, 164
Fleet Marine Force, United States, 56
Folgore Brigade, Italy, 37
Folgore Saboteur Batallion, Italy, 37
Force Reconnaissance, United States, 22, 56
Foreign Legion, France, 28-30
Spain, 38
Fort Bragg, John F Kennedy Special Warfare Center, **181**
Fourth generation rounds, bullets, 160-2, **161**
Framing charges, 157
France, 28-31
Battalion Etranger de Parachutistes, 28
Foreign Legion, 28-30
Paratroops, 31
pistols, 168-9
sub-machine guns, 190-1
Franchi, Luigi, 187
Franchi SPAS 12, shotguns, **186**, 186-7
Franchi SPAS 15, shotguns, **36**
Frangibility, 160
Frangible training, bullets, **162**
Frogman Group, COMSUBIN, Italy, 35
Fromandskorpset, Denmark, 23
Frontier Troops, East Germany, 64
Fulton STAR system, 219
Fusil Automatique, Manufacture d'Armes de St Etienne (FA MAS), 168

G

G3SG/1 Sniper, rifles, 170, **171**
GECO,
bullets, 163, **163**
plastic, **158**
GIGN, **151**
GPMG General Purpose Machine Gun (and see machine guns, sub-machine guns), 47
GRU Soviet Military Intelligence, 64, 69
GSG 9 Grenzschutzgruppe 9 (West Germany) 121, 126-7, **126**, **127**, **166**, 32-3
Gaddaffi, Colonel, 107
Gal, Uziel, 194
Gala, Captain Hani, **116**
Galaxy, C-5, aircraft, 55
Galil, rifles, 77, 119, 172, **172**, 172, **173**
Gallah-wallahs, 39
Garand M1, rifles, 175
Gecko, Soviet Air Defence Batallion, 67
Gemini, boats, 43
General Purpose Machine Gun (GPMG) (and see machine guns, sub-machine guns), 47
Germany (Democratic Republic),
29th (Ernst Moritz Arndt) Regiment, 64
40th (Willi Sanger) Airborne Battalion, 64
Frontier Troops, 64
National People's Army, 64
Germany (Federal Republic),
Border Police, 167
Bundesgrenzschutz, 32
Fernspahkompanie, 32
GSG 9, 32-3, 121, 126-7, **126**, **127**, **166**
pistols, 166-7
rifles, 170-1
sub-machine guns, 192-3
Ghusha, Dr Samir, 110
Giorgieri, General Licio, 112
Glaser, bullets, **158**, **161**, **162**, 162-3
Glock 17, pistols, 153
Golan Heights, **110**
Golani Infantry Brigade, Israel, 119
Grayback, submarines, **61**
Grease guns, 57, 200
Greece, 24
Alpine Raiding Company, 24
Helios Lokos, 24
Paratroop Regiment, 24
Sacred Squadron, 46
Special Forces, 24
Green Berets, United States, **183**
Grenada, 54, 116, **118**, 143-5
Grenade launchers, 204-9
M79, 57
M203, 43, 57, **57**, 182, **203**, 206, **206-7**
Soviet Union, 204-5
United States, 206
Grenades (and see ammunition, missiles),
Haley & Weller E182 Multi-burst, **155**
MISAR MU-50G, 154
Grenzschutzgruppe 9 (GSG 9), West Germany, 32-3
Gruppo Operativo Subacquei, Italy, 35
Guns (and see machine guns,pistols, rifles, shotguns, sub-machine guns),
ASU-57, 63
ASU-85, 63, 210, **211**
M12, 138
Matra Manurhin Defense Disrupter, **157**
Gunships, AC-130A Spectre, 48, 218
Gur, Lieutenant General Mordecai, 119, **119**
Gurkhas, United Kingdom, 39-40

H

H&K,
rifles, 85, 170, **170-1**
pistols,

P11, **35**
P7M13, 166, **166**
P7M8, 166, **166**
P9S, 167, **167**
sub-machine guns, 33, **47**, 47
MP5, 150, **151**, 192-3, **192-3**, 192-3, **192-3**
MP5 K, **193**
MP5 SD, **192**
H-53, helicopters, 48
HC-130 Hercules, aircraft, **219**
HE slug, cartridges, 164
HMG, machine guns, 58
HMSU, Headquarters Mobile Support Units, 105
Haboob, 130
Haley & Weller Dartcord, **156**
Haley & Weller E182 Multi-burst, grenades, **155**
Halo Mi-26, helicopters, **216**, 217
Harke Mi-10, helicopters, 210
Harrier AV-8B, aircraft, 58
Hatton, cartridges, 164, **165**
Hawkeye E-2C, aircraft, 146
Hayward, Admiral Thomas, 130
Heckler & Koch,
machine guns,
HK21, 57
pistols,
P7M8, 166, **166**
P7M13, 166, **166**
P9S, 167, **167**
P11, **35**
rifles, 85, 170, **170-1**
sub-machine guns, 33, 47
MP5, 150, **151**, 192-3, **192-3**
MP5 K, **193**
MP5 SD, **192**
Hegarty, David, **103**
Hek G3SG1, sub-machine guns, 33
Hek P9P, pistols, 32
Helicopters, 216-18
Agusta 109, 47
AH-1 Cobra, 55
AH-1 Sea Cobra, 56, **57**
Alouette III, 77
Black Hawk UH-60, 55
CH-35, 56
CH-46, 56
CH-53E, 58, **58**
CH-53G, **76**
H-53, 48
Halo Mi-26, 71, **216**, 217
Harke Mi-10, 210
Hind Mi-24, **216-7**, 217
Hip Mi-8, 69, 216, **216**
Hook Mi-6, 71, 210, 217
Huey UH-1H, 55
Kiowa OH-58, 55
MH-53H Pave Low, 48
MH-53H/J Pave Low, 218, **219**
Mi-6, 71
Mi-6 Hook, 71, 210, 217
Mi-8 Hip, 69, 216, **216**
Mi-10 Harke, 210
Mi-24 Hind, **216-7**, 217
Mi-26 Halo, 71, **216**, 217
OH-58 Kiowa, 55
Pave Low MH-53H/J, 48, 218, **219**
RH-53D Sea Stallion, 128, **128**, **129**, **130**, 131
S-76, 77
Sea King, **35**
Sea Stallion RH-53D, 128, **128**, **129**, **130**, 131
Soviet Union, 216-17
UH-1 Huey, **48**, 55, 56
UH-60 Black Hawk, 55
Helios Lokos, Greece, 46
Hensoldt 6x42, scopes, 170
Hercules, aircraft,
AC-130, 144
C-130, 48, 55, 119, **119**
C-130B/H, aircraft, 77
HC-130, aircraft, **219**
MC-130E, aircraft, 144, **145**
Hind Mi-24, helicopters, **216-7**, 217
Hip Mi-8, helicopters, 69, 216, **216**
Hollow, bullets, 160
Hook Mi-6, helicopters, 71, 210, 217
Hornet F-18, aircraft, 56, 58
Howitzers, 218
M198, 58, **58**
Oto Melara 105mm Model 56, 34-5
Huey UH-1H, helicopters, 55
Hungary, Hungarian People's Army, 38

Hunt, Leamon, 112
Hush-Puppy, pistols, 62
Hussars, Canada, 26
Hydro-shock, bullets, **159**, **164**

I

IBS Inflatable Small Boats, **61**
IED Improvised Explosive Device, 157
Il-76 Candid, aircraft, 66
INLA Irish National Liberation Army, 45, 96-107, 98, 100, 105
weapons, 107
IRA Irish Republican Army, 45, 96-107, **183**, **205**
Iceland, 23
Ikar descender, **33**
Improvised Explosive Device (IED), 157
incendiary, cartridges, 164
Incursori, COMSUBIN, Italy, 36
India, Parachute Brigade, 74-5
Individual Weapon, L70A1, 42
Ingram,
Gordon B, 200
sub-machine guns, 200-1, **200-1**
Interior Army, Soviet Union, 64
Intruder A-6, aircraft, 56
Iran, Desert One, 128, 129-30
Iranian Embassy Seige, London, 45, 132-6
Irish Industrial Explosives, 107
Irish National Liberation Army (INLA), 96-107
Irish Republican Army (IRA), 96-107
Israel,
35th Parachute Brigade, 119
Elite Units, 76
Golani Infantry Brigade, 119
Paratroops, 76
reconnaissance units, 76
rifles, 172-3
Sayeret, 76
sub-machine guns, 194-5
Italy,
Alpine Troops, 34-5
COMSUBIN, 35-6
Folgore Brigade, 36, 37
Frogman Group, 35
Incursori, 36
Leatherheads, 112, 137-9
Nucleo Operativo Centrale di Sicurezza, 112, 137-9
Raider Operations Group, 35, 36
rifles, 174-5
shotguns, 186-7
Ithaca, shotguns, 188, **188-9**
Ithaca Gun Company, 188

J

JSOC Joint Special Operations Command, 56-7
Jaeger platoon, Norway, 24
Jaegerkorps, Denmark, 23
Jandara, Turkey, 24
Jibril, Ahmad, 110
Joint Special Operations Command (JSOC), 56-7
Jones, General David, 129
Jordan, Special Forces, 76-7

K

K-Bar, knives, 154
KC-130, aircraft, 56
KGB Soviet State Security, 64
KTW, bullets, 163
Kaida, 119
Kalashnikov AK-47, rifles, 79, 172, **178**, 178-9, **179**
Kennedy, President John F, 49
Kepi, 30
Kestrel, boats, 43
Kieth, Elmer, 160
Kiowa OH-58, helicopters, 55
Klepper, canoes, **42**
Klepper Mark 13, boats, 43
Klinghoffer, Leon, 146
Knives,
Camillus, 154
K-Bar, 154
Kukri, 40, 154
M7 bayonet, **180**
Parkerized Tanto, 154
Warlock, 82
Korea (North), Special Purpose Forces, 79

Korea (South),
shotguns, 187
Special Forces, 80-1
Kukri, knives, 40, 154
Kyle, Colonel James, 129

L

L1A1, rifles, 42, 47, 74
L4A4, machine guns, 75
L7A1, machine guns, 203
L7A2, machine guns, 42, 203, **203-4**
L34A1, sub-machine guns, 74, 75
L70A1, Individual Weapon, 42
LAAB Light Armored Assault Battalions, 58
LAV Light Armored Vehicles, 58
LAW80, anti-tank weapons, 206, **206-7**
LMT Radio Professionelle RB12A, radar, **156**
LMT/RP (Thomson-CSF) Rasit 3190B, radar, **156**
LPD Landing Platform Dock, 69
LRRP Long Range Reconnaissance Patrol, 84
LST Landing Ship Tanks, 69
Polnocny class, **68**
Landing Platform Dock (LPD), 69
Landing Ship Tanks (LST), 69
Lavasani, Abbas, 132
Leatherheads, Italy, 112, 137-9
Leupold Stephens 16xM1 Ultrascope, **153**
Light Armored Assault Battalions (LAAB), 58
Light Armored Vehicles (LAV), 58
Long Range Patrol Company, Royal Netherlands Army, 24
Long Range Reconnaissance Patrol (LRRP), 84
Long-Range Amphibious Reconnaissance Commandos, Taiwan, 84-5
Lufthansa, 125
Luxembourg, 23
Luzycka Naval Assault Division, Poland, 64

M

M2 Carl Gustav antitank recoilless, rifles, **46**
M3A1, sub-machine guns, 57, 81, **184**, 200-1, **200-1**
M7 bayonet, knives, **180**
M8 Gecko, Soviet Air Defence Battalion, 67
M12,
guns, 138
sub-machine guns, 112
M16, rifles, 43, **50**, 56, 74, 77, 79, 85, **98**, 106-7, 206, **206**
M16A1, rifles, **39**, 52, 62, 81, 85, **151**, 182, **183**
M16A1/2, rifles, 206, **206**
M16A2, rifles, 52, **57**, 182, **183**
M21, rifles, 184, **184**
M41, tanks, 38
M60, machine guns, 57, 62, 77, 81, 85, 203, **203**
M60A1, tanks, **57**, 58
M79, grenade launchers, 57
M101A1, canon, **58**
M198, howitzers, 58, **58**
M203, grenade launchers, 43, 57, **57**, 182, **203**, 206, **206-7**
M249, Squad Automatic Weapon, 56
M551 Sheridan, armored reconnaissance vehicles, 55
M-3,
armored personnel carriers, 38
armoured personnel carriers, 38
M-60, tanks, **173**
MAC-10, rifles, 119
MAG Mitrailleuse d'Appui General, 202
MAS 49/56, rifles, 30
MAT49, sub-machine guns, 190, **190-1**
MAW Marine Aircraft Wing, 56
MC1-1B steerable, parachutes, **55**

MC-130 Combat Talon, aircraft, 218, **218-19**

MC-130E Combat Talon, aircraft, 48

MC-130E Hercules, aircraft, 144, **145**

MC-130H Combat Talon II, aircraft, 48

MH-53H Pave Low, helicopters, 48

MH-53H/J Pave Low, helicopters, 218, **219**

Mi-6 Hook, helicopters, 71, 210, 217

Mi-8 Hip, helicopters, 69, 216, **216**

Mi-10 Harke, helicopters, 210

Mi-24 Hind, helicopters, **216-7**, 217

Mi-26 Halo, helicopters, 71, **216**, 217

MILAN, missiles, **34**, **37**, **40**, 140, 141

MISAR MU-50G, grenades, 154

Mk19, machine guns, 58

MP-5, sub-machine guns, **32**, 44

Machine guns (and see general purpose machine guns, guns, sub-machine guns), 202-3

FN MAG, 27, 77, 82, **83**

general purpose, **41**, 47, 62

Heckler & Koch HK21, 57

HMG, 58

L4A4, 75

L7A1, 203

L7A2, 42, 203, **203-4**

M60, 57, 62, 81, 85, 203, **203**

M60 MG, 77

Mk19, 58

RPK, 67

United Kingdom, 202-3

United States, 203

Madsen, sub-machine guns, 190, **190-1**

Madsen Industrial Syndicate, 190

Mahmoud, 125, 127

Manzarieh airfield, 128

Marine Corps, Netherlands, **23**, 24

United Kingdom, **42**, 43 144

Mark VIII MOD-6, SDV, Swimmer Delivery Vehicles, 60

Mark XII-C Pepper Fog, tear gas/fog generators, 185, **185**

Massu, General Jacques, 31

Matra Manurhin Defense Disrupter, guns, **157**

Mauser 66, rifles, 32

Merrill's Marauders, United States, 54

Micro-Uzi, sub-machine guns, 195, **195**

Military Transport Aviation (VTA), Soviet Union, 66

Mini-Uzi, sub-machine guns, 195, **195**

Missile launchers, SA-7, 71, 79

Missiles (and see ammunition, grenades), 204-9

AT-6 Spiral, 217

Dragon, 54, 77, 208, **208-9**

MILAN, **34**, **37**, **40**, 140, 141

Sagger, 210

Spiral AT-6, 217

Stinger FIM-92A, 208, **208-9**

TOW, 55, 77

United Kingdom, 206

United States, 208

Mobile Command, Canada, 26

Model 22 Type, pistols, 62

Mogadishu, Somalia, 32, 45, 125-7

Moluccan Train Incident, Netherlands, 116, **116**, 122-4

Moro, Prime Minister Aldo, 112, 137

Mortars, 79

ECIA, 38

Mossberg 500 ATPS, shotgun, 188, **188-9**

Mountain Brigades, Romania, 64

Mubarak, President Hosni, 146

Murphy, Lenny, 102

N

NATO North Atlantic Treaty Organization, 23-5

NAVSPECWARGRU Naval Special Warfare Groups, 60

NICRA Northern Ireland Civil Rights Association, 101, 102

NOCS Nucleo Operativo Centrale di Sicurezza, Italy, 137-9

NSP-2 (IR), night sights, 204

National People's Army, East Germany, 64

Nautiraid, canoes, **155**

Naval Infantry, Soviet Union, 67-9

Naval Special Warfare Groups, 20, 60

Neave, Airey, 107

Netanyahu, Lieutenant-Colonel Jonathan, 119, 120

Netherlands, 24

Bovensmilde school seige, 124

Long Range Patrol Company, 24

Marine Corps, **23**, 24

Marine Corps Special Assistance Unit, 24

Moluccan Train Incident, 116, **116**, 122-4

New Zealand, Special Air Service, 46, 78

Newman, Sir Kenneth, 105

Night sights, NSP-2 (IR), 204

Rank Pullin Controls SS80, **154**

RPG-7D, 204

Nike tracer, cartridges, **165**

North Atlantic Treaty Organization (NATO), 23-5

North Korea, Special Purpose Forces, 79

Northern Ireland, 41, 45, 96-107

B Specials, 102

Northern Ireland Civil Rights Association (NICRA), 101, 102

Norway, 24, **24**

Jaeger platoon, 24

Readiness Troop, 24

Nucleo Operativo Centrale di Sicurezza (NOCS), Italy, 112, 137-9

O

OCS Officers Candidate School, 58

OH-58 Kiowa, helicopters, 55

OLEU Legion Special Operations Unit (Spain), 38

OSS Office of Strategic Services, 49

OT-64, armored personnel carriers, 120

Oan, 132

Officers Candidate School (OCS), 58

O'Hara, Patsy, **97**

Operation Eagle Claw, 48, 128-31

Operation Evening Light, 128-31

Operation Jonathan, 119-21

Operation Urgent Fury, 143-5

Operational Research Wing, SAS, 150

Orange Volunteers, 102

organization, 82nd Airborne Division (United States), 55

Airborne Force (Soviet Union), 66

COMSUBIN (Italy), 35

Delta (United States), 56

Foreign Legion (France), 20

GSG 9 (West Germany), 32

Gurkhas (United Kingdom), 39

Marines (United States), 56

Parachute Brigade (India), 74

Parachute Regiment (United Kingdom), 41

Rangers (United States), 54

SAS (Australia), 74

SAS (United Kingdom), 46

SEALs (United States), 60

Special Army Forces (Thailand), 84

Special Forces (Jordan), 77

Special Operations Forces (United States), 51

Special Purpose Forces (North Korea), 79

SPETSNAZ (Soviet Union), 69

Oto Melara Model 56, howitzers, 34-5

P

P-6, pistols, 71

PFLP Popular Front for the Liberation of Palestine, 108-9

PFLP-GC Popular Front for the Liberation of Palestine-General Command, 110

PGO-7, sights, 204

PGO-7V, sights, 204

PIRA Provisional Irish Republican Army, 96-107, **98**, **99**, **102**, 105, 107 weapons, 107

PLF Palestine Liberation Front, 110-11, **117**

PLO Palestine Liberation Organization, 107, 108-11, 146

POST Passive Optical Seeker Technique, 208

PPSF Palestine Popular Struggle Front, 110

PRI, pistols, 71

PT-76, Soviet Tank Battalion, 67 tanks, 67, **68**

PTFE, bullets, **159**

PX 1 Mark 4, parachutes, **42**

Palestine Liberation Front (PLF), 109, 110-11

Palestine Liberation Organization (PLO), 108-11

Palestine Popular Struggle Front (PPSF), 110

Parachute Batallions, Belgium, 46

Parachute Brigades, India, 74-5 Israel, 119

Parachute Regiments, 2nd Battalion, 140-3 United Kingdom, 41-2

Parachutes, D-1, **66**, 67

EFA 672-12 (IS), 77

MC1-1B steerable, **55**

PX 1 Mark 4, **42**

Paracommando Regiments, Belgium, 23

Paracudisti, BM59 rifles, 37, **37**

Paratroops, France, 31 Greece, 24 Israel, 76

Parker-Hale, rifles, 74, **152**

Parkerized Tanto, knives, 154

Passive Optical Seeker Technique (POST), 208

Patchett, G W, 196

Pave Low MH-53H, helicopters, 48

Pave Low MH-53H/J, helicopters, 218, **219**

Peled, Major General Benny, 120

Pepper Fog, tear gas/fog generators, 185, **185**

Personnel carriers, M-3, 38 OT-64, 120

Phantom F-4, aircraft, 56

Pistols (and see guns, rifles, shotguns), 166-7

Beretta, 92S, **36** Corto (.380 ACP), 37

Browning, 47, 79, **134**, **152**

Colt .45, 57

France, 168-9

Germany, Federal Republic, 166-7

Glock 17, 153

Heckler & Koch, P11, **35**

P7M13, 166, **166**

P7M8, 166, **166**

P9S, 167, **167**

Hek P9P, 32

Hush-Puppy, 62

Model 22, 62

P-6, 71

PRI, 71

Smith & Wesson M59, 160

Sterling MkVII, **198**, **199**

Tokarev automatic, 79

US Navy Model 22, 62

Plus P, 160

Point Salines, **143**

Poland, 6th Pomeranian Air Assault Division, 64

7th Luzycka Naval Assault Division, 64

Blue Berets, 64

Coastal Defence Unit, 64

Police Ordnance Company, 200

Polnocy class, LST, **68**

Popular Front for the Liberation of Palestine (PFLP), 108-9

Popular Front for the Liberation of Palestine-General Command (PFLP-GC), 110

Portugal, 24

Corpo de Fuzileiros, **25**

Special Forces Brigade, 24

Prazisionsschutzengewehr (High Precision Marksman's Rifle), 170

Protestant Action Force, 102

Provisional Irish Republican Army (PIRA), 96-107

Prowler EA-6B, aircraft, 146

Psychological Warfare Center, Fort Bragg, 49

R

R-4, rifles, **83**

R-4 Galil, rifles, 172

R-350M, radios, 71

RB15, craft, **81**

RH-53D Sea Stallion, helicopters, 128, **128**, **129**, **130**, **131**

RIP Ranger Indoctrination Program, 54

ROK Republic of Korea (South), 80-1, 187

RPG-2/7, 79

RPG-7, anti-tank weapons, 77 rocket launchers, 79, **111**

RPG-7D, night sights, 204

RPG-7V, rocket launchers, 67

RPG-7V AT, rocket launchers, 204, **204**

RPG-16, anti-tank weapons, 204

RPK, machine guns, 67

RPKS-74, rifles, **177**

RSA Republic of South Africa, 82-3

RUC Royal Ulster Constabulary, 96, 102-5, **104**

Rabin, Prime Minister, 119

Radar, A-7D, **219**

LMT Radio Professionelle RB12A, **156**

LMT/RP (Thomson-CSF) Rasit 3190B, **156**

Radios, AN PRC6, **30**

R-350M, 71

Raider Operations Group, COMSUBIN, Italy, 35, 36

Rank Pullin Controls SS80, night sights, **154**

Readiness Command, United States, 20

Readiness Troop, Norway, 24

Reagan, President Ronald, 143

Recce Commandos, South Africa, 82-3

Recon Company, United States, **22**

Reconnaissance Commandos, South Africa, 82-3

Reconnaissance Marines, United States, 56

Reconnaissance vehicles, M551 Sheridan, 55

Red Brigades, 112-13, 137-9

Red Hand Commando Group, 102

Redfield, telescopic sights, 57

Rejection Front, 109, 110

Remington 40XB, rifles, 57

Remington 870, shotguns, 163

Remington Woodmaster, rifles, 107

Rifled slug, cartridges, 164

Rifles (and see guns, pistols, shotguns), 168-83

Accuracy International PM, **153**

AK-47, 79, 172, 178-9, **178**, **179**

AK-74, 176-7, **176-7**

AKD, 176

AKM, **66**, 67, 178-9, **178**, **179**

AKMS, 67, **177**

AKS-74, 66, 71, 176-7, **176-7**

AR70/223 Beretta, 174, **174**

Armalite M16 (and see M16), 43

Beretta, AR70/223, 174, **174**

BM59, 175, **175**

BM59 Mark Ital TA, 34

BM59 Paracudisti, 37, **37**, **175**

SC70, 174, **174**

Special Troops Carbine, 174, **174**

Browning Hi-Power, 74

Bullpup FA MAS, 30, **168-9**

C1A1, 27

C-7.A, **27**

CAR 15, 57

CETME Model 68, 38, **38**

Colt Commando, 53, 180, **180-1**

Dragunov, 178-9, **178**, **179**

FA MAS, **29**, **30**, 168, **168-9**

FAL, 82

FN FAL, 75

FR-F2, **153**

FRF-1, **151**

G3SG/1 Sniper, 170, **171**

Galil, 77, 119, 172, **172**, 172, **173**

Garand M1, 175

Germany, Federal Republic, 170-1

Heckler & Koch 33, 85

PSG1, 170, **170-1**

Hek G3SG1, 33

Israel, 172-3

Italy, 174-5

Kalashnikov AK-47, 79, 172, **178**, 178-9, **179**

L1A1, 42, 47, 74

M16, **50**, 56, 74, 77, 79, 85, **98**, 106-7, 206, **206**

M16A, 27

M16A1, **39**, 52, 81, 85, **151**, 182, **183**

M16A1/2, 206, **206**

M16A2, 52, **57**, 182, **183**

M2 Carl Gustav antitank recoilless, **46**

M21, 184, **184**

M161A, 62

MAC-10, 119

MAS 49/56, 30

Mauser 66, 32

Paracudisti, 37, **37**

Parker-Hale Model 82, 74

Parker-Hale Model 85, **152**

Prazisionsschutzengewehr, 170

R-4, **83**

R-4 Galil, 172

Remington 40XB, 57

Remington Woodmaster, 107

RPKS-74, **177**

SA80, 42, **154**

SC70 Beretta, 174, **174**

SKS, **179**

Soviet Union, 176-9

Special Troops Carbine, 174, **174**

Springfield 03, **97**

SVD, 66, 67, 178-9, **178**, **179**

Type 65, 85

United States, 180-4

Rigid Raider, boats, 43, 154

Road Watch Team, 129

Rocket launchers, AT-3 Sagger, 79

BM-14, 69

BM-21, 69

RPG-7, 79, 107, **111**

RPG-7V, 67

RPG-7V AT, 204, **204**

Romania, 161st Paratroop Regiment, 64

2nd Mountain Brigade, 64

4th Mountain Brigade, 64

Royal Canadian Horse Artillery, 26

Royal Canadian Regiment, 26

Royal Marines, United Kingdom, **42**, 43

Royal Netherlands Army, Long Range Patrol Company, 24

Royal Netherlands Marine Corps, **23**

Special Assistance Unit, 24

Royal Small Arms Factory, Enfield, 196, 202

Royal Small Arms Limited, 184

Royal Ulster Constabulary (RUC), 96, 102-5, **104**
Rubber bullets, **159**
Rubber cartridges, 164
Ruslan An-124, aircraft, 66

S

S-76, helicopters, 77
SA80, rifles, 42, **154**
SA-7, missile launchers, 71, 79
SAS Special Air Service, 44-7, 105, 127, 132-6, 192
  Australia, 46, 74
  New Zealand, 46, 78
  Operational Research Wing, 150
  United Kingdom, 44-7
SAW Squad Automatic Weapon M249, 56
SBS Special Boat Squadron (United Kingdom), **42**, 43
SDV Swimmer Delivery Vehicles, Mark VIII MOD-6, **60**
SEAL Sea, Air, and Land, 60-2, 144
  Delivery Vehicle Teams (United States), 60
  Team 6 (United States), 57
SG, cartridges, **165**
SKS Semi-automatic Karbine Simonov, rifles, **179**
SOCCT Special Operations Combat Control Team, 48
SOCEUR Special Operations Command Europe, 20
SOCPAC Special Operations Command Pacific, 20
SOF Special Operations Forces, 20-7
  expenditure, 22
  structure, **22**
SOS Special Operations Squadrons (United States), 48
SOW Special Operations Wing (United States), 48
SPAS Special Purpose Automatic Shotgun, **36**, **186**, 186-7
SPAS penetrator, cartridges, **165**
SPETSNAZ Spetsialnoye Nazranie (Soviet Union), 64, 69-71
SPLAT Synthetic Splastic Ammunition for Training, **158**, **159**, **162**, 163
STAR Surface-To-Air Recovery, 219
SVD, rifles, 66, 67, 178-9, **178**, **179**
Sacred Squadron, Greece, 46
Sagger,
  missiles, 210
  rocket launchers, 79
Saiqa, 108
Salewski, Wolfgang, 126
Saracen, armored cars, **104**
Sayeh, Suhaila, **126**, 127
Sayeret, Israeli reconnaissance units, 76
Schaefer, Colonel, **128**
Schumann, Jurgen, 125, **127**
Scimitar, cannon, 140
Scoones, Sir Paul, 144
Scopes,
  Hensoldt 6x42, 170
  Leupold Stephens 16xM1 Ultrascope, **153**
  Zeiss diavari 1.5x6X, 170
Scorpion,
  sub-machine guns, **153**
  tanks, 140
Sea Cobra AH-1, helicopters, **57**
Sea King, helicopters, **35**
Sea Stallion RH-53D, helicopters, 128, **128**, **129**, **130**, **131**
Seafox, boats, 62, 154
Seawolf, amphibious aircraft, **155**
Selection and training,
  82nd Airborne Division (United States), 55
  Alpine Troops (Italy), 34
  COMSUBIN (Italy), 36
  Delta (United States), 57
  Folgore Brigade (Italy), 37
  Foreign Legion (France), 29-30
  Foreign Legion (Spain), 38
  GSG 9 (West Germany), 32-3

Gurkhas (United Kingdom), 39-40
Israeli units, 76-7
Marine Corps (United States), 58
Naval Infantry (Soviet Union), 67
Parachute Brigade (India), 75
Parachute Regiment (United Kingdom), 41-2
Paratroops (France), 31
Rangers (United States), 54
Reconnaissance Commandos (South Africa), 82
SAS (Australia), 74
SAS (United Kingdom), 46-7
SBS (United Kingdom), 43
SEALS (United States), 60-2
Special Forces (Jordan), 77
Special Forces (South Korea), 80-1
Special Operations Forces (United States), 51-2
Special Purpose Forces (North Korea), 79
Special Army Forces (Thailand), 84
SPETSNAZ (Soviet Union), 69-71
Semi-wad cutter, bullets, 160
Shepherd, Major R V, 196
Sheridan M551, armored reconnaissance vehicle, 55
Shomron, Brigadier-General Dan, 119, **119**, 120-1
Shotguns (and see guns, pistols, rifles, 186-9
  Armsel Striker, 186-7, **187**
  Daewoo USAS-12, 187, **187**
  Deerslayer, 188
  Featherlight, 188
  Franchi SPAS 12, **186**, 186-7
  Franchi SPAS 15, **36**
  Italy, 186-7
  Ithaca Model 37, 188, **188-9**
    pump, **188**
    Stakeout, **189**
  Mossberg 500 ATP8, 188, **188-9**
  Remington 870, 163
  South Africa, 186-7
  South Korea, 187
  SPAS Franchi, **36**, **186**, 186-7
  United States, 188-9
  USAS-12, 187, **187**
  Winchester Marine, 163
Sieffert, Major, 130
Sights, 57, 204
Sinn Fein, 100
Skorpion, sub-machine guns, 112, 152
Skyhawk A-4, aircraft, 56
Small Arm for the 80s, SA80, 42
Smith & Wesson M59, pistols, 160
Soft-point, bullets, 160, **162**
South Africa,
  Reconnaissance Commandos, 82-3
  shotguns, 186-7
Soviet Union,
  Air Assault Brigade, 64
  Airborne Force, 65-6
  Airborne Rifles Divisions, 210
  aircraft, 214-17
  Airmobile Assault Regiment, 64
  ASU, Aviadezantnaya Samochodnaya Ustanovka, 66, 210
  Attack Helicopter Regiment, 64
  Black Berets, **68**
  Border Guards, 64
  elite forces history and structure, 63-4
  and Grenada, 144-5
  grenade launchers, 204-5
  GRU, Military Intelligence, 64, 69
  helicopters, 216-17
  Interior Army, 64
  KGB, Soviet State Security, 64
  M8 Gecko Air Defence Batallion, 67
  Military Intelligence, 64, 69
  Military Transport Aviation (VTA), 66
  Naval Infantry, 67-9
    rifles, 176-9
  SPETSNAZ, 69-71

Tank Battalion, 67
  vehicles, 210, **211**
  ZSU-23-4 Air Defence Batallion, 67
Spain, Foreign Legion, 38
Spartan, bullets, 162-3
Special Air Service,
  Australia, 46, 74
  New Zealand, 46, 78
  Operational Research Wing, 150
  United Kingdom, 44-7
Special Army Forces, Thailand, 84-5
Special Assistance Unit, Netherlands, 24
Special Boat Squadrons,
  United Kingdom, **42**, 43
  United States, 60
Special Forces,
  Greece, 24
  South Korea, 80-1
Special Forces Brigade, Portugal, 24
Special Intervention Squadron, Belgium, 23
Special Operations Combat Control Team, United States, 48
Special Operations Command Europe (SOCEUR), 20
Special Operations Command Pacific (SOCPAC), 20
Special Operations Squadrons, United States, 48
Special Operations Unit, Spain, 38
Special Operations Wing, United States, 48
Special Purpose Forces, North Korea, 79
Special Reconnaissance Company (Jaegerkorps), Denmark, 23
Special Service Force, Canada, 26-7
Special Troops Carbine (Beretta), 174, **174**
Special Warfare Department, Turkey, 24, **25**
Spectre, boats, 62
Spectre AC-130, aircraft, 218
Spectre AC-130A, gunships, 48
Spence, Gusty, 101
Spetsialnoye Nazranie (SPETSNAZ), Soviet Union, 69
Spiral AT-6, missiles, 217
Springfield 03, rifles, **97**
Squad Automatic Weapon M249, SAW, 56
Stanley, John, **40**
Star Z-70B, sub-machine guns, 38
Starfighter F-104, aircraft, 122
Starlifter C-141, aircraft, 55, 128, 129, **130**
Sten Gun, sub-machine guns, 196-7, **196-7**
Sterling,
  pistols, MkVII, **198**, **199**
  sub-machine guns,
    L2A3, 42, 75, 196-7, **196-7**
    L34, 152
    L34A1, 43
    L34A1 Silenced, 198-9, **198-9**
    Mk4, 74
Sterling Engineering Company, 196
Stinger FIM-92A, missiles, 208, **208-9**
Stoppers, 158, **158**
Sub-machine guns (and see general purpose machine guns, machine guns), 190-201
  Beretta,
    M4, 112
    Model 12, 36, **36**
    Model 38/49, 34
  Danish, 190-1
  Denmark, 190-1
    France, 190-1
    Germany (Federal Republic), 192-3
    Heckler & Koch, 47
      MP, 33
      MP5, **32**, **44**, **47**, **107**, **133**, **135**, 150, **151**, 192-3, **192-3**
      MP5 K, **193**
      MP5 SD, **192**
    Ingram, 200-1, **200-1**
    Israel, 194-5
      L34A1, 74, 75
      M3A1, 57, 81, **184**, 200-1, **200-1**

M12, 112
Madsen Model 53, 190, **190-1**
MAT49, 190, **190-1**
Micro-Uzi, 195, **195**
Mini-Uzi, 195, **195**
Skorpion, 112, 152
Star Z-70B, 38
Sten Gun, 196-7, **196-7**
Sterling,
  L2A3, 42, 75, 196-7, **196-7**
  L34, 152
  L34A1, 43
  L34A1 Silenced, 198-9, **198-9**
  Mk4, 74
  Type 36, 85
United Kingdom, 196-9
United States, 200-1
Uzi, 77, 152, 194-5, **194-5**
V261 Scorpion, **153**
Sub-skimmer, **155**
Submarine Products Ltd, **155**
Submarines,
  Grayback, **61**
  mini, **154**
Suicide Commandos, Turkey, 24
Super Vel, bullets, 160
Swedish soap, 163
Swimmer Delivery Vehicles, Mark VIII MOD-6, (SDV), **60**

T

T-54, tanks, 69, 120
T-55, tanks, 69
TC armor piercing, cartridges, 164
THV, bullets, **158**, **159**, **161**, 163
TOW, missiles, 55, 77
Taiwan, Long-Range Amphibious Reconnaissance Commandos, 84-5
Tanks,
  AMX-13, 38
  M41, 38
  M60A1, **57**, 58
  M-60, **173**
  PT-76, 67, **68**
  Scorpion, 140
  T-54, 69, 120
  T-55, 69
Tarantelli, Ezio, 112
Tear gas/fog generators, 185
Teheran, 48, 56
  US Embassy Siege, 128-31
Telescopic sights, Redfield, 57
Tercio de Extranjeros, Spain, 38
Thailand, Special Army Forces, 84-5
Thunderbolt (PLO faction), 108
Tiedemann, Gabrielle, 121
Tokarev automatic, pistols, 79
Tomcat F-14, aircraft, 146, 147, **147**
Train 747 (Moluccan Train Seige, Netherlands), 116
Transall C-160, aircraft, **30**
True Blue Medical School, Grenada, 143
Tulle (Manufacture d'Armes de Tulle), 190
Tungsten AP, cartridges, **165**
Tunnels, **78**, 80
Turkey, 24
  Jandara, 24
  Special Warfare Department, 24, **25**
  Suicide Commandos, 24
Turner, Sir Ralph, 40
Turpin, H S, 196

U

UDA Ulster Defence Association, 96, 102
UDR Ulster Defence Regiment, 96, 102-5
UDT Underwater Demolition Teams, 60
UFF Ulster Freedom Fighters, 96, 102
UH-1H Huey, helicopters, **48**, 55, 56
UH-60 Black Hawk, helicopters, 55
USAS-12, shotguns, 187, **187**
USS Nimitz, 128, 130, **131**
USS Saratoga, 146, **147**
USSOC US Special Operations Command, 20
UVF Ulster Volunteer Force, 96, 101, 105

UWC Ulster Workers Council, 98, 102
Ulster Army Council, 102
Ulster Defence Association (UDA), 96, 102
Ulster Defence Regiment (UDR), 96, 102-5
Ulster Freedom Fighters (UFF), 96, 102
Ulster Special Constabulary, 102
Ulster Volunteer Force (UVF), 96, 101, 105
Ulster Workers Council (UWC), 98, 102
Uniforms,
  23rd Air Force (United States), 48
  82nd Airborne Division (United States), 55
  Airborne Force (Soviet Union), 67
  Alpine Troops (Italy), 35
  Canada, **26**, 27
  Folgore Brigade (Italy), 37
  Foreign Legion (France), 30
  Foreign Legion (Spain), 38
  GSG 9 (West Germany), 32
  Gurkha (United Kingdom), 40
  Israeli units, 77
  Long-Range Amphibious Reconnaissance Commandos (Taiwan), 85
  Naval Infantry (Soviet Union), 69
  Parachute Brigade (India), 75
  Parachute Regiment (United Kingdom), 42
  Paratroops (France), 30, **30**
  Rangers (United States), 54
  Reconnaissance Commandos (South Africa), 83
  SEAL (United States), 62
  SAS (Australia), 74
  SAS (New Zealand), 78
  SAS (United Kingdom), 47
  SBS (United Kingdom), 43
  Special Army Forces (Thailand), 85
  Special Forces (Jordan), 77
  Special Forces (South Korea), 81
  Special Operations Forces (United States), 53
  Special Purpose Forces (North Korea), 79
  SPETSNAZ (Soviet Union), 71
United Kingdom,
  anti-riot weapons, 184-5
  Gurkhas, 39-40
  machine guns, 202-3
  missiles, 206
  Parachute Regiment, 41-2
  Royal Marines, **42**, 43
  Special Air Service, 44-7, 105, 127, 132-6, 192
  Special Boat Squadron, **42**, 43
  sub-machine guns, 196-9
United States,
  23rd Air Force, 48, 57
  160th Aviation Group, 57
  Air Force, SOF, **180**
  aircraft, 218-19
  Amphibious Unit, 22
  anti-riot weapons, 185
  Army,
    5th Special Forces Group, **21**
    8th Army, 80
    82nd Airborne Division, 55
    Delta Force, 56
    Ordnance Corps, 200
    Rangers, **21**, 54, 144, **151**
    SEAL Team 6, 57
    Special Operations Forces, 49-53
    Civil Irregular Defense Groups, 49
    Darby's Rangers, 54
    Delta Force, 56, 128-31
    Embassy Siege, Teheran, 128-31
    Fleet Marine Force, 56
    Force Reconnaissance, 56
    Forces, 20-7
      command chain, 20-2
      grenade launchers, 206
      machine guns, 203
    Marine Corps, 22, **22**, 56-9, 144

Amphibious Unit, 22
Force Reconnaissance, 22
Recon Company, **22**
Merrill's Marauders, 54
missiles, 208
Navy,
Amphibious Base,
Coronado, **20**
SEAL Delivery Vehicle
Teams, 60
SEAL Forces, **20**, 60-2
Special Boat Squadrons, 60
Special Warfare Team, **21**
Readiness Command, 20
Recon Company, **22**

Reconnaissance Marines,
56
rifles, 180-4
shotguns, 188-9
SEAL Forces, **20**, 60-2
Special Boat Squadrons, 60
Special Operations Forces,
182
Special Operations
Squadrons, 48
Special Operations Wing, 48
Special Warfare Team, **21**
sub-machine guns, 200-1
Uzi, sub-machine guns, 77, 152,
194-5, **194-5**

V261 Scorpion, sub-machine
guns, **153**
VTA Voyenno Transportnaya
Aviatsiya, 66
Valle, Vitorio, 174
Vaught, Major General James,
129
Vehicles, 210-13
Soviet Union, 210, **211**
Vietnam, 49
Vietor, Jurgen, 125

Volksmarine, East Germany, 64
Voyenno Transportnaya
Aviatsiya (VTA), Soviet
Union, 66
Vulcan, cannon, 218
Vysadkova Brigade,
Czechoslovakia, 64

W

Warlock, knives, 82
Warsaw Pact, elite forces
history and structure, 63-4
Wegener, Colonel Ulrich, 121, 126

Wheelbarrow, **156**
Winchester Marine, shotguns, 163
Wireless Ridge, 140-3
Wischnewski, Hans-Jurgen, 126

ZSU-23-4,
anti-aircraft guns, 69
Soviet Air Defence Battalion, 67
ZU-23, anti-aircraft guns, **63**
Zeiss diavari 1.5x6X, scopes,
170
Zodiac, boats, **75**

PICTURE CREDITS

Front cover: AP, US Department of Defense (DoD). Endpapers: DoD. Page 1: Accuracy Int. 2-3: P Valpolini/Milpress. 4-5: Bernard & Graefe Verlag. 6-7: DoD. 9: DoD. 10-11: DoD. 12: DoD. 12-13: Spooner/Gamma. 13: DoD. 15(top): DoD. 15(bottom left): Rex/SIPA. 15(bottom right): Ministry of Defence. 16: DoD. 16-17: Rex/SIPA. 17(top): Rex/SIPA. 17(bottom): Spooner/Gamma. 18-22: DoD. 23(top): Royal Netherlands MoD. 23(bottom): MoD. 24: NATO. 25(top):GIAT. 25(bottom): Turkish MoD. 26-27: Canadian Armed Forces. 28: ACMAT. 29-30: Rex/SIRPA. 31: DoD. 32-33: Bernard & Graefe Verlag. 34-35(left): Italian Army. 35(top & right): P Valpolini/ Milpress. 36(top & bottom left): P Valpolini/Milpress. 36(top & bottom right): Raids/JP Hussom. 37: P MacDonald. 39(top): Brigade of Gurkhas. 39(bottom): Sgt Kelly. 40(top): Brigade of Gurkhas. 40(centre): Sgt Kelly. 40(bottom): Brigade of Gurkhas. 41-42: MoD. 42(top): Associated Press. 43: Avon Rubber plc. 46: UPI(top). 46(bottom): Photographers Int/T Fincher. 48-59: DoD. 60-62: US Navy. 63: MoD. 70(bottom): DoD. 74-75: Australian DoD. 75(top): Australian War Memorial. 75: Australian DoD. 76: Israeli Defence Force. 77(left): IMI. 77(right): Israeli Defence Force. 78(left): NZ MoD. 78(right) – 81: S Korean MoD. 82-83: Spooner/Gamma. 84-87: DoD. 88-89: Rex. 90-91: DoD. 92: Rex. 93(top): Rex/SIPA. 93(centre): Rex. 93(bottom): DoD. 96(top): Pacemaker Int. 96(bottom) – 97(top): Rex. 97: Rex. 99(top): Photo Source. 99(bottom) – 100: Rex. 101: AP. 102-107: Pacemaker Int. 108: DoD. 109-111: Rex/SIPA. 112: Photo Source. 113(top left): Spooner/Gamma. 113(top right): Rex/SIPA. 113(bottom) – 115: Rex. 116-117: Rex/SIPA. 118(top): MoD. 118(bottom): DoD. 119(top): Rex. 119(bottom) – 120: Spooner/Gamma. 121-122(top): Rex/SIPA. 122(bottom):

Spooner/Gamma. 123-125: Rex/SIPA. 126: Spooner/Gamma. 127(top & centre): Rex/ SIPA. 127(bottom left): Rex/SIPA. 128: DoD. 130(bottom left): Rex/SIPA. 131: DoD. 132: Photo Source. 133: Rex. 134: London Express News. 135(top): BBC. 135(bottom): Rex. 136(top): BBC. 136(bottom): PA. 137(top): UPI. 137(bottom): Spooner/Gamma. 138: UPI. 138-139: DoD. 140-141: Parachute Regt. 141-142: LEN. 143-145: DoD. 146(top): Rex/SIPA. 146(bottom): DoD. 147: Rex/SIPA. 148-149: P Valpolini/Milpress. 150(top): DoD. 151: Spooner/Gamma. 152(left): D Grant Assoc. 152(bottom) – 153(right): Accuracy Int. 153(bottom): Franchi. 154: Rank Pullin Controls. 154(centre) – 155(centre): Subskimmer. 155(top left): Haley Weller. 155(top right): Nautiraid. 155(bottom): Lake Aircraft. 156(bottom left): LMT Radio. 156-157: Thompson-CSF. 157(top): MoD. 157(centre): British Aerospace. 166-167: Heckler & Koch. 168-169: GIAT. 170-171: Heckler & Koch. 172-173(top): IMI. 173(bottom left): T Gander. 173(bottom right): Israeli Defense Forces. 174-175: Beretta. 176-177: Tass. 177(bottom right) – 178(top): DoD. 178(bottom): Tass. 179(bottom): DoD. 180: MARS. 180-181: Royal Ordnance. 181(bottom): I Hogg. 182-184: DoD. 185(bottom left): Pacemaker Int. 185(bottom right): DoD. 187: Daewoo Precision Ind. 188-189(top): I Hogg. 188(bottom) – 189(bottom): Intergun. 190: I Hogg. 191(centre): I Hogg. 193(bottom): Heckler & Koch. 196(bottom): MoD. 197(top): IWM. 197(bottom): Sterling. 199(centre & bottom): Sterling. 201(bottom right): DoD. 202(top): NATO. 202(bottom): MoD. 203-205(top left): DoD. 206: Colt Ind. 206-210(top): DoD. 210(bottom): Tass. 211(top): Novosti. 212-213(top & centre): Glover Webb. 212-213(bottom): LTV. 213(top): Glover Webb. 213(bottom): LTV. 214-215(top): DoD. 215: Tass. 216: DoD. 216-217(top): DoD. 216-217(bottom): Tass. 218-219: DoD.